A GUIDE TO UNDERSTANDING
THE BIBLE

Harper ▲ ChapelBooks

A GUIDE
TO UNDERSTANDING
THE BIBLE

The Development of Ideas within the
Old and New Testaments

BY

HARRY EMERSON FOSDICK

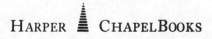

HARPER CHAPELBOOKS

Harper & Row, Publishers
New York

CONTENTS

There are heavy sins of commission to be charged against the so-called Higher Criticism that, from its lair in Germany, raged over the world during the nineteenth century—many extravagances of conjecture and not a few absurdities. All this is plain enough to any one who plods through that enormous literature. But it was not entirely labour lost. Some results have come out of it that may be accepted as permanent and salutary; and among these must be reckoned the discovery of the evolutionary character of the Bible. . . . We have learned a good deal of the history of Israel; in its larger outline we know how their sacred books were finally put together from successive strata, and how these strata represent the developing religious sense of the people. This change of attitude towards the sacred Scripture of the Jews I hold to be of almost incalculable importance for the future of religion: it takes the ground from under the older criticism of the book from the angle of fact and ethics; it supports and clarifies the teleological relation between the two Testaments, and it puts the claims of revelation in a new and thoroughly consistent light.

PAUL ELMER MORE

INTRODUCTION

One major result of the last half-century of Biblical scholarship is ability to arrange the documents of Scripture in their approximately chronological order. The typical questions asked by scholars concerning Biblical writings—Who wrote them? When, to whom, and why were they written?—while still presenting many baffling difficulties, have been answered sufficiently to clarify the broad outlines of the Bible's chronological development.

An important result of thus seeing the Biblical writings in sequence is ability to study the development of Biblical ideas. Upon this problem some of the best scholarly work in recent years has been expended. Seen as informed students now regard it, the Bible is the record of an incalculably influential development of religious thought and life, extending from the primitive faith of early Hebraism into the Christianity of the second century. Such a bald statement, however, does scant justice to the illumination which has thus fallen on the Jewish-Christian writings. The first results of critical research into the Bible seemed disruptive, tearing the once unified Book into many disparate and often contradictory documents. The final result has turned out to be constructive, putting the Bible together again, not indeed on the old basis of a level, infallible inspiration, but on the factually demonstrable basis of a coherent development. The Scriptures reflect some twelve centuries and more of deepening and enlarging spiritual experience and insight, in the written record of which nothing is without significance, and everything is illumined by its genetic relationships.

In general, this view of the Scriptures has become the common property of the well-informed, but it still remains, in many minds, a mere framework without substantial content. That the Bible is the record of centuries of religious change, that its early concepts are allied with primitive, animistic faiths, that between such origins and the messages of Hebrew prophets and Christian evangelists an immensely important development is reflected in the Book—this general view is the familiar possession of many in both synagogue and church. All too few, however, have any clear and specific conception of the ways in which the Biblical

ideas unfolded from their beginnings until they became one of
the most potent influences in Western culture.

One reason for this situation is that scholars, who know the
fascinating story of the development of Biblical ideas, have commonly written of it in technical terms, so that while the average
minister, the intelligent layman, and the college student may
know by hearsay the outline of their findings, the books where
the substance of the matter lies are often too recondite for general
reading. Yet the story of developing Scriptural ideas ought to
be popularly known. It is fascinating in itself; it throws light on
every portion of the Bible; it clears up obscurities, explaining
what is else inexplicable; it distinguishes the minor detours from
the major highways of Biblical thought; it gives their true value
to primitive concepts, the early, blazed trails leading out to great
issues; and, in the end, it makes of the Bible a coherent whole,
understood, as everything has to be understood, in terms of its
origins and growth. This illuminating outlook on the Scriptures
ought somehow to be made a more available possession than it
is for the general reader.

This present book is written neither by a technical scholar
nor for scholars. It is written for the interested student and
endeavors to build a bridge over which available information
concerning developing Biblical ideas may pass into the possession
of a larger public. To be sure, no device can translate so weighty a
matter into light and casual reading. The subject is serious and, at
its simplest, requires serious consideration. Nevertheless, with the
Bible still the world's "best-seller," there must be many whose
reading of it would gain meaning and interest if the knowledge
possessed by the expertly informed were more easily at their
disposal.

Readers unaccustomed to think of the Biblical literature in
terms of its chronological development are advised to consult
the approximate dating of the documents presented in the Appendix. The unsolved problems in this realm are many and in some
cases wide variations exist between the estimates of different
scholars, but the main outline seems dependable as a basis for
so general a statement as we are here attempting. Since the
chronological arrangement of the Biblical writings is fundamental
to this book's discussion, two thorough and readable treatments
of the matter are specially recommended: *The Literature of the
Old Testament in Its Historical Development*, by Julius A. Bewer,

and *The Literature of the New Testament*, by Ernest Findlay Scott, both published by the Columbia University Press.

In trying to achieve the object we have just described, two major methods have been used in this book.

First, six main strands of developing thought have been, so far as possible, disentangled from their mutual complications, and have been separately presented. The ideas of God, Man, Right and Wrong, Suffering, Fellowship with God, and Immortality have been traced, each by itself, as each progresses through the two Testaments. The alternative method, often used by scholars, considers one epoch of Biblical religion at a time, presenting the entire complex of ideas which characterized that era, and then moves on to study the next succeeding epoch as a whole. For the general reader, however, this method adds the confusion of complexity to the natural difficulties of the subject. I have hoped that, by driving six separate roadways through Scripture, clarity might be gained without serious sacrifice of balance and proportion, and that the very fact of repetition, as each roadway inevitably brings the traveler within sight of familiar scenes common to all six, would help rather than hinder comprehension.

Second, these lines of developing thought have been traced, one at a time, through both Testaments. The specialization of surgeons, who will not invade one another's domain, is hardly more precise than is the specialization of Biblical scholars. In particular, the Old Testament, the inter-Testamental writings, and the New Testament, represent areas of well defined and highly differentiated expertness. The result is that while the general reader may find available the story of developing thought in one era, or in the Old Testament, or in the New Testament, no first-rate scholar has written or would be likely to write a book carrying the course of thought through the Bible as a whole. Only some one with no reputation for original scholarship to maintain, free to avail himself of any scholar's work, professing only a transmissive and interpretive function, and interested not in moot details but in general results, would have the hardihood to undertake the task. Having, therefore, lived for years with Biblical scholars as my friends and colleagues and in the classroom having dealt with students, trying to gain a coherent and usable understanding of the Bible for practical purposes, I have dared the attempt to put together developments of ideas which the separate Biblical disciplines leave apart. I am under no illusion as to the adequacy of the result. This book is now published only after two of my colleagues, Professor Julius A. Bewer and Professor James E. Frame, one an authority on the Old Testament and the other on the New, have read the manuscript with painstaking care. I may not hold them responsible for any opinion expressed in this book, but to their criticism and guidance I am unpayably indebted and only because of it dare hope that I have presented without undue distortion or prejudice a picture of the major trends of thought in the Jewish-Christian scriptures.

In writing the book I have constantly encountered four difficulties, and since the author has been acutely aware of them they will probably be visible to the observant reader—oversimplification, inadequate exposition, the chronological fallacy, and modernization.

Over-simplification is inevitable in the very process of selective attention involved in the method of this book. To disentangle from its many complications the idea of God, for example, and to follow through from early Hebraism to second-century Christianity this idea's progress, while it makes the story more easily understandable, obscures the actual confusion of cross-currents, back-eddies, stagnant shallows, whirlpools, rapids, and cataracts present in history itself. It tends toward over-clarifying the picture and, in the end, it may even draw a diagram, rather than reproduce in the reader's imagination the total struggle involved in the working out of Biblical ideas. Of this danger I have been constantly aware and have endeavored to guard against it. If the reader will do the same, he may avail himself of such simplification as has been achieved, without too serious loss of historic realism.

Inadequate exposition of the matured convictions of Scripture is also necessarily involved in the purpose and method of this book. Its major interest is not expository but genetic; it tries to trace the highroads traversed by Biblical ideas from their origin to their culmination; when they have reached their culmination it makes no endeavor to give a systematic and adequate exposition of them. It is not primarily a book on Biblical theology but a genetic survey of developing Biblical thought. To be sure, if the reader shares at all the author's experience, he will find that clear light is shed on the mature convictions of Judaism and Christianity by such a study of their origins and growth. To know where Scriptural doctrines came from is in itself an indispensable help in understanding what they mean. Nevertheless, if the reader wishes an adequate theological treatment of such a theme as Biblical monotheism, he should look elsewhere; here he will find only the story of the way in which Biblical monotheism emerged from early origins.

The chronological fallacy haunts such a study as this and is difficult to avoid. The very fact that six historically influential ideas are presented in terms of development, with their later formulations on an altitude immeasurably higher than the low-lands from which they came, may produce the illusion of constant ascent, as though being posterior in time always meant being superior in quality. But truth and chronology are incommensurable terms. A poet writing in the twentieth century A.D. may be a puny figure compared with the titanic stature of a Greek dramatist five centuries before Christ, and ethical insight cannot be graded on the basis of the calendar. The fact that one Biblical book is later in time than another is in itself not the slightest indication that it is superior in quality—Nahum is on a much lower spiritual level than Amos, and the Book of Revelation in the New Testament is morally inferior to the writings of the Great Isaiah in the Old Testament. Of this fact the reader is continually reminded in this book, and no statement, I think, denies or neglects it. I have tried to make plain the retrogressions in Biblical thought, the irregularities of change, with its ups and downs, its persistent lags, and its moral surrenders. There is no smooth and even ascent in the Book. There are, instead, long detours, recrudescences of primitivism, lost ethical gains, and lapses in spiritual insight. There are even vehement denials of nascent truth, and high visions that go neglected for centuries. At this point I am solicitous that my desire for clarity in tracing development may not beguile any reader into the illusions of the chronological fallacy.

Modernization dogs the footsteps of any one who endeavors to make ancient developments of thought live for contemporary readers. By subtle, unnoticed gradations the presentation of old patterns of thinking slips over into twentieth-century categories and phrases. The more one perceives in ancient literature, whether of Judea or Greece, values of permanent validity, the more one tends to lift them out of their original frameworks of concept and present them in modern terms and ways of thinking. But 'corporate personality,' demonology, Messiahship, apocalypticism, the Logos-doctrine, and many other mental categories in the Bible are not modern. It requires a difficult thrust of historic imagination to understand at all what they meant to their original users. It may be comforting to translate them into present-day equivalents but that always involves an historic fallacy. This difficulty is everywhere present in this book and I wish the reader to be aware of it. I have honestly tried never to picture an ancient way of conceiving facts as though it were identical with modern thinking, but always to portray the Biblical writers as using their own mental forms of thought in their own way, however diverse from ours those forms may be. Such is the difficulty involved, however, in making modern language serve this purpose that in this regard the coöperation of the reader is imperative.

The implications of this book with regard to theories about the Bible are not discussed in the text. Obviously, any idea of inspiration which implies equal value in the teachings of Scripture, or inerrancy in its statements, or conclusive infallibility in its ideas, is irreconcilable with such facts as this book presents. The inspirations of God fortunately have not been thus stereotyped and mechanical. There is, however, nothing in the process of development itself, whether in the organic world in general or in the realm of mind and morals, to call in question the creative and directive activity of God.

Needless to say, the author is a theist. The process of spiritual development reflected in the Bible seems to him to involve not only human discovery but divine self-disclosure. Indeed, the unfolding of ideas which the Scripture records would represent not so much discovery as illusion, were there not an objective spiritual world to be discovered. Any one, therefore, holding a religious rather than a materialistic philosophy, will think of the process of Biblical development as dual—seen from one side, a human achievement; seen from the other, a divine self-revelation.

Nevertheless, there is no finality about it in the sense that the ideas which the Scriptures opened up were finished when the Scriptures stopped. Neither Judaism nor Christianity, despite their theories, has in practise succeeded in so treating the Book. Every one of the six lines of unfolding thought traced in this volume has had a long subsequent history of continuing development, and the end is not yet in sight. The God of the Bible has proved his quality as "the living God," who has not said his last word on any subject or put the finishing touch on any task. The supreme contribution of the Bible is not that it finished anything but that it started something. Its thinking is not so much a product as a process, issuing from a long precedent process and inaugurating an immeasurably important subsequent development.

To be sure, as Copernicus achieved a finality in establishing a heliocentric universe, so the Bible represents final gains in thought and insight—apprehensions of truth which, once laid hold on, need not be discovered all over again. The real glory of Copernicus, however, is revealed not so much in what he finished as in what he started—initiating an insight of incalculable future promise, which modern astronomy is unfolding yet. So, the finalities of Scripture are mainly important because they are germinative. They are misinterpreted and misused when employed to stop further development rather than to encourage it. One reason for such a study as this book presents is that one cannot understand Western thought in any era, or our own thought in this modern age, without knowing the Biblical origins of our ideas in religion and morals.

It would be less than the truth, however, if the author's interest in writing the book were represented as merely the desire to explain ideologies. I have faithfully tried to present an objective, factual picture of unfolding Biblical thought, but it will doubtless be evident that the central ideas of Scripture, in whatever changing categories they may be phrased, seem to me the hope of man's individual and social life.

One major problem in writing this book has been the difficulty of deciding when to quote the Scriptures fully in the text and when merely to refer to them in the footnotes. I have used such judgment as I possess in this matter, but obviously much of the Biblical evidence that confirms and illumines the statements made is concealed in the unquoted Scriptural references. No one, therefore, can read the book thoroughly who does not read it with a Bible at hand for constant consultation. Except when otherwise indicated, the American Standard Edition of the Revised Bible is used, save that 'Jehovah' is replaced by the more correct form, 'Yahweh.'

That I am at every point indebted to the work of others is evident in the text, and in major matters this has been made explicit in the footnotes. The larger field of the book's indebtedness is indicated in the appended bibliography. As to obligations of a more personal nature I have many people to thank—colleagues who have advised me, students at Union Theological Seminary who have stimulated me with their responsive interest, members of the congregation of The Riverside Church, New York, who, by their attentive listening to mid-week lectures on the subjects handled in this book, have kept alive my confidence that even difficult and recondite problems concerning the Bible are of vital, contemporary importance. Nor would it be fair to publish this book without acknowledging my debt to the tireless patience of my secretaries, and especially to the painstaking care of Miss Margaret Renton in correcting and preparing the manuscript.

HARRY EMERSON FOSDICK

June 30, 1938

A GUIDE TO UNDERSTANDING
THE BIBLE

CHAPTER I

THE IDEA OF GOD

I

Nowhere do the early documents of the Bible more obviously carry us back to the ideas of primitive religion than in dealing with the concept of God. The first chapter of Genesis reveals a confident monotheism, but that represents centuries of developing life and thought from the time the Hebrews were introduced at Sinai to their god, Yahweh. At the beginning, the distinctive deity of the Hebrews was a tribal divinity to whom the clans of Joseph first gave their allegiance at the time of the Exodus from Egypt. That previously the Israelites had not known their god, Yahweh, by his name is explicitly stated in the Bible: "God spake unto Moses, and said unto him, I am Yahweh: and I appeared unto Abraham, unto Isaac, and unto Jacob, as El Shaddai; but by my name Yahweh I was not known to them."[1] This passage appears in the late Priestly Document and all the more because of that the probabilities favor its truth. Without a solid basis in historic fact, such a delayed beginning of Yahweh's worship would not have been invented by succeeding generations. The natural tendency of loyal devotees would be to carry back the name of their god to their most ancient patriarchal legends and to confirm his worship with the sanctions of antiquity. So, one story in Genesis, referring to the days of Seth, son of Adam, says, "Then began men to call upon the name of Yahweh."[2]

The statement in Exodus is more convincing than this contradictory account in Genesis, not only because of intrinsic probability but because the evidence available in the Bible clearly indicates that it was in connection with the Exodus from Egypt that Yahweh first became god of the tribes of Israel. Although, centuries afterward, the name Yahweh was commonly put upon the lips of ancestral heroes and patriarchs and was used even in the narrative of man's creation in Eden, the bona fide historic fact

---

[1] Exodus 6:2–3 (marginal reading). The meaning of El Shaddai is dubious, and "God Almighty" a very questionable rendering.
[2] Genesis 4:26.

1

was too firmly set to be eliminated—at the Exodus, for the first time, Yahweh and Israel had met and sworn mutual allegiance. The Ephraimite Document of narratives, for example, carefully avoids the name Yahweh in all the early stories until the Exodus is reached and then warns the people to "put away the gods which your fathers served beyond the River [Euphrates], and in Egypt; and serve ye Yahweh."[1] Commonly also in the prophets, the beginning of Yahweh's relationship with Israel is associated with the Exodus, as when Hosea twice represents the deity as saying, "I am Yahweh thy God from the land of Egypt,"[2] or Jeremiah places Yahweh's espousal of his people in the Mosaic period,[3] or Ezekiel represents God as calling Moses' generation "the day when I chose Israel."[4]

According to the available evidence, Moses first came upon Yahweh at "the mountain of God,"[5] called both Sinai and Horeb.[6] Like Zeus upon Olympus and many another primitive deity, Yahweh, at the first, was a mountain god. Indeed, he was so confined to his habitat that, when the tribesmen under Moses left Sinai, the problem of believing in Yahweh's continuing presence with them was serious. According to the oldest traditions they did not suppose Yahweh himself would go with them—he was attached to his mountain home. Three times it is explicitly stated that not he but his angel was to accompany them on the journey to Canaan.[7]

For centuries this special attachment of Yahweh to his wilderness mountain remained vivid in the imagination of his devotees. When Deborah won a victory far north in Palestine, she still pictured Yahweh as coming in thunderous power from Sinai to his people's help.[8] When Elijah, dismayed by the apostasy of Israel, wished to stand in the very presence of his deity, he fled to "Horeb the mount of God."[9] Deuteronomy and Habakkuk, in the seventh century B.C., still kept in their symbolism the old picture of Yahweh coming from Sinai;[10] and a post-Exilic psalmist thought of God and Sinai together.[11]

As for the train of events which led to the momentous introduction of Israel to Yahweh at the "mountain of God," the proba-

---

[1] Joshua 24:14.
[2] Hosea 12:9; 13:4.
[3] Jeremiah 2:1-2.
[4] Ezekiel 20:5.
[5] Exodus 3:1 ff.
[6] Horeb and Sinai are presumably different names for the same mountain variously located. Horeb may be the more primitive. See W. J. Phythian-Adams: *The Call of Israel*, pp. 131-133.
[7] Exodus 23:20-23; 32:34; 33:1-3.
[8] Judges 5:4-5.
[9] I Kings 19:8.
[10] Deuteronomy 33:2; Habakkuk 3:3.
[11] Psalm 68:7-8.

bilities are strong. Moses, fleeing from Egypt to the wilderness, joined himself to the Kenites, a Midianite tribe of nomads living in the desert about Sinai. Into this tribe Moses married. His father-in-law was its religious head, "the priest of Midian,"[1] and Moses, associating himself with his wife's clan, became a devotee of Yahweh, the Kenite god. In such an incident as is presented in Exodus 18:1–12, revealing the pride of Jethro, priest of Yahweh, in the conquests of his tribal deity, this "Kenite hypothesis" seems to fit the facts.

Far down the course of Hebrew history, the Kenites continued to appear as uncompromising devotees of Yahweh. They associated themselves with the tribes of Israel and, settling in southern Canaan, continued there on the edge of the wilderness a semi-nomadic life.[2] Jael, a Kenite woman and a worshiper of Yahweh, smote Sisera;[3] the son of Rechab, a Kenite, supported Jehu in the bloody revolt of Yahweh's devotees against the apostasies of Ahab;[4] and even in Jeremiah's time, the Rechabites, driven from their ancient nomadic ways by guerilla warfare, could in Jerusalem be used to shame the Hebrews by their uncompromising devotion to the laws of their fathers.[5]

This Kenite hypothesis may be modified in detail as new evidence becomes available,[6] but its core of truth seems solid and dependable. Interpreted in terms of it, the scene at Sinai gains substance and clarity. Moses, himself a convert to the worship of Yahweh, led his fellow tribesmen from their bondage and at the "mountain of God" converted them to the same allegiance. There Yahweh and the tribes from Egypt were wedded with mutual exchange of vows. The tribal deity of the Kenites took a new people as his own and a confederation of clans that never before had served Yahweh swore fealty to him as their divinity.

To be sure, Yahweh was not a new god; at least the Kenites had been acquainted with him; the Judean Document, which scholars call "J," in its final form holds that the fathers had known him, and he may have been a deity of the tribe of Judah.[7] Even a more ancient and extensive history may have been his. "We find," says Lods, "in cuneiform documents of the pre-Mosaic age, a great number of personal names compounded with the syllables *ya, yau,*

[1] Exodus 3:1.
[2] Judges 1:16.
[3] Judges 5:24–27.
[4] II Kings 10:15–18 (cf. I Chronicles 2:55).
[5] Jeremiah, chap. 35.
[6] See Theophile James Meek: *Hebrew Origins*, pp. 86 ff.
[7] Exodus 3:16–18.

yami (or *yawe*), and even *jahveh*."[1] Some, therefore, think that
this god to whom Moses introduced the tribes from Egypt, while
new to them as their tribal deity, was not a stranger in the traditions of their race. This, however, does not affect the crucial fact,
from which the subsequent development of Israel's religion proceeds, that the distinctive faith of the Hebrews began with the
covenant between them and a deity new to their allegiance. Moreover, this relationship was not determined by mere chance of locality in accordance with which a static people naturally served
the god of their territory, but was an alliance voluntarily assumed
by migrating tribes. Yahweh was conceived as graciously choosing
a new people and the people were conceived as deliberately
accepting a new god.

Thus to emphasize the fresh start initiated by the creative
influence of Moses need not involve forgetfulness of the ancestral
background. Religion among the Semites had had a rich history
before Moses, and he and his people were the inheritors of a long
and significant tradition. Doubt of Abraham's personal existence,
for example, once prevalent, is surrendering to an increasing
confidence in the Biblical accounts of his migration from "Ur
of the Chaldees."[2] New in name, therefore, Yahweh may have
been old in meaning, and into Moses' creative faith doubtless
went long accumulating ideas and attitudes from his ancestral
heritage. Substantial truth may lie in the Scripture's verbal anachronism which represents Yahweh as saying: "I am the God of
thy father, the God of Abraham, the God of Isaac, and the God
of Jacob."[3]

II

Some of the major characteristics of Yahweh, the mountain
god of Sinai, stand out plainly in the narrative.

1. He was a storm god, associated with violent exhibitions of
nature's power. According to the written tradition, the first
experiences that the liberated clans from Egypt had with him
at Sinai were accompanied by thunderings and lightnings and
the mountain's smoking—"the smoke thereof ascended as the
smoke of a furnace, and the whole mount quaked greatly."[4]
This suggests a volcano, and Sinai may have been that or legend

---

[1] Adolphe Lods: *Israel from its Beginnings to the Middle of the Eighth Century*,
translated by S. H. Hooke, p. 320.

[2] See Stephen L. Caiger: *Bible and Spade*,
pp. 30 ff.

[3] Exodus 3:6,15,16; 4:5.

[4] Exodus 19:18; 20:18.

may have exaggerated such storms of thunder and lightning as still occur about the huge granite massif of the traditional Sinai, with mist pouring up like smoke from its flanks.

At any rate, as is true among all early peoples, from the beginning till far down the course of Hebrew thought, thunder and lightning were regarded as special exhibitions of superhuman power.

> They that strive with Yahweh shall be broken to pieces;
> Against them will he thunder in heaven[1] —

so sang the devotees of Sinai's god long after they were in Palestine, and in specific cases they attributed victory to the interposition of his thunderbolts—"Yahweh thundered with a great thunder on that day upon the Philistines, and discomfited them."[2] When Yahweh came from Sinai to Deborah's help, he was pictured riding the storm,[3] and even a psalmist saw the help of the Lord when he "thundered in the heavens," hurled "hailstones and coals of fire" and, like arrows, sent out his "lightnings manifold."[4]

It is impossible to tell when the idea that in thunder "the Most High uttered his voice" and in lightning shot his arrows[5] ceased being literal and became symbolic. The story of Elijah's sacrifice on Carmel with Yahweh sending down his lightning to burn the altar and its offering[6] is literal enough. Certainly at the first, the deity of Sinai was a god of storm.

2. Even more significantly, he was a god of war, battling for his people and leading them to victory. The ascription in the so-called Song of Moses,

> Yahweh is a man of war:
> Yahweh is his name,[7]

is typical of the earliest traditions. Concerning the triumph of Joshua on the day when "the sun stood still," we read, "Yahweh fought for Israel";[8] David defied Goliath, crying, "I come to thee in the name of Yahweh of hosts, the God of the armies of Israel";[9] and even a psalmist wrote,

> He teacheth my hands to war;
> So that mine arms do bend a bow of brass.[10]

[1] I Samuel 2:10.
[2] I Samuel 7:10.
[3] Judges 5:4.
[4] Psalm 18:13–14.
[5] Ibid.
[6] I Kings 18:38.
[7] Exodus 15:3.
[8] Joshua 10:13–14.
[9] I Samuel 17:45.
[10] Psalm 18:34.

Indeed, one compiler quotes from a book no longer extant, "the book of the Wars of Yahweh."[1]

Any god, vitally believed in at any time, is conceived as the backer of man's necessary enterprises. So the early Hebrews, whose most constant activity, next to sustaining life by labor, was war, needed a "Lord of hosts," a superhuman leader of armies, and Yahweh met that need. When camp was broken and the Ark was lifted, they cried, "Rise up, O Yahweh, and let thine enemies be scattered."[2] When the captured Ark was carried into the Philistine towns, the Israelite chronicler delighted to picture the Philistines' fear as they cried: "God is come into the camp. . . . Woe unto us! who shall deliver us out of the hand of these mighty gods?"[3] This interpretation of Yahweh's most sacred palladium, the Ark, was of one piece with the people's interpretation of Yahweh's most necessary function as their fighting chief. As another has put it, the Ark was "at one and the same time the primitive sanctuary and the battle standard."[4]

A storm god, dwelling on a mountain, whose major activity was war—such was the beginning of the development of the Jewish-Christian idea of God.

3. Involved in such a beginning is the further fact that Yahweh was a tribal god. That he loved Israel and graciously entered into covenant with his chosen people, far from implying love and grace in other relationships, involved vehement hatred of Israel's enemies.

An integral part of Yahweh's covenant with Israel was his declaration, "I will be an enemy unto thine enemies, and an adversary unto thine adversaries."[5] Indeed, Yahweh was represented as outdoing Israel in sustained and lethal hatred against non-Israelites, as, for example, the Canaanites—"It was of Yahweh to harden their hearts, to come against Israel in battle, that he might utterly destroy them, that they might have no favor, but that he might destroy them."[6] This capacity in Yahweh for prolonged and violent hatred of Israel's foes is set down in the record with unashamed emphasis, whether in the traditions of the wilderness, where "Yahweh will have war with Amalek from generation to generation,"[7] or in the early days of the kingdom in Palestine, when Yahweh commanded Saul to "go and smite

---

[1] Numbers 21:14.
[2] Numbers 10:35.
[3] I Samuel 4:7-8.
[4] H. Wheeler Robinson: *The Religious Ideas of the Old Testament*, p. 56.

[5] Exodus 23:22.
[6] Joshua 11:20.
[7] Exodus 17:16.

Amalek, and utterly destroy all that they have, and spare them not; but slay both man and woman, infant and suckling, ox and sheep, camel and ass."[1]

This god of war, with his relentless hatred of his people's enemies, was even supposed to be pleased by the sacrifice of prisoners taken in battle. In the history of primitive religions this form of human sacrifice is familiar. "It was also the custom from very early times," says Lods, "to slay adults, especially prisoners of war and criminals, with rites more or less resembling those of sacrifice. Among the pagan Arabs, captives were slain under every form of sacrifice. . . . Long after the slaughter of prisoners had become a purely secular act in Arabia, the term *hadij*, sacrificed, still denoted the slain captive. Similarly, the Carthaginians, after the defeat of Agathocles in 307 B.C., slew the prisoners of rank 'before the altar, in front of the sacred tent.'"[2] The wonder is not that this practise obtained but that it is so seldom evident in the Hebrew records. That it existed, however, is plain from an indubitable instance when Samuel, angry at the reservation of the Amalekite king from the general massacre, "hewed Agag in pieces before Yahweh in Gilgal."[3]

In many passages, moreover, this same usage is indicated, when the meaning of the English Version's words 'utterly destroy' is correctly given in the margin as 'devote.' That is, when "they smote the Canaanites that inhabited Zephath, and utterly destroyed it,"[4] what they really did was to 'devote' it to Yahweh. So Mesha, King of Moab, completely wrecking a town and killing its male inhabitants, said, "I slew all the men of the city for a spectacle to Chemosh"[5]—the Moabite god. Under this innocent translation in our English Versions, therefore, where 'utterly destroy' is substituted for 'devote,' there lies an idea of deity rejoicing in the human sacrifice of his people's foes. As the story in Numbers 21:1–3 reveals, one way to secure Yahweh's help in battle, so Israel believed, was to promise him the complete 'devotion' of all captured property and persons. So jealous was the god thought to be of this 'devoted' loot that when, as at Jericho, tabooed property was secreted, his wrath was ruinous,[6] or when, as late as the ninth century, Ahab spared the life of the captured king of Syria, Yahweh was pictured as saying, "Because thou

---

[1] I Samuel 15:3.
[2] Adolphe Lods: *Israel from its Beginnings to the Middle of the Eighth Century*, translated by S. H. Hooke, p. 287.
[3] I Samuel 15:33.
[4] Judges 1:17.
[5] The Mesha Stone II, 11–12. See Lods: *op. cit.*, p. 288.
[6] Joshua, chap. 7.

hast let go out of thy hand the man whom I had devoted to destruction, therefore thy life shall go for his life."[1]

The long-drawn-out story of the Jewish-Christian endeavor to outgrow nationalism in theology as well as in practise began in this belligerent and ruthless tribalism of Israel's primitive war god.

4. Involved in this early idea of Yahweh was, of course, anthropomorphism. At first he was pictured with frank physical realism. It is difficult to determine when the ascription to him of hands, feet, face, eyes, ears, and nose, passes over into symbolism, but such expressions have behind them, as the records show, a thoroughly anthropomorphic idea of deity. He walked in the Garden of Eden in the cool of the day and talked familiarly with Adam;[2] he ate and conversed with Abraham;[3] he wrestled with Jacob so that the patriarch said, "I have seen God face to face, and my life is preserved."[4]

The origins of the sacrificial system in Israel, as elsewhere, imply this physical realism in the thought of deity. Back of more sophisticated meanings, which later were seen in the temple sacrifices, and more rarefied interpretations of the effect of ritual offerings on Yahweh, was the idea of the communal meal where deity and people shared the same feast and the god of the tribe enjoyed with his devotees their sacrificial food. This is explicitly stated and indirectly implied in many passages of the Old Testament. The fat and blood of the sacrifices were reserved for Yahweh; they were his portion of the feast. At first they were rubbed upon the sacred stone or altar; later, when offerings of fat were made by fire, Yahweh partook of them only through the sense of smell—"the priest shall burn them upon the altar: it is the food of the offering made by fire, for a sweet savor; all the fat is Yahweh's."[5] The age-long persistence of outward forms of animal sacrifice along with profound changes in the interpretation of their meaning presents one of the commonest phenomena of religious history—preservation of custom accompanied by alteration of theory. At the origin of food offerings to the god was the primitive idea that the god shared the enjoyment of them.

This physical participation of Yahweh in the sacrifices was plainly implied in the prophetic reaction against such anthropomorphism. No explanation of the specific points selected by

[1] I Kings 20:42.
[2] Genesis, chap. 3.
[3] Genesis 18:1 ff.
[4] Genesis 32:24–30.
[5] Leviticus 3:16.

the prophets for attack seems probable except that those points constituted a continuing danger to the spiritual idea of the divine nature. When, therefore, <u>Isaiah's Yahweh</u> scorned "the burnt-offerings of rams, and the fat of fed beasts,"[1] or the psalmist's Yahweh cried,

> Will I eat the flesh of bulls,
> Or drink the blood of goats?[2]

we have not only an emphatic insistence that God is not the kind of being who partakes of physical food, but also a clear indication that the popular view, against which this protest was being made, held the contrary.

Moreover, the sublimation of actual eating and drinking into smelling the offerings was probably an endeavor to rarefy the more gross conception of the god, and it revealed in the background the primitive ideas it sought to overpass. The Deluge Tablet of Babylonia says concerning the sacrifice after the Flood:

> The gods smelled the odor,
> The gods smelled the sweet odor.
> The gods gathered like flies around the sacrificer.[3]

The Hebrew rendition of the same story chastens the details but retains the anthropomorphism—"Yahweh smelled the sweet savor."[4] From being food for Yahweh's eating, sacrifice thus became what Deuteronomy called "incense in thy nostrils,"[5] and so literally was this conceived that against it also the prophets launched their protest. Isaiah's Yahweh cried, "Incense is an abomination unto me,"[6] and Amos' Yahweh declared, "I will not smell a savor in your solemn assemblies."[7]

The early narratives concerning the Sinaitic deity to whom Moses introduced Israel are outspoken in their anthropomorphism. Apart from details which are probably symbolic, such as Yahweh's writing the original tables of the law with his own finger,[8] we have a physical vision of Yahweh by Moses, which must have originated in a primitive story of a man seeing his god. "Yahweh said, Behold, there is a place by me, and thou shalt stand upon the rock: and it shall come to pass, while my

---

[1] Isaiah 1:11.
[2] Psalm 50:13.
[3] As quoted by Morris Jastrow: *Hebrew and Babylonian Traditions*, p. 332.
[4] Genesis 8:21.
[5] Deuteronomy 33:10 (marginal translation).

[6] Isaiah 1:13.
[7] Amos 5:21 (marginal translation).
[8] Exodus 31:18. Cf. The Rosetta Stone, where hieroglyphs are called "the writing of divine words, written by the god Thoth himself."

glory passeth by, that I will put thee in a cleft of the rock, and will cover thee with my hand until I have passed by: and I will take away my hand, and thou shalt see my back; but my face shall not be seen."[1]

One of the notable achievements of later Judaism was the abolition of idolatry—the complete suppression of all pictorial and plastic representations of Yahweh and all images of man or beast associated with his worship. This, however, was not the primitive beginning. Even the later rewriting of the records, pushing back the command against images into the law of Moses and denying in every way the allowance of idols, did not destroy the plain evidence of Yahweh's physical representation in the early days. Micah, the Ephraimite, had an image of Yahweh;[2] Gideon made one out of captured gold;[3] the teraphim were household gods, human enough in appearance to supply David with a substitute when he fled from his foes;[4] and, indeed, so customary were "graven images" that while early protests were made, as in the law of Exodus, "Thou shalt make thee no molten gods,"[5] and in the story of the golden calf,[6] probably dating from the time of Jeroboam's apostasy, the first prophet plainly to take his stand against them was Hosea, in the eighth century.[7]

The inevitable companion of anthropomorphism was anthropopathism, ascribing human emotions to the god. Hatred, jealousy, vindictiveness, disappointment at unforeseen events, regret for mistaken decisions—the common characteristic attitudes of man at his worst, as well as at his best, were attributed to the god. At the beginning, therefore, the god of the Bible was a person, physically embodied although superhumanly powerful, who could conceivably be seen, who in the earliest strata of the Scripture walked, talked, wrestled, dined, and smelled, and who shared with man a wide gamut of good and bad emotions.

III

One of the most important occasions of change in Israel's idea of Yahweh came when this primitive mountain god became the territorial deity of the land of Canaan. As time went on, Yahweh was detached in the imagination of his people from his exclusive

[1] Exodus 33:21–23.
[2] Judges 17:3–4.
[3] Judges 8:24–27.
[4] I Samuel 19:12–16 (cf. Genesis 31:17–35).
[5] Exodus 34:17.
[6] Exodus 32:1 ff.
[7] Hosea 11:2; 8:4–6. See Adolphe Lods: "Images and Idols, Hebrew and Canaanite," III, 2, in *Encyclopædia of Religion and Ethics*, edited by J. Hastings.

residence on Sinai, and he became acclimated in Canaan as lord of the land. In this process, according to the finished tradition, the Ark—a sacred coffer whose attendance with the wandering tribes was understood to involve either the real or deputed presence of Yahweh—played a significant part. While, at the first, it was his angel rather than himself who went with the migrant clans, the shading between Yahweh and his angel in the early documents is so vague that in the same story both forms of representation may be used.[1] So, as the Biblical records present the picture, Yahweh, whether in his proper person or by deputy in an angelic representative, traveled with his nomadic devotees, and of his abiding presence the Ark was the visible symbol and vehicle. Where the Ark was, he was; when the Ark was not carried into an important enterprise, his guidance and power were absent.[2]

This identification of the Ark with the special presence of Yahweh is repeatedly shown in the narratives, until, as the most sacred palladium of the nation, it was placed in the Holy of Holies of Solomon's temple. When David was bringing it up to his capital, he and the people played and danced "before Yahweh"[3] and when on the first stage of its journey a helpful man tried to steady the sacred fetish as it jounced over the rough road, he fell dead because, so they thought, "Yahweh had broken forth upon Uzzah."[4] Whatever may have been the historic facts about the Ark in the wilderness,[5] the written tradition in the end pictured God as traveling with his people in this sacred chest, and while Sinai for centuries was thought of as his special home, the Ark, whether as history or legend, may well have been a bridge by which in popular imagination Yahweh passed over into Canaan. There, at any rate, he was acclimated and naturalized until Palestine became what Hosea called it, "Yahweh's land."[6]

This process carried with it at least two attendant results.

1. Becoming the god of Israel's land, Yahweh was limited in his sovereignty to the territory of his people. At this stage, not only were tribal deities confined in their goodwill to their own clans but, as well, they were generally imagined as confined in their presence and power to their own lands. The Philistine cities were hardly twenty-five miles from Bethlehem but, when David by Saul's jealousy was forced to take refuge there, he complained,

[1] Genesis 16:7–14; 21:17–19.
[2] Numbers 14:41–45.
[3] II Samuel 6:2–5, 12–15.
[4] II Samuel 6:6–8.
[5] See Louis Wallis: God and the Social

Process, pp. 107–109; Elmer A. Leslie: Old Testament Religion in the Light of its Canaanite Background, pp. 121 ff,
[6] Hosea 9:3.

"They have driven me out this day that I should not cleave unto the inheritance of Yahweh, saying, Go, serve other gods."[1] This idea of Yahweh's available presence as limited to his territory, so that only a few miles away one must worship other deities, constituted the background from which larger ideas of God emerged, and far down in Israel's history its sway was felt. Even a late and nobly international tract, the Book of Jonah, recalls it, picturing Jonah as taking ship to another country that he might flee "from the presence of Yahweh."[2] In many ways, direct and indirect, this limitation of the Hebrew god to his own geographical demesne is revealed in the early documents of the Bible, as, for example, when Naaman, the Syrian, healed by Elisha, carried "two mules' burden of earth" from Israel's land back to Damascus, that he might have, even in a foreign country, some of Yahweh's soil on which, standing, he could worship the god of Israel.[3]

This attachment of a god to his territory obviously involved the recognition of other gods as real and powerful in their own lands. So Jephthah, claiming for Israel what Israel's god had given her, granted to Moab the right to "possess that which Chemosh thy god giveth thee."[4] The Hebrew records even attribute the retreat of an Israelitish army, which had been successfully invading Moab, to the "great wrath against Israel" that the Moabites aroused, presumably in their god Chemosh, by the human sacrifice of their own crown prince.[5]

When, therefore, by choice or necessity one was in other lands, one would naturally worship other gods, as David in Philistia felt coerced to do. Even a post-Exilic book, Ruth, pictures its heroine as changing gods when she passed from Moab to Bethlehem, although the two were scarcely thirty miles apart and could be plainly seen, one from the other, across the Jordan gorge—"Whither thou goest, I will go; and where thou lodgest, I will lodge; thy people shall be my people, and thy God my God."[6] As late as Jeremiah's time, exile from the Holy Land was popularly interpreted as forcing the worship of strange deities—"Therefore will I cast you forth out of this land into the land that ye have not known, neither ye nor your fathers; and there shall ye serve other gods day and night."[7]

---

[1] I Samuel 26:19.
[2] Jonah 1:3,10.
[3] II Kings 5:17.
[4] Judges 11:23–24.
[5] II Kings 3:26–27.
[6] Ruth 1:16.
[7] Jeremiah 16:13.

As this necessity was laid on Israelites in foreign territories, so, in reverse, foreigners in Palestine fared ill if they failed to worship Yahweh. When the Northern Kingdom fell, in 721 B.C., and the Assyrian monarch settled strangers in Samaria, it was in vain that they brought their own gods with them. "Yahweh sent lions among them," and it was only when a Hebrew priest was furnished to "teach them the law of the god of the land .... how they should fear Yahweh," that they felt safe.[1]

This extension of the idea of Yahweh, until, no longer merely or mainly a storm god dwelling on Sinai and furnishing leadership in war, he became the god of the land of Canaan, was one of the first long steps out into new conceptions of deity.

2. Yahweh, becoming the territorial god of Canaan, became of necessity an agricultural deity. This he never had been in the wilderness, where agriculture and its accompanying needs, habits, and ideas did not exist. To pass, as the Hebrews did, from nomadic wanderings to a settled residence, from the exclusive tending of herds to the culture of crops, from tents to villages and walled towns, involved a profound change in the life and thought of the people, and, not least of all, in their religion. This process, the military part of which has been artificially foreshortened in the Biblical story of the conquest of Canaan, was really long drawn-out and gradual. For generations the Israelites clung, as it were, by their eyebrows to a small section of the hill country of Ephraim amid bitter enemies—Ammonites and Moabites, to the east; the Philistines invading the seacoast lands to the west; the Amorites still possessing a score of strong towns and the farm lands around them.

At first the inveterate prejudice of the nomad against the agriculturist held its ground. Of this stage the legend of Cain and Abel is representative, in which Yahweh is pictured as welcoming the offerings of the herdsman, Abel, and refusing the offerings of the farmer, Cain.[2] But, after all, the Israelites and the Amorites were cousins; they came alike of Semitic stock; their traditions were rooted in a common soil; the commercial civilization of the Amorites was far more rich, varied, and advanced than that of the rough and virile adventurers under Joshua and his successors, so that, as generations passed, with the two peoples living side by side and the more robust and energetic Israelites gaining increased ascendency, an inevitable process of syncretism went on and the two cultures blended.

[1] II Kings 17:24-33.   [2] Genesis 4:2-5.

The Canaanitish baals were gods of agriculture. As the conquering clans of Israel had needed their god chiefly as the "Lord of hosts," so the Canaanites needed their gods to give rain and bestow fertility. Each locality had its baal or baals, and the "high places," where these ancient deities were worshiped, still have their lineal descendants in Palestine, often doubtless identically situated, in the local shrines of Mohammedan and Christian saints. The Israelites did not so much choose between Yahweh and the baals as blend the worship of Yahweh with the customs of the high places until Yahweh himself became a baal. So, long afterward, Hosea in the name of Yahweh protested: "Thou . . . shalt call me no more Baali."[1] This process of syncretism was doubtless greatly encouraged when David, in order to conquer the Philistines, substituted alliance with the Amorites for the traditional hostility against them and so built a kingdom which included Yahweh-worshipers and baal-worshipers together. Long before that, however, the baals, as historically established gods of the land, had exercised a profound influence on Hebrew ideas of Yahweh and on methods of worshiping him.

At first Yahweh and the baals were so different in function that coördinate loyalty to both was possible. The local baals were the sources of agricultural plenty—so wide areas of the people still believed when in the eighth century Hosea thundered against the idea[2]—while Yahweh was the god of nomadic life and the leader of his clans in battle. This distinction can be pressed too far but it was real. An Israelite, therefore, might retain genuine loyalty to his tribal god, turning to him when his needs were military, and still make sacrifices to the local baal when he wanted rain. This initial division of function, however, could not last; syncretism was inevitable; alike in idea and custom, Yahweh borrowed from the baals and the baals, presumably, from Yahweh. So, in the end, while the Ark may have been the special palladium of the people and the initial pledge of Yahweh's presence, he was so far from being confined to it that he was available throughout his land in the high places where his people worshiped. Indeed, a justification of this was read back into tradition and put upon the lips of Yahweh in his conversation with Moses on Mount Sinai: ("In every place where I cause my name to be remembered I will come unto thee and I will bless thee."[3])

[1] Hosea 2:16.
[2] Hosea 2:5–13.
[3] Exodus 20:24 (marginal translation).

As soon as this idea of the approachability of Yahweh at the local shrines was well established, the blending of Yahweh and the baals was certain to proceed apace. The powerful hold of Yahweh on the grateful memory and devotion of Israel is, indeed, made evident by the fact that they did not surrender him to the Canaanitish gods of the land, but kept him, added to him the functions, powers, and ceremonies of the baals, until the prophets rose in a desperate and magnificent attempt to conserve the good and eradicate the evil of this perilous syncretism.

Such a process as this is a commonplace in the history of religion. When Christianity moved into northern Europe, the old shrines of the pre-Christian deities, instead of being abolished, were often taken over and absorbed. Where some heathen god had been adored, now the Virgin or a saint was worshiped, and as had happened in Rome itself when the Saturnalia was transformed into the Christmas festival, old customs were given new meanings. "In like manner," says Kautzsch, "among the Arabs, long after the victory of Islam, the local cult of the pre-Islamic gods persisted, partly in the popular usages (forbidden by Islam), partly in some usages incorporated with Islam itself."[1] If this happened in the face of a victory as complete as Islam's over Arabia, how much more would such syncretism take place when, as in Israel's case in Palestine, the Canaanites could not be utterly conquered but, sustained and empowered, so current beliefs would suggest, by their native gods, lived on with the Israelites!

One effect of this syncretism was greatly to enlarge and diversify the functions of Yahweh until, to the faithful Israelite, he became the source of agricultural plenty. Thence arose the agricultural festivals, such as the Feast of Unleavened Bread, the Feast of Tabernacles, the Feast of Weeks, the Feast of Harvest, whose origin was read back into the Mosaic Law but whose existence could have had no meaning until the Israelites were in Canaan. In the end a prophet could ascribe to Yahweh the revelation of all man's knowledge concerning the technique of farming.[2]

Nevertheless, the cost of such syncretism was heavy. Yahweh had always been conceived as powerful and ruthless in war—even brutal from the standpoint of later ideals—but he had been

---

[1] E. Kautzsch: "Religion of Israel," III, iii, 2, in Hastings' *Dictionary of the Bible*, Extra Vol., p. 645.

[2] Isaiah 28:23-29.

virile, austere, and chaste. If he had the faults of a war god he also had the virtues—he was hard and disciplined, an inflexible sponsor of rigorous self-control and of the social solidarity of the nomads. The gods of agriculture, however, have uniformly been licentious. There never failed to exist in Israel a protestant party, holding to the primitive austerity of Yahweh's worship and resisting the encroachments of the new pollutions—the Rechabites, for example, who would not even dwell in houses or touch wine.[1] Moreover, the Israelites on the ridge of Ephraim evidently maintained in their kinship groups many basic nomadic ideas of social justice sponsored by Yahweh and were consciously and even violently at variance with the inequities of Amorite commercialism sponsored by the baals. Nevertheless, when two cultures live so closely together, mutual contagion across all barriers is inevitable and Israel was profoundly affected by ideas and customs associated with the baals.

The Hebrews, for example, took over the imitative magic in accordance with which the sexual act, performed at the shrine of the god, was supposed to encourage the soil's fertility. So prostitution and sodomy crept into the worship of Yahweh and were found even in the central temple at Jerusalem as late as the reform of Josiah in the seventh century.[2] Here, too, grew up the worship of Yahweh under the likeness of bulls, such as Jeroboam set up at Dan and Bethel.[3] The story of Aaron and the golden calf[4] in all probability was written in this later age to help withstand the polluting identification of Yahweh's worship with the adoration of bulls.

It is not possible to trace to their origins the many factors which made up Israel's popular religion. The Yahweh tradition was only one strand in a tangled complex where old Semitic inheritances, animistic survivals, and syncretic appropriations were confusedly mingled. Israel's religion was not an individualistic faith but a social culture which affected every hour of every day and penetrated conduct at every point. In it were included curious taboos,[5] primitive cults such as serpent worship,[6] the use of ordeal in judicial cases,[7] the power of the curse,[8] the employment of magic in battle;[9] and as for sacred stones, trees, waters, caves, the early records are full of them. Such common factors

---

[1] Jeremiah 35:1–10.
[2] II Kings 23:7; Hosea 4:13–14.
[3] I Kings 12:26–29.
[4] Exodus 32:1 ff.
[5] E.g., Exodus 23:19; Leviticus 22:28.
[6] II Kings 18:4.
[7] Numbers 5:11–31.
[8] Numbers 22:6.
[9] Exodus 17:8–13.

in primitive religion doubtless came out of Israel's background but Canaan supplied endless opportunity for their application. The Hebrews took over the sacred places, constructed patriarchal legends concerning them, absorbed their customary rituals, and wove them into the complex fabric of Yahweh's faith and worship. And, as the prophets later saw, all this presented two focal points of peril to the best traditions that had come from the desert: it substituted for the old austerity the alluring licentiousness of baal worship, and it sanctioned the commercial inequalities and tyrannies, which the baals of sophisticated Canaan sponsored against the ancient ideas of social solidarity, equality, and justice for which Yahweh stood.

IV

No historic imagination can adequately canvass the varied causes and occasions which led to the gradual enlargement and elevation of the Hebrew idea of deity, but some of the process is visible.

1. Yahweh became god of the sky.[1] The very fact that he was a mountain god controlling thunder and lightning would associate him with the sky, and while we are dealing with legend in Jacob's vision of the celestial ladder with Yahweh above it,[2] and in the story of the tower of Babel, where Yahweh jealously protects from men's invasion his heavenly dwelling,[3] such representations reveal the extension of Yahweh's sovereignty, far above solitary mountain or earthly territory, to the sky.

This idea, at the beginning, doubtless coexisted with earlier and more mundane conceptions; it was thought by a few before it was held by many; it was conceived by many before it became practically operative in their daily religion. At last, however, it occupied the minds and imaginations of the people and tended inevitably toward universalism. A god who, as the Eighteenth Psalm put it, "bowed the heavens"[4] was escaping from the limited ideas by which his earlier followers had conceived him.

Indeed, the word Elohim, the ordinary Hebrew name for God, belonging as it does to a large family of Semitic words which spring from the same stem, is thought by some to have denoted originally a sky god. So inevitably is universal dominion suggested by such a concept of deity that some even suspect a kind of

[1] E.g., Psalm 2:4; 11:4; 103:19; II Chronicles 6:18.
[2] Genesis 28:12–13.
[3] Genesis 11:1–9.
[4] Psalm 18:9.

primitive Semitic monotheism as a background against which the mass of lesser gods arose.[1](In the Bible itself, however, no evidence exists of such original monotheism, nor is any contribution made toward explaining the detailed data of Scripture by supposing it.) Moreover, the word Elohim is of dubious origin and meaning; quite probably it denotes not the sky in particular but strength in general; variously translated in our English Versions, it is used in the Bible of household gods,[2] of supernatural spirits,[3] even of earthly judges,[4] and to build on its higher developments a doctrine of original monotheism is not convincing. Rather, the universality of the "God of heaven" was a long postponed conviction in Israel's thinking.[5]

2. Along with this elevation of the thought of Yahweh as god of the sky went the even more practical idea that, however geographically bounded he might be within his people's land, he still could display his power outside it. On the basis of Israel's own traditions, both historic and legendary, he long since had operated over all the known world. Had he not given an illustrious exhibition of his power in favor of his people in Egypt? As the written stories of the patriarchs stand in the "J" Document, had he not called Abraham in "Ur of the Chaldees" and dealt intimately with the patriarchs all the way from the Euphrates to the Nile? An earthly king may have his own limited territory and still be able to strike far beyond its boundaries to protect his subjects and assert his majesty. So Yahweh, while the god of the Holy Land, was conceived as possessing ever extended powers, and while this could be roughly harmonized with belief in many gods, it broke through the strictness of the earlier territorial ideas and opened the way to expectations of Yahweh's effective action, anywhere, at any time, as he might please.

3. After kingship was established in Judah and Ephraim, such enlarged ideas were given visible form and practical effect by alliances between princely houses. One of the first results of international royal marriages is to be seen in statements like this: "Then did Solomon build a high place for Chemosh the abomination of Moab, in the mount that is before Jerusalem, and for Molech the abomination of the children of Ammon. And so did

---

[1] See Stephen Herbert Langdon: *Semitic Mythology*, p. 93.
[2] Judges 17:5; Genesis 31:19,32.
[3] I Samuel 28:13.
[4] Psalm 82:1.
[5] On fallacy of pre-Mosaic monotheism see Adolphe Lods: *Israel from its Beginnings to the Middle of the Eighth Century*, translated by S. H. Hooke, pp. 253–257; Theophile James Meek: *Hebrew Origins*, pp. 180 ff.

he for all his foreign wives, who burnt incense and sacrificed unto their gods."[1] The theological inference implied in such inter-territorial worship is clear: gods can be served outside their own domains; they are more or less interlocking in their directorates; if Chemosh, who had been the fierce enemy of Yahweh and his people, can be worshiped on the Mount of Olives, presumably Yahweh can be worshiped in Moab. To be sure, such inferences were not generally drawn. The practise of inter-territorial worship, exhibited by Solomon in Judah or by the house of Omri in Ephraim, far from being used as a proposition from which to draw theological deductions, was abhorred by the vigorous devotees of Yahweh as sacrilege and apostasy. Nevertheless, the practise was there: gods were becoming intermingled across all boundaries; a change in lands did not, at least for royal folk, necessitate a change in deities.

Many more influences, doubtless, than the Biblical records reveal or our insight can recapture played thus on the enlarging conception of Yahweh. Obviously, however, as god of the sky, able to display his power across the known world and conceivably to be worshiped outside his own land, he was on the way toward universal sovereignty. Still he was far from it. At that stage a pious Hebrew was no monotheist. He might be a henotheist—worshiping one god himself while not doubting the existence of others. Monolatry he might practise but monotheism he had not yet grasped.

V

Far more important than the influences which we have named in deepening the idea of Yahweh's character was the social conflict involved when the nomadic ethics of Israel faced the commercial civilization of the Amorites. The baals were gods not simply of agriculture but of the economic and social relationships which had developed in the comparatively sophisticated, stratified, commercialized town life of the Amorites. The struggle on the crest of Ephraim's hills, where the Israelites precariously held their ground, was not between two sets of religious ideas in the abstract, but between two economic and social cultures, one sponsored by the baals, the other by Yahweh. On the one side was a stratified society, with a few rich and many poor, with private property in land and water, with money, trade, and credit and the inequalities and tyrannies incident to a commer-

[1] I Kings 11:7-8.

cialized regime—all this under the ægis of the baals. On the other side was a tribal brotherhood of nomads where, amid the penury of the wilderness, all must be for each and each for all, where land and water were never private but always communal, where none was very rich or very poor, where every one was known to all and the exigencies of desert life forced a rough but sturdy justice. So Doughty speaks of the nomad tribes as "commonwealths of brethren" and says that "in the opinion of the next governed countries, the Arabs of the wilderness are the justest of mortals."[1] Of this social solidarity and fraternal fair play among the Israelite tribes Yahweh was the divine patron. A great tradition lies behind the statement in the later law, "Thou shalt love thy neighbor as thyself: I am Yahweh."[2] The crux of the struggle, therefore, between the Hebrew invaders and the Amorites was indeed between their gods, but between their gods as sanctifying two deeply antagonistic economic and social systems.

The translation of economic class struggle into terms of religious conflict is a familiar phenomenon in history. So Mr. George Henry Soule says of the Puritan revolution in the sixteenth century: "The conflict of religious ideas was indeed important, but it was important not so much because of the abstract significance of these ideas as because they represented the mechanism of attack and defense between economic and social classes who were struggling for power."[3] Similarly no one can understand the long conflict between the baals and Yahweh, with its story of attraction and repulsion, assimilation and revulsion, culminating in the prophetic determination, from Elijah on, to tear Yahweh's worship free from baal entanglements, unless one sees, underneath, the fierce hostility between two economic and social cultures. The Amorite lords and nobles—called baalim like their gods—hated and feared the equalitarian ideas and practises of the nomads, and the Israelites with similar revulsion despised the city-dominated social order with its private ownership of land and water and its bitter inequalities of station.

This conflict, which existed from the first and which accounts for much of the unappeasable hostility, became explicit in the ninth century in a titanic figure, Elijah.[4] Under the royal patronage of Queen Jezebel, Melkart, Baal of Tyre, rose to such prom-

---

[1] Charles M. Doughty: *Travels in Arabia Deserta* (3d ed., 1925), Vol. I, pp. 345, 249.
[2] Leviticus 19:18.
[3] *The Coming American Revolution*, p. 23.
[4] I Kings, chaps. 17–19.

inence and power that the party of Yahweh were in despair and Elijah towered up in protest. The greatest prophetic figure between Moses and Amos, his significance lay in his intense devotion to Yahweh as the god of the old, fair folk-ways of Israel. He himself came from Gilead, east of Jordan, and therefore close to desert life. He found, so we are given to understand, seven thousand in Israel who had not bowed the knee to Baal,[1] a strong party of Yahweh's devotees, who had refused to be assimilated. They represented the old ideals; they were often, it may be, of semi-nomadic habits; they were reactionaries against the new customs and especially the new luxury and inequality represented by the nobles and the court. Their social protest took form and gained point when a foreign baal, Melkart, was introduced by Jezebel of Tyre. Here was a visible symbol of the social system which they hated.

By this time the local baals had been largely absorbed, their agricultural functions had been taken over into a syncretic blend, and Elijah raised no protest against the worship of Yahweh at the high places, such as Carmel. The conflict which he led broke out over a foreign baal, supported by royal authority and symbolizing the entire system of alien customs, selfish luxury, and iniquitous commercialism that threatened not alone Yahweh's worship but Yahweh's social justice.

The importance of the economic factor in this protest is apparent in Elijah's sponsorship of Naboth against Ahab.[2] The motive power of Elijah lay in the indissoluble blend of his religion with social justice. He stood in vehement opposition to the modern customs, which presumably included the luxurious court, the collapse of old simplicities, the conscription of farmers and shepherds into military service, mounting taxation, the decay of old nomadic ideals of brotherhood. 'Yahweh against baal' was identical in his mind not so much with a theological discussion as with a social revolt. Yahweh stood for justice and brotherhood, against luxury for the few and want for the many, and especially against the iniquitous accretion of oppressive power by which a family heritage like Naboth's could be seized by the king even at the cost of murder. Here we run upon the most significant of all factors in the development of Israel's idea of God, and the ultimate outcome, long afterward, was not simply monotheism but *ethical* monotheism.

That this prophetic idea of Yahweh's character and of his

[1] I Kings 19:18.   [2] I Kings, chap. 21.

demand for personal and social righteousness was a development and was not to be found in full flower in the original Sinaitic deity as the later legends pictured him, is clear. Yahweh, the mountain storm god, was not ethical in any such sense as was Yahweh, 'Lord' of the prophets. To be sure, a deeply ethical element existed in the religion of Yahweh from the start, for it was based on the mutually exchanged vows of a voluntary covenant. Yahweh, at first, was, like Chemosh, a mountain god, but a significant fact distinguished them. Chemosh was a natural god to Moab—the lord and owner of Moabite territory and therefore the inevitable god of any folk who lived there. Yahweh, however, by free selection had of his own grace chosen a people who were strangers to him and they in turn had chosen a god whom hitherto they had not known. It was a religion by marriage rather than by birth, by grace rather than by geography, and, in so far, it was from the beginning moral, involving duties voluntarily assumed.

To this basic covenantal relationship the prophets constantly appealed; into its mutual obligations they poured ever new meanings; and at the center of its tradition they had the solid virtues of nomadic life where human ties are close, interdependent and coöperative, where men exist as brothers on a fairly equalitarian level and with a strong democratic sense of personal right. Elijah, therefore, is notably important as a creative influence in the developing idea both of Yahweh's sole supremacy over Israel and of his profoundly ethical character.

VI

In theology Elijah represented monolatry—believing other gods to be existent but recognizing Yahweh as the one and only god for Israel. Monolatry, however, to a vigorous and growing faith is monotheism in the bud, and the gradual flowering out of Israel's idea of God was evident in the eighth-century prophets. Still to Hosea and Amos, Canaan was especially Yahweh's land and other lands were "unclean."[1] Within Canaan Yahweh was to be worshiped at the high places; not until generations later was prophetic protest made against this custom and an idea of God developed that required one central and exclusive shrine. Still the ceremonial and ethical conflict was on between Yahweh and the baals—a certain irreducible hostility along with an inevitable syncretism. So Hosea insisted on crediting to Yahweh

[1]Amos 7:17; Hosea 9:3.

the agricultural functions which once belonged to the baals, while at the same time he protested against the licentious worship that the baals had sponsored.[1] Out from this old background, however, the first writing prophets can be seen moving, by a road familiar in the history of religion, toward monotheism.

The theistic question was asked then in a way far different from ours: it did not concern primarily the origin and maintenance of the universe. The Hebrews had scientific curiosity and, as the first chapter of Genesis reveals, ascribed to their God the creation of the world. Even Amos called Yahweh "him that maketh the Pleiades and Orion."[2] In the earlier prophets, however, this emphasis was rare. The vivid and imperious question then was: Among the gods of the nations, which god is most real and powerful? Sennacherib's message to the besieged people of Jerusalem touched their theology where it really was when he said: "Beware lest Hezekiah persuade you, saying, Yahweh will deliver us. Hath any of the gods of the nations delivered his land out of the hand of the king of Assyria? Where are the gods of Hamath and Arpad? where are the gods of Sepharvaim? and have they delivered Samaria out of my hand? Who are they among all the gods of these countries, that have delivered their country out of my hand, that Yahweh should deliver Jerusalem out of my hand?"[3] In answering this question about relative power among the deities, the early writing prophets moved out into practical monotheism, for they ascribed to Yahweh the successes and disasters even of their foes, and thought of him as in commanding control of all mankind.

So Isaiah's Yahweh addressed the world's most powerful king: "Ho Assyrian, the rod of mine anger, the staff in whose hand is mine indignation!"[4] and, according to Amos, Yahweh directed the migrations not only of Israel from Egypt, but of the Philistines from Caphtor and the Syrians from Kir.[5] A god whose sovereignty thus includes all men and nations is a god whose rivals will soon cease to seem real.

Moreover, in the prophets of the eighth and seventh centuries, along with this emergence of practical monotheism went an even more astonishing development of moral ideas. Here we are faced with a contribution to human thought easier to admire than to explain. With all available theological and sociological factors

[1] Hosea 2:8–9; 4:12–14.
[2] Amos 5:8.
[3] Isaiah 36:18–20.

[4] Isaiah 10:5.
[5] Amos 9:7.

in our hands, we still are thrown back in wonder upon the "abysmal depths of personality" in the great prophets. The lowest point in conceiving the moral character of Yahweh is probably to be found in a strange encysted bit of folklore in the Book of Exodus. There Yahweh is pictured as bloodthirstily wanting to kill Moses at a wayside lodging place, for no apparent reason at all, and is dissuaded by Zipporah's swift circumcision of Moses' child, at the sight of which the god "let him alone."[1] The difference between this primitive folklore and the moral dignity and quality of God in the greatest of the pre-Exilic prophets, from Hosea to Jeremiah, represents one of the most significant revelations in human history.

To be sure, the prophets lost their battle; they did not succeed in preserving the social justice of the early nomadic brotherhood. As tyrannical kingship had taken the place of paternal chieftainship and a stratified society based on slave labor had crowded out earlier equality, so the social organization of Israel continued to take form from the patterns of the day. The very sophistications and inequities against which the partisans of Yahweh had vehemently contended became acclimated in Israel. "They covet fields, and seize them; and houses, and take them away: and they oppress a man and his house, even a man and his heritage"[2]— so to the end of the story the prophets fought a losing battle.

Nevertheless they won a war. They successfully prevented the identification of Yahweh with the social and economic inequities of his people. Far from allowing the Hebrew god to become mere sponsor of the Hebrew *status quo*, they associated him with an ethical standard which judged and condemned it. That they were able to do this because the nomadic traditions of their race had come into violent conflict with a more sophisticated civilization, so that, in the name of conservatism, they could appeal to old folk-ways against the new commercialism, does not detract from their credit. They never succeeded in making the old folk-ways regnant in the new civilization but they did succeed, as no other religious teachers of antiquity ever succeeded, in elevating their god above both the nationalistic policies and the economic customs of their people. Yahweh, in their thought, became not merely a nationalistic deity or a divine patron of an existent order, but a moral judge who would throw into the discard even his chosen people if they violated his ethical standards.

[1] Exodus 4:24-26.   [2] Micah 2:2.

In this lies one of the main elements of uniqueness in the Old Testament's developing idea of God. The temptation of all believers in any kind of god is to use him as the sanctifier of the *status quo*. Tribal and nationalistic deities in particular have commonly been associated with the dominant customs and the ruling class, have been regarded as committed to the support of national policies, have become often gods of the powerful rather than of the weak, of the rich rather than of the impoverished, of the existent system rather than of social reformation. Thus was Yahweh conceived in Israel by many a king and priest, by many a member of the land-owning, slave-owning, creditor class, and doubtless also by wide areas of popular opinion. He was thought of as unqualifiedly committed to Israel's support, no matter what Israel might do, and as sanctioning the social system customary at the time. The prophets, however, won a victory of permanent consequence over that idea. Yahweh, as the Old Testament in the end presents him, is supernationalistic, the judge of nations, unqualifiedly committed to social righteousness and to those who practise it. He is for the weak against the oppressive strong, for the poor against the selfish rich. He is thus a standard of social change, not a sanctifier of existent circumstance. He is a disturbing moral judge of men and nations, not a comfortable divine sponsor of their customs. And he is of this quality because he comes to us not by way of king and priest, but through insurgent prophets identifying him with an unattained social ideal.

One of the noblest figures in this great succession was Hosea. He, too, like Amos before him, pronounced an austere judgment of doom on his apostate people,[1] but, in a way none before him had ever achieved, he went beyond the idea of God as judge to the idea of God as savior. Himself the victim of domestic tragedy, he loved his wife even in her faithlessness. His rage and shame at his wife's betrayal of him, his grief and anguish, and his unconquerable love for her despite her sin, seemed to him an experience like that of God himself, dealing with faithless Israel. In undiscourageable compassion he loved his false wife, "even as Yahweh loveth the children of Israel, though they turn unto other gods."[2] Far from identifying God, therefore, with the dominant customs of contemporary Israel or stopping with the divine condemnation of them, Hosea saw God with passionate earnestness refusing to give up his people and determined to save them from their evil:

[1] Hosea 4:1 ff.　　　　[2] Hosea 3:1.

How shall I give thee up, Ephraim?
  how shall I cast thee off, Israel?
How shall I make thee as Admah?
  how shall I set thee as Zeboim?
My heart is turned within Me,
  My compassions are kindled together.
I will not execute the fierceness of Mine anger,
  I will not return to destroy Ephraim:
For I am God, and not man,
  the Holy One in thy midst, and not mortal.[1]

Of such insurgent prophecy up to the Exile Jeremiah was the consummation. In him practical monotheism, supernationalistic and thoroughly ethical, was achieved. In his eyes nothing happened anywhere without Yahweh. He is even credited with writing: "Am I a God at hand, saith Yahweh, and not a God afar off? Can any hide himself in secret places so that I shall not see him? saith Yahweh. Do not I fill heaven and earth? saith Yahweh."[2] The prophetic movement, as expressed in Deuteronomy, lifted the idea of Israel's god to such a point of solitary uniqueness that it is difficult, if not impossible, to distinguish the conception from theoretical monotheism. "Yahweh he is God in heaven above and upon the earth beneath: there is none else"[3]—this phrasing in Deuteronomy may mean simply that Yahweh is incomparable, but the difference between that and his sole existence is manifestly growing diaphanous. As for Jeremiah, he plainly universalized and spiritualized Yahweh and so identified him with righteousness that, in the prophet's eyes, to be unrighteous was in itself to "serve other gods."[4]

VII

Nevertheless, a long and tragic road lay ahead of the Hebrews before ethical monotheism became the common property of their people. The very difficulties confronting the prophetic party in teaching monotheism reveal the background of thought and imagination whose history we have been tracing. For example, they could not persuade their people that Yahweh was one God while he was being worshiped at many local shrines. Granted that Amos, Hosea, and Isaiah conceived Yahweh as managing the movements of world empires, still the ordinary Hebrew was far from having one god. Deity was dispersed in many sanctu-

---

[1] Hosea 11:8–9 as translated by Julius A.
Bewer: *The Literature of the Old Testament
in its Historical Development*, p. 96.

[2] Jeremiah 23:23–24.
[3] Deuteronomy 4:35, 39.
[4] Jeremiah 11:10; 16:11–13; 25:6.

aries—the Yahweh of this place and the Yahweh of that. If one starts with clear belief in the divine unity and omnipresence, one may safely worship in many places, as we do, without losing the sense of God's oneness; but when the presuppositions of thought and imagination are polytheistic, as with the early Hebrews, many shrines keep alive and vivid the tradition of many gods.

The prophetic movement represented in Deuteronomy, therefore, wishing to make real to the people the doctrine, "Hear, O Israel: Yahweh our God is one Yahweh,"[1] adopted as its program the suppression of the local shrines and the establishment of an exclusive, centralized worship in the temple at Jerusalem. This program was brought into practical effect in the Josian reform,[2] and the theological position which that reform attacked was stated by Jeremiah, whose ministry was then beginning: "According to the number of thy cities are thy gods, O Judah."[3]

This centralization of worship in one exclusive temple, which looked at from our standpoint might seem reactionary, was in fact a necessary step toward unifying the idea of Yahweh. The Hebrews never had one god in the full sense of that term until they had one central place of worship. Here the prophets were surprisingly effective in their approach to a difficult theological problem; they rightly estimated the importance of imagination to religion.

Whereas Elijah, therefore, had been in despair because the local altars of Yahweh were being cast down, the prophetic party some two centuries later were in despair because they were not cast down. So Deuteronomy, proclaiming the doctrine of Yahweh's unity, proclaimed as an indispensable accompaniment the law of one sanctuary.[4]

Despite lapses from the idea and infidelities to its practise, the more or less successful centralizing of Yahweh's worship in Jerusalem was a forward step. With Yahweh adored in an exclusive temple while his sovereignty extended over all the earth, many in Judah doubtless felt, to a degree not true before, the divine unity. The danger, however, involved in this method of unifying the idea of deity came on apace in the speedy and complete destruction of the temple by the Babylonians and the exile of the Jews in Mesopotamia. The question raised by that disaster was not only practical but acutely theological: What,

[1] Deuteronomy 6:4.
[2] II Kings 23:1-25.
[3] Jeremiah 2:28.
[4] Deuteronomy 12:1-18; 16:5-6, etc.

now, had become of their god? With the destruction of the Northern Kingdom in 721 B.C., Yahweh's holy land had been restricted
to Judah; with the exclusive unification of Yahweh's worship
in Jerusalem the oneness of their god had been clearly symbolized.
Now, however, this trellis on which the imagination of his unity
had twined was utterly abolished. The Forty-second Psalm is a
first-hand document filled with the poignant anguish not only
of practical misery but of religious despair occasioned by the
Exile:

> As with a sword in my bones, mine adversaries reproach me,
> While they continually say unto me, Where is thy God?[1]

In history there are few instances of the transmutation of
tragedy into gain so impressive as the achievement of the later
prophets, using the disaster of Zion's ruin and the temple's
destruction to spiritualize and universalize the idea of God. To
this end Jeremiah already had blazed the trail. This prince of
prophets, combining in himself the sensitiveness of a poet, the
clear vision of a statesman, and the stuff of which martyrs are
made, had foreseen, long before it happened, Zion's downfall and
the people's exile. He had, therefore, faced in advance the problem
of his religion minus land and temple, altar and cultus, and had
adjusted himself to that revolutionary situation. He had achieved
for himself and vicariously for his people an idea of God and a
faith in him so profoundly personal that it could operate wherever
persons were, and so spiritual that, when deprived of land,
temple, and altar, it could rise to new heights and possess itself
of new horizons. When, therefore, in Babylonia the Jews were
dismayed by the question, "Where is now thy God?" Jeremiah
wrote them a letter, one of the most notable documents in our
religious tradition, in which he declared the universal availability
of Yahweh, to be sought and found in personal prayer, anywhere,
at any time. With city and temple, altar and sacrifice gone, still
Jeremiah wrote in the name of Yahweh: "Ye shall call upon me,
and ye shall go and pray unto me, and I will hearken unto you.
And ye shall seek me, and find me, when ye shall search for me
with all your heart."[2]

The full flower of the monotheistic development in the Old
Testament, therefore, came from the Exile and from the influences which that disastrous experience released. Strangely symbolic though Ezekiel's pictures of deity are, one perceives in them

---

[1] Psalm 42:10.   [2] Jeremiah 29:12–13.

an awed endeavor to express an ineffable vision of the unity, transcendence, spirituality, and universal availability of the one God, and in more intimate and sympathetic moods he represented Yahweh as saying: "Whereas I have scattered them among the countries, yet will I be to them a sanctuary for a little while in the countries where they are come."[1] It is, however, to the Great Isaiah of the Exile that we must look for the most explicit statements of thoroughgoing monotheism. "Deutero-Isaiah," says H. W. Robinson, "drops the keystone of the monotheistic arch into its place."[2]

One pictures him in Babylonia, facing a crucial situation in the religion of his people. On the one side was the utter ruin of the old, sustaining sacred places and customs with which their faith in God had been identified, and on the other side was the competition of the brilliant gods of Babylon, who, according to ancient theory, had proved their reality and power by the ascendency of their people. In this situation the prophet's strategy was not defensive but offensive. He asserted the absolute sovereignty of Yahweh, his sole existence and the nothingness of all other deities, with an explicit, sustained, uncompromising monotheism never hitherto found among the Hebrews. Yahweh, as the Great Isaiah understood him, could say, "Before me there was no God formed, neither shall there be after me";[3] "I am the first, and I am the last; and besides me there is no God";[4] "My hand hath laid the foundation of the earth, and my right hand hath spread out the heavens: when I call unto them, they stand up together";[5] and, as for other gods, they are "of nothing" and their "work is of nought."[6] Whether in his positive assertion of the one universal God, as in the fortieth chapter, or in his scorn of all competitors, whom he placed in the category of worthless idols, as in the forty-fourth chapter, he "held his monotheism *with all his mind*," as Sir George Adam Smith said, and treated the gods of the nations "as things, in whose existence no reasonable person can possibly believe."[7]

The full significance of this is clear only as we visualize the prophet proclaiming the unity, eternity, and omnipotence, not of the deity of an ascendent and victorious people, but of a humiliated, decimated, and exiled nation, "despised, and rejected

[1] Ezekiel 11:16.
[2] H. Wheeler Robinson: *The Religious Ideas of the Old Testament*, p. 60.
[3] Isaiah 43:10.
[4] Isaiah 44:6.
[5] Isaiah 48:13.
[6] Isaiah 41:24.
[7] *The Book of Isaiah*, Vol. II, p. 40.

of men." Out of the depths of abysmal national ruin rose this full-orbed confidence in the sole existence and absolute power of the nation's God. It is this fact, among others, which gave to Jewish monotheism a character of its own. Monotheism was not new in the world. The Hebrews were not the first to reach it. By way of the cult of the sun god, for example, Egyptians long antedated Hebrews in ascribing to one deity sovereignty over the whole world. Even the Egyptian sun god at first was territorial; the sun hymn of the Pyramid Texts represents him as standing guard on Egypt's frontiers; but in the sixteenth century B.C. Thutmose III conquered the known world and became "the first character of universal aspects in human history." The theological consequence was immense, for the sun god also became universal. Said Thutmose, "He seeth the whole earth hourly." In a word, as Dr. James H. Breasted puts it, "Monotheism was but imperialism in religion"[1]—a fact reflected two centuries after Thutmose in an ascription to the sun, "Sole lord, taking captive all lands every day." This Egyptian monotheism long antedated the monotheism of the Hebrew prophets, and it is incredible that with Palestine often under Egyptian suzerainty it should not have affected the theological thinking of the Hebrews.[2] The quality of the Hebrew result, however, was very different from the Egyptian, and the reason, in part, lies in the fact that the full-orbed monotheism of the Hebrews was not "imperialism in religion" but the very reverse; it was the upthrust of a heart-broken and defeated people, defying plausibilities and, in the face of the seemingly triumphant idols of imperialistic Babylon, claiming sole existence, absolute sovereignty, and righteous character for their God. Monotheism as religious imperialism is a familiar and easily understandable phenomenon, but, so far as I know, the monotheism of the Old Testament, the defiant faith of a humiliated and crushed people in the sole reality and sovereign omnipotence of their God, is alike in its quality and consequence unique.

Such monotheism, astonishing though it is, sprang logically from the insurgent stand of the pre-Exilic prophets. They had identified their God with righteousness. Righteousness, however, in its principles and demands, is not local but universal. It is no respecter of persons or nations. It lays its obligations impartially on all alike. By way of the universality of righteousness, therefore,

[1] See James H. Breasted: *The Dawn of Conscience*, chap. 15.   [2] *Ibid.*, chap. 17.

the prophets had come to the universality of God, until against all competitors they believed in the sole existence of the one Deity, who stood for justice and would protect no nation that violated justice. When, therefore, the tragedy of the Exile came, insurgent prophecy faced not its refutation but its vindication. The prophetic school, at its best, went on proclaiming the supreme devotion of Yahweh to righteousness, above even his devotion to his chosen people. In the eyes of this prophetic school, the Exile was not an evidence of Yahweh's defeat but an expression of his just indignation against Israel's sin. As Dr. George Foot Moore puts it: "It was not the Babylonians in the might of their gods who had triumphed over Judah and its impotent god; it was Jehovah himself who had launched Nebuchadnezzar and his hosts against the doomed city to execute his judgment on religious treason."[1] So the Exile produced new dimensions in the Hebrew conception of God.

VIII

Among the Hebrews the achievement of faith in one God was thus supremely a moral victory. The alternative to it was not theoretical atheism but belief in the reality and power of the gods of victorious Babylon. The dominant motive which led to it was neither curiosity about the creation of the world nor philosophic interest, as in Greece, about the divine immateriality and interior unity, but faith that the social justice for which Yahweh stood would conquer. The chief obstacle to it was not doubt springing from "science" but doubt springing from the inveterate association of nationalistic hatreds with tribal gods. The major result of it was not so much a unifying philosophy of the physical cosmos as a new, revolutionary, international outlook on human life.

This is most clearly revealed in the great passages on the Servant of Yahweh now incorporated in the Book of Isaiah.[2] Whoever wrote these passages won an amazing victory, not simply for the idea of one God against many, although absolute monotheism is unmistakably proclaimed; nor simply for the idea that the one God is Israel's Yahweh, although under the circumstances of the Exile that is astonishing; but, even more, for the idea that this one God cares for all mankind and mercifully purposes the salvation of the whole world. This is monotheism

[1] *Judaism in the First Centuries of the Christian Era*, Vol. I, p. 222.

[2] Isaiah 42:1–4; 49:1–6; 50:4–9; 52:13—53:12.

taken morally in earnest, and it is the glory of the Old Testament at its best. Of the Servant of Yahweh it is written, "He will bring forth justice to the Gentiles"[1] and "He will not fail nor be discouraged, till he have set justice in the earth; and the isles shall wait for his law";[2] and Yahweh himself says, "It is too light a thing that thou shouldest be my servant to raise up the tribes of Jacob, and to restore the preserved of Israel: I will also give thee for a light to the Gentiles, that thou mayest be my salvation unto the end of the earth."[3] This is universalism in the thought of God allied with universalism in the thought of man. It is a new outreach of mind achieved only by an extraordinary expansion of moral vision and sympathy.

It would be too much to expect, however, that so great an adventure of mind and conscience as was involved in such an outlook would be shared by the nation as a whole. The practical exigencies which faced the Jews, first in Babylon and then during the wretched years when the restored community in Jerusalem struggled precariously for its existence, militated against any such lofty universalism. Looking at events in retrospect, we can see that the temple's destruction and the Exile were, humanly speaking, necessary for the spiritualizing and universalizing of Israel's faith in God. So Sir George Adam Smith says:

> It was well that this temple should enjoy its singular rights for only thirty years and then be destroyed. For a monotheism, however lofty, which depended upon the existence of any shrine . . . was not a purely spiritual faith. . . . The city and temple, therefore, went up in flames that Israel might learn that God is a Spirit, and dwelleth not in a house made with hands.[4]

The exiled Hebrews, however, desired nothing quite so much as the rebuilding of that destroyed city and temple; their persistent ambition centered in the restoration of the very shrine whose ruin had done so much to refine and elevate their faith.

Ezekiel's ideal, as from the Exile he dreamed the future, was a church state on Zion, centered in the temple, governed by the priests of Yahweh, and distinguished by carefully defined ceremonial peculiarities. The same Exile, which released Israel's faith from old dependences and helped to universalize it, also forced

[1] Isaiah 42:1.
[2] Isaiah 42:4.
[3] Isaiah 49:6.

[4] *The Book of Isaiah* (revised ed., 1927), Vol. II, pp. 44, 45.

upon the Jews, in self-defense, the stressing of particularisms that would prevent their assimilation into Babylon's life. It was in the Exile that the "Holiness Code" of Leviticus[1] was written, emphasizing purity from the contamination of surrounding paganism. It was in the Exile that the story of creation was brought to its climax in the admonition to keep the Sabbath, made sacred from the world's foundation.[2] It was in the Exile that the laws were rewritten and codified stressing Jewish differentials. The returning Jews, therefore, came back to Zion in no spirit of universalism. They had been compelled to magnify their particularisms if Babylon was not to absorb them, and they had done this with such notable success that then, as now, they maintained their unconquerable distinctness. Moreover, the new community on Zion was able to maintain itself only by vehement exclusiveness, so that in the end the survival of Israel would hardly have been possible without fierce nationalism, uncompromising racial prejudice, and bigoted devotion to religious peculiarities. If before the Exile the temple was holy, it was thrice holy and exclusive afterward, and all the national, racial, and religious differences that law and ritual could create and enforce were, more than ever before in Hebrew history, meticulously respected.

At the Old Testament's end, therefore, we face contradictions, everywhere to be found in living religions, between the great insights of the prophets and the common faith and practise of the people. Even the Isaiah of the Exile, despite his vision of a worldwide salvation, was a vehement nationalist when he thought of that salvation's medium; even he had proclaimed to his people that the world's kings and queens should "bow down to thee with their faces to the earth, and lick the dust of thy feet."[3] Post-Exilic Judaism, therefore, far from being unanimous, presents in its theology a profound variance—monotheism, taken morally in earnest, mingled with old ideas involved in tribal deities, racial prejudices, religious bigotries, and national hatreds.

In the Old Testament this variance is clearly reflected. On the one side is the Book of Esther, revealing "the fiery heart of Jewish nationalism in the third century B.C.," and on the other the Books of Ruth and Jonah with their appeals against racial

[1] Leviticus, chaps. 17–26.   [3] Isaiah 49:23.
[2] Genesis 2:1–3.

prejudice and international hostility. On the one side is a god
before whom men cry:

> O daughter of Babylon, that art to be destroyed,
> Happy shall he be, that rewardeth thee
> As thou hast served us.
> Happy shall he be, that taketh and dasheth thy little ones
> Against the rock,[1]

and on the other side is God, saying, "In that day shall Israel
be the third with Egypt and with Assyria, a blessing in the midst
of the earth; for that Yahweh of hosts hath blessed them, saying,
Blessed be Egypt my people, and Assyria the work of my hands,
and Israel mine inheritance."[2] On the one side is Yahweh the
lawgiver, requiring indiscriminately both moral conduct and
ritual correctness, and accepting sacrifice only at one temple,
and on the other side is the Yahweh to whom a psalmist sings,

> Thou delightest not in sacrifice; else would I give it:
> Thou hast no pleasure in burnt-offering.[3]

In a word, history had brought Judaism face to face with an
unavoidable antinomy—a God at once national and universal,
deity of a special people and yet God of the universe, lord of a
particular temple and yet everywhere accessible to prayer,
pledged to the ultimate victory of his purged and redeemed people
and yet the savior of all mankind. This antinomy the Old Testament never satisfactorily resolved, save in the "poems of the
Servant of Yahweh," and that solution was not accepted.
Rather, Zechariah's attitude is typical. "Yahweh shall be King
over all the earth: in that day shall Yahweh be one, and his
name one"[4]—such is the universal outlook of his monotheism.
But all this will come about with Jerusalem for its center, and
with no prerogative of Judaism surrendered, when "many nations
shall join themselves to Yahweh."[5] Indeed, "whoso of all the
families of the earth goeth not up unto Jerusalem to worship
the King, Yahweh of hosts, upon them shall there be no rain."[6]

A just appraisal of the Old Testament, however, must put its
emphasis on the great insights of the prophets. The future
belonged and still belongs to them. The lesser ideas were the old,
inherited jungle of primitive religion; the great prophets were
the road-builders laying down a highway through the jungle

[1] Psalm 137:8–5.
[2] Isaiah 19:24–25.
[3] Psalm 51:16.

[4] Zechariah 14:9.
[5] Zechariah 2:10–13.
[6] Zechariah 14:17.

and out of it. From a local, tribal god they found their way through to the sovereign Creator of the universe, in whose hands were the reins of all history, and from whose control no star and no nation could escape. From being a hard hater, their God became, in their imagination and belief, a merciful lover of his people, the depth of whose sacrificial compassions it strained their language to fathom: "In all their affliction he was afflicted, and the angel of his presence saved them: in his love and in his pity he redeemed them; and he bare them, and carried them all the days of old."[1] A mountain god of war and storm they left behind, to believe at last in a universal Spirit, everywhere available to the seeking soul, the one God of all mankind, who asks for his service only justice, mercy, and humility, and from whose presence there is no escape:

> Whither shall I go from thy Spirit?
> Or whither shall I flee from thy presence?
> If I ascend up into heaven, thou art there:
> If I make my bed in Sheol, behold, thou art there.
> If I take the wings of the morning,
> And dwell in the uttermost parts of the sea;
> Even there shall thy hand lead me,
> And thy right hand shall hold me.[2]

IX

It is not easy for a Christian to be objective and just in describing the difference between the ideas of God in the Old Testament and those in the New. The Christian reader feels a contrast but to locate its source and describe its nature is so difficult that many popular attempts have been and are demonstrably unfair. Yet injustice to the Old Testament at this point is also ingratitude. The great prophetic tradition had gone so far in the apprehension of God before Christianity began that the first prerequisite for a true estimate of the New Testament is grateful appreciation of the Old.

The fact, for example, that the idea of God in the Old Testament never entirely escaped the bondage of nationalism can easily be overstressed and misunderstood. God was always so exclusively Israel's deity, it has been said, that while Israel was to be his missionary and martyr nation to save the world, still Israel was always the chosen people not only in point of service but in point of privilege and prestige. The universalism of the

[1] Isaiah 63:9; cf. Hosea 11:8-9.   [2] Psalm 139:7-10.

Old Testament, it is claimed, did not go beyond the prayer of a nation, regarding itself as the divine favorite:

> God be merciful unto us, and bless us,
> And cause his face to shine upon us;
> That thy way may be known upon earth,
> Thy salvation among all nations.[1]

Not only is this true but from the standpoint of history it was unavoidable, and so far as comparison with the New Testament is concerned it is, at its best, similar to the attitude of Christians with reference to the church. Israel did regard herself as the peculiar trustee of a unique faith and conceived the protection of that faith from contamination and the propagation of it to the world as her duty, and so, thinking of her religion as a greenhouse in which to grow priceless things for later transplanting to the larger field of the world, she endured indescribable suffering on behalf of her heritage. That this attitude often involved constricting prejudices and bigotries is clear, but in its highest forms it is comparable with the loyalty of New Testament Christians, at their best, to the church as the object of God's special care and the chosen agency for the world's redemption.

It has also been commonly said that God, in the Old Testament, is primarily interested in the nation as a whole and not in persons one by one, so that he is a racial and national deity and not the God of personal religion. So far as the earlier portions of the Old Testament are concerned, this is true, but the much more considerable truth is that, starting with tribal religion, as all early peoples did, the Jews through their prophetic souls made one of the greatest contributions ever made in the spiritual history of man, by blazing the trail out from religion as merely a national cult to religion as also a profound, inward, personal experience. In great appeals such as the one beginning, "Ho, every one that thirsteth, come ye to the waters,"[2] or in revealing statements of the divine abode as being "with him also that is of a contrite and humble spirit,"[3] there is no mistaking the personal nature of the experience intended. As for Jeremiah, this is his unique distinction, making him, as Wellhausen said, "the father of true prayer,"[4] and elevating him to be the supreme exemplar of personal faith before the coming of Jesus. When he pictures God as

---

[1] Psalm 67:1–2.
[2] Isaiah 55:1.
[3] Isaiah 57:15.

[4] J. Wellhausen: *Israelitische und Jüdische Geschichte* (3d ed.), p. 144.

saying, "I will put my law in their inward parts, and in their heart will I write it,"[1] he is obviously thinking of transformed individuals as the basis of a transformed nation.

Even more commonly it has been said that God in the Old Testament is a king while in the New Testament he is a father, or, in other language, that justice is his attribute in the one and love in the other. This, however, is to fly in the face of the evidence and to set up a false antithesis. Montefiore says truly: " 'Our Father and King' remains for all Jews a most familiar invocation of God."[2] To be sure, in the Old Testament the divine fatherhood is almost always used with reference to the nation rather than to the individual,[3] but this is not exclusively so.

> A father of the fatherless, and a judge of the widows,
> Is God in his holy habitation[4]

is personal.

> Like as a father pitieth his children,
> So Yahweh pitieth them that fear him[5]

is personal. As for Jewish thought between the Testaments, this intimate, individual, fatherly love of God is so clear and so beautifully expressed that the idea involved is indistinguishable from similar passages in the New Testament. So in Ecclesiasticus stands the prayer, "O Lord, Father and Master of my life . . ."[6] and the Book of Jubilees, written in Palestine in the second century B.C., says: "Their souls will cleave to Me and to all My commandments, and they will fulfil My commandments, and I shall be their Father and they will be My children. And they will all be called children of the living God, and every angel and every spirit will know, yea, they will know that these are My children, and that I am their Father in uprightness and righteousness, and that I love them."[7]

X

Nevertheless, when one passes from the Old Testament into the New, one does move into the presence of fresh ideas about God and experiences with him. A major factor in producing this

[1] Jeremiah 31:33.
[2] C. G. Montefiore: *Some Elements of the Religious Teaching of Jesus According to the Synoptic Gospels*, p. 91.
[3] Deuteronomy 32:6; Isaiah 63:16; 64:8; Hosea 11:1–3; Jeremiah 3:4,19.

[4] Psalm 68:5.
[5] Psalm 103:13.
[6] Ecclesiasticus 23:1.
[7] *The Book of Jubilees, or The Little Genesis*, 1:24–25, translated by R. H. Charles, p. 7.

change in spiritual climate and scenery was the expulsion of the Christian movement from the synagogue. Just as Wesleyanism started as a phase of Anglicanism and remained so until it was coerced into separatism by the Church of England itself, so the first Christians were simply Jews who had found the Messiah and who intended remaining as the true Judaism within the larger matrix of the national faith. When they were driven out from synagogue and temple, they faced a disruption in their religious thought and practise comparable with the shock of the Exile to the Jews over six centuries before. That is, they lost the old trellis on which their faith had twined. The temple was no longer theirs; they were denied the sacrifices; they were outlawed from both cult and legal system; they were expelled from the synagogue and regarded as aliens by the Jewish community. The theological effect of all this was immense. What had happened partially when the physical temple had been destroyed and the nation exiled in Babylon now happened thoroughly. Yahweh lost his coercive entanglements with national loyalty and racial cult, and in a new liberation, unimaginable had not the expulsion of Christianity from Judaism taken place, he became a universal God, with no local temple or chosen people to limit him, and with worshipers of all tongues and nations on equal terms— neither Jew nor Greek, neither Scythian, barbarian, bond nor free, but one man in Christ.

The New Testament as a whole comes to us out of this completed separation of church from synagogue, with Christianity rapidly becoming more Gentile than Jewish. Paul had done his work and the church was an inter-racial, international brotherhood. The God of the New Testament, therefore, is universal, not only in the sense of being cosmic, but in the deeper and more difficult sense of being God of all mankind alike and "no respecter of persons."[1]

The direct effect of this in freeing monotheism from the Old Testament's constricting particularisms was great, but perhaps even more important was its indirect effect: it opened the idea of God in Christian minds to the influence of all the theologies of the Greco-Roman world. Long before Christ, the Jews in Alexandria had felt the nobility of Plato's theistic philosophy and had labored to blend their religious traditions with the best thought of Greece. To men like Philo, a contemporary of Jesus, Platonic philosophy was at one with Old Testament doctrine,

[1] Acts 10:34.

and this difficult syncretism was achieved by so allegorizing even
the "Books of Moses" as to find Platonic ideas there. Such
acceptance of Hellenistic thought, however, while typical of
Alexandrian Judaism, had little, if any, influence in Palestine
and, although mildly evident in the Apocrypha, it did not
affect the Hebrew Old Testament. Only after the Old Testament
canon was complete and in 70 A.D. the temple was destroyed
by the Romans, was Jewish thought, as a whole, finally cast
out of its local matrix, and even then the legal system, with its
particularistic minutiæ, was the more insisted on because the
sacrificial cult was gone.

The thought of the New Testament, however, had no such
protection against the influential philosophies of the Greco-
Roman world. To be sure, the Old Testament was at first the
only Christian Bible, and Christian doctrine was validated by
appeal to the sacred Book. Alexandrian Judaism, however, long
since had shown that the Old Testament could be interpreted
by allegory so as to abstract from it any philosophy one pleased.
In the Christian thinking of the first century, therefore, the
liberation of church from synagogue inaugurated a new era;
the apologetic necessity of being persuasive to Gentiles overbore
the tendency to be content with Hebraisms; and even in the
New Testament, predominantly Jewish though it is in its backgrounds, one sees the beginning of that larger mental hospitality
which led at last to the overwhelming influence of Greek thought
on Christian theology.

In the opening verses of the Fourth Gospel, for example, we
are in the presence of the Logos—the outgoing of eternal God in
the creation of his world and the salvation of his people. Stoics
and Neo-Platonists alike had their doctrine of the Logos—the
creative effluence of the transcendent God, forever going forth
into his world and, above all, lighting "every man."[1] The essential
doctrine of the first few verses of the Fourth Gospel would not
have been unfamiliar to educated people in Ephesus; only at
the identification of the Logos with Jesus would difficulty
have arisen.

When it is said, therefore, as it commonly is said, that the
New Testament simply takes over the Old Testament's theocratic
idea of God, wide areas of fact are forgotten. The God of the
New Testament is the eternal Spirit, God of no special nation
and of no chosen race, accessible everywhere to every soul

[1] John 1:9.

without requirement of special ritual or legalistic act, who, being spirit, can be worshiped only in spirit, who, being love, dwells wherever love dwells, and who supremely has shined in the face of Jesus Christ.

XI

In achieving this result, while the separation of church and synagogue furnished the necessary setting, the personality of Jesus was the major creative force. It was he who mainly made the difference between the ideas of God in the two Testaments. Strangely enough, he did this without saying anything new about God or even trying to. He used no new words concerning deity. He was in the lineal succession of the great prophets—Hosea, Jeremiah, the Isaiah of the Exile. What they had tried to do in their times and fashions he tried to do in his—take monotheism morally in earnest. Where they stopped he began, taking over from them the most expanded and ethically cogent ideas of God to which they had attained and so identifying himself with the great tradition of his people. As with the prophets, so with him, the major motive in all thinking about God was not cosmic curiosity but moral seriousness.

The common statement, therefore, that Jesus took over unchanged the Jewish idea of God needs at least an initial qualification. Which Jewish idea of God did he take over? His ministry was a concentrate protest against ideas and practises that had sprung from the lower levels of Hebrew tradition. His God was the God of the supreme prophetic passages—spiritual and universal, caring for all mankind across all boundaries of race and nation, near at hand to the humble and the contrite, a God of grace and forgiveness as well as of justice and retribution, redemptively merciful to sinners, demanding not ritualistic conformity but moral genuineness within and brotherly conduct without. Here, as everywhere in dealing with his people's heritage, Jesus practised selective attention. He picked the diamonds from the slag. Far from being negligible, such selective attention has often been one of the most creative processes in human thinking. It can so alter the entire composition of a religion or a philosophy, can so reorient and redistribute man's thinking, as to achieve, without the contribution of a single brand-new element, a startlingly new result.

To say, therefore, that Jesus took the Jewish idea of God at its best but had no new idea of his own presents a false antithesis.

The truth is that *by* taking the Jewish idea of God at its best and *by* treating this idea with thoroughgoing moral seriousness, sloughing off hostile adhesions and limitations, Jesus achieved a consequence so new as to be revolutionary.

In this achievement two factors are prominent. The first is Jesus' insight into the moral meanings of monotheism. His struggle was not to sustain faith in one God against either polytheism or atheism, but to persuade people who already believed in God to think and live as though they did. It was because of his morally majestic idea of God that the trivial legalisms of the Pharisees seemed intolerable. It was because he took the universal sovereignty of God in moral earnest that racial exclusiveness, directed, for example, against Samaritans, seemed to him inde‑fensible. He even conceived God as judging men only by tests of philanthropy,[1] and thus universalized God's requirements so that, regardless of race or nation, they could be met by a good life anywhere. The full extent of the revolution involved in this ethical monotheism of Jesus was not at first evident even to his most ardent disciples. On the basis of certain passages, notably the one concerning the Syrophœnician woman,[2] some have judged that it may not have been fully evident to Jesus himself. His enemies, however, sensed in his emphasis the potential ruin of their racial and religious particularisms. They were right about that. The New Testament's later development of an international and inter-racial faith was the logical conclusion of Jesus' way of thinking about God, and so notable was this contribution that he has been credited with being the first one in history to take monotheism with thoroughgoing moral earnestness.

The second factor prominent in this achievement was the intense reality of God in the personal experience of Jesus. Words about God are, after all, only verbal counters, and in themselves alone are inadequate as tests of the religious experience they are used to reveal. Two persons calling God Father may express by that name widely divergent meanings. It is beside the point, therefore, simply to catalogue the words of Jesus about God or to count the times he used a special name. To be sure, he did not discover *de novo* the fatherhood of God. Only in Matthew's Gospel is the word Father, as applied to God, his distinctive and constant usage, and he is never represented as speaking of 'love' as a divine attribute. This verbal test, however, does not reach

[1] Matthew 25:34–36.
[2] Mark 7:24–30. See, e.g., Charles Guigne‑ bert: *Jesus*, translated by S. H. Hooke, p. 317.

bottom. The effect which Jesus produced upon his disciples reveals a personality to whom God was overpoweringly real in spiritual experience. Austere as well as paternal, authoritative and kingly as well as merciful and gracious, terrific in judgment against selfishness, cruelty, and sham as well as forgiving to outcasts and prodigals, Jesus' God was revealed not so much in the words he used about him as in the life he lived with him. This life was of such a quality that those who knew Jesus best sought from him the secrets of prayer,[1] and those who came after him called God by a new name, "God the Father of our Lord Jesus Christ."[2]

So Dr. Buckham states the case:

> It is not the priority of Jesus' teaching of Fatherhood that makes it so significant, but its intense realism. Priority counts for little in such a matter as this, compared to a living and confident realization and the power to convey this realization to others. It was in this that Jesus was creatively original. Upon his lips *Abba* meant more than any name for God ever meant before. So purely and ardently did it issue from the depths of his own experience as to communicate itself to his disciples and through them to others in such vivid reality as to make a new and transforming epoch in the life of the human spirit. This is originality. By this token Divine Fatherhood may be rightly regarded as a discovery, and Jesus as the discoverer.[3]

XII

It is difficult to be accurately certain of Jesus' private ideas, as distinguished from the impressions of them reported by his disciples, just as it is difficult to be accurately certain of Socrates' own thoughts, disentangled from their rendition by Plato and Xenophon. Despite many questions in detail, however, such contributions as we have ascribed to him—selective attention in dealing with his religious heritage, profound insight into the moral meanings of monotheism, and contagious reality in his experience of God as a towering and penetrating fact—seem assured. The newness of the Christian idea of God, however, went deeper still.

[1] Luke 11:1.
[2] Colossians 1:3.
[3] John Wright Buckham: *The Humanity of God; An Interpretation of the Divine Fatherhood*, p. 45.

On this point the early Christians have a peculiar right to be heard. In the first instance they themselves were Jews, devoutly familiar with the Old Testament's ideas of God. So reverently did they regard their ancestral faith that, the Jewish Scripture being at first their only Bible, their new experiences and hopes were seen as the fulfilment of its prophecies. "Whatsoever things were written aforetime," said Paul, "were written for our learning."[1] Nevertheless, the newness of their faith, as followers of Christ, seemed to them unmistakable. They recorded the first impression of Jesus' preaching in terms of astonished exclamation—"What is this? a new teaching!"[2] From recollections of Jesus' own words describing his gospel as new wine, not to be put into old bottles, and new cloth, not to be sewed as a patch on old garments,[3] the conviction runs through the New Testament that, in the faith which it records, a fresh, original creative invasion of the world by the living God had taken place. The gospel is a new covenant;[4] one who accepts it becomes a new man;[5] the Christian's access to God is a new and living way,[6] related to the old order as reality is to dim foreshadowing; newness of life[7] comes to those who are united with Christ, and, indeed, "if any man is in Christ, he is a new creature: the old things are passed away; behold, they are become new."[8]

It stands to reason that this consciousness of creative originality in their faith could not have belonged to the early Christians apart from a fresh conception of God and experience of him. Nor does the New Testament leave in doubt the nature of this innovation in the Christian thought of deity—"It is God, that said, Light shall shine out of darkness, who shined in our hearts, to give the light of the knowledge of the glory of God in the face of Jesus Christ."[9] That is to say, the God of the early Christians was not so much the deity Jesus *taught* as the deity they believed him to *be*. He came from the divine realm, belonged to it, in his own person revealed it, and so brought to man a fresh and saving manifestation of God's nature and purpose. Paul preached "the gospel of the glory of Christ, who is the image of God";[10] John presented the Christ who could say, "He that hath seen me hath seen the Father."[11]

[1] Romans 15:4.
[2] Mark 1:27.
[3] Matthew 9:16–17.
[4] I Corinthians 11:25; II Corinthians 3:6; Hebrews 8:13; 9:15; 12:24.
[5] Ephesians 2:15; 4:24; Colossians 3:10.
[6] Hebrews 10:20.
[7] Romans 6:4.
[8] II Corinthians 5:17.
[9] II Corinthians 4:6.
[10] II Corinthians 4:4.
[11] John 14:9.

To be sure, this association of Jesus with the divine realm exists in the New Testament in various gradations and is set not in one pattern of thought, but in diverse categories familiar in the ancient world. Nowhere in dealing with the faith of New Testament believers is the modernizing of early Christian thought more false and dangerous. They were thinking of Jesus not in our categories but in theirs. In the belief of the first Jewish Christians, Jesus was the Messiah—that is, the Christ—divinely anointed for his supreme and saving mission. This Jewish category of Messiahship was not primarily metaphysical; it did not so much concern the essential nature of the divine missioner as his vocation; it could be applied on different levels—to one conceived as a "son of David" specially anointed to fulfil the divine purpose, or to one conceived as a preëxistent being, come at last to earth to achieve God's will. By means of this category, Jesus, at the first, was associated with the divine realm.

When, however, the gospel was carried from the Jewish to the Gentile world, the idea of Messiahship lost its cogency. The Gentiles did not traditionally know its meaning. 'Christ,' as a descriptive title, containing in itself a confession of faith in the divine mission of Jesus, was not easily intelligible to Greek and Roman Christians. So it came to be no longer a title and a creed combined, but only a proper name, and 'Jesus, the Christ' became 'Jesus Christ.' In Paul's Epistles especially, another name for Jesus tends to supplant 'Messiah.' He is 'the Lord.' This title, too, associated him with the divine realm but it came from other backgrounds and suggested other connotations than 'Christ.' 'Lord' was habitually used in the Greek sacramental cults as the title of the god, the cult's supernatural head, with whom the devotees were joined through their initiatory rites. Writes Professor Lake:

> A 'Lord' had a supernatural nature, which may or may not be described as divinity in proportion as Greek or Jewish forms of thought are being observed. To the Jew 'God' means the Creator, an omnipotent being beside whom there is no other. To the Greek 'God' is a generic title of a whole class of supernatural beings who are neither creators of the world, nor omnipotent, nor omniscient. . . . In this sense, the lords of the various cults were all gods and it would be natural enough for

the Greeks to interpret thus the statement that Jesus
was the Lord.[1]

To be sure, when the Jewish name of God, Yahweh, was
rendered into Greek, the same word, 'Lord,' was used. So a
fruitful source of confusion existed in the nomenclature of the
early church, and probably there is no solution of the contro-
versial problem as to the precise meaning in Paul's mind when
he called Jesus 'Lord.' That he himself felt the problem, as he
carried out into the world of Greek cults this presentation of
Jesus, seems plainly indicated in his saying, "For though there
be that are called gods, whether in heaven or on earth; as there
are gods many, and lords many; yet to us there is one God,
the Father, of whom are all things, and we unto him; and one
Lord, Jesus Christ, through whom are all things, and we through
him."[2] At any rate, it is clear that in categories of understanding
familiar to the non-Jewish mind 'the Lord Jesus Christ' was
preached to the Gentiles as belonging to the superhuman world.

This development reached its climax in the interpretation of
Jesus as the Logos, the eternal Word of God. The use of this
term in the prologue of the Fourth Gospel is familiar, but the
basic idea behind the term is present elsewhere in the New
Testament where the term itself is not used. Indeed, the idea had
already passed over from Gentile to Jewish thought in works
such as the Book of Wisdom, called in our Apocrypha "The
Wisdom of Solomon," where Wisdom is presented as the vice-
gerent of God—"She pervadeth and penetrateth all things,"
"a breath of the power of God," "a clear effluence of the glory
of the Almighty," "an effulgence from everlasting light," "an
unspotted mirror of the working of God," and "an image of his
goodness."[3] Here was a prevalent medium of thought ready for
Christian use in the interpretation of Jesus and by means of it
he was identified with the divine realm. He was preached as
"the image of the invisible God, the first-born of all creation,"[4]
as "the effulgence of his [God's] glory, and the very image of
his substance,"[5] as the Logos who in the beginning was with
God and was God.[6]

[1] Kirsopp Lake and Silva Lake: *An In-*
troduction to the New Testament, p. 238.
　[2] I Corinthians 8:5–6.
　[3] The Wisdom of Solomon 7:22–30.

[4] Colossians 1:15.
[5] Hebrews 1:3.
[6] John 1:1.

Unquestionably something new had happened to the idea of God, not only absent from the Old Testament but contrary to some of its strongest predispositions.

XIII

In this process by which Jesus was progressively reinterpreted in new patterns of thought, it is customary to see the gradual elevation of a man to the divine realm. In the simplest presentation of Jesus in apostolic preaching, he was called "a man approved of God unto you by mighty works and wonders and signs which God did by him in the midst of you, even as ye yourselves know . . . . who went about doing good, and healing all that were oppressed of the devil; for God was with him."[1] Before the New Testament writers were through interpreting him, however, the most august categories of the ancient world had been employed, and he was the Messiah, the Lord, the Logos. He had been deified. That this led Christian thinking far beyond the original historical facts concerning his life, teaching, and ministry is commonly emphasized. It is more important for our purpose, however, to observe the effect which the deifying of Jesus had, not on the Christian conception of him, but on the Christian conception of God. When Jesus, in the interpretation of his followers, became the divine Lord and Logos, not only was their thought of Jesus elevated but their thought of God was changed. Christ became the dominant factor in it. It was now in his face that they saw the light of the knowledge of God's glory. As New Testament thinking developed, not only did Christ become more and more identified with the divine world but the divine world became more and more identified with Christ. His character became central in the idea of God and the concept of God was thereby Christianized. So profound were the changes involved in this, that, from the point of view of the New Testament believer, Paul was justified in writing to his converts, whatever their previous religious allegiance might have been, "Now that ye have come to know God, or rather to be known by God."[2]

To put the matter simply, in Christian thinking God became Christlike. The divinity of Jesus became not only an assertion about Jesus but about divinity. Still the Most High was the majestic sovereign of the universe, "who created all things,"[3] and whose invisible might is revealed "through the things that

[1] Acts 2:22; 10:38.
[2] Galatians 4:9.
[3] Ephesians 3:9.

are made, even his everlasting power and divinity."[1] Into this inherited framework, however, Jesus was introduced as the essential portrait of the divine nature, the very "image of God."[2] When the early Christians thought of the divine, therefore, they thought of Jesus, so that while their theological reinterpretations of him, often in contravention of historical accuracy, changed their ideas of his earthly life and ministry,[3] his earthly life and ministry still exercised a profound influence on their theology.

The effects of this were so pervasive that to define them is like describing a change of climate. Nevertheless, some of the fruits of the change can be identified.

The individual extension of God's care to people one by one was clearly emphasized as it had never been in the Old Testament scriptures. Intimate care for individuals was characteristic of Jesus and if he was the "image of God," such must be the nature of the divine interest.

God's saving grace and mercy gained new positiveness and new dimensions, becoming more actively seeking and sacrificial than it had ever before been pictured as being. Jesus' life was love in motion, outgoing determination to save, free grace expended without regard to merit, and on the terms of the New Testament's thought of Christ, God *so* loved the world.[4]

The special care of God for sinners was made central and emphatic. That the righteous were to be loved and the iniquitous hated by both God and good men was the natural attitude of the early Old Testament, and no development of thought was more difficult of achievement than the extension of merciful, forgiving, saving love to sinners. In Jesus, however, this became one of religion's specialties, exhibited with tireless patience in his ministry and commended by him as the evidence of godlikeness.[5]

The purpose of God was conceived as represented in and carried out by Christ. Still the "Majesty in the heavens"[6] exercised sovereignty over the course of history, and with prevenient ordination, as well as grace, the potter had "a right over the clay,"[7] but this directive control of the Most High was now conceived

---

[1] Romans 1:20.
[2] II Corinthians 4:4.
[3] E.g., on the way John's Gospel changes the picture of Jesus' attitude toward sinners from that presented in the Synoptics, see Ernest Cadman Colwell: *John Defends the Gospel*, chap. 4.

[4] Cf., e.g., Pauline passages on the grace of God: Romans 3:23–25; 5:15–21; Ephesians 1:3–7; 2:4–8.
[5] Matthew 5:43–48; cf. Romans 5:8.
[6] Hebrews 8:1.
[7] Romans 9:20–21.

as "the eternal purpose which he purposed in Christ Jesus our Lord."[1]

The dominant attribute of God, the criterion of judgment with reference to which other aspects of the divine nature were estimated, became the kind of love the New Testament writers found in Christ. The paucity of Pauline references to the earthly ministry of Jesus is commonly emphasized, but when one takes the full measure of them, and adds all the intimations of Paul's insight into Jesus' quality and character, one may reasonably decide that the apostle understood his Master very well. He besought his readers "by the meekness and gentleness of Christ";[2] he based his admonition concerning the duties of the strong toward the weak on the example of Christ, who "pleased not himself";[3] he urged generosity on the Corinthians after the manner of Christ—"Though he was rich, yet for your sakes he became poor, that ye through his poverty might become rich";[4] he pleaded for the virtues of humility, harmony, magnanimity, saying, "Treat one another with the same spirit as you experience in Christ Jesus";[5] he saw the bearing of one another's burdens as the fulfilment of the "law of Christ";[6] he urged on his readers forgiveness, "even as the Lord forgave you,"[7] and considerate love, "even as Christ also loved you."[8] This centrality of love in Paul's thought of Christ was carried up into Paul's thought of God, and as Christ's love "passeth knowledge"[9] so, too, God's love is to Paul tireless, potent, holding believers in a bond so strong that nothing in the universe can separate them from it.[10] As for John, who certainly tried to understand his Master's earthly ministry, the consequence of Christ's influence is plain: "God is love; and he that abideth in love abideth in God, and God abideth in him."[11]

Obviously something new had entered into the idea and experience of God. This creative factor was not so much a concept as a personality. Old frameworks of thought were carried over from Jewish tradition and new ones were added from the Hellenistic world, but for Christians the portrait in all of them was "the face of Jesus Christ."

[1] Ephesians 3:11.
[2] II Corinthians 10:1.
[3] Romans 15:1–3.
[4] II Corinthians 8:9.
[5] Philippians 2:1–5 (Moffatt translation).
[6] Galatians 6:2.
[7] Colossians 3:13.
[8] Ephesians 5:2.
[9] Ephesians 3:18–19.
[10] Romans 8:38–39.
[11] I John 4:16.

XIV

Even this, however, does not carry our thought far enough. The center of the New Testament's interest is not so much an idea as a deed. In Christ God had performed a supremely important act for the world, so climactic that prophecy found there its culmination and so determinative that all man's future was conditioned on it—such is the Christian Scripture's dominant conviction. Like the Old Testament, the New does not move in realms of calm, philosophic discourse; all its writings have some practical intention, such as the upbuilding of the church, the defensive presentation of truth, the overthrow of gainsayers, and the winning of converts. Both Gospels and Epistles are engaged not mainly in the careful balancing of ideas but in the militant presentation of a crucial deed, the very hinge of history, on which swings the world's fate and each man's destiny. The characteristic attributes of the early Christian idea of God, therefore, cannot be fully understood apart from this consummate and creative act which he had wrought in Christ.

In this regard a deep difference separated the Hebrew and the Hellenistic world views. As Professor Edwyn R. Bevan puts it,[1] the Hebraic view of the world was based on "an apprehension of God as righteous Will, Some One who does definite 'mighty acts' in the world-process"; it conceived history as "a Divine plan beginning in God's mighty act of creation and leading up to a great consummation in the future"; it associated "the Divine plan with a Divine community, a 'people of God' chosen to be the vehicle of God's purpose." In the Hellenistic world view, however, God "tended to become immovable Being, to which men might indeed strive to attain, but which did not do particular acts in the world-process"; the course of history itself "was a vain eternal recurrence, a circular movement, leading nowhere"; "deliverance was attained by the individual when he detached himself in soul from the world."[2] As between these two ways of regarding the cosmos, the New Testament is predominantly Hebraic. Many influences of Hellenism are discernible in the Christian scriptures, some of them potent in their effect, but as for the underlying idea of God and the world, the Jewish view maintained its hold. God is righteous

---

[1] For the following antithesis see "Hellenistic Judaism," in *The Legacy of Israel*, edited by Edwyn R. Bevan and Charles Singer, p. 50.
[2] *Ibid.*

and loving Will, a doer of mighty deeds; history is a process, under his sovereign control, in which he performs decisive acts; the church is the chosen vehicle of his purpose—such is the New Testament's world view.

As in the Old Testament, therefore, the idea of God had been progressively formulated, not so much in the light of philosophic disquisition as in the light of his mighty acts for Israel, from the deliverance out of Egypt to the least and latest sign of his effective control over human affairs, so in the New Testament the idea of God was centered not in a concept but in a deed. God had sent his Son into the world;[1] what the prophets had desired to see and hear had now come to pass;[2] of the most hopeful foresights of ancient seers it could be said, "To-day hath this scripture been fulfilled;"[3] believers had "passed out of death into life,"[4] and had been "delivered . . . out of the power of darkness, and translated . . . into the kingdom of the Son of his love."[5] A supreme and saving deed had been done, an unprecedented act of God for man's salvation, and in the light of *that* the ideas of God's nature, character, and purpose grew to new amplitude and bore new fruit.

It is the more important to emphasize this because of the prevalent stress in our time upon the apocalyptic hopes of early Christians as altogether centered and absorbed in a future event— the triumphant return of Christ from heaven. Granted the dominance of this hope in the New Testament! The early disciples did live with a glowing expectation of a divine climactic act that would usher in a "new heaven and a new earth, wherein dwelleth righteousness."[6] Nevertheless, this ardent hope cannot be adequately understood save as an integral result of a supreme event which had occurred already. God's greatest deed was not to be done; it had been done. What was to come by way of culmination was corollary and consequence. The transcendent act had already been performed: "No man hath seen God at any time; the only begotten Son, who is in the bosom of the Father, he hath declared him."[7]

The idea of God in the New Testament stems out from this deed. "God commendeth his own love toward us," writes Paul— not in a philosophy but in an act—"in that, while we were yet

[1] John 3:16–17.
[2] Matthew 13:17.
[3] Luke 4:17–21.
[4] John 5:24.
[5] Colossians 1:13.
[6] II Peter 3:13.
[7] John 1:18.

sinners, Christ died for us."[1] The early Christians, therefore, lived not simply in expectation of the future but in glad appropriation of a deed already done. They were convinced that the kingdom of God had come upon them;[2] that "the darkness is passing away, and the true light already shineth";[3] that here and now they had entered into "eternal life";[4] that already they had been "begotten again,"[5] saved "through the washing of regeneration and renewing of the Holy Spirit,"[6] and given "the right to become children of God."[7] No deed comparable with this, they were sure, had ever been done before, and to them God was primarily the kind of being who could and would do it. As the early Hebrews thought of Yahweh first of all as the one who had delivered them out of Egypt, so the early Christians thought of God as the one who had rescued them out of the power of darkness and translated them into the kingdom of his Son.

Particularly pertinent to our present theme is the fact that by this saving deed believers conceived themselves as ushered into a new experience of sonship to God. The fatherhood of God in the New Testament is most explicitly manifest, not in what is said about God, but in what is said about the Christian experience of sonship. God desires sons—in that idea his fatherhood is most emphatically made plain. Paul says, "The earnest expectation of creation waiteth for the revealing of the sons of God."[8] The act of God wrought in Christ had this for its aim: "When the fulness of the time came, God sent forth his Son . . . that we might receive the adoption of sons."[9] In the eyes of the New Testament this deed has now been done. The right has been given "to become children of God";[10] "as many as are led by the Spirit of God, these are sons of God";[11] no longer slaves, they have become sons and heirs, and their address to God is, "Abba, Father."[12] From Jesus' remembered admonition, "that ye may be sons of your Father,"[13] to the Epistles rejoicing in the Christians' "adoption as sons through Jesus Christ,"[14] this idea runs. They were using an old phrase but it seemed to them packed with new meaning. Far from being wholly a postponed expectation of Christ's return, as

[1] Romans 5:8.
[2] Matthew 12:28.
[3] I John 2:8.
[4] John 3:36.
[5] I Peter 1:23.
[6] Titus 3:5.
[7] John 1:12.
[8] Romans 8:19.
[9] Galatians 4:4,5.
[10] John 1:12.
[11] Romans 8:14.
[12] Galatians 4:6-7; Romans 8:15.
[13] Matthew 5:45.
[14] Ephesians 1:5.

extreme eschatologists affirm, the glory of the early Christians lay in their appropriation and exploration of the experiences already opened to them by the great deed of God in Christ— "Blessed be the God and Father of our Lord Jesus Christ, who hath blessed us with every spiritual blessing in the heavenly places in Christ."[1]

XV

Indeed the richness and variety involved in the developing experience and idea of God in the New Testament began to overflow the customary forms of historic theism. There was one God, but there was also one Lord, belonging to the divine world, who supremely revealed him; and, as well, there was one Spirit—"his Spirit that dwelleth in you."[2] Jewish monotheism stood for the sole existence and sovereignty of the one God; Christianity was soon trying to secure new dimensions in its theism by thinking of the Father as revealed in the Son and made immediately available to every believer by the indwelling Spirit. This enrichment of the idea of God Paul expressed in a benediction, now a familiar formula, but which, at first, voiced the amazed and grateful experience of discoverers who saw theism unfolding into new dimensions—"The grace of the Lord Jesus Christ, and the love of God, and the communion of the Holy Spirit, be with you all."[3] The life and ministry of Christ had been divine; their own interior experience of spiritual renewal and sustentation was divine; their God was no longer a cosmic creator, father, and king only, but, as well, a revelatory character, "full of grace and truth," and an indwelling spiritual presence. All this was not yet trinitarian dogma. It was rather an expansion and enrichment of theism, an overflowing of the idea of divinity into new forms of thought. The unilinear nature of the old monotheism seemed to the new experience inadequate. The early Christians could not say about God all they wished to say in the mental patterns and terminology of traditional monotheism. Their experience had too many facets, was too rich and copious. Quite without intending to start a development that would issue in the classic creeds, they saw themselves, as a matter of fact, dealing with the Divine in three major ways—as the cosmic Creator and Father, as the incarnate Savior and Character, as the interior Spirit of Power.

Far from being, as it later became, a too precise surveying of the

[1] Ephesians 1:3.
[2] Romans 8:11.
[3] II Corinthians 13:14.

divine nature, this trinitarian experience involved, at first, a humble and grateful acknowledgment of unfathomable mystery in the Eternal. The Bible's greatest passages concerning God, in Old and New Testaments alike, are suffused with this sense of mystery. The Book is not a good forest to cut timber in for theistic dogmatism. Not only are its ideas of God in constant process of change, but it is everywhere conscious of depth beyond depth in the divine nature, uncomprehended and incomprehensible. The questions of Zophar in the drama of Job are true to the spirit of Scripture:

> Canst thou by searching find out God?
> Canst thou find out the Almighty unto perfection?
> It is high as heaven; what canst thou do?
> Deeper than Sheol; what canst thou know?[1]

Indeed, as we might expect, it is the most confident believers who acknowledge most humbly their limited insight into what Paul called "the deep things of God,"[2] and say with the Great Isaiah, "There is no searching of his understanding."[3] In the New Testament this sense of God's unfathomable profundity, "dwelling in light unapproachable,"[4] is nowhere more plainly indicated than in the idea that while God is one, as contrasted with polytheistic ideas, this unity is diversified and copious, and not confined, as a bare monotheism implies. When Paul talked about God he used ampler language than monotheism had ever before been equipped with— "filled unto all the fulness of God";[5] "Christ in you, the hope of glory";[6] "The Lord is the Spirit."[7] In all this he was not metaphysically analyzing the divine nature but was indicating the manifoldness of the divine approach to man, and was endeavoring, in the spirit of his own words, to express the ineffable—"O the depth of the riches both of the wisdom and the knowledge of God! how unsearchable are his judgments, and his ways past tracing out!"[8]

Incredibly difficult it would have been to imagine such an outcome from the early beginnings of the theistic idea in Israel. Indeed, in retrospect, the road traveled by the idea of God through the Bible as a whole presents a fascinating spectacle.

Beginning with a storm god on a desert mountain, it ends with

---

[1] Job 11:7–8.
[2] I Corinthians 2:10.
[3] Isaiah 40:28.
[4] I Timothy 6:16.
[5] Ephesians 3:19.
[6] Colossians 1:27.
[7] II Corinthians 3:17.
[8] Romans 11:33.

men saying, "God is a Spirit: and they that worship him must worship in spirit and truth."[1]

Beginning with a tribal war god, leading his devotees to bloody triumph over their foes, it ends with men seeing that "God is love; and he that abideth in love abideth in God, and God abideth in him."[2]

Beginning with a territorial deity who loved his clansmen and hated the remainder of mankind, it ends with a great multitude out of every tribe and tongue and people and nation,[3] worshiping one universal Father.

Beginning with a god who walked in a garden in the cool of the day or who showed his back to Moses as a special favor, it ends with the God whom "no man hath seen ... at any time"[4] and in whom "we live, and move, and have our being."[5]

Beginning with a god who commanded the slaughter of infants and sucklings without mercy, it ends with the God whose will it is that not "one of these little ones should perish."[6]

Beginning with a god from whom at Sinai the people shrank in fear, saying, "Let not God speak with us, lest we die,"[7] it ends with the God to whom one prays in the solitary place and whose indwelling Spirit is our unseen friend.

Beginning with a god whose highest social vision was a tribal victory, it ends with the God whose worshipers pray for a world-wide kingdom of righteousness and peace.

[1] John 4:24.
[2] I John 4:16.
[3] Revelation 5:9.
[4] John 1:18.
[5] Acts 17:28.
[6] Matthew 18:14.
[7] Exodus 20:19; cf. Deuteronomy 5:25.

CHAPTER II

THE IDEA OF MAN

I

The development of the Old Testament's idea of man involves two main matters: first, the relationship of the individual to his social group, and second, the nature of the individual within himself. Using modern terms, we should say that the Bible records a development of thought about human nature in both its sociological and psychological aspects.

The Old Testament's early idea of man in his social relationships could be inferred on a priori grounds from the early Biblical idea of God. The conception of Yahweh as a tribal deity, caring for his clans as a group and warring against other clans as groups, implied not simply a theology but a sociology. At this level of thought, the individual man was submerged in his tribal relationships. Human beings, one by one, did not stand plainly out as having separate importance or rights. The social fabric was everything and in it the separate threads were barely distinguishable items.

Even such a comparison does scant justice to the absorption of the individual's meaning and value in the meaning and value of his tribe. We habitually think of persons, one by one, as the constituent elements of society, and we regard the social whole as made up of their enforced or voluntary blending. The primitive mind, however, in the Bible as elsewhere, thought of the social group—family, clan, tribe—as the original and creative fact, the continuous reality from which individuals came, to which they inseparably belonged, and apart from which they had no meaning, status, or rights. The center of worth lay not in persons, who conferred worth on the group, but in the group, which gave to persons any significance they might possess.

This presupposition is so diverse from our thinking that only with difficulty can a modern mind grasp it. With us the social organization exists, or ought to exist, to serve persons; to the primitive mind persons existed as phases of the group and their

55

meaning lay primarily in group functions. Indeed, no early Hebrew ever would have distinguished thus between the tribe as a whole and individuals as separate entities so that he could have discussed which was prior or which existed for the other. Even in his unconscious assumptions he was totalitarian. When, therefore, we think of the development of social consciousness as a distinctively modern gain, we have reversed the actual historic process. Mankind's early eras were dominated by social consciousness; to a degree difficult for us to imagine, the tribe was all. The shaking loose of the ordinary individual from this identification with his society until, as a personality, he had worth, rights, and hopes of his own, was a supreme achievement.

This submergence of the individual in the social group has been called 'corporate personality' and the name accurately indicates the nature of the fact. Personal life among primitive peoples was rather the tribe's possession than the individual's. It was the tribe that corporately had plans and purposes, suffered or prospered, was punished or rewarded by the god. To be sure, the individual shared in all this, had his vivid experiences and interests as a part of it, was doubtless on occasion independently rebellious and aggressive. Moreover, while the vivid stories of the Hebrew patriarchs and their dealings with God are largely legendary, they doubtless represent a fact always true in any era, that outstanding personalities have outstanding experiences. Nevertheless, in primitive society the abiding entity was conceived to be the social group as a whole rather than its individuals.

One of the unintentional cruelties sometimes practised by the United States Government in dealing with American Indians has sprung from failure to understand this contrast between primitive and modern culture. To a notable degree even yet, the unmodernized Indian's life is corporate, and the individual exists only in his tribal relationships and functions, so that when the Government, even with good intentions, has tried to serve the Indian on a different basis, taking him away from home for education, discouraging old folk-ways as heathenish, assuming individualistic thinking in his treatment, the result has commonly been the disintegration of the Indian's life. He could not make the adjustment swiftly enough. The chief meaning of his existence had lain in group relationships, group functions, and group purposes. He had not even pictured himself as a personality separate from the group. Treated individualistically, therefore, he felt like a branch cut from the tree; his life was gone. To him the continuous tribe was the abiding reality of which he was a phase.

II

That the Old Testament's thinking began with such corporate personality is plainly indicated in the record. The early social life of Israel was centered in the patriarchal family. The master fact in the experience of the people was blood-kinship, first in the household, whose head was alike priest, owner, and judge, and then in the wider circle of clan and tribe, traced back to some progenitor whose blood was supposed to flow in the veins of all. Whatever social solidarity existed depended on the coherence of these family groups. If outsiders were admitted into the tribal relationship, they were conceived as assuming blood-brotherhood. The members of the tribe were not primarily individuals; they were the offspring and representatives of one kindred; because of that they existed, and in that they found life's meaning. They did not make the tribe but the tribe made them, and the consequent obligations of loyalty and sacrifice were absolute. They lived, yet not they; the tribe lived in them.

In general such social organization was everywhere the background of the early Hebrew records and its illustrative evidences are unmistakable.

1. Vengeance was a tribal obligation. If any wrong was done to a member of the blood-brotherhood, every member was in duty bound to take up the feud. "The one great obligation upon all the members of a tribe or clan," writes Dr. John Peters, "was to avenge the shedding of the blood of any member of that tribe or clan."[1] Vengeance might, indeed, be individual, as it was represented to be in Lamech's case, although probably a tribal experience was the source of the ancient folk-song:

> . . . I have slain a man for wounding me,
> And a young man for bruising me:
> If Cain shall be avenged sevenfold,
> Truly Lamech seventy and sevenfold.[2]

Far beyond individual retribution, however, the duty of vengeance was an affair of social solidarity. The wrong of one was the wrong of all within the blood-brotherhood, as when Abram took to himself the harm done to his brother.[3] The entire tribe was in a

---

[1] John Punnett Peters: *The Religion of the Hebrews*, p. 62.

[2] Genesis 4:23–24.
[3] Genesis 14:14–16.

sense a single personality, which, hurt anywhere, resented it everywhere.

2. This vengeance was directed, not necessarily against the individual who had done the wrong, but against the whole family, clan, or tribe to which he belonged or against any single member of it, however innocent himself. Far from thinking it unfair to visit on an innocent man retribution for a deed he had not done, it seemed then the essence of justice that any or all members of a kinship-group should suffer for wrong done by one of its members. As late as David's time, when a devastating famine was blamed by the oracle on Saul's slaughter of the Gibeonites, two of Saul's sons and five of his grandsons, entirely innocent, were put to death and their bodies hung up "before Yahweh."[1] When in the ninth century Jehu's revolt avenged the death of Naboth, not only were the perpetrators of the deed, Ahab and Jezebel, slain, but also their sons.[2] That is, the individual, submerged in his blood-brotherhood, had no separate rights of his own; a sin committed by one man was conceived as committed by all his kin and all were as liable to vengeance as was the guilty person.

3. This principle of vengeance was, as well, a basis for sober judicial action, as the Code of Hammurabi shows. Written at the latest between 1955 and 1913 B.C., this code of Semitic law reveals basic ideas and particular applications so akin to later Hebrew legislation that either direct influence or, more probably, a common heritage is indicated. According to Hammurabi, if a builder had constructed a house so poorly that it fell and caused the death of the occupant's son, it was not the builder, but the builder's son, who was to be killed;[3] and if a woman's death was caused in a particular way by an evil man, not the man but his daughter was to be slain.[4] Such applications of the law of retaliation in terms of a family's solidarity would have been completely at home in early Hebrew thought. In the Old Testament not cruelty but well-considered judicial procedure, based on blood-brotherhood, was responsible for the wholesale destruction of a family in punishment for the sin of a single member of it, as in the case of Achan.[5] His special iniquity, hiding a portion of the devoted loot of Jericho, was in Yahweh's eyes—so the story runs—the sin of the whole people, and on the whole people Yahweh's anger fell. So, too, the

[1] II Samuel 21:1–14.
[2] II Kings 9:24–26; 10:1, 7–11 (cf. I Kings, chap. 21).
[3] *The Code of Hammurabi*, sec. 230, translated by Robert F. Harper, p. 81.
[4] *Ibid.*, sec. 210, p. 77.
[5] Joshua, chap. 7.

leaders of Israel saw the sin of Achan not as his alone but all his family's, and on his family as a whole the death penalty was executed.

4. So profound and serious were these ideas of solidarity through kinship, together with their accompanying conceptions of justice, that they were read up into theology. The familiar passage where Yahweh calls himself "a jealous God" and threatens to visit "the iniquity of the fathers upon the children, upon the third and upon the fourth generation of them that hate me,"[1] has been commonly interpreted as an ancient prevision of the hereditary results of sin. That interpretation is an anachronism; the passage really represents tribal justice, in accordance with which the sin of one involves in guilt and penalty the entire kinship-group to which the wrongdoer belongs. Not heredity but corporate personality explains Yahweh's far-flung punishments upon even the great-grandchildren of his enemies; it was the whole tribe that sinned in any member's sin and it was the whole tribe that suffered. The total social group was conceived as an active and responsible agent, and, so far as justice in our modern sense was concerned, the individual did not stand out distinctly enough to have separate status.

5. Still another evidence of this early totalitarianism is presented in the absolute ownership of its members by the group. Jephthah, for example, was the *baal*, the owner, of his entire household, both property and persons. On that basis he had the right to 'devote' to Yahweh by oath "whatsoever [marginal translation, "whosoever"] cometh forth from the doors of my house to meet me."[2] When it turned out to be his daughter, her doom was sealed. She had no rights of her own as a separate personality, just as Iphigenia had no rights when Agamemnon, for the tribe's sake, needed a sacrifice to allay the wrath of Artemis.

One important consequence of this complex of ideas associated with corporate personality appears in the Old Testament's conception of atonement. Substitutionary atonement, where one suffers in place of others and clears them by bearing the penalty that they deserve, is in view of modern ideas of justice to the individual an immoral outrage. But modern ideas of justice to the individual were not in the background of the Old Testament's thought, and nowhere in the Bible does 'atonement' mean what modern theologies, presupposing modern legal systems, have made it mean. The basis of Biblical ideas of substitution—one bearing

[1] Exodus 20:5. [2] Judges 11:30-40.

the sin and penalty of all—was corporate personality, where in deepest earnest the sin of one was regarded as being the sin of all, the punishment due to one as being due to all, and the sacrifice of one, as in the case of Jephthah's daughter, as being offered by all. Biblical ideas of atonement root back in this basic soil and stem out from it; and while the development later carried them to branches far distant from the roots, there is no understanding the topmost twig—for example, "as in Adam all die, so also in Christ shall all be made alive"[1]—without reference to this origin.

When in unmodernized areas of Chinese life today, the legal authorities, unable to capture the real culprit in a felony, seek his son instead to be punished as his substitute, the same ideas and customs are evident with which the Old Testament began. The clear visualization of individual personality as in itself and for itself worthful and significant, with rights and hopes of its own, came only after a long development of life and thought.

6. This early absorption of the individual in the social group is made clear in the Old Testament by the further fact that, at the start, there was no such experience as would be called now 'personal religion.' Religion was of tremendous and penetrating import; nothing was proposed, undertaken, or done, even in what we would call secular affairs, without reference to the divine powers; but all this was a public, tribal concern rather than an inward, private experience. This had been true of Semitic religion, in general, long before the distinctive Hebrew development began. "It was not the business of the gods of heathenism," wrote W. Robertson Smith, "to watch, by a series of special providences, over the welfare of every individual. . . . The god was the god of the nation or of the tribe, and he knew and cared for the individual only as a member of the community."[2]

That this held true at the beginning of Israel's relationship with Yahweh is revealed in the narratives of Sinai. Moses, as representative of the tribes, dealt directly with Yahweh, but the individual tribesmen, earnestly as they desired the god's favor on the group and willingly as they might perform all necessary acts to secure it, wanted nothing intimately to do with the god himself. They were commanded not even to touch the mountain where he dwelt; and, as for their own feeling, Yahweh was so fearful in their

---

[1] I Corinthians 15:22.   [2] *Lectures on the Religion of the Semites,*
pp. 258, 259.

eyes that they begged he might not speak to them directly in their assembly lest they die.[1]

At the beginning of the development of the Old Testament, therefore, individual personality was largely submerged in the social mass. The fact of sin and the assurance of punishment, the sense of wrong and the practise of vengeance, the ideal of justice and the power of religion—all were operative forces but no one of them primarily concerned the individual; he came under their sway mainly as a member of the community.

III

The major factors that caused the break-up of this original solidarity and the emergence of the individual into personal worthfulness and meaning can be, at least in outline, seen and described.

1. The passage from nomadic to agricultural life, and so out into the commercialized town life of Palestine, inevitably encouraged a growing individualism. Tribal solidarity, especially in the desert, exists in large part because it is demanded by the situation. The social arrangements of nomadic clans must of necessity be collectivist. The individual cannot escape his incorporation in the group and his never ending dependence on it; it is the master fact of his experience; his whole life, apart from his most intimate bodily aches, pains, and delights, consists in the shared life of the group. Having seen an Arab chieftain's son, who had attended the American University in Beirut, make his decision between the old nomadic life of his clan, still living in tents, and the new town life which his education made possible, one vividly understands that, choosing the former, he inevitably chose submergence in the social solidarity of his group as against emergence into the individualism of a commercial community.

The very fact, therefore, that the Hebrews conquered Palestine, settled in towns, developed private property in land, broke up into economically unequal classes, chose various crafts and businesses, and, as the centuries passed, became part of the diversified international civilization of their day, meant of necessity the gradual diminution of the old tribal cohesion and its associated ideas. The individual in every aspect of his life—economically, socially, intellectually, morally—was increasingly thrown on his own as his nomadic forefathers never could have been. Without this underlying social factor, the emergence of the Bible's later evaluation of

[1] Exodus 20:19.

the individual is not conceivable; with it the way was opened for powerful forces to operate in shaking personality free from its complete incorporation in the group.

2. One of the most evident forces working to this end was the growth of moral and religious nonconformity. In a completely tribal organization of society nonconformity was intolerable. The welfare of the whole group, and especially the favor of the divine powers, were thought to depend upon unanimous respect for tribal customs and taboos and unanimous performances of religious rites. A single man's moral defection, as in Achan's case, or a single family's refusal to follow the leader, as in Korah's jealousy of Moses,[1] might bring down on all the group the divine disfavor. Corporate personality, therefore, involved moral and religious uniformity, with the least possible allowance for original thought and action.

Such uniformity, however, never easy to maintain, was impossible amid the moral and religious conflicts into which the new civilization of Canaan and the new worship of the baals plunged the Hebrews. Choices of profound importance had to be made, not only by clans and tribes as a whole, but by minority groups and individuals, and nothing more imperiously calls out the sense of personal worth and dignity than the exercise of moral choice. At this point the prophets, demanding ethical and religious decisions, achieved not only direct results deliberately sought but an indirect result full of future consequence—they put a premium on nonconformity.

Beginning with Elijah on Carmel, clearly distinguishing Yahweh from Baal and crying, "How long go ye limping between the two sides? if Yahweh be God, follow him; but if Baal, then follow him,"[2] the prophets, explicitly appealing to the people as a whole for decision, implicitly involved in their appeal a challenge to the moral competence of individuals. The messages of Amos, Hosea, Micah, and Isaiah, while addressed to Israel as a whole, demanded decision and action on the part of the Israelite, and this appeal to intellectual discrimination and ethical choice involved a consequence more important than the prophets probably guessed.

Isaiah, for example, based his hope for Israel not on Israel as a whole—Israel as a whole was too corrupt and disobedient—but on a righteous "remnant." For the first time in our religious tradition, this prophet stated the doctrine of salvation by a minority. The nation as a whole could not be saved—only the purged and

---

[1] Numbers 16:1 ff.   [2] I Kings 18:21.

righteous portion of it.[1] The saving power lay not in the total group but in the true Israel within Israel, "the church within the church." The prophet named his own son, "A remnant shall return [i.e., to Yahweh],"[2] and looked to his band of disciples, his spiritual offspring, as the hope of the future.[3] In a word, he might be said to have formed the first *ecclesia*, the earliest church, called out from the doomed majority to be a redeeming minority. In this true Israel within Israel, Isaiah saw the vital seed of the nation's hope—"as a terebinth, and as an oak, whose stock remaineth, when they are felled; so the holy seed is the stock thereof."[4]

Of this insurgent independence Isaiah's own life was an illustration. He belonged to the ruling class in Judah but he refused to be a partisan of its class interests. He attacked its misuse of prerogative, denounced its social iniquities, vigorously championed the cause of the impoverished, and became in consequence an object of hostility and ridicule. Once, when he came upon a drunken scene, probably in connection with the temple sacrifices, where priests and prophets, as he says, reeled with wine and staggered with strong drink until the tables were full of "vomit and filthiness," he was greeted with the intoxicated jeers of the people's religious leaders: "Whom will he teach knowledge? and whom will he make to understand the message? them that are weaned from the milk, and drawn from the breasts? For it is precept upon precept, precept upon precept; line upon line, line upon line; here a little, there a little."[5] That is to say, his drunken adversaries imitated baby-talk as a caricature of the prophet's teaching,

> Saw lasaw saw lasaw
> Kaw lakaw kaw lakaw
> Zᵉir sham zᵉir sham.

It was because he found himself and his followers in so despised a minority that he wrote his message down that some future time might vindicate his truth against his gainsayers. "Now go," Yahweh commanded him; "write it before them on a tablet, and inscribe it in a book, that it may be for the time to come for ever and ever. For it is a rebellious people, lying children, children that will not hear the law of Yahweh."[6] Out of such moral insurgence

---

[1] Isaiah 1:24–31; 10:20–23.
[2] Isaiah 7:3 (marginal translation).
[3] Isaiah 8:16–18.
[4] Isaiah 6:13 (The final phrase was possibly written by a later hand).
[5] Isaiah 28:9–10.
[6] Isaiah 30:8–9.

and nonconformity grew the emerging sense of personal worth among the Hebrews.

When, in the century after Isaiah, the prophetic movement, cherishing the faith and morals which the nation as a whole had deserted or had failed to reach, came to explicit expression in the reform under Josiah,[1] it necessarily involved an appeal to individual courage and cost the break-up of kinship-groups. Of this we have an illustration in Jeremiah. His loyalty to the prophetic party and to his own profound insights cost him such enmity from his own clan, whose prestige and perquisites were being hurt, that they plotted his death.[2] When the later Judaism saw in retrospect this conflict between prophetic ideals and popular religion, it was clear that the social solidarity of the nation had been on the wrong side of the issue and that Jeremiah, in his courageous and sacrificial isolation, had been right. In this regard the Bible records a significant reversal of moral values. Whereas at first nonconformity within the tribe had been an intolerable sin, it now became a necessary virtue. Unanimity with the group as a whole had been at the beginning the *sine qua non* of Yahweh's favor; now such submergence of moral conviction in the majority's opinion seemed to the real devotees of Yahweh to be supine apostasy. To stand with the solidly coherent group had been at first both ethics and religion; now neither ethical excellence nor the highest religious loyalty was possible without standing out from the group. And along with this appeal to, and response from, the moral competence of individuals had gone an increasing emphasis on personal rights and duties and a general collapse of old ideas associated with solidarity. It is no accident that Deuteronomy, which sums up the ideals of the pre-Exilic prophetic party, contains an explicit denial of the ancient theory that an innocent person can rightly be punished for another's sin: "The fathers shall not be put to death for the children, neither shall the children be put to death for the fathers: every man shall be put to death for his own sin."[3]

3. Powerful as were such pre-Exilic influences—the rise of a complex civilization and the moral demand for nonconformity—it was the Exile itself that forced the issue of individualism. So long as social solidarity existed as a fact in Israel and the national group was still coherent, traditional ideas of social solidarity were bound to persist. When, however, the temple was destroyed, the

---

[1] II Kings 23:1–25.   [3] Deuteronomy 24:16.
[2] Jeremiah 11:21–23 (cf. Jeremiah 1:1).

Holy City razed, and the Jews scattered from Babylonia to Egypt, a new and powerful influence was injected into the situation.

Jeremiah represents this influence at work in his own personal experience. Loyal to the prophetic movement of his day, his ideas at the beginning of his ministry were at one with Deuteronomy and the reform under Josiah. His clear foresight, however, soon outran the superficial success of the reform and previsioned the ultimate downfall of the nation. This forced upon him, first in his inner experience and then in his message, a profound deepening of his religious ideas. His own life was lonely—"I sat not in the assembly of them that make merry, nor rejoiced; I sat alone because of thy hand."[1] A sensitive and conscientious man, who to his own grief foresaw the destruction of his nation and could not prevent it, he was hated by his people for his foreboding and thrown inward upon his own soul for his resource.

As a result, he made one of the supreme contributions in man's spiritual history to the significance of the individual as the religious unit. He was "loyal to the royal" in himself at a time when social solidarity was rapidly disintegrating. He never ceased caring primarily for the nation, but, if he was to sustain his private integrity and his public prophethood, he was compelled to fall back on God in secret and to find an inner temple when the outer temple was destroyed. That he did this is evidenced in many passages that reveal his intimate, inward struggle with God and reliance on him. "O Yahweh, thou knowest; remember me, and visit me. . . . Thy words were found, and I did eat them; and thy words were unto me a joy and the rejoicing of my heart. . . . O Yahweh, my strength, and my stronghold, and my refuge in the day of affliction"[2]—that is personal religion.

No factor has been more closely associated with the sense of individual dignity and worth, whether as cause or consequence, than such personal faith. When God was conceived as caring only for the tribal group, only the tribal group was conceived as worth caring for, while the thought of God as the patron and lover of individuals was inevitably associated with the thought of individuals as clearly visualized centers of value. The experience of a personal relationship with God, of which Jeremiah was one of the creative forerunners, thus made an incalculable contribution to the emergence of the individual from the mass. Moreover, this experience with God, while in part dependent on factors of intimate temperament, was accentuated in, and urged upon, needy

[1] Jeremiah 15:17.   [2] Jeremiah 15:15,16; 16:19.

souls by the removal of all outward props for religion in temple and cult and by the break-up of the nation. For two generations the Jews were forced to a more personal concept of religion in order to have any vital religion at all.

The Jews, therefore, outgrew the original narrowness of their tribal ideas of God, not only, as we saw in the last chapter, because of a new extensiveness of vision in the direction of an international faith, but also because of a new intensiveness of experience in the direction of an individual faith. In the end, Yahweh was no longer a tribal god in the old sense of caring solely for the social group; he was a personal god as well, in the sense of caring for and bringing interior sustenance to individuals, one by one. Out of this new dimension in Israel's experience came such hymns of the post-Exilic temple as the 139th Psalm:

> O Yahweh, thou hast searched me, and known me.
> Thou knowest my downsitting and mine uprising;
> Thou understandest my thought afar off.
> Thou searchest out my path and my lying down,
> And art acquainted with all my ways.
> For there is not a word in my tongue,
> But, lo, O Yahweh, thou knowest it altogether.
> Thou hast beset me behind and before,
> And laid thy hand upon me.[1]

Obviously, any individual who thus could speak had emerged from absorption in the group into personal self-consciousness and self-respect.

4. Along with this change in the nature of religious experience, until instead of being a circle with its single center in the tribe it became an ellipse with the nation and the individual for its two foci, went a profound change in moral strategy. After the Exile, as before it, the saving of the nation, whether for its own sake or for the world's, was for all the prophets the ultimate goal. But the sin from which the nation needed to be saved was more and more located within the lives of individuals, and the hoped-for salvation was increasingly seen to depend on individual transformation. Here too, Jeremiah, following the tradition of Hosea and Isaiah, played an important role. He traced national evil back to its ultimate sources in the thoughts and attitudes of persons. If the social group as a whole was sunk in iniquity, the reason lay deep in the quality of the group's constituent individuals—"The heart is de-

[1] Psalm 139:1-5.

ceitful above all things, and it is exceedingly corrupt: who can know it?"[1] If on the social group as a whole Yahweh's wrath was falling, the punishment was an inevitable consequence of the way individuals were thinking—"Hear, O earth: behold, I will bring evil upon this people, even the fruit of their thoughts."[2] And if salvation was to come, the only hope of it lay in the interior cleansing of the people's spirit—"O Jerusalem, wash thy heart from wickedness, that thou mayest be saved. How long shall thine evil thoughts lodge within thee?"[3] While, therefore, as always, national reformation was the desired end, a significant deepening was going on in estimating the conditions which would make that possible, and ever more clearly it was seen that no national reformation could be permanent without individual regeneration.[4]

5. Under such influences as these, the social mass lost its indiscriminateness and the constituent persons emerged into clarity and importance, until the ideas of justice associated with the old social solidarity became intolerable. Men, one by one, now had status, each in his own right, and the sense of equity, no longer satisfied by mass judgment on mass sin, demanded fair play for every individual. The innocent ought not to suffer for the guilty; each should stand on his own feet and be responsible only for his own deeds—such flat denial of the ideas with which the Old Testament started now became the express teaching of the later Judaism.

Of this new doctrine Ezekiel was the most uncompromising spokesman. This is the more notable because Ezekiel was the advocate of a restored church state on Zion, and was one of the most effective forces in reëstablishing the social structure whose breakdown had encouraged individualism. He was far from being as profound a soul as Jeremiah, but in his youth he had been under Jeremiah's influence and he carried through to a logical extreme the doctrine of individualism that the older prophet had encouraged.

The old orthodoxy, born out of tribal solidarity, Ezekiel could not tolerate. That one should suffer penalty for another's sin or for the group's sin as a whole seemed to him essentially unjust. So thoroughgoing was his revolt that he swung to the opposite extreme and in his individualism became a veritable atomist. No punishment from God, he taught, ever leaks through from a guilty man to an innocent, even in the intimate relationships of the family; each is penalized exclusively for his own iniquity.

[1] Jeremiah 17:9.
[2] Jeremiah 6:19.
[3] Jeremiah 4:14.
[4] E.g., Jeremiah 31:31–34.

"The soul that sinneth, it shall die: the son shall not bear the iniquity of the father, neither shall the father bear the iniquity of the son; the righteousness of the righteous shall be upon him, and the wickedness of the wicked shall be upon him."[1]

This extreme statement of the case was called out from Ezekiel by the situation in Babylonia. The exiled Jews were blaming their disaster on their fathers. Unwilling to assume responsibility for the sin that had caused the nation's downfall, they found their defense mechanism in ascribing the guilt to their ancestors. "The fathers have eaten sour grapes," they said, "and the children's teeth are set on edge."[2] Such refusal to accept responsibility for the crisis was so easy a method of avoiding obligation in the crisis that Ezekiel found in the ancient orthodoxy, according to which one suffers for another's sin, a dangerous stumblingblock to the nation's reconstruction. If the earlier prophets had been forced to appeal to individuals for decision, even more was Ezekiel constrained, amid the disintegration of the nation, to arouse individual minds and consciences and to gather a responsible and convinced minority. He launched his attack, therefore, against all excuses for evading obligation and especially against the doctrine that God rewards and punishes men in masses. That never happens, the prophet taught. God deals with individuals, one by one, and each receives the just recompense of his own deeds:

> What mean ye, that ye use this proverb concerning the land of Israel, saying, The fathers have eaten sour grapes, and the children's teeth are set on edge? As I live, saith the Lord Yahweh, ye shall not have occasion any more to use this proverb in Israel. Behold, all souls are mine; as the soul of the father, so also the soul of the son is mine: the soul that sinneth, it shall die.
>
> But if a man be just, and do that which is lawful and right . . . he shall surely live, saith the Lord Yahweh.
>
> If he beget a son that is a robber, a shedder of blood . . . he [the son] shall surely die; his blood shall be upon him.
>
> Now, lo, if he beget a son, that seeth all his father's sins, which he hath done, and feareth, and doeth not such like . . . he shall not die for the iniquity of his father, he shall surely live. . . .

[1] Ezekiel 18:20.   [2] Ezekiel 18:2.

Yet say ye, Wherefore doth not the son bear the iniquity of the father? When the son hath done that which
is lawful and right . . . he shall surely live. The soul that
sinneth, it shall die. . . .

Therefore I will judge you, O house of Israel, every
one according to his ways, saith the Lord Yahweh.[1]

It is difficult to imagine a more emphatic statement of thoroughgoing individualism or a more explicit denial of the old doctrine
that Yahweh visits "the iniquity of the fathers upon the children."[2] So extreme was the statement that it rose later to plague
Judaism. Taken by itself, without the balancing truth contained
in the idea of social solidarity, Ezekiel's teaching was no adequate
account of the facts. Men do not stand, one by one, like bottles in
the rain; rather, like interflowing streams, they share their fortunes. The consequences of personal goodness and badness are not
confined to the individual; they spill over through multitudinous
channels into other persons and into society at large. Ezekiel's
extreme doctrine of individualism, therefore, far from settling the
question, started a controversy which Judaism never finished, as
is plain in Job's unconquerable doubt of divine justice to individuals, and Ecclesiastes' scornful denial of it.

While, however, Ezekiel's words, as now recorded, overstate the
case by a wide margin, he made a necessary contribution to the
emergence of personal rights. The individual now stood clear of
the mass, an object of divine care, reward, and punishment, and
never afterward could Judaism lose sight of him as one indispensable focus in the religious ellipse.

6. Partly as a consequence of this rise of interest in individuality, and partly as a cause of deepening concern with it, came belief in the resurrection of at least some persons from Sheol, the
land of the dead. Obviously, men could not pass through the experience of death and out again into a resurrected life in masses;
death in any generation is not like a wide thoroughfare but like a
turnstile, through which men go one by one. The emergent belief
in resurrection from Sheol, therefore, both sprang from and re-
acted upon the increasing importance of personality. Even when
life after death was a very vague hope, held by only a few, scorn-
fully denied by some, supposed to affect only a selected group of
saints and sinners,[3] the fact that the possibility of resurrection was
in Judaism's thought incalculably heightened the importance of

[1] Ezekiel, chap. 18.   [2] Exodus 20:5.   [3] E.g., Daniel 12:2.

personality. To some, at least, it had become so worthful that God cared for it intimately, dealt with it separately, and would preserve it eternally. This influence on the increasing sense of individual importance was heavily accentuated between the Testaments.

IV

When one passes from the Old Testament into the New, one finds Christian thinking, in this regard as in every other, rooted in the prophetic tradition. One factor, however—the complete separation between church and synagogue—made possible to the early Christians a much more unimpeded treatment of the individual soul as the religious unit.

However much original insight and thought may have contributed to the high estimate of personality that is one of the chief characteristics of the New Testament, the fact remains that, until religion was disentangled from nationalism, the full meaning of personality could not stand clear. Judaism, in the centuries between the Exile and the coming of Jesus, was inextricably identified with a special race and a special national state. Indeed, after the Exile, nationalism and racialism came back with a vengeance. The evils endured by the returning exiles, the need of uncompromising separateness if they were not to be assimilated and lost, the bitter resentment aroused by the cruelty of Hellenistic and Roman conquerors, constrained Judaism not only to social solidarity but, in Palestine especially, to extreme racial, national, and religious particularism. While, therefore, the lessons of the prophets, far from being forgotten, bore fruit in great examples of personal piety, the prophetic tradition could not break through to its logical conclusion—religion as a free, individual choice, regardless of race or nation.

To be sure, from the days of the Exile on, the majority of Jews lived not in Palestine but in foreign lands, where they were played upon by alien customs and ideas, and in such a situation continued fealty to the ancestral faith was far more a matter of individual choice than it was in the homeland. Thus, among the dispersed Jews, as Dr. George Foot Moore writes, "The older ideas of national solidarity were supplemented and to some extent superseded by personal responsibility."[1] It is true, therefore, that universalistic tendencies in Judaism outside Palestine were emerg-

---

[1] *Judaism in the First Centuries of the Christian Era*, Vol. I, pp. 224-5.

ing, that proselytism was active, that a relaxation of ritualistic and legalistic requirements was in process, that men of other races and nations were being drawn to the synagogue by Jewish monotheism and morality, and that profound changes were taking place in certain areas of Judaism under Hellenistic influence. Nevertheless, whatever loosening of religious demands or of theological orthodoxies may have taken place among dispersed Jews, Jewish nationalism continued unabated, and not until the highest levels of the prophetic teaching had been released from it could religion become a matter of free, personal choice, determined not by racial stock or national allegiance but by individual conviction.

In the Old Testament taken as a whole, the controlling and creative factor is the social group. This is the abiding reality from which individuals spring and in loyalty to which they find their meaning. In the New Testament taken as a whole, while the church is always in the forefront of attention, the dominant, creative factor is individuals. They are the primary participants in religious experience; they are the unit of value; the social group, the church—while it is conceived to be in unbroken continuity the true "commonwealth of Israel"[1]—is produced and sustained by their freely chosen, coöperative fidelity; and entrance into God's kingdom, whether on earth or in heaven, depends on personal quality. It is difficult to exaggerate the importance of this shift in emphasis. The Old Testament starts with social solidarity so complete that the individual has practically no rights, and achieves at last profound insight into the meaning, worth, and possibility of personal life. The New Testament starts with personalities as in themselves supremely valuable, and conceives the "beloved community" in terms of their free coöperation and the social hope of the kingdom of God the crowning evidence of their faith and loyalty. The opportunity to try this significant experiment in an inter-racial, international religion of converted individuals was given to the early Christians and indeed was forced upon them by Judaism itself when it drove them from the synagogue.

While, however, this disentangling of the Hebrew-Christian tradition from its incorporation in a special race and state provided the indispensable setting for a religion of free, personal choice, the influence of Jesus himself is needed to explain what happened. He himself never broke away from Judaism, but he did, like a greater Jeremiah or Ezekiel, carry the principle of in-

[1] Ephesians 2:11-12.

dividuality into the forefront of his faith. He found the center of all spiritual values on earth in personal lives and their possibilities. "Jesus Christ," says Harnack, "was the first to bring the value of every human soul to light."[1]

By whatever road one approaches the message or ministry of Jesus, one finds this factor dominant and determining.

1. In the religious experience which Jesus wished to share with his disciples, inwardness was an essential quality. He was unashamedly subjective in his description of vital religion's nature. At its creative center was an intimate personal relationship with God;[2] its ethical fruitage came from rightness of interior disposition;[3] nothing outward, however worthy in itself, could be a substitute for such goodness of character and motive.[4] In this Jesus was the fulfiller of Jeremiah with his emphasis on "thoughts of naughtiness"[5] as the source of outward evil and on regeneration of spiritual quality as the basis of social reformation.[6] In the Jewish law, three of the main areas of legislation concerned murder, adultery, and perjury, and in the Sermon on the Mount Jesus took pains to trace all three back to intimate, personal dispositions revealed in "the angry word, the lustful look, the evasive formula."[7] Such inwardness is inexplicable save as one sees Jesus taking the principle of individuality in thorough earnest and conceiving the religious life as rooted inside persons, one by one.

2. Along with this went Jesus' faith in the moral competence of personality. Granted his vivid recognition of the disastrous individual effects of evil social conditions, it still remains true that he believed in the ability of persons to resist environment and rise above it. He appealed confidently to man's capacity for moral choice. Repent, he said—that is, change your mind—in the assurance that despite outward conditions men could do that if inwardly they would. It was within the power of the Prodigal Son to say, "I will arise and go to my father";[8] it was within the power of the sinful woman to "go . . . sin no more."[9] In Jesus' thinking, God was so committed to the support of right choices that the divine resources could be counted on by all who threw their

[1] Adolf Harnack: *What Is Christianity?* translated by Thomas Bailey Saunders (2d revised ed., 1912), p. 73.
[2] E.g., Matthew 6:6.
[3] E.g., Matthew 7:16–20.
[4] E.g., Matthew 6:1–4, 5–15, 16–18.
[5] Jeremiah 4:14 as translated by S. R. Driver: *The Book of the Prophet Jeremiah*, p. 24.
[6] Cf. Matthew 15:19–20.
[7] H. Wheeler Robinson: *The Christian Doctrine of Man*, p. 94. Cf. Matthew 5:21 ff.
[8] Luke 15:18.
[9] John 8:11.

wills on the right side. Thus the primary center of ethical decision was within the individual, and like Ezekiel Jesus would have resisted any person's endeavor to evade responsibility for his own conduct. In this regard he was fulfilling the prophetic tradition and would have agreed with the writer of the Apocalypse of Baruch: "Each of us has been the Adam of his own soul."[1] In consequence, his moral appeal was habitually directed to individual consciences and his moral blame was visited on refractory wills. Personalities stood out, clearly visualized in his imagination, and one by one he called them, even while in the world, not to be of it.

3. Along with this went Jesus' use of ideas and language drawn from the family. In his religious heritage, fatherhood, motherhood, marriage, sonship, and brotherhood had been familiar descriptions of divine-human relationships. Nevertheless, when the Old Testament refers to God's fatherhood, it is almost always Israel as a whole rather than the individual Israelite that is the son,[2] and when in a few instances individuals are referred to as sons of God, it is either Israelites in general[3] or their Messiah[4] in particular that is intended. While, therefore, as we have said,[5] the divine fatherhood in the Old Testament is personal as well as national, it remains true that in the Hebrew Scripture the idea that God's fatherhood, whether of nations or of persons, extends beyond the borders of Jewry is nowhere explicitly stated. The universality of God is typically expressed by calling him "a great King over all the earth,"[6] but his fatherhood is spoken of as the prerogative of Israel and the Israelites.

Few factors were as influential in Jesus' teaching as the seriousness with which he appropriated from his Old Testament heritage these home relationships as symbolizing divine-human kinship, and the insight with which he enlarged and deepened this use of the family. The home was normative in Jesus' thought of God and man. The divine fatherhood, true religion as filial relationship with God, God's cosmic goodwill to all his children whether deserving or not,[7] God's undiscourageable care for each child, however wayward,[8] the ideal of human relationships as a social order where the principles of the family shall be universalized—all such conceptions, familiar in Jesus' teaching, go back to the home

---

[1] II Baruch 54:19.
[2] E.g., Deuteronomy 32:6; Isaiah 63:16; 64:8; Hosea 11:1-3; Jeremiah 3:4, 19; cf. Isaiah 1:2; Deuteronomy 1:31.
[3] E.g., Hosea 1:10.
[4] E.g., II Samuel 7:14; Psalm 2:7; 89:26.
[5] Chap. I, p. 37.
[6] Psalm 47:2.
[7] Luke 6:35-36; Matthew 5:45-48.
[8] Luke, chap. 15.

for their rootage and sustenance. "The family," wrote Professor George William Knox, "is by nature the social unit, and Jesus makes its terms dominate the whole series of his conceptions."[1]

Now, the family is the one social group, so far developed in human history, in which each personality is of essential value. In a good home, no matter how many children there may be, each possesses individual status and rights, and in the eyes of all the rest has separate and inalienable meaning and worth. This conception characterized Jesus' outlook on mankind. His was the astounding faith that, in this regard, the attitude of a good home could be carried out into an evil world. His view of man, therefore, is throughout conditioned by the family and, in consequence, each person is regarded as a child of God, possessing intrinsic value.

4. Along with this went Jesus' conviction that moral destinies, here and hereafter, are personal affairs. One of the major factors in concentrating attention on the individual has always been faith in some form of immortality. Between the Testaments this belief became the assured conviction of those Jews who belonged to the dominant school of the Pharisees, and in Jesus and the Christian community after him this confidence rose into triumphant certainty.

Immortal destinies, however, are individual affairs. To be sure, under the influence of social solidarity, Hebrew hopes of the future were in the beginning centered on an undying nation upon earth, but when hope outgrew this early stage and resurrection from Sheol became a Jewish expectation, it took of necessity the form of an individual return. While at first the individual was pictured as returning to join the undying and triumphant nation on the earth, still the door, once opened to personal hope, could not be closed and the future world involved promise of individual, heavenly destinies. In the light of eternal life in its developed forms, even the most cohesive national solidarity tends to disintegrate. One need not surrender a primary loyalty to one's own race, but one tends to spiritualize the meaning of one's race, to teach, for example, as Jesus did, that to be a true son of Abraham is a matter of moral quality and that God could out of the stones of the field make Abraham's sons, if the lineal descendants of his flesh proved false.[2]

---

[1] *The Gospel of Jesus the Son of God; An Interpretation for the Modern Man*, p. 65.

[2] Matthew 3:9.

In the New Testament, beginning with Jesus himself, the projection of personal destinies into the future world plainly accentuated the importance of the individual and made souls the objects of solicitude and the subjects of salvation. Exhortations to flee the wrath to come and promises of eternal life were alike addressed to individuals. In this regard the indirect results of the rising faith in immortality seem at times as important as the substance of the faith itself.

5. Of one piece with this thorough acceptance of individuality in Jesus' teaching was his faith in the care of God for persons. The contrast here between the beginning of Israel's development and the outcome in the New Testament is clear. Jesus' God was primarily the father of souls, whose will it was that not "one of these little ones should perish,"[1] whose joy it was to see one sinner repent,[2] whose intimate care could even be symbolized in such terms as numbering the very hairs of our heads.[3]

This idea is so emphatic in the Gospels that it can easily be interpreted as individualistic in a narrow and imprisoning sense. As a matter of fact, the result of it was not confining but liberating; up this road early Christianity moved into a universal gospel. For if God is conceived as caring for persons as persons, and so in the end as caring for personality everywhere, no boundaries of state or race can be thought of as circumscribing his relationship with souls. Far from being individualistic in an imprisoning sense, Jesus' exaltation of the worth of personality was an open road toward the universality both of his God and his gospel.

This is clear when one interprets Jesus' thought of God's care for individuals as a reflection of his own life. He himself cared supremely for individuals. There is little chance of exaggerating the fact that the central object of Jesus' concern was persons, that in personality he found life's supreme value, that in the possibilities of personality he put his faith and invested his service. He himself thus interpreted the principle of his ministry and the secret of his divergence from current orthodoxy.[4] So caring for persons, he found it impossible to stop caring when faced with the artificial boundary lines of race or nation. He cared for a Roman centurion[5] and for a Samaritan.[6] The logical outcome, therefore, of his type of individualism was universalism, with the center of value and the object of devotion shifted from special race or nation to per-

[1] Matthew 18:14.
[2] Luke, chap. 15.
[3] Matthew 10:30; Luke 12:6–7.
[4] Matthew 12:11–12; Mark 2:27.
[5] Matthew 8:5–13.
[6] Luke 10:25–37.

sonality wherever found and within whatever social group incorporated. This is an historic paradox of the first importance—
Christian universalism came out of Christian individualism. To
this day the national and racial prejudices which disgrace Christendom are due to the failure of Christians to care so supremely
for personality that no boundaries can confine their sense of its
value.

6. Far from being a denial of such emphasis on individuality or
even a limitation of its meaning, Jesus' proclamation of the kingdom of God was of one piece with what we have been saying.
Jesus' message certainly was not individualistic in the sense that
he put souls over against God's universal and consummated
sovereignty, as though he cared for the first and neglected the
second. Rather, the primary element in his preaching was the
proclamation of the coming of God's righteous reign, but both the
motive and the meaning of his faith in that new order of life were
inseparable from his care for personality.

In Jesus' thought the divine kingship is here already, to be
acknowledged in the doing of God's will. God's sovereignty a
present reality to be sometime consummated in his universally
acknowledged reign—such is the meaning of the 'kingdom' in
Jesus' teaching. God is sovereign now *de jure;* sometime he will be
de facto. To identify this transcendent hope with the temporal
details of a new social order on the earth is to miss its full significance. Belief that the eternal sovereign would assert his universal
sway in a new realm of righteousness required more superhuman
and inclusive factors than any social reform could supply. Nevertheless, this coming reign of God involved the ending of social
wrongs, and it is of importance to note that, so far as the records
reveal, Jesus' concern about social iniquities always sprang from
his indignant perception of their ill effect on individuals. The
victim of the bandits on the Jerusalem-Jericho road,[1] the widow
mistreated by an unjust judge,[2] the unfortunates on whom publi-
cans like Zacchæus practised extortion,[3] the destitute at a rich
man's door,[4] prisoners unvisited and hungry folk unfed[5]—always
it was wronged individuals who called out from Jesus a social
message. To him the greatest of evils was represented by personality mistreated and unfulfilled; the greatest of good was represented by personality released into abundant life. One cannot

[1] Luke 10:30–37.
[2] Luke 18:2–6 (cf. Mark 12:40).
[3] Luke 19:2–10.
[4] Luke 16:19–31.
[5] Matthew 25:42–43.

imagine any picture of the kingdom, satisfying to Jesus, that did not involve this fulfilment of personal life. He doubtless conceived the method of the kingdom's coming in apocalyptic terms, as a dramatic overthrow of the earthly *status quo* by a heavenly invasion, but the meaning of the kingdom to him was centered, not in the victorious supremacy of one race and nation. but in the conferring of abundant life on human beings.

v

Passing from the ministry of Jesus into the New Testament as a whole, one finds the principle of individuality uncompromisingly stated. The teaching of the Master in this regard fitted, as hand in glove, the practical situation that the early Christians faced. Whether expelled from the synagogue or won over from Gentile faiths, they perforce became Christians as individuals. Moreover, the intrinsic value of the human soul was made central in their thought, not only by the teaching of the Master but, even more, by the doctrine of the church concerning him. Christ died for every man[1]—that conviction put the capstone on the arch. Each soul was lifted into inestimable worth as being the object of divine sacrifice. Loved of God, died for by God's Son, carrying in itself eternal destinies, the human soul became far and away the most valuable reality with which human life and thought could be concerned. To use Browning's phrase, in the thinking of the New Testament, "thy soul and God stand sure."[2]

Climactic though this is, however, to the special development we have been tracing, human life is far too complicated to be comprehended by an individualistic formula. No sooner had early Christianity thus carried the insights of great prophets, like Jeremiah and Ezekiel, through to their logical conclusion, than it found itself facing the profound and inescapable truths involved in social solidarity.

1. For one thing, the early Christians, stepping out from old social groups, were at once compelled to begin building a group of their own. The New Testament clearly reveals with what insistent certainty, as one decade followed another, the church took an ever more central and important position in the experience of Christians. Converted individuals they were, to be sure, but they found themselves engaged with increasing concentration on the task of creating a fellowship. In this "beloved community" their faith was kindled, by its consensus of opinion their thinking was

---

[1] II Corinthians 5:14-15; Hebrews 2:9.   [2] Robert Browning: "Rabbi Ben Ezra."

directed, and in its mutual encouragement they gained stimulus and stability. Even within New Testament times, the church became the body of which individual Christians were organic members.[1]

Indeed, at this point we stand in danger of misrepresenting what went on in the mind of an early Christian like Paul. Basic in his thought was the unbroken continuity between the old dispensation and the new. As Martin Luther, aware of the abrupt transition he was making, was even more convinced that his movement, far from deserting Christianity, represented the true Christian church, so Paul conceived his gospel as the fulfilment of the Old Testament and believers in Jesus Christ as the true Israel. In his thinking, therefore, there was no break in the continuity of the social group; the church was God's true people, inheriting the promises and carrying on the great tradition of Israel. For this idea he had support in the ancient prophetic conception of a faithful and saving remnant standing out from a disobedient and apostate people. "Even so then," he wrote, "at this present time also there is a remnant according to the election of grace."[2] To Paul, therefore, the church was the continuation of the assembly of Israel, in which the eternal purpose of God was being worked out and whose head was the Messiah.[3]

Even the very early Christians could thus conceive themselves as children of the church rather than as its creators. New though it was, in a deeper sense it was old and out of its long accumulated heritage had come the gospel they professed. So started a development of thought that later led to the declaration that the church is the mother of all to whom God is the father. The priority of the social group over the individual naturally returned. The church could discipline its members, expel heretics, command assent.[4] According to Paul, not only did Christ die for every man, he died for the church.[5] This group consciousness, accentuated by persecution from without, rose to such power and became so central in the thinking of Christians that, in the First Epistle of John, the test of genuine faith and life is love of the Christian brethren.[6]

To suppose, therefore, that the New Testament disciples, carrying to high fulfilment the principle of individuality, escaped the problems of social solidarity is to misread the situation. They

---

[1] I Corinthians, chap. 12.
[2] Romans 11:5.
[3] This idea underlies such passages as Galatians, chaps. 3–4; Romans, chaps. 9–11; Colossians 1:1–23.
[4] E.g., I Corinthians, chaps. 5–11.
[5] Ephesians 5:25.
[6] Cf. I John 3:14.

met those problems on the new level of an inter-racial, international fellowship entered by free personal choice, but all subsequent Christian history bears witness to the fact that the adjustment between society and the individual, both within the church and out of it, still remained one of the most crucial problems of mankind.

2. Moreover, by no manner of emphasis upon the importance of individuals could early Christians escape, any more than we can, the towering evils of society at large. To be sure, their hope of a "new heaven and a new earth"[1] was cast in apocalyptic molds. By a divine invasion of the world, stopping history in mid-course and suddenly inaugurating the new age, God, not man, would bring the kingdom of heaven to earth. In the meantime, salvation was individual, not social. Paul never dreamed of gradually saving the Roman Empire; he gloried in saving souls out of the Empire, persuading them to turn "from idols, to serve a living and true God, and to wait for his Son from heaven."[2] Protected by this apocalyptic hope from any sense of obligation to reform society, New Testament Christians concentrated attention on individual quality. The end of the world was at hand, and in view of this ultimate and swiftly approaching judgment day, personal readiness to meet it was the main desideratum, and personal morals fit to meet it were described in terms of the highest idealism. As Professor Alfred Whitehead puts it: "The result was that with passionate earnestness they gave free rein to their absolute ethical intuitions respecting ideal possibilities without a thought of the preservation of society."[3]

Protected from undertaking the reformation of this present world, therefore, by its apocalyptic faith in the divine invasion soon to come, early Christian individualism ran headlong into the danger of being as unbalanced on its side as the ancient Hebrews had been on the side of social solidarity. Moreover, this danger was accentuated when Christian thought and Greek thought coalesced. The human soul as the supreme reality next to God was no discovery of Hebrew or of Christian faith. That idea was an organic part of the Platonic philosophy. "For six hundred years," writes Professor Whitehead, "the ideal of the intellectual and moral grandeur of the human soul had haunted the ancient Mediterranean world."[4] It is no accident that Platonic philosophy and the Christian religion readily discovered common ground,

---

[1] Revelation 21:1.
[2] I Thessalonians 1:9-10.
[3] *Adventures of Ideas*, p. 19.
[4] *Ibid.*, pp. 17-18.

and that, in particular, Platonic ideas of the sublimity of the human soul were assimilated by Christian doctrine. Moreover, the Greek mystery religions, the influence of which on certain areas of the New Testament seems clear, were primarily means of personal salvation out of this world into the present possession and the future assurance of eternal life.

So difficult is the achievement of balance in human thought and experience that one sees even the Bible moving from an original sense of social solidarity, lacking adequate recognition of individuality, to a sense of the value of the single human soul, in danger of lacking adequate consciousness of social obligation. It is at this point that Christians should feel profoundly grateful for the Old Testament and for the persistent effect of its great prophetic tradition. From the days of Marcion in the second century, certain Christians, troubled by the anthropomorphisms of the early Old Testament and by the immoralities attributed to Yahweh, have discredited the Hebrew books and have even wished to drop them from the Christian Bible. The fact is, however, that not only is it impossible to understand the New Testament without the Old, but that the New Testament alone presents an incomplete statement of the range of moral obligation.

The reason for this is patent. No Christian writer of the New Testament, so far as our records reveal, ever faced the responsibility of applying high moral principles to preserving the institutions of society, administering governments, handling international relationships, prosecuting social reforms, or even mitigating by public measures the inequities of an economic system. When we have emphasized to the full the immense gains made possible by the separation of the Christian movement from a special national state, we need also to remember that thereby the early Christian movement escaped practical administrative responsibility for the most difficult social problems that mankind faces. With these social problems the Hebrew prophets were continually concerned, and to their solution gave such creative thought that to this day all revivals of social conscience among Christians draw inspiration and direction from them.

Indeed, so integral are the Old and New Testaments to each other and so truly was Jesus a Hebrew prophet in the great succession from Amos and Hosea on, that from the beginning a powerful social conscience was injected into Christianity. In the light of its own records in the Gospels, it never could so individualize its thought as to be satisfied by subjectivism alone.

The hope of the "new earth," whatever the method of its coming, was a revolutionary social expectation. Far from being secondary, it was primary—the first element in Jesus' original preaching and the ultimate consummation of the "eternal purpose." Despite all influences to the contrary, it lifted a standard of judgment in the light of which the Christian conscience at its best could not be content with social evil. From its early days, therefore, until the present, Christianity never has been able completely to reduce itself to a circle with one center, the soul; always the great tradition has called it back to be an ellipse around two foci, the individual and society. In this regard the debt of Christians to the Old Testament's sturdy, realistic consciousness of social solidarity is immeasurable.

As for the New Testament's special contribution, that too has proved to be of incalculable importance in the history of ideas. It carried to fulfilment a long development of thought, disentangling persons from submergence in the social mass and giving to each one status, meaning, and rights of his own; it concentrated attention on the spiritual value of personality and its possibilities; it created a religion to be entered by free personal choice, regardless of race or nation; it set persons to building a social fellowship for the redemption of souls; and it proclaimed as the ultimate goal of divine creation and human hope the kingdom of God in "new heavens and a new earth, wherein dwelleth righteousness."[1]

VI

Accompanying this development of thought concerning the relations between the individual and society, the Bible records another development concerning man's interior nature without tracing which the first cannot be fully understood. Words, for example, which we have been freely using, such as 'personality' and 'soul,' require interpretation. They never have had a static meaning and their modern connotations are misleading when applied to ancient thought. Indeed, it requires a difficult *tour de force* of imagination for the modern mind to grasp the ideas of man's inner nature characteristic of Biblical religion.

In general it may be said that just as the early Hebrews had never in their thinking broken up the social mass so as clearly to visualize the individual, they never had broken up the individual so as to distinguish between what we should call 'soul' and 'body.' The primitive mind started with man as he visibly

[1] II Peter 3:13.

appeared, a physical organism, and even when primitiveness had been overpassed and ideas had begun to move out toward more adequate conceptions, alike the thoughts of men and the words they used moved still on the physical plane.

For example, the idea of soul among the Hebrews, as among early peoples generally, started with the physical breath. The obvious difference between the quick and the dead lies in the presence or absence of breathing. The first 'soul,' therefore, that man had was not metaphysical or spiritual but material. So the Latin word for soul is *anima*—breath—from which comes our word 'animated'; the Japanese word for soul originally meant 'wind-ball,' and for death, 'breath departure'; the Hindu word for soul is *atman*, from which comes our word 'atmosphere.' Similarly, the Hebrew word *nephesh* may best be translated 'breath-soul,' as is clear, for example, in the early story of man's creation: Yahweh shaped man from dust out of the ground, and blew into his nostrils the breath of life, so that man became a *nephesh*—that is, an animated being.[1]

This intriguing word cannot be translated by any single English expression without doing violence to its original meaning. Probably no instance occurs where 'breath' in a purely literal sense is a completely adequate translation; there is another word, *neshāmāh*, for that. The meaning of *nephesh*, however, ranges all the way from a significance difficult to distinguish from physical breath up to connotations clearly spiritual, so that no English word can sweep the gamut, and in consequence our English Versions are commonly misleading. When Elijah complained, "They seek my *nephesh*, to take it away,"[2] he doubtless meant 'life,' as the Revisers have rendered it; and when the psalmist cried, "Let them be put to shame and brought to dishonor that seek after my *nephesh*,"[3] he also meant 'life' and not 'soul,' in our modern sense, as the translation suggests. When Elijah raised the son of the widow of Zarephath and "the *nephesh* of the child came into him again, and he revived,"[4] the rendering would be far more truly 'breath' than 'soul.' Sometimes the word connoted the seat of emotional life—"the distress of his *nephesh*";[5] sometimes the seat of physical appetite—"our *nephesh* loatheth this light bread";[6] sometimes the seat of desire in gen-

[1] Genesis 2:7.
[2] I Kings 19:10.
[3] Psalm 35:4.
[4] I Kings 17:22.
[5] Genesis 42:21.
[6] Numbers 21:5.

eral—"whatsoever thy *nephesh* desireth."[1] But the word also ranged up until it stood for the whole inner life of man: "The law of Yahweh is perfect, restoring the *nephesh*";[2] "A sojourner shalt thou not oppress: for ye know the *nephesh* of a sojourner, seeing ye were sojourners in the land of Egypt."[3] Nevertheless, however wide and high its range, the word always kept the flavor of its origin. This first breath-soul of man never involved so clear a discrimination between the physical and the non-physical that its existence apart from a physical organism was conceivable.

Indeed, the identification of what we call spirit with the material body is clearly seen in the Old Testament, as among all early peoples, in the functions ascribed to the bodily organs. Some eighty different portions of the body are named in the Hebrew books. The brain, strangely enough, is not mentioned and there are no terms for nerves, for lungs, or for diaphragm. Thinking is associated with the heart, not with the brain.[4] In the ancient world in general, such ideas held sway and even Aristotle conceived no function for the brain except to cool the blood. While the Hebrews, however, had only a rough and ready knowledge of bodily functions, they experienced the intimate identification of mental and emotional life with them. A man to them was primarily a body, animated, to be sure, with a breath-soul, but still basically a body, and all his experiences, intellectual and emotional as well as physical, were conceived in bodily terms.

Three organs, in particular, were regarded by the Hebrews as the seats of what we should call psychical activity—heart, kidneys, and bowels. Of these the heart came, in the end, to have the widest usage and the most abiding importance, so that it has passed over into modern speech and we still symbolize our emotions in terms of it. At the beginning, however, this usage was not confined to one organ, and far from being figurative, it represented the literal thinking of the people.

In the Old Testament the heart is used, as we use it, to express emotional experiences, such as anxiety—"his heart trembled";[5] joy—"the priest's heart was glad";[6] love—"the king's heart was toward Absalom";[7] even intoxicated gaiety—"Nabal's heart was merry within him, for he was very drunken."[8] But it is also used

[1] I Samuel 20:4.
[2] Psalm 19:7.
[3] Exodus 23:9.
[4] Isaiah 10:7; Matthew 9:4.
[5] I Samuel 4:13.
[6] Judges 18:20.
[7] II Samuel 14:1.
[8] I Samuel 25:36.

to express mental activity, such as meditation—"Thou shalt say in thy heart";[1] or the achievement of wisdom—"an understanding heart to judge thy people."[2] Even beyond this the word is used to express, as *nephesh* does, the whole inner life and character—"Man looketh on the outward appearance, but Yahweh looketh on the heart."[3]

The naturalness of this manner of speech in our usage should not deceive us as to its original meaning. To us it is figurative; at the beginning of our Hebrew-Christian tradition it was literal. The meaning then was not that personality, conceived somehow in metaphysical terms as a soul, had sensations and experiences mediated through or associated with its physical organism. Then the physical organism *was* the man and the bodily organs were the active agents of experience. 'The heart' was not a metaphor for 'the spirit,' nor was there any psychological theory to explain that the experiences of the self are associated with organic sensations. All such sophisticated thinking was still centuries ahead. It was the heart itself that felt, thought, desired, and decided. As H. W. Robinson summarily puts it: "The body, not the soul, is the characteristic element of Hebrew personality."[4] In a word, the Old Testament began with a thoroughgoing primitive behaviorism.

This is the more easily seen when we turn to the Old Testament's use of bodily organs other than the heart. So alien to our manner of speech are certain passages that when the bowels, for example, are employed to express love[5] or compassion[6] or distress,[7] the Revised Version declines a literal rendering and disguises what the Hebrew says in euphemisms—'heart' or 'inward parts.' In the same way, the kidneys are used as the seat both of discontent[8] and of wise meditation,[9] but in our translations we must turn to the margin to discover that the word rendered 'heart' really means 'reins.' The Old Testament, therefore, plainly begins with man as a physical being, whose emotional and intellectual life is a physical function.

Indeed, this entirely realistic view of human nature is further shown in the identification of life with blood. Not only loss of breath but loss of blood means death, and this fact was seized upon by the early Hebrews, as by other peoples, as the basis of

[1] Deuteronomy 7:17.
[2] I Kings 3:9.
[3] I Samuel 16:7.
[4] *The Christian Doctrine of Man*, p. 12.
[5] Song of Solomon 5:4.
[6] Isaiah 16:11.
[7] Jeremiah 4:19.
[8] Psalm 73:21.
[9] Psalm 16:7.

an elaborate superstructure of religious ritual. The blood was sacred; in the sacrifices it belonged to the god; for a man to partake of it was to break an important taboo. Behind this sanctity of blood in sacrificial ceremonies stood a profoundly influential idea concerning the nature of life: "The blood is the life";[1] "As to the life of all flesh, the blood thereof is all one with the life thereof."[2] So basically physical was human nature as the Hebrew religion first conceived it.

Moreover, within the boundaries of the Old Testament, the Hebrew religion never outgrew the idea that man's life is indissolubly associated with his body. This is evident from the fact that when the hope of life after death emerged, it took the form of bodily resurrection. The Hebrews, prior to the days when the Neo-Platonic philosophy affected Alexandrian Judaism, never thought of life after death except in terms of a resurrected body. The Old Testament reflects not at all Platonic teaching about the soul as imprisoned in the flesh and escaping at death to the realm of pure spirit, but rather Egyptian teaching, with its hope of a physical resurrection. What the Egyptians pictured the sky goddess as doing when she raised up the departed, an early Hebrew, beginning to believe in life after death, might have pictured Yahweh as doing: "She sets on again for thee thy head, she gathers for thee thy bones, she unites for thee thy members, she brings for thee thy heart into thy body."[3] As we shall see in a succeeding chapter, so persistent was this realistic manner of thinking that, however sublimated, it still underlies and is necessary to explain the Jewish-Christian passages on immortality in the New Testament. In Paul's thought, to be sure, the resurrected body was to be spiritualized; it was to be no longer "flesh and blood," but his desire was not to be "unclothed" in the future world but "clothed upon" with a body.[4] The age-long and still influential Christian doctrine of bodily resurrection thus goes back to primitive Hebrew behaviorism, which always conceived soul as a function of the material organism and never, like Greek philosophy, conceived immortality as escape from the imprisoning flesh.

[1] Deuteronomy 12:23.
[2] Leviticus 17:14.
[3] As quoted by James H. Breasted: *The Dawn of Conscience*, p. 48.

[4] I Corinthians, chap. 15; II Corinthians 5:4.

VII

The development that took place in the Old Testament, however, was profoundly important and was achieved in characteristic Hebrew fashion. The Jews in their native estate were not given to metaphysical speculation. Their minds were practical, their interests ethical, their manner of thinking picturesque and dramatic. They did not leap to all-inclusive, abstract generalizations such as one finds in Greek or Hindu philosophy. Whether in working out their idea of God or man, one sees them thinking their way through practical situations a step at a time, and nowhere is this matter-of-fact, realistic method of making progress more evident than in their developing idea of human nature. They neither started nor ended with sweeping generalizations about a metaphysical soul; they simply became more and more concerned with, intent upon, and intelligent about those aspects of human life which we call ethical and spiritual.

One of the most interesting consequences of this is seen in the expanding meaning of one supremely important Hebrew word, *ruach*. Just as the word *nephesh*, beginning with a significance difficult to distinguish from physical breath, enlarged its horizons until it came to stand for the interior life of man as a whole, so the word *ruach* began its career on the physical level. In pre-Exilic literature it was used mainly in two meanings: the blowing of the wind and the heavy breathing of men under strong feeling. Which was original is not certain, but probably, in view of its kinship with the word for smelling in Hebrew and some cognate languages, *ruach* at first signified the heavy breathing of man and later the blowing of the wind as the breath of God. In any case, the word's usage is closely associated with the more urgent and powerful emotions of men. Anger,[1] restored vital energy,[2] extraordinary outbursts of strength,[3] abnormal obsessions of feeling,[4] profound grief[5]—such highly emotional experiences were covered by the word *ruach*. Moreover, it is clear that this range of meaning was suggested by the association of powerful emotion with heavy breathing, and that it came to include both the passions of men and the winds of God.[6]

---

[1] Judges 8:3.
[2] I Samuel 30:12.
[3] Judges 14:6.
[4] I Samuel 16:14–15.

[5] Genesis 26:35.
[6] E.g., II Samuel 22:16; Psalm 18:15; Exodus 15:8; Job 4:9.

The journey which the Hebrews traveled by means of this word, as they pushed out its significance like an advancing roadway, could not have been foreseen but in retrospect it is clear. As their interest and care centered increasingly on man's inner life, on spiritual quality and ethical devotion, as the stronger emotions ceased being merely anger or grief and became also penitence, aspiration, moral idealism, and the love of God, the word *ruach* expanded its meanings to cover the case. It came to represent the interior life of man on its highest altitudes. And because in its origin the word had meant not simply man's breathing but God's wind, it became the verbal agent by which man could say that his best life is inbreathed by God—inspired, as we say, using the same metaphor Latinized—so that *ruach* at last meant the Spirit of God inspiring the spirit of man.

To be sure, as is the habit of words, *ruach* never altogether lost its earlier significance. Both Job and a psalmist used it to mean the breath of life in their nostrils,[1] and Ezekiel in one of his most splendid passages deliberately played on the word's double meaning as he pictured the spiritual resuscitation of his dead nation: "Thus saith the Lord Yahweh: Come from the four winds, O breath, and breathe upon these slain, that they may live."[2] Moreover, *ruach* carried other words, such as *nephesh* and 'heart' up with it, so that, as is the way with words, they borrowed meaning from each other and were used together when an emphatic statement of the whole man's inner devotion was wanted. "With my *nephesh* have I desired thee in the night," said Isaiah; "yea, with my *ruach* within me will I seek thee earnestly."[3]

In the end, the loftiest experiences of man's spirit and the quickening influences of God's spirit found in *ruach* their congenial agent of expression. It was by means of this word that the Old Testament rose to its heights, as in the Fifty-first Psalm—

> Cast me not away from thy presence;
> And take not thy holy Spirit from me[4]—

or in the sixty-first chapter of Isaiah—"The Spirit of the Lord Yahweh is upon me; because Yahweh hath anointed me to preach good tidings unto the meek."[5] To watch this word grow from

---

[1] Job 27:3; Psalm 104:29.
[2] Ezekiel 37:9.
[3] Isaiah 26:9.
[4] Psalm 51:11.
[5] Isaiah 61:1.

meaning 'wind' to meaning 'holy Spirit' is to watch one of the most significant developments in the Old Testament.

By this method of approach, the Jews never reached, as the Greeks did, a doctrine of a metaphysical soul separable from the body. They laid no speculative foundation for anything that could be called a psychology. They took man realistically as he was—as we should say, a psycho-physical organism—and across many centuries profoundly deepened their insight into the supreme meaning and value of his ethical and spiritual life. To them, at their best, this became in practical fact man's real life. The body was taken for granted as the basic and necessary constituent of a man—so much taken for granted that there is no special and distinct word for body in the Old Testament at all. But man's distinguishing characteristic, the core of his being and the meaning of his existence, lay elsewhere—in his spirit. They had started with the individual as a physical organism animated by a breath-soul; they ended with the individual as primarily a character, his major concern moral conduct, his real value spiritual quality, the source of his power the Spirit of God.

VIII

Nowhere is our dependence on the Old Testament for the understanding of the New more evident than in this realm. The early Christians were Jewish in their conception of the interior nature of man and they never became anything else until they fell under the influence of Greek philosophy. In this regard Jesus was a true son of his race. He never speculated about the relations of soul and body or thought theoretically about philosophies of personality. His interest was overwhelmingly ethical. The important discrimination, as he saw it, was not between material and immaterial—a distinction with which he never dealt—but between moral and immoral. In so far as this involved the body as a possible enemy of spiritual living, he counseled the utter subordination of the body, saying with characteristic hyperbole that hands and feet were to be amputated and eyes plucked out if they caused the higher life of a man to stumble.[1] He never thought, after the Greek fashion, of soul as pure being, capable of disembodiment, but spoke, as his Jewish contemporaries did, of future life in terms of bodily resurrection, and on that basis he discussed life after death with the skeptical Sadducees, protesting only against the popular, contemporary ways of conceiving the raised

[1] Mark 9:43-47.

body and its uses in the next world.[1] In a word, he traveled the same road the Hebrew prophets had surveyed, making a profound ethical discrimination between the higher and the lower man, the inner and the outer man, the spiritual and the carnal man. To Jesus, as to the prophets, a man was a being with two major capacities, moral life and fellowship with God.

The close kinship between the Testaments in this regard is manifest in the very words used. 'Heart,' in Jesus' speech as in the Old Testament, covered man's interior life: "pure in heart;"[2] "Where thy treasure is, there will thy heart be also";[3] "Out of the heart come forth evil thoughts";[4] "Out of the abundance of the heart the mouth speaketh."[5] This usage in the Gospels reveals the development that had preceded it. Gradually through the Old Testament, reference to bodily organs as the seat of intellectual, emotional, and moral life had ceased being literal and had become metaphorical. Just as truly as Greek philosophy differentiated within the individual between the material body and the immaterial soul, Hebrew religion differentiated between the moral man and his physical organism. Conceiving the two not as separable but as distinguishable, the Old Testament put the emphasis overwhelmingly on the side of mind and character. Of this tradition Jesus was the inheritor and the fulfilment.

In giving expression to it in Christian form, the New Testament uses words that cannot be adequately understood except as Greek translations of the Hebrew. *Nephesh* became *psyche*, carrying over into the Greek word the flavor of its origin. Sometimes it signifies physical life: "They are dead that sought the young child's *psyche*";[6] "Is not the *psyche* more than the food?";[7] "hazarding his *psyche*."[8] But as with *nephesh*, so with its Greek rendering, the word ranges up into higher meanings which leave English translators in perplexity. "He that findeth his *psyche* shall lose it; and he that loseth his *psyche* for my sake shall find it"[9]—there is no adequate English rendering for that. 'Life,' 'soul,' and 'self' have all been tried, but it means more than physical life, less than metaphysical soul, and other than psychological self. One has to come up to it from its Hebrew heritage and *feel* its significance. So one of the greatest of the sayings of Jesus, "What doth it profit a man, to gain the whole world,

[1] Matthew 22:23 ff.
[2] Matthew 5:8.
[3] Matthew 6:21.
[4] Matthew 15:19.
[5] Matthew 12:34.
[6] Matthew 2:20.
[7] Matthew 6:25.
[8] Philippians 2:30.
[9] Matthew 10:39.

and forfeit his *psyche?*"[1] may mean, What good is the possession of the whole world to a man who must die? or, What good is material gain if it cost spiritual loss? or, What good is the ownership of the world for a time to one who pays for it eternally with a forfeited soul? Probably, were Jesus to interpret his own saying, we should find that something of all three entered into its significance. At any rate, there is no understanding the New Testament's *psyche* without understanding the Old Testament's *nephesh*. In the later Book as in the earlier, the word sweeps the gamut from breath-soul, which was its origin, to interior spiritual life and character, which was its culmination. At one end of the gamut is Acts 20:10, where Paul, finding a supposed dead man still breathing, cries, "Make ye no ado; for his *psyche* is in him"; at the other is I Peter 2:11, where the full spiritual meaning of the term is evident—"Abstain from fleshly lusts, which war against the soul."

As for *ruach*, that became *pneuma*, a Greek word which also had started by meaning wind and had come to mean spirit. In the New Testament the word's old association was not altogether lost—"The wind bloweth where it will . . . so is every one that is born of the Spirit."[2] By this word, in the New Testament as in the Old, the noblest altitudes and attributes of the human spirit and the saving influences of the divine spirit were expressed. Especially was this true of Paul, to whom the essence of Christian living was to "walk not after the flesh, but after the *pneuma*."[3]

IX

Indeed, it was in Paul that the development we have been tracing came to its culmination. His distinctive view of man's interior nature involved a sharp contrast between flesh and spirit. With reiterated emphasis in the eighth chapter of Romans, for example, he sets over against each other "the mind of the flesh" and "the mind of the Spirit." This has been commonly interpreted as the result of Greek influence. Certainly Paul must have been affected by contemporary Hellenism, for no man can use a language as he used Greek without carrying over in the very words meanings and mental patterns from the current thinking out of which the words come. When, therefore, along with phrases like the "old man,"[4] "the law in my members,"[5]

---

[1] Mark 8:36.
[2] John 3:8.
[3] Romans 8:4.

[4] Ephesians 4:22; Colossians 3:9; Romans 6:6.
[5] Romans 7:23.

"your members which are upon the earth,"[1] Paul used 'flesh'[2] as representing the seat of sin, some at once suspect the influence of Hellenism, with its immaterial, pure spirit on one side and its material, sinful flesh on the other.

To grant that Paul's use of 'flesh' as the seat of sin was colored by contemporary Hellenism, however, is one thing, and to see Paul as in any important sense a Hellenist is quite another. It has long been recognized, for example, that some relationship existed between Paul and his contemporary, Seneca, the Stoic philosopher. The kinship of thought and language between them is too close in too many instances for any theory of chance to cover the case.[3] Either there was direct contact between them, which seems improbable, or else they both reflected a common area of contemporary thought and speech. While, however, the similarity between Paul and Seneca in many passages is unmistakable, this does not make Seneca a Christian or Paul a Stoic. All the presuppositions of Paul's thought were Jewish, and his kinship with Seneca lay either in special phrases, such as 'Spend and be spent,' which might easily have been in common vogue, or in large matters like the brotherhood of all men, where Paul shared a universalism long current in the Greco-Roman world. When St. Jerome in the fourth century tried to represent the Stoic philosopher as a Christian, calling him "our own Seneca,"[4] he was stretching the matter out of all semblance of truth. But truth is as badly stretched when one sees the fundamentally Jewish Paul as a Hellenistic or Stoic philosopher.

In many Pauline passages one suspects the influence of the world in which as a boy Saul of Tarsus had lived and through which Paul the Apostle traveled widely as a man. He used the phrase 'the good' ($\tau\grave{o}$ $\kappa\alpha\lambda\grave{o}\nu$) with a Hellenistic flavor;[5] he appealed to 'nature' as standard in a way a Stoic might have done;[6] his praise of moderation and his use of 'virtue' were in good current form;[7] his employment of the word 'mind' was Greek rather than Hebrew;[8] his sense of God's immediate presence, whether shown in his ideal of being "filled unto all the fulness of God"[9] or in a

[1] Colossians 3:5.
[2] Romans 7:18; 8:6; Galatians 5:17.
[3] See J. B. Lightfoot: *Saint Paul's Epistle to the Philippians*, Appendix II, "St. Paul and Seneca," listing similarities of expression, pp. 287–290.
[4] S. Eusebius Hieronymus (St. Jerome): Adversus Jovinianum, I, par. 49, in J. P.

Migne's *Patrologia Latina*, Vol. XXIII, p. 279.
[5] Romans 7:18; II Corinthians 13:7; Galatians 4:18; 6:9; I Thessalonians 5:21.
[6] I Corinthians 11:14–15.
[7] Philippians 4:8.
[8] Romans 7:23,25.
[9] Ephesians 3:19.

quotation from Aratus, "In him we live, and move, and have our being,"[1] was excellent contemporary religion; and his contrast between 'flesh' and 'spirit' doubtless gained sharpness from Hellenistic thought.

Nevertheless, in the bases of his thinking Paul was a Jew. When he used 'flesh' as the seat of sin he was not, after the Hellenistic fashion, thinking of the material body as essentially evil. Traditional Hebrew that he was, his ultimate ideal was not escape from the body but "the redemption of our body."[2] Meanwhile, this mortal flesh, far from being essentially evil, was potentially good—to be dedicated, "your members as instruments of righteousness unto God."[3] If Paul had thought of physical flesh as inherently the source of evil, he could not have thought of Christ as perfect when incarnate or of demons as wicked when discarnate, and yet he did both. While, at times, he talked as a Greek in setting flesh and spirit in sharp opposition, he always was thinking as a Jew; he was contrasting, not material flesh and immaterial spirit, but the natural man uninspired by the divine Spirit, on one side, and the spiritual man transformed by God's grace, on the other. 'Flesh,' therefore, in Paul's usage was a metaphor for all the lower, unredeemed side of human nature and, so far from being confined to or even indissolubly connected with the material body, it might, as in the phrase 'fleshly wisdom,'[4] refer to idle speculation, or, in the phrase 'fleshly mind,'[5] to pagan thinking, such as Gnosticism.

All this lights up Paul's view of man's interior nature. Man to Paul was a twofold creature. First, as a natural being he was body-plus-soul. This does not mean 'soul' as we use it, a synonym for 'spirit,' but 'soul' in the old inherited sense, which carried its meaning back through the natural faculties of man to his physical life and breath. This animated being, body-plus-soul, was human nature unredeemed; it was simply what the first Adam was, a body with its *nephesh*. Christ, however, was more than that:

> '*The* first *man*, Adam, *became an animate being*,
> the last Adam a life-giving Spirit.'[6]

To Paul, therefore, the complete man was made possible only when this original body-soul was taken possession of by Spirit,

[1] Acts 17:28.
[2] Romans 8:23.
[3] Romans 6:13; cf. Romans 12:1; I Corinthians 6:13,15,19.
[4] II Corinthians 1:12.
[5] Colossians 2:18, 21–23.
[6] I Corinthians 15:45 (Moffatt translation).

when the divine presence invaded and controlled the "old man" and made him new. First, last, and all the time, Paul's interest thus was in moral reclamation, not psychology, in salvation, not metaphysics, and his aim was the transformation of men, with their natural faculties of body, mind, and emotion, into spiritual persons. In pursuing this aim he developed peculiarities of thought and phrase. He made a much sharper distinction between soul and spirit than one finds elsewhere in the Bible; he associated soul with flesh and gave flesh an ethical significance quite his own; but all his ideas and verbal usages were instruments for a single purpose—the creation of complete persons, body-souls redeemed by the Spirit of God.

The difference is obvious between such mental patterns in the New Testament and most of our accustomed Christian thinking. Commonly with us, soul and body are sharply distinguished— soul, the immaterial, immortal part of man, and body, the material and perishable, with salvation concerning the soul, and death, the soul's release from its physical habitation. The explanation of this contrast lies in the fact that historic Christian thought in this regard, as in others, has been Greek rather than Hebrew. Claiming to be founded on the Scripture, it has, as a matter of fact, completely surrendered many Scriptural frameworks of thinking and has accepted the Greek counterparts instead. The Christian movement carried out into the Greek world a gospel of individual redemption from sin and death. Not only was the individual lifted out of the social mass, but within the individual a profound discrimination was made between his nature as a mere native of this earth and his nature transformed by the divine Spirit. This gospel of salvation, with its elevated estimate of human worth and possibility, possessed a close kinship with the Greek philosophy. Into the molds of that philosophy it was run, as the classic creeds bear witness, and in this process its ways of phrasing truth were altered, as they have been altered many times since. Within the New Testament, however, the controlling ways of thinking still are Hebrew. While the Greeks distinguished within the individual the immaterial soul from the material body, the Hebrews and the early Christians distinguished the natural man in his sin from the redeemed man, living "not after the flesh, but after the Spirit."[1]

[1] Romans 8:4.

x

The two lines of development in the Biblical idea of man, which we have been considering, may be combined and summarized thus:

At the beginning, a physical organism, whose life-principles were breath and blood, whose mental and emotional experiences were the functions of bodily organs, the ordinary man was submerged in the corporate mass of his tribe, without individual status, separate hopes, personal rights, or claim on divine care apart from the group. In the end, an immortal being, endowed with capacity for moral living and divine fellowship, man stood distinct from the mass, possessing in personality the supreme value, having separate status and individual rights of his own, and gifted alike with the privilege of sonship to God and the responsibility of an eternal destiny.

So abstract and general a statement, however, not only oversimplifies the long and complicated process it endeavors to describe but, in particular, neglects the natural human opposition which so high an estimate of personality encountered—the endless doubts, cynicisms, and denials with which this emerging estimate of man's value was inevitably met. The futilities and frustrations of human experience in any age are so many and so baffling that it is commonly easier to hold a high faith about God, whom we have not seen, than about man, whom we have. That the Hebrews found this to be the case is evident in their scriptures. The emergent individual, regarded as of intrinsic worth and possibility, was a conception which did not so much solve problems as raise them. As we shall see,[1] some of the most puzzling difficulties which the later writers of the Old Testament faced grew out of the developing sense of personality's importance. Was life just to individual persons? Did each man receive the fair recompense of his deeds? Did God treat men, one by one, as he might be expected to if he were just and men were valuable? And behind such theological and cosmic questions was always the more immediate, inescapable fact of man's stupidity, squalor, futility, and sin, seeming to deny outright a high estimate of his worth.

The development which we have been describing, therefore, had no easy road to travel. There were doubtless many cynics who shared the opinions of the writer of Ecclesiastes that "man hath no preëminence above the beasts";[2] that it is not even

[1] Chap. IV.   [2] Ecclesiastes 3:19.

clear "what advantage hath the wise more than the fool";[1] and that, in general, no man knows what is good for him "all the days of his vain life which he spendeth as a shadow."[2] The candor of the Old Testament in expressing not only its emerging faith but, as well, its cynicisms and denials, is in this realm clearly exhibited. The Hebrews suffered tragically at man's hands; they were under no optimistic illusions about man's natural quality; just as, against all the plausibilities, they asserted their profoundest faith in God when they were a defeated people in exile, so they wrought out a positive, triumphant faith in man, although they knew, as few peoples in history have ever known, how cruel man can be. Some Old Testament passages still reflect the moods that in multitudes of individuals must have opposed the rising faith in personal worth and possibility—

> I loathe my life; I would not live alway:
> Let me alone; for my days are vanity.
> What is man, that thou shouldest magnify him?[3]

Moreover, the Hebrews felt, as thoughtful men have always felt, the difficulty of holding a high estimate of man's worth in the face of the vast cosmos which is his dwelling. While the immense universe, humbling man into diminutive insignificance, was far smaller in early Hebrew eyes that it is in ours, still, then as now, stars were visible and man's imagination felt the disparity between the cosmos and the human individual. Frail, tenuous, and temporary was man's hold even on existence— "Cease ye from man, whose breath is in his nostrils; for wherein is he to be accounted of?"[4] He is as transient as the grass;[5] he is but flesh, "a wind that passeth away, and cometh not again."[6] Above man's littleness and ignorance the universe towers overwhelmingly, so that one who takes true account of its marvels will cry, "I abhor myself."[7] It was not because the Hebrew failed to feel this mood of insignificance and transiency that he wrought out his faith in man. In the same psalm he mingled confidence in human greatness with the sense of mystery that in a universe so vast man should count for so much:

> When I consider thy heavens, the work of thy fingers,
> The moon and the stars, which thou hast ordained;

[1] Ecclesiastes 6:8.
[2] Ecclesiastes 6:12.
[3] Job 7:16–17.
[4] Isaiah 2:22.
[5] Psalm 103:15.
[6] Psalm 78:39.
[7] Job 42:6; see also Job, chaps. 38–42.

What is man, that thou art mindful of him?
And the son of man, that thou visitest him?
For thou hast made him but little lower than God,
And crownest him with glory and honor.[1]

Despite the size of the cosmos, two elements in human nature seemed to the Hebrew more significant and more indicative of ultimate reality than all the outer framework of the world— man's capacities for moral living and for fellowship with the Eternal. On these facts of moral and religious experience the Hebrew took his stand; he saw the universe itself as the predestined home for their development; he told the story of cosmic creation as culminating in man;[2] and he wrought out an estimate of personality's worth and destiny which, passing by way of Christianity into confluence with Greek thought, is still part of the great tradition of the Western world. When a modern scientist says that "personality is the great central fact of the universe,"[3] he is in lineal descent from Paul, who, both as a Jew and as a Christian, believed that "the earnest expectation of the creation waiteth for the revealing of the sons of God."[4]

The importance of this tradition is accentuated when it is compared with what had been going on in India. The Hindu-Buddhist development, starting from primitive ideas kindred with the Old Testament's early tribalism, traveled a far different road. There one feels the controlling sense of the misfortune of man's self-conscious existence, its endless transmigrations, vain illusions, and insatiable desires. There the solution was sought in a denial of individuality rather than in its affirmation, in a renunciation of man's clamorous wants rather than in their encouragement and satisfaction. In Buddhism the presupposition is that the universe contains no food for the ultimate feeding of man's many hungers, no living water for his insatiable thirsts, so that restless hunger and thirst are man's worst enemies, to be subdued and at last eliminated, until even the desire for self-conscious existence is gone and Nirvana is attained. In the Hebrew-Christian tradition the presupposition is that the universe does contain satisfaction for man's highest desires, that those who hunger and thirst after righteousness are blessed and shall be filled, that there is living bread and water for the spirit, not in a negative peace of renounced desire but in the positive achieve-

---

[1] Psalm 8:3–5.
[2] Genesis 1:1—2:3.

[3] J. Scott Haldane: *Mechanism, Life and Personality*, p. 139.
[4] Romans 8:19.

ment of triumphant personality, both here and in an eternal kingdom of souls. No such summary contrast can possibly be just to either side; the Buddhist would say that his Nirvana is the satisfaction of his worthiest desires and the Hebrew knew well the need of subjugating, disciplining, and eliminating clamorous wants; but with whatever qualifications, this contrast roughly indicates the far dissevered roads which the two traditions traveled. The distinction of the Hebrew-Christian development of thought about man lies in its insistent affirmation of personality as boundless in value and possibility, and in its faith that God and his universe are pledged to the satisfaction of personality's inherent promise.

As for the modern scene with its contemporary problems, the New Testament's idea of man faces immense difficulties in maintaining itself. The vast enlargement of the physical cosmos, the evolutionary origin of man, materialistic theories which endeavor to explain him, brutality of social life involving low conceptions of him, the innumerable masses of men such that old cynicisms gain new force,

> The Eternal Sákí from that Bowl has pour'd
> Millions of Bubbles like us, and will pour[1]—

these and other factors tend in many minds to undo what the Hebrew-Christian development did. Yet the most humane elements in our civilization are rooted in the estimate of human nature that the Jewish-Christian faith and the Platonic philosophy bequeathed to the Western world. Indeed, in a day when behaviorism as a psychological theory and coercive collectivism as a social ideal are popular, it may be salutary to recall that, far from being modern, both behaviorism and collectivism were primitive. The Hebrew-Christian tradition began with them, and for nearly two millenniums was mainly engaged in breaking free from their impoverishing effects. From this and from the further fact that mankind keeps swinging back to them, it may be fair to infer that there is indeed truth in them, but not enough truth to fit all the evidence or enough satisfaction to meet man's deepest needs.

---

[1] Omar Khayyám: "The Rubáiyát," XLVI.

CHAPTER III

THE IDEA OF RIGHT AND WRONG

I

It is always possible to express an ideal of duty by an abstract noun and so, having used a generalized name for it, to discover that ideal in all ages and places. The primitive man depended on 'justice' as much as the modern man does, and the Sinais of history have as emphatically demanded it as have modern codes of ethics. Such verbal usage, however, easily produces a mistaken impression of similarity where, as a matter of fact, the differences have been profound. Justice, *mishpat*, was the central ethical concept of the Hebrews, but the word was an omnibus into which many meanings were packed and from which many meanings were dropped in the long traveling of the Hebrew mind.

Alike the major virtue and the major limitation of the tribal justice with which the Old Testament began are plain. The virtue lay in the strong cohesion of the group of kinsmen, in their mutual interdependence and loyalty, in their approximate equality of estate, and in the intimacy with which each was known by all. "Seldom the judge and elders err," writes Doughty with reference to modern Arab tribes, "in these small societies of kindred, where the life of every tribesman lies open from his infancy and his state is to all men well known."[1] The major limitation imposed on tribal justice by its environment lay in the narrow boundaries of blood-kinship within which it was virtuous to be just. In a society based on kinship, especially under circumstances of severe inter-tribal rivalry for the means of subsistence, one finds high ideals of just conduct within the group combined with the absence of the sense of moral obligation beyond the group. To love the clan and to hate its rivals, to feel responsibility for just dealing within it and no such responsibility beyond it, were two sides of the same thing.

With such a moral heritage, combining both high value and

[1] Charles M. Doughty: *Travels in Arabia Deserta* (3d ed., 1925), Vol. I, p. 249.

narrow limitation, the tribes of Israel entered Palestine and, after a long conflict with the previous inhabitants, settled down to adjust and synthesize their cultural traditions in the midst of the much more complicated agricultural and urban society which they had conquered. Around the problems involved in this situation the stream of ethical thinking in the early Old Testament swirls.

One result was to have been expected. Whenever a sudden readjustment of cultural life and moral standards is forced by a fresh situation, society faces the peril of losing old safeguards and sanctions before it gains new ones. Just as in China, this last generation, the passage from a patriarchal to a political and commercial civilization has been attended by turmoil, so the Hebrews made the transition only at the cost of practical and moral confusion. As the ancient record puts it, "In those days there was no king in Israel: every man did that which was right in his own eyes."[1] Despite the powerful cohesion of the tribal life, the readjustments in Palestine produced a period of comparative individualism which in retrospect looked to the narrator like moral anarchy.

Nevertheless, the old ideals of justice never died out. The resistant power of Hebrew character and the sturdy refusal of tribal morality to be assimilated gave to the early prophets a strong basis of appeal. From Elijah on, they were not, as they commonly are pictured, progressives, but conservatives; they were contending for an ethical heritage in peril of being lost. To be sure, in thus contending for it and applying it to contemporary life, they expanded it. One never understands them, however, if one supposes that they thought of themselves as projecting a new ethic. They were consciously trying to conserve an old ethic, and are among the chief illustrations in history of the statement that all reformation is restoration. For intentionally restorative though the prophets were, they were too vigorous in their nonconformity not to be revolutionary in the end. Ideas of right and wrong were incalculably enlarged and deepened under their influence, and in this process they had to deal with certain outstanding limitations in their moral tradition.

II

The most obvious of these limitations was the narrowness of the area within which moral obligation was recognized. The idea

[1] Judges 17:6.

of duty involves not simply a question of quality but of quantity—To how wide a circle of persons is one under obligation to be just? In any modern society are multitudes of people in whom the sense of moral responsibility is a matter of kinship and propinquity. Beyond a constricted inner circle their imagination fails and their consciences do not function. This natural poverty of imagination and conscience in dealing with people either distant in space or not intimately connected with the group was intensified indefinitely in primitive society, where 'stranger' and 'enemy' were so similar in meaning that one word commonly covered both. Customarily the tribe was at war with all other tribes it touched except kinsfolk, and the spirit that once said in America the only good Indian was a dead Indian said in Palestine, with complete satisfaction of conscience, that the only good Amalekite was a slain one. That is to say, no moral obligations were recognized toward Amalekites, so that while within the tribal group ideals of fair play and humane dealing might rise to great heights, this vertical reach of moral responsibility was not matched by its horizontal extension. So Professor J. M. Powis Smith moderately sums up the ancient situation in Israel: "A foreigner has few rights that an Israelite is bound to respect. The ordinary claims of humanity are largely ignored in dealings with non-Israelite groups and individuals."[1]

In so far as this restriction of the sense of duty to the kinship group was illustrated in war, modern life presents lamentable parallels. Hostility creates hatred and contempt; the necessity of either killing or being killed obliterates humaneness; and even those who in times of peace have been cosmopolitans, with international interest and goodwill, become under the spell of war intense group-loyalists with no sense of moral obligation to the enemy. Much more was this restriction of the area of ethical responsibility vivid and controlling in days when war was constant and internationalism had not yet dawned. The utmost cruelty was not only allowed but commanded by Yahweh against Israel's rivals, and in the presence of habitual conflict fine ideals of humaneness had their chance to develop only within the circle of the blood-brotherhood.

The oft-quoted saying of Samuel, "To obey is better than sacrifice," was associated with the idea that, along with the captured animals, the captured king of Amalek should be put to death as a human offering, 'devoted' to Yahweh.[2] This does

---

[1] *The Moral Life of the Hebrews*, p. 12. [2] I Samuel, chap. 15.

not imply that Samuel was an inhumane man. He may have been, as the records suggest, a high-minded, intensely conscientious, devotedly loyal, and kindly person. The area, however, within which he conceived himself as under obligation to exercise such qualities was strictly limited to his tribal confederation.

This development of high moral quality within a restricted field of application is best illustrated in the Book of Deuteronomy. Written in the seventh century, a summary of the prophetic ideals leading up to the Josian reformation, it is one of the great documents of history in its expression of social goodwill. It is notable for laws to protect the poor, mitigate the treatment of debtors, ease the lot of slaves, and in general to encourage humaneness. All this, however, was for domestic consumption within Israel, not for foreign export; such ideas of fair play and goodwill toward foreigners as are found in the book apply only to those sojourning in Israel. A distinction was made between resident and non-resident aliens, and while injustice toward outsiders living in Israel was forbidden[1] and even love toward them commanded,[2] no obligations to other foreigners were acknowledged. Still in this remarkable document of merciful laws, massacre and extermination are the ideal treatment of conquered enemies— "Thou shalt make no covenant with them, nor show mercy unto them."[3] The only qualification of this statement which the evidence allows is that in Deuteronomy we find the idea of relative foreignness with a consequent gradation of responsibility. If an edible beast dies of itself, that is, of disease or old age, a Hebrew might not eat it; he might, however, give it away to an alien sojourner within the Hebrew community; but in dealing with a foreigner all barriers were down and diseased meat might be sold for what it would bring.[4] So in gaining admission to the Hebrew congregation, an Ammonite or a Moabite might not "enter into the assembly of Yahweh; even to the tenth generation."[5] In the case of others, however, there were special mitigations: "Thou shalt not abhor an Edomite; for he is thy brother: thou shalt not abhor an Egyptian; because thou wast a sojourner in his land. The children of the third generation that are born unto them shall enter into the assembly of Yahweh."[6] Indeed, as though positively fearing that growing humaneness within

---

[1] Deuteronomy 1:16; 27:19. This distinction runs through the entire Law; cf. Exodus 20:10; 22:21; 23:9; 23:12.
[2] Deuteronomy 10:19.
[3] Deuteronomy 7:2.
[4] Deuteronomy 14:21.
[5] Deuteronomy 23:3.
[6] Deuteronomy 23:7–8.

Israel might be carelessly applied to foreigners, the restrictions of mercy were meticulously noted. Every seven years there was to be a moratorium on all debts owed by Hebrews to Hebrews, but this neighborly provision was not binding if the debt was owed by a non-Israelite: "Of a foreigner thou mayest exact it."[1] As for loans, it was illegal for a Hebrew to take any interest from a Hebrew, but from a foreigner he might take all that the traffic would bear.[2]

Against this background the succeeding course of ethical development in the Bible must be seen. For centuries the area of moral obligation was limited to fellow Hebrews, and the struggle of the greater spirits to outgrow this limitation and universalize the realm of ethical responsibility was one of the most difficult and important which the Bible records.

III

A second limitation of Biblical morality at the beginning concerned classes of people within the tribal group to whom full personal rights were not conceived as due. The early Hebrews, for example, were at one with their race and time in giving to woman a low social status and narrowly limited rights. In the older story of creation, she was even pictured as an afterthought, made not on an equality with man but as a by-product; and, along with the serpent, she was represented as responsible for Adam's fall and was specially cursed with travail in childbirth as a penalty.[3]

In the tribal set-up of society a woman was the property first of her father and then of her husband. The word *baal*, used of a god as owner of the land, is commonly used in the Old Testament also for the male head of a household, and in our versions is translated 'owner,' 'master,' or 'husband,' according to the context. The word correctly represents the social fact of male supremacy in the Hebrew family, where the man was owner of his household—wives, children, slaves, herds, and properties. In the same code of laws a man is spoken of as 'the baal' of an ox and 'the baal' of a woman—that is, her owner and proprietor.[4] Since, therefore, such legal ownership inhered in the male head of a household, he could do what he would with his persons as with his properties, even selling his daughters into slavery.[5]

---

[1] Deuteronomy 15:1–3.
[2] J. M. Powis Smith: *The Moral Life of the Hebrews*, p. 129.

[3] Genesis 2:18 ff.
[4] Exodus 21:4,28.
[5] Exodus 21:7.

At marriage a girl who was not a slave passed for a financial consideration from her father's ownership to her husband's. Indeed, so important to the father was this potential property value in a daughter that the law code carefully protected his right to it in case a girl was wronged by a man before marriage.[1] This conception of woman as a chattel led, of course, to grave abuses. So Lot felt free to offer his two virgin daughters to the passions of the men of Sodom in order to save his male guests from their lust.[2] He could do what he would with his own, and a woman's rights were not comparable with a man's. This chattel relationship in which from birth the woman stood to the male head of her family is consistently present in the background of the early Old Testament. Even in the Ten Commandments, as recorded in Exodus 20:17, woman was listed along with the house, slaves, ox, and ass, belonging to one's neighbor, which one should not covet.

Among the Hebrews, therefore, as among early peoples generally, and, indeed, down to modern times, the process of courtship involved a commercial transaction. "Ask me never so much dowry and gift," cried one eager suitor to the girl's father, "and I will give according as ye shall say unto me: but give me the damsel to wife."[3] The same buying of a bride is seen in the case of Rebekah's espousal[4] and more clearly in the story of Rachel and Leah;[5] and everywhere it is evident that a woman was always possessed by some man who exercised over her a proprietorship which only gradually was mitigated and guarded against abuse.

This picture of woman's chattel relationship can, however, be overdrawn. For one thing, personality will out and, in a society as simply organized as the clan group, women of notable gifts could not be and were not kept down. Such names as Miriam, Deborah, Esther, and Judith in Jewish history and tradition are typical of an important fact about womanhood's estate in Israel. Women could and did rise to leadership then as in all ages and no theory of status could prevent it.

Moreover, not only is it true that personality will out, but love will too. The romances of Isaac and Rebekah, of Jacob and Rachel, are among the most beautiful love stories in ancient literature. "Isaac brought her into his mother Sarah's tent, and took Rebekah, and she became his wife; and he loved her";[6]

---

[1] Exodus 22:16-17.
[2] Genesis 19:8.
[3] Genesis 34:12.

[4] Genesis 24:53.
[5] Genesis 29:1-30.
[6] Genesis 24:67.

"Jacob served seven years for Rachel; and they seemed unto him but a few days, for the love he had to her"[1]—such romance is not dependent on social status and can flourish along with any custom of purchase which the existent society may have inherited. While, therefore, under the early Hebrew system a shocking absence of regard for womanhood is revealed in some narratives, so that Professor J. M. Powis Smith can even say that in the early traditions of Israel, "Chivalry is conspicuous by its almost total absence,"[2] that is not by any means the whole story. Love had its way and the traditional romances of Rebekah and Rachel were doubtless reproduced in many families.

Moreover, to overstress the chattel aspect of woman's status neglects the fact that in her functions as wife and mother she was, in a society organized around the family, the very center of the structure. An old background of custom is doubtless represented in Yahweh's reported remark to Moses about Miriam: "If her father had but spit in her face, should she not be ashamed seven days?"[3] Evidently a father's rights over the dignity of his womenfolk were very wide. He could do what he pleased and even if, as in Jephthah's case, his vow involved the sacrifice of his daughter's life,[4] his was the right and even the obligation to slay her. On the other hand, the exalted place of Leah and Rachel as the traditional mothers of the race and such stories as that of Hannah and Samuel[5] indicate another line of evidence.

Moreover, the rigid laws governing women's chastity, the severe penalties meted out for harlotry,[6] for rape,[7] for adultery,[8] even in the early traditions and confirmed in the later laws, while showing a narrowly constricted interest in the sexual side of woman's meaning to the tribe, reveal also a high estimate of the social values of wifehood and motherhood. It is true that in one of the Ten Commandments woman is classed with chattel property, but in another she is raised to coördinate dignity with man—"Honor thy father and thy mother."[9] One need only read the story of Abigail to see that then, as now, many a wife and mother had the brains and character of the family and by one device or another successfully expressed them.[10]

Indeed, seen against the background of their time and in comparison with the customs of surrounding civilizations, the

---

[1] Genesis 29:20.
[2] *The Moral Life of the Hebrews*, p. 41.
[3] Numbers 12:14.
[4] Judges 11:30–40.
[5] I Samuel 1:1 ff.
[6] Genesis 38:24.
[7] Genesis, chap. 34.
[8] Genesis 26:10–11.
[9] Exodus 20:12; cf. Exodus 21:15,17.
[10] I Samuel 25:9 ff.

noteworthy matter is not the degree to which the Hebrews shared the prevailing depreciation of woman but the degree to which they transcended it. The story of Eve in the Garden of Eden, judged by our standards, seems shocking to the dignity of womanhood, but in comparison with its Babylonian counterpart it is, as Stade says, "as a clear mountain spring to the slough of a village cesspool."[1]

Nevertheless, the early organization of society bore heavily on women. As has been the case for ages since, they were valued for their sexual uses rather than as ends in themselves. The perpetuity of the family name depended on their fertility and the levirate marriage laws, whereby when a man died without issue his brother took the widow to wife,[2] make plain how central and controlling this test of woman's value was. Always along with this primacy of her sexual uses, the Old Testament reveals a strong sense of her worth as property, so that even in the late and beautiful description of a wife and mother in the Book of Proverbs,[3] the commercial method of estimate is not excluded— "Her price is far above rubies." Never does woman escape the ownership of a proprietor, her father or husband or the patriarch of the clan, and against his will her rights are meager. Even her vows to Yahweh might be abrogated by father or husband[4] for, being the property of her family's head, she is not free to involve herself in any oaths conflicting with his wishes.

One of the most important corollaries of this status of woman was polygamy. If women could be bought and sold, so that a father could even sell his daughter as a slave, the only limitation on the number of wives a man possessed lay in the available supply of women and in his financial resources to procure them. Polygamy, therefore, was taken for granted in the domestic arrangements of early Israel. How thoroughly it was taken for granted is amply revealed in the Old Testament with even statistical details. "Gideon had threescore and ten sons of his body begotten; for he had many wives."[5] David had eight wives individually mentioned, married more unmentioned in Jerusalem, and when he fled from Absalom left ten concubines behind him in the city. In this regard Solomon was, of course, notorious—

---

[1] D. Bernhard Stade: "Der Mythus vom Paradies Gn 2.3 und die Zeit seiner Einwanderung in Israel," in *Zeitschrift für die alttestamentliche Wissenschaft*, 1903, p. 174.

[2] Deuteronomy 25:5–10.
[3] Chap. 31.
[4] Numbers 30:3–16.
[5] Judges 8:30.

"He had seven hundred wives, princesses, and three hundred concubines."[1]

As for more normal domestic establishments, the stories of the Hebrew patriarchs reveal households differing little in essentials from the family life of modern nomadic tribes. One who has seen a new wife welcomed to a chief's tent among the Adwan Arabs—the new arrival recommended and selected by the first wife, alike for the chief's satisfaction and to assist in the daily work now grown too onerous—feels himself at home in the Old Testament. When Sarah bore no children, she urged Hagar on Abraham as a concubine.[2] Jacob had two sisters to wife at the same time.[3] As for the common people, their economic status doubtless limited the size of their households and, as among all polygamous peoples, any rise in affluence was accompanied by an increase of wives. The ordinary situation was probably described in the case of the home in which Samuel was born: Elkanah "had two wives."[4]

Even in the later law codes, the old status of woman was retained without substantial change, although the Deuteronomic edition of the Ten Commandments amended the edition of Exodus by lifting the wife into special mention apart from the rest of the household.[5] Far from being man's equal, however, she was continually reminded of her inferiority. The legal value of a woman was only a little over half that of a man.[6] A mother who bore a daughter was 'unclean' twice as long as one who bore a son.[7] Polygamy still was taken for granted, slightly mitigated by provisions to guard against extremes. In post-Exilic times for instance, any Jacob possessing two sisters as wives at the same time would have found himself condemned.[8] Likewise, to have a mother and daughter to wife synchronously was forbidden.[9] The very presence of such prohibitions, however, makes clear how thoroughly polygamy in its ordinary forms must have been assumed.

As for divorce, the man alone had rights. Any husband could divorce a wife for any reason—"some unseemly thing in her"—of which he himself was the sole judge, but no provision was made for a wife's escape from a cruel husband.[10] The process of divorce was altogether in the man's control, at a moment's notice,

---

[1] I Kings 11:3.
[2] Genesis 16:1–2.
[3] Genesis 29:21–30.
[4] I Samuel 1:1–2.
[5] Deuteronomy 5:21.

[6] Leviticus 27:3–7.
[7] Leviticus 12:1–2,5.
[8] Leviticus 18:18.
[9] Leviticus 20:14.
[10] Deuteronomy 24:1–4.

without appeal to impartial arbitrament—"He shall write her a bill of divorcement, and give it in her hand, and send her out of his house"—yet even this was an advance over the customs that had preceded it. In this regard the Hebrew law was far less humane and civilized than was the Code of Hammurabi drawn up centuries before.[1]

IV

Slaves constituted another class denied full personal rights. The fact that slavery, like polygamy, was taken for granted is disguised in our English Versions by the euphemisms 'man-servant' and 'maid-servant,' but in the Hebrew there is no mistaking the established institution of slavery with its characteristic customs and consequences. Indeed, one law in Exodus, intended to make the lot of slaves more tolerable, goes only so far as to declare the owner liable to punishment if, in beating a slave, he kills him outright, whereas if the wounded slave "continue a day or two" the owner escapes penalty, "for he is his money."[2]

Among the Hebrews, as always where slavery has flourished, the institution presented an endless series of moral and legal problems. The constant endeavor was to make the system as humane as possible, but the very laws to that effect reveal how inhumane it was. Early codes limiting the rights of masters concern themselves with Hebrew slaves only, implying that at first only fellow Hebrews in bondage were conceived as having rights, while foreign slaves were still regarded as having none. Hebrews became slaves to Hebrews mainly in two ways, for debt or by the sale of daughters, and the following statutes are characteristic of early endeavors to mitigate the misfortune of such bondmen and bondwomen: Hebrew male slaves were to be given their freedom after six years[3]—an ideal law more honored in the breach than the observance; Hebrew female slaves, if used as concubines and found displeasing, might be sold to Hebrews but not to foreigners;[4] if a man and his wife went into slavery for debt together, they should go free together the seventh year, but if the man, entering bondage alone, was given his wife by his owner, even though children were born, only the man could go free;[5] a master who put out a slave's eye or knocked out a

[1] *The Code of Hammurabi*, translated by Robert Francis Harper, sec. 142, p. 51.
[2] Exodus 21:20-21.
[3] Exodus 21:2.
[4] Exodus 21:7-8.
[5] Exodus 21:3-4

tooth must as compensation free the slave;[1] one who kidnaped another and sold him into slavery was to be put to death.[2] Such laws reveal a humane intention but they also disclose the inhumanity of the accepted system which they were intended to control. Doubtless the widow's desperate cry was often heard in the land: "The creditor is come to take unto him my two children to be bondmen."[3]

How resistant to improvement the institution was is made plain when the slave laws of Deuteronomy are compared with the earlier codes. In this later rendition of the statutes under the influence of the prophetic school, the woman, equally with the man, might go free the seventh year;[4] the departing slave was to be furnished with sufficient goods to give him opportunity for readjustment;[5] an escaped Hebrew slave should not be returned to his master and should be protected from oppression.[6] Evidently the conscience of the Hebrews was struggling with the cruel details of their slave system, but the institution itself was taken for granted as an integral part of their society.

To be sure, mitigating circumstances were doubtless present in many cases. To this day inter-tribal competition for the slender means of subsistence reduces individual nomads to such need that slavery is a blessing to them. Accepted as bondsmen in some clan, they can, at least, be assured of enough to eat. Similarly, provision was made in Israel's laws of the seventh century for the kind of slave who, offered freedom the seventh year, preferred the safety of his bondage to the responsibilities of liberty. "If he say unto thee, I will not go out from thee; because he loveth thee and thy house, because he is well with thee," then, at his own request, his bondage might be made perpetual.[7]

Indentured servants, such as were familiar in the Colonial days of America, were probably comparable to Hebrews in bondage to fellow Hebrews when conditions were at their best. In the American Colonies men and women bound themselves to several years of servitude and after that went free, their passage money from the old country and their maintenance in the meantime being provided by their masters. They were technically enslaved for debt but one of them, Alsop by name, wrote as follows concerning his condition: "The four years I served there

[1] Exodus 21:26–27.
[2] Exodus 21:16.
[3] II Kings 4:1.
[4] Deuteronomy 15:12.
[5] Deuteronomy 15:13–14.
[6] Deuteronomy 23:15–16.
[7] Deuteronomy 15:16–17.

were not to me so slavish as a two-years' servitude of a handicraft apprenticeship in London."[1] Doubtless many Hebrews, enslaved for debt, were in a similar case.

While, however, a sensitiveness of conscience about the bondage of fellow Hebrews can be seen developing, no such mitigation is suggested in the early Old Testament with regard to foreign slaves. To be sure, there are exceptions even to most rigid rules, and able personality, in slavery as out of it, makes itself felt. So in the story of Abraham, unless as some think the text at this point is corrupt, the patriarch's plea for a son is based on the fact that, if he lacks a child as heir, Eliezer of Damascus, a bondman born in Abraham's house and apparently an able manager of his estate, will inherit his property.[2] Indeed, it should be noted that slavery itself was a social advance—a substitute for massacre and exile in dealing with peoples conquered in war: "It came to pass, when Israel was waxed strong, that they put the Canaanites to taskwork, and did not utterly drive them out . . . . but the Canaanites dwelt among them, and became subject to taskwork."[3] Whether this explanation of the servile classes of aliens in Israel be taken as adequate or not, it clearly indicates a servile class to be explained. Indeed, the excuse for holding alien bondsmen was carried back into legend, and the Canaanites, as descendants of Ham, were represented as having been cursed by Noah and so doomed to servitude—

> Cursed be Canaan;
> A servant of servants shall he be.[4]

Far from being a minor matter, therefore, slavery was one of the dominant facts in the social situation that the prophets faced. A stratified society, with wealthy landowners at the top and slaves at the bottom and, in between, a mass of poor folk skirting precariously the edge of servitude for debt and in times of depression forced into it or compelled to sell sons or daughters to redeem the family's fortunes—such a picture is revealed by a careful reading of the records. Even in the comparatively simple society of 1000 B.C., one household of which we read had at least twenty slaves,[5] and the rumbling of servile discontent was evidenced in Nabal's word to David: "There are many servants now-a-days that break away every man from his master."[6] As

---

[1] Quoted by Alice Morse Earle: *Colonial Dames and Good Wives*, p. 11.
[2] Genesis 15:2–4; cf. I Chronicles 2:34 ff.
[3] Judges 1:27–33.
[4] Genesis 9:18–27.
[5] II Samuel 19:17.
[6] I Samuel 25:10.

the social structure became more complicated, with increasing power in the hands of a few and increasing uncertainty in the status of the many, economic inequality became more, rather than less, pronounced and the slave system was alike more firmly established and more ethically troublesome.

V

In addition to the narrowness of the tribal boundaries within which the sense of moral obligation functioned and the supression of classes, especially women and slaves, within the tribal circle itself, a third limitation affected, at the beginning, the Old Testament's ideas of right and wrong. As among early peoples generally, morals were to the ancient Hebrews what the etymology of the word suggests—*mores*, 'customary behavior.' The observance of tribal taboos and ritual ceremonies, along with such restraint on daily conduct as would protect and further the interests of the tribe, constituted a man's duty, and every detail of this complicated obligation was regarded as the will of the tribal gods. Such observances and restraints, however, were almost altogether a matter of external behavior, while concern about motives and attitudes, about quality of spirit and purpose, was absent from the ethical picture.

This customary morality of prohibition and taboo was inextricably associated with early tribalism. Attention was concentrated on the tribe's success and on those ways of acting that would secure the favor of the tribal gods. "Religion," as W. Robertson Smith puts it, "did not exist for the saving of souls but for the preservation and welfare of society, and in all that was necessary to this end every man had to take his part, or break with the domestic and political community to which he belonged."[1] The result was that the whole duty of man was summed up in the observance of established tribal customs, and the utmost rigor was used in compelling conformity. Any irregularity was likely to bring down, not on the individual sinner alone but on the whole group, the god's ruinous disfavor, and therefore the coercion of customary conduct and the extirpation of irregular conduct were ruthless. A typical illustration is to be found in Yahweh's supposed insistence on circumcision—"The uncircumcised male . . . shall be cut off from his people; he hath broken my covenant."[2]

[1] *Lectures on the Religion of the Semites,*   [2] Genesis 17:13-14.
p. 29.

Far down in history such insistence on uniform custom has commonly emerged when any group, especially if it has conceived itself to be a theocracy, has faced a severe struggle for existence in which social cohesion was indispensable. So Miss Agnes Repplier says of the Massachusetts Bay Colony:

> It is hardly worth while to censure communities which were establishing, or seeking to establish, "a strong religious state" because they were intolerant. Tolerance is not, and never has been, compatible with strong religious states. The Puritans of New England did not endeavor to force their convictions upon unwilling Christendom. They asked only to be left in peaceful possession of a singularly unprolific corner of the earth, which they were civilizing after a formula of their own. Settlers to whom this formula was antipathetic were asked to go elsewhere. If they did not go, they were sent, and sometimes whipped into the bargain—which was harsh, but not unreasonable.[1]

If the endeavor to build a strong religious state under pioneering conditions could work such consequence among notable individualists like the Puritans, much more would primitive Hebrew tribalism emphasize the necessity of conformity with custom. The idea of right, therefore, in the beginning of the Old Testament, suffered the limitation of externality, and this limitation continued to be, as Jesus found it, one of the outstanding problems of Hebrew ethics.

The nature of the problem appears in two main aspects.

1. A man could observe the tribal customs outwardly without deep concern about his inner quality. Customary ethics demand at the most respectability, but they do not lead a man to pray,

> Create in me a clean heart, O God;
> And renew a right spirit within me.[2]

The Old Testament came at last to such praying but it did not start there.

In one of the renditions of the Decalogue,[3] thought by scholars to be the earliest, are such commands as these: "Thou shalt worship no other god"; "Thou shalt make thee no molten gods"; "The feast of unleavened bread shalt thou keep"; "All that

---

[1] *Under Dispute*, pp. 8–9.   [3] Exodus, chap. 34.
[2] Psalm 51:10.

openeth the womb is mine"; "Six days thou shalt work, but on the seventh day thou shalt rest"; "Thou shalt not offer the blood of my sacrifice with leavened bread"; "Thou shalt not boil a kid in its mother's milk." These and similar commands are external regulations, which can be observed with no deep searching of conscience and with no concern about personal motive and quality.

When, beyond customary behavior associated with rubric, one considers actions associated with human relationships, a similar externality obtains. Murder, adultery, false witness, the covetous seeking of a neighbor's goods—such prohibited conduct was anti-social and could be externally refrained from by any one who was determined to respect the established customs of the tribe.

Here, then, in primitive tribal life was laid the foundation of the later legalism which at its best was the boast and at its worst the disgrace of Judaism. The idea of customary ethics kept a persistent grip on the developing morals of Israel, all the more persistent because every detail of the customary ethics was regarded as the will of God. In modern thought and parlance, ethics and religion are separable; in Hebrew thought and parlance they were inseparable and even indistinguishable. Like heat and light in sunshine they came as one, and only later more sophisticated thinking differentiated between them. Whatever was customarily right was God's will; whatever was God's will was profoundly important and urgent. Thus the sacredness with which religion always endues whatever it touches clung even to the minutiæ of duty. In order to protect the will of God from being in the least transgressed, the good life was defined and set down in laws. But laws can be expanded, interpreted, refined, evaded, and explained away, so that in the fully developed legal system the ideals of goodness were commonly externalized by the ingenuity of lawyers. As for early Hebrew legislation, it was largely absorbed in details of outward behavior, much of it entirely non-moral, with much of what was moral so set in terms of customary action that the keeping of the law made only a small demand on ethical insight and personal quality.

2. This limitation of externality appeared in a second aspect. When the laws of early Israel were in process of formation, rubric and ethic were combined and, thus deposited together in the written statutes, they continued to exercise together a binding control over life. In consequence, even in the later codes, what we would call religious etiquette and humane ethic were

often put upon a level, with the constant danger that the first would become a substitute for the second in the service of God. This is too obvious in the earlier codes to need special illustration. The laws about sacred seasons, Sabbath observance, details of sacrifice, clean and unclean foods, bulk much larger than legislation on ethics, and this lack of perspective and proportion, this inveterate idea that Yahweh was appeased by ceremonial behavior, obtained so firm a grip that even the prophets who contended against it never broke its hold, as orthodox Judaism today bears witness. Indeed, a great prophet, Ezekiel, lumped together adultery, idolatry, bloodshed, and the eating of meat improperly prepared, as alike displeasing to Yahweh.[1]

In this regard the early Hebrews faced a problem, common not only to all primitive faiths but to all advanced faiths too, in which humane conduct has to compete for primacy with ritual observance. The task of the Hebrew prophets at their best, insisting on the absolute supremacy of righteousness as the requirement of God, has never yet been anywhere completely finished. In the Old Testament this problem took shape from current circumstance and inherited tradition and in many forms is present in the writings of Israel. Even a late rendition of Hebrew history in Chronicles ascribes a pestilence to David's presumption in taking a census of the people.[2] The banning of a census as a presumptuous exhibition of curiosity, seeking information which only the god has a right to possess, is a familiar taboo in primitive religion, and opposition to a census on religious grounds arose even in New Jersey before the American Revolution.[3] When one considers the appalling cruelties of which David was guilty,[4] to say nothing of his perfidy in the case of Uriah,[5] one feels a profound lack of ethical perspective in associating so severe a punishment as a wide-spread pestilence with the crime of census-taking.

Legalism and ritualism, therefore, tempted the Hebrews to externality in their idea of right living, and with this temptation the great prophets and Jesus were intimately and constantly concerned.

VI

Such were the three main limitations on early Hebrew morals: the field of ethical obligation was tribally constricted; within

---

[1] Ezekiel 33:25–26.
[2] I Chronicles 21:1–17.
[3] See Henry Pratt Fairchild: *General Sociology*, p. 311.

[4] E.g., I Samuel 27:9; I Samuel 27:11; II Samuel 8:2–6.
[5] II Samuel, chap. 11.

the tribal circle certain classes were denied full personal rights; and the nature of moral conduct was interpreted in such external terms of custom and ritual as to make small demand on internal insight and quality. The progress made, therefore, in the later stages of the Old Testament, in the inter-Testamental period, and in the New Testament, may be interpreted as the overpassing of these three inadequacies.

Considering them in reversed order, it is plain that the great prophets and Jesus insistently drove back the moral problem into the inner quality of personal life. The prophetic leaders of Israel were as much interested as any members of the nation in the success of the social group; the beginning and end of their thought was Israel redeemed, purified, and fulfilling her mission in the world. Their interpretation of what this involved, however, went far beyond meticulous legalism and ritualism into ethical insight and creative moral living, saying with Micah, "What doth Yahweh require of thee, but to do justly, and to love kindness, and to walk humbly with thy God?"[1] The progress involved in this creative work of the Hebrew conscience was one of the supreme contributions to human life which the Old Testament records.

The increasing humaneness and inwardness of moral life under the influence of the great prophets and Jesus is illustrated in the changing ideas about forgiveness of enemies. In the older strata of documents, retaliation was distinctly taught as the proper principle of legal procedure—"Life for life, eye for eye, tooth for tooth, hand for hand, foot for foot, burning for burning, wound for wound, stripe for stripe."[2] Justice between man and man and between nation and nation was thus pictured in retaliatory terms; history was written to illustrate the principle of retaliation in God's dealings with men, and even psalms celebrated the people's hope of seeing it executed upon their enemies.[3]

Far from being inhumane, such strict adherence to the principles of retaliation represented, at first, progress in goodwill, for it put boundaries around man's natural desire to wreak on personal and social enemies an unlimited and abandoned vengeance. In Lamech's claim to the right of revenge "seventy and sevenfold,"[4] we have the historic starting point for a study of the growing ideal of forgiveness, and the first step up from such unrestricted vengeance was the adoption of retaliation as a substitute. The

[1] Micah 6:8.
[2] Exodus 21:23-25.
[3] Psalm 137:8-9.
[4] Genesis 4:23-24.

law of 'eye for eye,' therefore, was at first a moral advance, curbing extravagant vindictiveness and allowing only the strict return of injury for injury, no more, no less.

A further enlargement of thought was associated with the idea that the requiting of evil upon enemies was not so much man's business as God's. This idea lay behind even Paul's argument against vindictiveness—"Avenge not yourselves, beloved, but give place unto the wrath of God: for it is written, Vengeance belongeth unto me; I will recompense, saith the Lord."[1] In this statement Paul showed himself a good Jew, true to his racial heritage. Human vengeance in the Old Testament was restricted, not simply by being reduced to retaliation but by being handed over to the divine executioner. By this means the outward wreaking of vengeance could be forgone without giving up the interior hope of it. So Deuteronomy rejoices in Yahweh because "he will avenge the blood of his servants,"[2] and a psalmist cries,

> Yahweh is on my side among them that help me:
> Therefore shall I see my desire upon them that hate me.[3]

Obviously, while such methods of handling the passion of vindictiveness may be externally ameliorative, they are not inwardly curative, and they lend color to the words of Jesus, "Ye have heard that it was said, Thou shalt love thy neighbor, and hate thine enemy."[4] Nevertheless, this substitution of God for man in dealing with enemies, as Paul's employment of it reveals, was capable of high usage. It could be extended and deepened to mean a deliberate willingness to forgo either vengeance or retaliation, leaving the issue with God. So the Book of Proverbs puts it:

> Say not thou, I will recompense evil:
> Wait for Yahweh, and he will save thee.[5]

A further advance was made when vindictiveness, or even retaliation toward a personal enemy, was under certain circumstances visited with moral disapproval. Even in the early law codes, special situations were visualized where not retaliatory justice but positive mercy toward a foe was commanded—"If thou meet thine enemy's ox or his ass going astray, thou shalt surely bring it back to him again. If thou see the ass of him that hateth thee lying under his burden, thou shalt forbear to leave

---

[1] Romans 12:19.
[2] Deuteronomy 32:43.
[3] Psalm 118:7.
[4] Matthew 5:43.
[5] Proverbs 20:22.

him, thou shalt surely release it with him."[1] By thus calling attention to the problem of treating enemies, not when they were triumphant but when they were in distress, a path of least resistance was indicated for the progressive spirit of magnanimity. A growing humaneness, expressed in positive mercy, was first commanded toward foes when they were in misfortune; generous treatment of enemies secured its foothold by appealing to pity. So said the Book of Proverbs:

> If thine enemy be hungry, give him bread to eat;
> And if he be thirsty, give him water to drink.[2]

To be sure, such magnanimity was far from perfect. The Book of Proverbs, in another passage, begins on a high note,

> Rejoice not when thine enemy falleth,
> And let not thy heart be glad when he is overthrown,

but, as for the inward motive, the passage ends on a low note,

> Lest Yahweh see it, and it displease him,
> And he turn away his wrath from him.[3]

Nevertheless, magnanimity, having secured a foothold in dealing with distressed foes, could not be denied its further way. The evidence of enlarged humaneness is unmistakable, as when Job pleaded his innocence of wrongdoing and revealed his detestation of vindictiveness—

> If I have rejoiced at the destruction of him that hated me,
> Or lifted up myself when evil found him
> (Yea, I have not suffered my mouth to sin
> By asking his life with a curse). . . .[4]

Within the limits of the Old Testament, the most precise statement of this growing ideal of magnanimity toward enemies is found in the Exilic law: "Thou shalt not hate thy brother in thy heart: thou shalt surely rebuke thy neighbor, and not bear sin because of him. Thou shalt not take vengeance, nor bear any grudge against the children of thy people; but thou shalt love thy neighbor as thyself."[5]

It is to be noted that only fellow Israelites were included within the scope of such magnanimity. This persistent constriction of developing humaneness within the racial group explains

---

[1] Exodus 23:4–5.
[2] Proverbs 25:21.
[3] Proverbs 24:17–18.

[4] Job 31:29–30.
[5] Leviticus 19:17–18.

otherwise strange contrasts in the Old Testament. Joseph's forgiveness of his brethren, for example, presents one of the most moving scenes in ancient literature,[1] while, on the other hand, the Book of Esther with unabashed gusto enjoys the Jewish *pogrom* in which multitudes of alien enemies were massacred in all the provinces of the Persian Empire.[2] This contrast in moral attitude, however, is only in appearance. Joseph forgave his *brethren* and the writer of Esther would have applauded that, while the writer of the Joseph stories would doubtless have agreed with the Book of Esther that alien enemies were not within the proper scope of such generosity and that to pardon them or even to refrain from vengeance on them was not virtue but disloyalty.

Between the Testaments, despite national evils which brought vindictiveness naturally in their train, there was a notable deepening of magnanimity. Vindictiveness there was a-plenty. Nothing in the Old Testament specifically condemned it when exhibited toward foreign foes. The unlimited outreach of divine mercy even toward Nineveh, such as the Book of Jonah represents, was the faith of a few and its human counterpart the attainment of only a small number. Rather, the Book of Nahum—a pæan of joy over the downfall of Nineveh—represented the popular attitude toward foreign foes, as it would today in Christendom under similar circumstances. Despite this, however, the wisdom of the forgiving spirit was ever more clearly seen and its statement became so universal in form as to suggest unlimited application. The Testaments of the Twelve Patriarchs, for example, was a Hebrew book written in the second century B.C., and was probably known to Jesus. At any rate, its kinship with his spirit is unmistakable—"Love ye, therefore, one another from the heart; and if a man sin against thee, cast forth the poison of hate and speak peaceably to him, and in thy soul hold not guile; and if he confess and repent, forgive him. . . . And if he be shameless and persist in his wrong-doing, even so forgive him from the heart, and leave to God the avenging";[3] "If any one seeketh to do evil unto you, do well unto him, and pray for him, and ye shall be redeemed of the Lord from all evil."[4] Indeed, everything that Jesus said on this matter[5] is to be found in germ in the Jewish literature which preceded him, sometimes with verbal resemblance

---

[1] Genesis, chap. 45.
[2] Esther, chap. 9.
[3] The Testament of Gad 6:3,7.

[4] The Testament of Joseph 18:2.
[5] See Mark 11:25; Luke 6:27-28; Matthew 18:21-22; 5:43-45.

so close that conscious quotation is suggested. The Book of Sirach
even says,

> Forgive thy neighbour the injury (done to thee),
> And then, when thou prayest, thy sins will be forgiven.[1]

Here, then, was a development of moral ideal in the Bible
that extended all the way from Lamech's claim to vengeance
"seventy and sevenfold" to Jesus' plea for forgiveness of
enemies "until seventy times seven." Such a development
called increasingly for inward quality of spirit, for rightness of
attitude and motive. Vengeance and retaliation could be outwardly administered; penal justice could be roughly managed by
legality; but the more magnanimity was called for, the more
inward quality was indispensable, until at last the Bible faced
man with an ideal that put upon him a profound demand for
interior regeneration—"Let all bitterness, and wrath, and anger,
and clamor, and railing, be put away from you, with all malice:
and be ye kind one to another, tenderhearted, forgiving each
other, even as God also in Christ forgave you."[2]

VII

The overpassing of the limitation of externality in early
Hebrew morals involved not only the development of ethical
ideals concerning special virtues such as magnanimity, but a
profoundly important evolution of thought about the nature of
sin in general and of what is necessary in securing salvation from
it. At first, sin was transgression of tribal custom and the penalty
was the displeasure of the tribal god, with its dire results. The
sum and substance of sin and salvation might then have been
described in such terms as these: obedience to tribal custom
means Yahweh's favor and the tribe's prosperity; transgression
of tribal custom means Yahweh's displeasure and the tribe's
disaster; therefore, do not transgress. The negativeness and
externality of this idea of wrongdoing and of salvation from it is
plain and, as well, the slight demand it makes on inward, personal resources of character. At this stage no question was raised
as to man's ability to refrain from transgression if he so desired,
and there was, in consequence, no conscious need of inner assist-
ance, much less of interior cleansing by the Spirit of God. One
of the most fascinating roadways along which the Old Testament's
thought traveled led from this beginning to the consciousness

---

[1] Sirach (Ecclesiasticus) 28:2.   [2] Ephesians 4:31–32.

of sin as inner defilement and of salvation as inner cleansing and renewal.

In this development Jeremiah played an eminent part. He too, an intense patriot, cared supremely for his nation's welfare, but, as the nation broke up under the shock of war and exile, his experience of God became a profound, inner possession in the strength of which alone he carried on through tragic days. Moreover, along with this experience of inwardness in his own religious life went his disillusionment over the external reform imposed by royal authority in the reign of Josiah.[1] The reform had seemed successful. It had achieved outwardly many of the ends the prophets sought. It had cast down the local high places, had centralized worship in Jerusalem, had eliminated the worst abominations of the heathen cults, and in the ethical realm had put in force the admirable law code of Deuteronomy. But it had remained an external reformation; the inner fountains of motive and desire had not been cleansed. So Jeremiah cried, "Wash thy heart from wickedness, that thou mayest be saved."[2]

Jeremiah's experience and ministry are chiefly notable because in him, for the first time in our religious tradition, the idea of sin emerged as inner pollution and that of salvation as inner regeneration. Still the goal sought was a righteous nation, but no social righteousness, he saw, could be achieved by external reformation only; right-minded and right-motived persons were the prerequisites of a fortunate society. In the sixth century before Christ, he understood with astonishing clarity the inward origins of public character and traced the good life back, behind taboo and custom, legality and form, to personal quality of spirit. Out of this insight came the prophet's vision of the new covenant by which alone Israel could be saved—God's law in the people's spirit and written on their hearts.[3]

This deeper current of thought in Israel made its way slowly. Before the Exile, old ideas of tribal morality withstood such inward conceptions of sin and salvation. During and after the Exile, the struggle of the Jews against being assimilated by paganism so coerced them into stressing their differentials and, as always in such a case, so led them to stress obvious peculiarities which are external, that Judaism emerged into a new era of accentuated legalism and ritualism.

Under the influence of this situation the duties of a Jew were

[1] II Kings 23:1–25.   [3] Jeremiah 31:31–34.
[2] Jeremiah 4:14.

formalized in written laws. What Deuteronomy began, Ezekiel and the Priestly Code carried on. Then the scribes arose and, by giving interpretations to, and drawing corollaries from, the Law, applied it with meticulous care to the minute affairs of daily life. Israel became a people of a book, the Torah, and the good life was defined in terms of written statutes. The trouble, however, with a written law is that, defining goodness in terms of statutory observance, it is tempted to set the standard low and to neglect the inner sources of great character and the interior need of spiritual renewal. Out of such legalism came the Eighteenth Psalm, which has seldom, if ever, been surpassed as an illustration of moral self-satisfaction,[1] and the remark of the complacent young ruler who said to Jesus, "All these things have I observed from my youth up."[2]

As morality was thus formalized in post-Exilic legalism, formalism developed in the temple worship, and all the dangers associated with ritualism and priestcraft befell Israel. The wonder is not that legalism and ritualism thus absorbed so large a share of Judaism's thought—the same has been true in all religions, not least in Christianity—but that the deeper stream of prophetic teaching still flowed on. Even Ezekiel, who contented himself too much with eddies of outward conduct rather than with main currents of inner purpose, and who indiscriminately mixed up ethics and tribal taboos, had caught the deeper truth for which Jeremiah stood, and appealed repeatedly for "a new heart and a new spirit."[3]

Indeed, the same Psalter, the hymn book of the second temple, which contains the complacence of the Eighteenth Psalm, contains also the profundity of the Fifty-first. There sin is a deep, inward defilement; goodness is an interior fountain of spiritual quality; penitence concerns what a man *is* behind what he does; and the desire for a good life calls out the prayer for spiritual rebirth,

> Create in me a clean heart, O God;
> And renew a right spirit within me.[4]

In this matter, once more, Jesus belonged to the great tradition of his people. Between the Testaments the stream had flowed on, whose springs in the Old Testament we have traced. The good life, being more than law and rubric, was seen to lie in moral

---

[1] Psalm 18:20–24.
[2] Luke 18:21.

[3] Ezekiel 18:31; 11:19–20; 36:26–27.
[4] Psalm 51:10.

insight, wisdom, and goodwill. As the Fifty-first Psalm had said, goodness was truth in the inward parts and, in the hidden part, wisdom, and the good man was washed thoroughly from iniquity and upheld by a willing spirit. The insight of Jeremiah, tracing evil back to private thinking, was taken for granted in the Testaments of the Twelve Patriarchs—"Fearing lest he should offend the Lord, he [the good man] will not do wrong to any man, even in thought."[1]

This quality of inwardness was of the very essence of Jesus' ethic. He saw anger as killing, hate as murder, lust as adultery, and insincerity as perjury. In his eyes genuine philanthropy and genuine prayer alike sprang from inner quality of spirit, for which no outward deed could act as surrogate. His ultimate moral philosophy lay in such propositions as that "from within, out of the heart of men, evil thoughts proceed,"[2] and that "a good tree cannot bring forth evil fruit."[3] In the New Testament's insistence, therefore, on the need of inner spiritual renewal and empowerment, fulfilment came to a development of life and thought which had begun in the insight of a few prophetic souls centuries before. The development began with the external observance of tribal taboos; it ended with men saying, "Except one be born anew, he cannot see the kingdom of God";[4] "Be not fashioned according to this world: but be ye transformed by the renewing of your mind";[5] "The ordinance of the law . . . fulfilled in us, who walk not after the flesh, but after the Spirit";[6] "If any man is in Christ, he is a new creature."[7]

This emphasis constitutes the essential matter in Paul's life and thought. He had been reared in a system where sin was regarded as transgression of law, and where repentance, forgiveness, and amendment of life were the cure. This legal estimate of sin's nature seemed to him utterly inadequate. Man's sin had deeper roots than wilful disobedience; it was, as it were, a demonic power so that it was not Paul who did evil but "sin which dwelleth in me."[8] Deep-seated and inveterate, sinfulness was now regarded as so essentially a part of human nature that no mere forgiveness of transgressions could salve its evil or volitional amendment undo its harm. A profound, interior deliverance was needed; one must pass from the dominion of the flesh into the

---

[1] The Testament of Gad: 5:6
[2] Mark 7:21.
[3] Matthew 7:18.
[4] John 3:3.

[5] Romans 12:2.
[6] Romans 8:4.
[7] II Corinthians 5:17.
[8] Romans 7:17.

dominion of the spirit. Short of that, the old moral cures of repentance and forgiveness were mere palliatives, failing to deal with the real disease—"In me, that is, in my flesh, dwelleth no good thing."[1]

To be sure, the experience of forgiveness is to be found in Paul,[2] but only as the beginning of a far deeper and more thoroughgoing event—the crucial passage of a man's life from being "in the flesh" to being "in the Spirit" or "in Christ Jesus."[3] The Apostle's estimate of the nature of sin and salvation, voiced in his cry, "Who shall deliver me out of this body of death?"[4] could not be matched by any legal transaction whatever—only by a profound deliverance, first, from the power of the flesh now, and second, from the very presence of the flesh in the great denouement. Then Christ "shall fashion anew the body of our humiliation, that it may be conformed to the body of his glory."[5]

This radical estimate of the nature of sin, with its accompanying demand for a radical deliverance, while phrased by Paul in terms uniquely characteristic of himself, is one of the major contributions of the New Testament. To be sure, Christianity could be and was interpreted as a new law, as for example in the Epistle of James.[6] Professor E. F. Scott, however, passes a not unfair judgment on James: "Conceiving of the new message as a 'law,' and not as a power which creates a new life, he misses what is deepest, both in the Christian religion and the Christian ethic."[7]

As for John, he had his own way of conceiving and phrasing man's need of deep, interior deliverance. He, too, saw in Jesus the one who "taketh away the sin of the world,"[8] and in a Pauline metaphor he pictured Christ's work as redeeming men from the slavery of sin to the freedom of sonship.[9] There are even faint intimations in John of a Pauline contrast between flesh and spirit—"It is the spirit that giveth life; the flesh profiteth nothing";[10] "That which is born of the flesh is flesh; and that which is born of the Spirit is spirit."[11] Here, however, the resemblance ends and the fact emerges, as elsewhere, that there is no such thing as New Testament theology—only New

---

[1] Romans 7:18.
[2] E.g., Romans 4:6–11; Colossians 1:14; 2:13; Ephesians 1:7; 4:32.
[3] Romans 8:9; 6:11.
[4] Romans 7:24 (marginal translation).
[5] Philippians 3:21.
[6] James 1:25; 2:8–12; 4:11–12.

[7] *The Literature of the New Testament*, p. 216.
[8] John 1:29.
[9] John 8:34–36.
[10] John 6:63.
[11] John 3:6.

Testament theologies. Indeed, so distinctive is John's idea of salvation that it has been said it does not conceive the saving work of Christ as deliverance from sin.[1] John says that men would have had no sin at all had not Christ "come and spoken unto them"[2] and that sin essentially lies in the refusal of the light so offered. The Spirit will convict men of sin, says the Johannine Jesus, "because they believe not on me."[3]

According to John, the evil from which Christ saves his people is not so much sin as it is an inner darkness of man's unregenerate nature, a profound privation of true light, true knowledge, and true life. Sunk and benighted in this native estate of all who are born "of the will of the flesh,"[4] man's existence is really death and salvation from it is not attainable by man's unaided will. In order to pass "out of death into life"[5] one must be "born anew."[6] A divine initiative from above regenerates the man so that he passes from a state of unspiritual darkness, illusion, and privation into the higher realm of being, concerning which John uses three major words—light, life, and love. To John, therefore, Christ is the life-giver. Coming himself from the realm of "eternal life," he confers it on those who receive him. They are reborn into a new world of being; they become children of God,[7] possess life "abundantly,"[8] no longer "walk in the darkness" but "have the light of life."[9] Christ is the vine, his disciples the branches, and in this vital union life flows inwardly to each believer so that abundant fruitage is possible.[10] This is the distinctively Johannine phrasing of salvation, and it represents the way some early Christians, deeply influenced by Hellenistic thought, described man's profound need of deliverance and conceived the inner regeneration which Christ brought in saving answer.

VIII

This overpassing of the limitation of externality, however, had it stood alone, might have led to a predominantly subjective religion, whereas the development of Biblical thought emphatically retained the unity of religion and ethics that Jeremiah

[1] Ernest Findlay Scott: *The Fourth Gospel; Its Purpose and Theology*, p. 218.
[2] John 15:22.
[3] John 16:9.
[4] John 1:13.
[5] John 5:24.
[6] John 3:3 (see also marginal translation).
[7] John 1:12.
[8] John 10:10; cf. 6:40.
[9] John 8:12.
[10] John 15:1 ff.

stressed when he identified humane conduct with knowing God.[1] In particular, one perceives in the later Old Testament and in the New Testament a growing respect for personality wherever found, and, in consequence, a deepening concern about unjustly treated classes of people.

No one acquainted with the history of slavery and of woman's status will expect to find, within the centuries covered by the Bible, either the elimination of the one or the emancipation of the other. Slavery still exists; its pressing consequences are today present in the United States and living men and women can remember the slave system in full swing. As for Greco-Roman civilization, it was based squarely on slave labor, and one of the profoundest differences between the ancient Mediterranean culture and our own is that there slavery was taken for granted along with a growing consciousness of the moral compromise it involved with man's best ideals, while with us liberty is taken for granted along with deep ethical discontent at the parallels of slavery, or worse, which exist under the wage system. As for womanhood, millions of women today have no status remotely approaching equality with man's. Throughout both the Old and the New Testaments, therefore, slavery was a recognized part of the social structure and woman was nowhere conceived as rightfully escaping from the proprietorship of father or husband. What the Bible does represent is a preparation of the moral soil for a new crop of ideas on these and kindred matters. Specifically, the Bible records a deepening sense of the value of personality wherever found and an increasing insistence on respect for it.

So far as woman was concerned, it is not so much in the Old Testament's laws as in its poetry that we catch a distinctly altered tone. The Song of Songs,[2] for example, is a love lyric often tropical in its passion, and very important as evidence that romance rather than convenience or barter was gaining recognition as the basis of marriage—

> . . . Love is strong as death,
> A passion as resistless as Sheol.
>
> .   .   .   .   .
>
> Water cannot quench it,
> Nor do rivers drown it;
> If one offer all the wealth of one's house
> For love, they will utterly reject it.[3]

---

[1] Jeremiah 22:15–16.
[2] Called The Song of Solomon, in the English Versions.

[3] Song of Solomon 8:6–7 as translated by Hinckley G. Mitchell: *The Ethics of the Old Testament*, p. 347.

This implies the ideal of personal choice rather than family sale as the basis of marriage, and indeed, if Budde's emendation of one sentence is correct, the Song of Songs leaves no room in true love for polygamy:

> Solomon had sixty queens,
> And eighty concubines,
> And maidens numberless;
> My dove, the faultless, is one.[1]

At any rate, this celebrated love lyric, whose admission to the Hebrew canon was vigorously withstood and was not finally settled until about 90 A.D.,[2] presents an ideal of love highly romantic and individualistic. When the idealized bridegroom found his bride the "fairest among women" and yet, in her control of his affections, "terrible as an army with banners," the relationship of marriage was plainly escaping its old tribal restrictions, the family was becoming more plastic, and the trail was being blazed from polygamy to monogamy.

The Book of Proverbs gives further evidence of the same trend. No specific condemnation of polygamy is to be found, but it is impossible easily to fit polygamy into the ideas of the writer—

> House and riches are an inheritance from fathers;
> But a prudent wife is from Yahweh.[3]

> He that hath found a [good] wife hath found a blessing,
> And hath obtained favor from Yahweh.[4]

> A worthy woman is the crown of her husband.[5]

Above all, in the thirty-first chapter occurs the description of a wife and mother in which she is elevated to such dignity that rivals in the household are not easily imaginable.

Along with such finer estimates of woman in Hebrew poetry went an inevitable tendency to improve the laws in her behalf. So Deuteronomy marked an advance over the earlier codes, and the Priestly Document of the Exile went further yet in ordaining, for example, woman's right of inheritance.[6] As for the integrity of family life on a monogamous basis, Malachi's protest against

---

[1] Song of Solomon 6:8–9 as translated by Karl Budde (see H. G. Mitchell: *op. cit.*, p. 348).

[2] At the Synod of Jamnia, although even later Rabbi Akibah pronounced condemnation on those who sang snatches from this book in wine houses.

[3] Proverbs 19:14.

[4] Proverbs 18:22 as translated by H. G. Mitchell in *op. cit.*, p. 330.

[5] Proverbs 12:4.

[6] Numbers 27:6–11.

divorce bears eloquent testimony to Israel's developing conscience: "And this again ye do: ye cover the altar of Yahweh
with tears, with weeping, and with sighing, insomuch that he
regardeth not the offering any more, neither receiveth it with good
will at your hand. Yet ye say, Wherefore? Because Yahweh hath
been witness between thee and the wife of thy youth, against
whom thou hast dealt treacherously, though she is thy companion,
and the wife of thy covenant. And did he not make one, although
he had the residue of the Spirit? And wherefore one? He sought
a godly seed. Therefore take heed to your spirit, and let none
deal treacherously against the wife of his youth. For I hate
putting away, saith Yahweh, the God of Israel."[1]

As among ancient people generally, the actual practise of monogamy among the Hebrews came not so much by direct legislation
as by the indirect influence of changed economic conditions, the
increase of individual freedom, the rise of romantic love, and the
deepening estimate of womanhood's worth in terms of personality.
The very fact that Jesus took monogamy for granted reveals
its prevalence in his day. He doubtless was appealing to the best
conscience of his people when, against current looseness and
especially against the injustice of husbands to wives in the matter
of divorce, he stated the ideal of marriage in terms of a single,
indissoluble bond—"Have ye not read, that he who made them
from the beginning made them male and female, and said, For
this cause shall a man leave his father and mother, and shall
cleave to his wife; and the two shall become one flesh? So that
they are no more two, but one flesh. What therefore God hath
joined together, let not man put asunder."[2]

The strictness of Jesus' command against divorce which immediately follows this passage, and the even stricter command
in Mark's earlier account,[3] can be understood only when set in
the historic situation and seen as a defense of womanhood. The
right of the husband to be judge, jury, and executioner in severing
the marriage tie and expelling the wife from her home and children
seemed to Jesus cruelly unjust, and with characteristic indignation
against arrogant misuse of power he denied this legal right conferred on husbands by Leviticus. He granted that such a high
standard as he set up was impossible as universal legislation,[4]
but as against the prevalent practise, according to which a husband could, without appeal beyond his own wish, expel his wife

[1] Malachi 2:13–16.
[2] Matthew 19:4–6.
[3] Mark 10:1–12.
[4] Matthew 19:11–12.

from the home, Jesus pleaded for the rights of the woman and for the duty of the man, save in extreme cases, to keep his marriage indissoluble. All this is of one piece with Jesus' general attitude toward women. It is impossible to distinguish women from men in the personal respect with which Jesus treated them. Repeatedly he came to their defense as he came to the defense of children. Despite its high estimate of womanhood, even the Book of Proverbs, in the many passages where it condemns harlotry,[1] habitually lays the initial responsibility on the woman, as though man were only the poor victim of her wiles. When Jesus, however, was presented with this problem, so the Fourth Gospel tells us,[2] he turned on the men as they prepared to stone an adulteress, saying, "He that is without sin among you, let him first cast a stone at her."[3]

Whether, therefore, one thinks of the prominence of women among the friends and followers of Jesus, or of his willingness to risk the wrath of the orthodox by dealing with sinful women as personalities in need of help, or of his spirited defense of women against the tyranny of husbands in a matter like divorce, or, in general, of his constant treatment of women as persons and, therefore, as ends in themselves, one understands the judgment that in Jesus woman found the best friend she ever had in the ancient world. It is no accident that in the movement which he originated it came soon to be understood that the distinction of sex represented no difference of spiritual status; there was "no male and female."[4]

Indeed, the fact that this particular phrase is Paul's should chasten the readiness with which many moderns, lacking an historical perspective, condemn him as an anti-feminist. He faced a perplexing practical situation. In Corinth, for example, only women of questionable reputation or of frankly public character as prostitutes commonly functioned outside the domestic circle as leaders in politics or religion. To allow the women of the Corinthian church public functions would have opened wide the door to a complete misunderstanding of Christian morals. As it was, the early Christians were generally believed to indulge in sensual orgies at their "love-feasts," and prudence was imperatively called for by the situation. His injunction against a woman's

[1] Proverbs 2:16; 5:3–5; 6:24–26; 7:5–27; 23:27–28.

[2] This passage in its present form is of doubtful authenticity, as the Revised Version indicates, but it represents a bona fide tradition of Jesus' attitude.

[3] John 8:7.

[4] Galatians 3:28.

speaking in the church, therefore, must be understood with the local situation in mind.[1]

Similarly, Paul's statement, lamentable in modern ears, that it is better to remain unmarried but that if one cannot remain unmarried without being unchaste, "it is better to marry than to burn,"[2] needs historic background for its understanding. Its origin was not ascetic but apocalyptic. Paul thought that the last days had come, that before his death the Messiah would appear, and that in the few remaining years there were more important tasks afoot than founding families. As in another period of crisis General Robert E. Lee said, "This is no time for marriage,"[3] so Paul felt as he surveyed the current scene in the light of the new church's tremendous tasks and of the Messiah's expected return. Granted that the expectation was mistaken and that the obsession of Paul's mind by it warped his perspective, yet he should be allowed to decry marriage for the reason he really thought he had and not be accused of decrying it for another reason altogether. Far from being ascetic, he not only idealized marriage as a true figure of Christ's union with the church, but he carefully prescribed the complete satisfaction of biological needs in the marriage relationship and commanded that neither party physically defraud the other.[4]

Nevertheless, when all allowance has been made, it remains true that Paul was limited not only by the practical situation which he faced but by the ideas which he had inherited. He never resolved the conflict between the larger vision of womanhood which he saw and the actual status of woman as man's inferior. On one side he was quaintly archaic, arguing that a man should not have his head covered in church "forasmuch as he is the image and glory of God," but that a woman should have her head veiled because she "is the glory of the man."[5] He retained even the ancient inference from the story of Eden: "Neither was the man created for the woman; but the woman for the man."[6] Having said this, however, he was troubled by its inadequacy, and tried to compensate for the historic and actual subjugation of woman to man by stating an ideal equality in the relationship of both to God—"Nevertheless, neither is the woman without the man, nor the man without the woman, in the Lord.

[1] I Corinthians 14:34–35.
[2] I Corinthians 7:9.
[3] Quoted by Mrs. Roger A. Pryor: *Reminiscences of Peace and War*, p. 327.
[4] I Corinthians 7:3–5.
[5] I Corinthians 11:7.
[6] I Corinthians 11:9.

For as the woman is of the man, so is the man also by the woman; but all things are of God."[1] Nowhere is Paul more human or more like ourselves than in this confused endeavor to harmonize a spiritual ideal with an actual situation plus an inveterate set of inherited ideas concerning it.

In particular, Paul never escaped the opinion that the only proper status of woman lay in the proprietorship of her husband—"Wives, be in subjection unto your own husbands, as unto the Lord. For the husband is the head of the wife, as Christ also is the head of the church. . . . But as the church is subject to Christ, so let the wives also be to their husbands in everything."[2] Doubtless if he had to legislate on this subject for the nascent churches, this was the only prudent legislation he could suggest, since any other would have wrecked the reputation of his movement. It required many centuries to prepare the race, even in its most civilized areas, for other ideas and other practises. Despite the boasted culture of Greece, Pericles in his great oration on Athenian liberality asserted that woman's glory consists in never being heard of at all, either for good or evil. Professor MacIver claims that in all his history Thucydides referred to a woman only twice—then only casually in passing—and that "in the majority of Greek cities women filled so small a part that we cannot even obtain information about them."[3] Indeed, even yet the status of womanhood is eminently unfair and the emancipation of women is attended by domestic and moral turmoil amounting at times to chaos.

Far from depreciating Paul, therefore, for attitudes that were inevitable in his time, a true historic judgment must applaud him for ideas ahead of his time. The supreme reforms of history can be traced back to ideals on the spiritual plane in direct antagonism to facts on the practical plane. Such equality in politics or before the law as man has attained began in the ideal of all men as equal before God, who is "no respecter of persons."[4] Similarly, such practical equality as obtains between man and woman has sprung from an ideal equality. In Paul's eyes there was one place where man and woman stood together with no preëminence of one over the other, and that was before the face of God. "In the Lord" they were equal.[5] At first this seems a poor substitute for the economic

---

[1] I Corinthians 11:11–12.
[2] Ephesians 5:22–24.
[3] R. M. MacIver: *The Modern State*, p. 89.
[4] Acts 10:34.
[5] I Corinthians 11:11.

and domestic freedom of womanhood but in fact it was not so much a substitute as a creative idea, which, once set at work, could not be stayed in its leavening power. When persons are believed to be equal as God sees them, the race must try to make them equal as man treats them.

In the New Testament, therefore, while we see no completed process in woman's elevation to an equal status, we do see the germinative ideas of equality, which today are still trying to grow into actualities. The New Testament presents God as "no respecter of persons" and, therefore, as no discriminator against women; it presents marriage as monogamy on a high level, comparable, as *The Book of Common Prayer* says, with the "mystical union that is betwixt Christ and his Church";[1] and, probably for the first time in human history, it presents a fellowship in which, so far as spiritual status was concerned, there was "no male and female."[2] As James Russell Lowell said about the New Testament in general, there was dynamite enough in such ideas to blow all our existing institutions to atoms.[3]

IX

So far as slaves were concerned, nowhere in the Bible is the institution of slavery, as such, attacked or even questioned. What Professor Whitehead says about the Greeks, however, applies in large measure to the Hebrews and to the early Christians—"The Athenians were slave-owners: but they seem to have humanized the institution. Plato was an aristocrat by birth and by conviction, also he must have owned slaves. But it is difficult to read some of his Dialogues without an uneasy feeling about the compulsory degradation of mankind."[4]

One of the early Hebrew laws, for example, forbade the holding of a Hebrew slave for more than six years.[5] Evidently this law was widely disobeyed, for it was suddenly treated with respect, as a means of placating Yahweh, when in the days of Jeremiah the Babylonian army besieged Jerusalem. When, however, the enemy temporarily departed to meet the attacking Egyptians in the plain, the masters in Jerusalem speedily took back their slaves again and Jeremiah lashed them for their perfidy.[6] Nevertheless, despite its treacherous abrogation, the original agreement

---

[1] Ephesians 5:25-33.
[2] Galatians 3:28.
[3] See his essay, "The Progress of the World."

[4] Alfred North Whitehead: *Adventures of Ideas*, p. 16.
[5] Exodus 21:2; Deuteronomy 15:12.
[6] Jeremiah 34:8-22.

which King Zedekiah had made with the people of Jerusalem—
"that every man should let his man-servant, and every man his
maid-servant, that is a Hebrew or a Hebrewess, go free; that
none should make bondmen of them, to wit, of a Jew his brother"[1]
—indicates a disturbed conscience about a Jew's enslavement
by a Jew.

Especially with reference to bondage for debt, the lot of
unfortunate Jews was mitigated by successive laws[2] and Nehemiah
was "very angry" and indulged in one of his most effective outbursts of indignation over the use of debt as a means of gaining
slaves.[3] This growing sensitiveness of conscience about Hebrew
slavery was doubtless responsible for the fact that, whereas
according to the earlier history Solomon prepared and trans-
ported the materials for his temple by "a levy out of all Israel,"[4]
later history reports that the 153,600 men engaged in this task
were "the sojourners that were in the land of Israel,"[5] and that
"of the children of Israel did Solomon make no servants for his
work."[6] This rewriting of the record plainly comes from a late
period, when opposition to the enslavement of fellow Hebrews
had won its way to general recognition and when it seemed
desirable to expunge from the historical record a precedent so
dangerous as Solomon's example would provide.

Aside from this effective protest of the Hebrew conscience
against the enslavement of their own brethren, the contribution
of the Old Testament to the problem is mainly by indirection
rather than by direct attack. Says Dr. Louis Wallis:

> Indeed, we may search the pages of the literary
> prophets in vain to find a single instance in which the
> question of human slavery in the abstract is discussed.
> Amos passes over it in silence. Micah says nothing about
> it. Isaiah makes no mention of it. Hosea does not raise
> the subject. And so with all the prophets.[7]

What the prophets did contend for, however, was a rising estimate of human value, which, while it did not cancel slavery,
affected deeply the treatment of slaves. This demand of the
prophetic school for humaneness is seen in Deuteronomy's plea
for mercy to slaves because the Hebrews had themselves been

[1] Jeremiah 34:9.
[2] Deuteronomy 15:12–18; Leviticus 25:
35–43.
[3] Nehemiah 5:6 ff.
[4] I Kings 5:13–16.
[5] II Chronicles 2:17–18.
[6] II Chronicles 8:9.
[7] Sociological Study of the Bible, p. 157.

slaves in Egypt,[1] and even more in the merciful law concerning the year of jubilee in the Levitican Code: "And if thy brother be waxed poor with thee, and sell himself unto thee; thou shalt not make him to serve as a bondservant. As a hired servant, and as a sojourner, he shall be with thee; he shall serve with thee unto the year of jubilee: then shall he go out from thee, he and his children with him, and shall return unto his own family, and unto the possession of his fathers shall he return."[2] So far as the Old Testament is concerned, humane consideration for slaves is most adequately expressed in the picture of the ideal man in Job:

> If I have despised the cause of my man-servant
> or of my maid-servant,
> When they contended with me;
> What then shall I do when God riseth up?
> And when he visiteth, what shall I answer him?
> Did not he that made me in the womb make him?
> And did not one fashion us in the womb?[3]

This insight and attitude of Job are continued and advanced in the New Testament. Jesus never explicitly questioned or discussed the institution of slavery. It was taken for granted in Palestine, as in the entire ancient world, as a natural part of the social structure. Jesus, therefore, assumed it as inherent in this present evil age, and in his parables slaves appear with no attack upon the economic institution that produced them. At that time no one, inside the New Testament or outside, had apparently thought of slavery as anything but inevitable or had dreamed of its eradication. What Jesus did was to elevate incalculably the status of personality as in itself intrinsically valuable. He treated all persons on that basis—slaves and freemen, rich and poor, men and women, elders and children—and, even if he did not foresee what this would do centuries afterward to some of the institutions of society, he made an inestimable contribution.

One of the first consequences was the admittance of slaves on equal terms with freemen into the first Christian churches. This represents the New Testament's greatest single contribution to the solution of the problem of slavery. "In Christ Jesus" there were no slaves—"neither bond nor free."[4] The Epistle to Philemon, far from deserving opprobrium because it takes

---

[1] Deuteronomy 15:15 (The same argument had already been made earlier, in the Book of the Covenant, Exodus 22:21).

[2] Leviticus 25:39–41.
[3] Job 31:13–15.
[4] Galatians 3:28.

slavery for granted without protest against the institution, represents one of the most indispensable forward steps in history toward the ultimate elimination of slavery. It presents an eloquent and persuasive plea for the welcome not only of a slave but of an "unprofitable" slave, as now converted to Christ and therefore to be regarded and treated "no longer as a bondservant, but more than a bondservant, a brother beloved."[1] So far is this from being a small matter that American Christians to this day find it easier to rejoice in the historic elimination of the slave system as a whole than to welcome into churches children of ex-slaves on terms of equality, as brethren beloved. The principle of action recorded in the New Testament was profound and revolutionary; it is not yet even remotely lived up to. Certainly the ideal equality of slave and freeman as members of the Christian community was one of the major ideas presaging slavery's ultimate downfall.

X

With regard to the institution of slavery and the status of woman, the writers of the late Old Testament and of the New probably saw least clearly the implications of their growing idea of personality's sacredness. They could no more have foreseen what the giving of full personal rights to women and slaves would involve than they could have foreseen aviation. They did, however, make an incalculable contribution to man's ethical life by their ever deepening recognition of inherent dignity in persons and their ever more sensitive demand for humaneness toward persons. The great prophets of the Old Testament were the defenders of the poor, the solicitous protectors of all the plundered and oppressed people of the land. In Deuteronomy, which is the early endeavor of the prophetic school to put its ideals into laws, this humane sympathy with all who suffer extends not only to the fatherless, the widow, the poor, and the stranger, but to criminals[2] and animals[3] as well.

Such humaneness was the direct result of the prophetic teaching—of Amos' indignation against those who "pant after the dust of the earth on the head of the poor";[4] of Isaiah's plea to "seek justice, relieve the oppressed, judge the fatherless, plead for the widow";[5] of Hosea's idea of the merciful Yahweh, who says, "My

---

[1] Philemon, vs. 16 (marginal translation).
[2] Deuteronomy 25:1–3.
[3] Deuteronomy 5:14; 22:6–7; 25:4.
[4] Amos 2:6–7.
[5] Isaiah 1:15–17.

heart is turned within me, my compassions are kindled together. "[1]
Within the changing national and economic setting the prophets
were constantly at work upon an underlying moral attitude. They
felt the value of human life, the sacredness of brotherhood, the
right of persons to justice, the shame of the plundered poor, the
supreme wickedness of cruelty. Of such teaching and, as well, of
the courage with which the prophets launched it in the face of the
powerful, Jeremiah may well be the exemplar as he addressed a
tyrannical king in his new palace—"Shalt thou reign, because
thou strivest to excel in cedar? Did not thy father eat and drink,
and do justice and righteousness? then it was well with him. He
judged the cause of the poor and needy; then it was well. Was not
this to know me? saith Yahweh. "[2]

In this regard the common opinion is mistaken that justice in
the Old Testament is negative and in the New Testament positive.
To be sure, various ancient writers stated the law of justice negatively, as Confucius did—what ye would not that men should do
to you, do ye not to them. Nevertheless, Leviticus said, "Thou
shalt love thy neighbor as thyself,"[3] extending this admonition
to cover the resident foreigner, "Thou shalt love him as thyself,"[4]
and in Ecclesiasticus Jesus may well have read: "Consider thy
neighbour's liking by thine own. "[5] In Judaism the ideal of personal
right and fraternal goodwill rose to great heights, involving the
obligation not only of negative justice but of positive mercy, so
that the virtuous man of the Book of Job is, above all, a philan-
thropist—

> If I have withheld the poor from their desire,
> Or have caused the eyes of the widow to fail,
> Or have eaten my morsel alone,
> And the fatherless hath not eaten thereof
> (Nay, from my youth he grew up with me as with a father,
> And her have I guided from my mother's womb);
> If I have seen any perish for want of clothing,
> Or that the needy had no covering;
> If his loins have not blessed me,
> And if he hath not been warmed with the fleece of my sheep;
> If I have lifted up my hand against the fatherless,
> Because I saw my help in the gate:
> Then let my shoulder fall from the shoulder-blade,
> And mine arm be broken from the bone.[6]

[1] Hosea 11:8.
[2] Jeremiah 22:15–16.
[3] Leviticus 19:18.
[4] Leviticus 19:33–34.
[5] Ecclesiasticus 31:15.
[6] Job 31:16–22.

In this realm, as in every other, it is inconceivable that the Jews should have lived in isolation from the thinking of the world at large. In any given case, the degree to which Old Testament ideas have been affected by influences from Egypt, Babylonia, Persia, or Greece, is difficult to estimate. In general, however, Dr. James H. Breasted's statement is true: "We are all aware that Egypto-Babylonian culture set European civilisation going; but few modern people have observed the fact, so important in the history of morals and religion, that *Egypto-Babylonian culture also set Hebrew civilisation going.*"[1] Certainly, in teaching the ideal of humaneness, the Egyptians long antedated the Hebrews. Beginning with a drama originating in Memphis in the middle of the fourth millennium B.C., and containing the earliest known discussion of right and wrong in man's history, the Egyptians progressively developed high standards of social justice and humane conduct. The lament of Khekheperre-soneb, born about 1900 B.C., "The poor man has no strength to save himself from him that is stronger than he,"[2] and the Heracleopolitan king's elevation of righteousness over sacrifice in pleasing the gods, "More acceptable is the virtue of the upright man than the ox of him that doeth iniquity,"[3] represent developing ideals kindred with Hebrew thinking ages before the Hebrews reached them. Long before the Hebrew tribes reached Palestine, the Coffin Texts represented the sun god as saying:

> I have made the four winds that every man might breathe thereof like his brother during his time.
> I have made the great waters that the pauper like the lord might have use of them.
> I have made every man like his brother, and I have forbidden that they do evil, (but) it was their hearts which undid that which I had said.[4]

Indeed, as a parallel to Job's ideal, written about 400 B.C., one may set Ameni's ideal, put on his Egyptian tomb-chapel in the nineteenth century B.C.:

> There was no citizen's daughter whom I misused, there was no widow whom I afflicted, there was no peasant whom I evicted, there was no herdman whom I expelled, there was no overseer of five whose people I took away

---

[1] *The Dawn of Conscience*, p. 14.   [3] *Ibid.*, p. 156.
[2] Quoted by Breasted in above volume,   [4] *Ibid.*, p. 221.
p. 179.

for (unpaid) taxes. There was none wretched in my community, there was none hungry in my time. When years of famine came, I ploughed all the fields of the Oryx barony (his estate) as far as its southern and its northern boundary, preserving its people alive, furnishing its food so that there was none hungry therein. I gave to the widow as to her who had a husband. I did not exalt the great (man) above the small (man) in anything that I gave. Then came great Niles (inundations), rich in grain and all things, but I did not collect the arrears of the field.[1]

Such general similarities, however, would not indicate any necessary dependence of Hebrew ethics on the preceding Egyptian development were it not for specific evidence. There is no doubt, for example, that the late Biblical Book of Proverbs, strongly impregnated with the feeling of Egypto-Grecian Judaism in Alexandria, is largely indebted to *The Wisdom of Amenemope*, written about 1000 B.C. Indeed, Proverbs 22:17—23:11 is an almost verbatim translation of the Egyptian book, and in many other passages the similarity is too close to be mistaken.[2] That there was effective influence, therefore, flowing from Egyptian to Hebrew thought is not only generally probable but specifically demonstrable, but how far that influence ran into the ideas of the great prophets or how important it was in shaping their teaching is uncertain. At any rate, nothing in ancient history equals the total moral quality and effect of the Hebrew prophets at their best.

Of this great tradition Jesus was the inheritor. Inwardness and humaneness were the twin qualities of his ethic. Moreover, his humaneness, far from being kindly sentiment alone, was solidly grounded in a well-considered estimate of personality's worth. This indeed constituted the morally creative factor in his attitude. Whether he dealt with women, children, or slaves, whether he described the Good Samaritan[3] or announced the principle of service on the basis of which God judges men,[4] whether he vehemently condemned selfish luxury in the face of human need[5] or died for man because he thought man worth dying for, the common principle of outgoing, sacrificial humaneness, based on the supreme value of personality, gave unity to it all.

To be sure, the self-regarding motives were prominent in Jesus'

---

[1] *Ibid.*, pp. 213–214.
[2] For these parallels see above volume. pp. 372–380.
[3] Luke 10:30–37.
[4] Matthew 25:31–46.
[5] Luke 16:19 ff.

teaching and any interpretation of unselfishness as meaning forgetfulness of the interests of one's own life found no support in
him. We are to judge not, that we be not judged;[1] to forgive, that
we may be forgiven;[2] to be merciful, since thus we shall obtain
mercy.[3] Repeatedly this rebound of blessing on the good man's life
was stressed in Jesus' message, and his injunction to the rich
young ruler to surrender present wealth was coupled with assurance that his loss was seeming, not real, and that he should have
"treasure in heaven."[4] Personality is sacred not only in the
human object of the serviceable deed but in the doer of it also, and
he is to love his neighbor even as he loves himself.[5] In this respect
Jesus frankly cherished self-regarding motives as part of the
ethical life.

Nevertheless, his ethic was centered in humane love and in the
New Testament love became the cardinal virtue. In Jesus' teaching, it is important to note that love, far from being mainly emotional, was a profoundly ethical attitude capable of deliberate
exercise and direction. It could be commanded. According to
Matthew, when Jesus said, "Love your enemies," he added,
"pray for them that persecute you";[6] according to Luke, he
added, "do good to them that hate you."[7] Loving one's enemies,
that is, involved both inward goodwill and outward helpfulness; it
required deliberate self-discipline; any emotional tone of kindly
feeling in it was subordinate to the resolute schooling of the spirit
in persistent beneficence; it was predominantly ethical, not senti-
mental.

In this regard Jesus was in the great succession of the Hebrew
prophets at their best. If justice and love together were primary in
the Old Testament, love and justice together were primary in the
New, and in the literature between the Testaments stood parallels
to many of the most characteristic sayings of Jesus in this realm.
Even his principle of equivalence between the mercy a man shows
to man and the mercy he receives from God[8] had been stated in
the Testaments of the Twelve Patriarchs—"In the degree in
which a man hath compassion upon his neighbors, in the same
degree hath the Lord also upon him."[9]

Nevertheless, there is no mistaking the clear emergence of
the ethic of love as the dominant and unique principle of conduct

[1] Matthew 7:1.
[2] Mark 11:25.
[3] Matthew 5:7.
[4] Matthew 19:21.
[5] Matthew 19:19.

[6] Matthew 5:44.
[7] Luke 6:27.
[8] E.g., Matthew 5:7; 18:23–25.
[9] The Testament of Zebulun 8:3.

in the ideals of the New Testament. Goodwill was to be exercised toward all persons, good and bad, grateful and ungrateful, friendly and hostile. It was to acknowledge no boundaries of race, nation, sex, or economic status. It was to be the sole reliance of Jesus' disciples in dealing with all sorts and conditions of men, and in Paul's thinking it was so comprehensive that the external law was displaced by it, since "love . . . is the fulfilment of the law."[1] Many differences in situation and opinion separated Jesus and Paul but with regard to the central ethical principle of whole-hearted reliance on the power and persuasiveness of sacrificial love, Paul, as the thirteenth chapter of First Corinthians shows, understood Jesus very well.

The unique position which the ethic of love holds in the New Testament is made plain by the very contradictions of it that occur. For example, while man was to practise tireless love, vengeance still belonged unto God, and the inherited idea of everlasting punishment was still retained. On the one side, Christians were to exercise undiscourageable goodwill toward evil men, even praying for those who slew them when no other manner of expressing goodwill remained; but, on the other side, the new faith retained the hopeless torture chamber of Gehenna, where punishment was supposed to go on in endless agony long after moral purpose in the torture had been lost. Here was a clear contradiction in moral principle between a primitive idea of cosmic penology and a new ethic.

Moreover, the ethical teaching of the New Testament faced antagonistic elements not only in its religious tradition but, as well, in the current situation. On the growing churches fell such difficult days, full of hardship and persecution, that the ethic of love in its pure form proved impracticable. Concerning our present civilization Professor Whitehead says, "As society is now constituted a literal adherence to the moral precepts scattered throughout the Gospels would mean sudden death."[2] Likewise in the Greco-Roman world the pure ethic of love faced a desperate trial, and the marvel is not that the New Testament contains contradictions and qualifications of it, but that such elevated and triumphant faith in it was voiced at all and has remained to chasten and guide the conscience of the world.

Any Christian tempted to condescend to the Old Testament because the Book of Nahum is there with its unabashed delight in

[1] Romans 13:10.   [2] Alfred North Whitehead: *Adventures of Ideas*, p. 18.

the catastrophic downfall of Nineveh, should read the eighteenth chapter of the Book of Revelation, with its similar delight over the prophesied ruin of Rome, disguised under the title of Babylon. And any Christian, failing to see how inevitably a cruel and tragic world forced on the Jewish community a greater humaneness toward its own members than they could possibly extend to the Moabites, should read the First Epistle of John, where love is expressed with supreme beauty but is always to be understood as love of the brethren.

The New Testament, that is, launched the ethic of love into a world whose inherited ideas and practical situations limited its application and denied its claims. Nevertheless, the New Testament did launch the ethic of love, and by persuasive statements of it and, above all, by the presentation of its incarnation in Christ made an incalculable impression on the world. The real contrast between Judaism and Christianity, at their best, is to be found in the fact that whereas the proper symbol of the one is the Torah, a great statute book of moral law, the proper symbol of the other is the cross, a supreme expression of adventurous, sacrificial love. This contrast is not mutually exclusive but it is characteristic and significant. Christianity has no more lived up to the meaning of the cross than Judaism has lived up to the meaning of the Torah, but the two are not identical. With the advent of the New Testament, centered in the cross, a new and revolutionary era, not even yet fairly under way, began in man's ethical ideals.

XI

Along with the overpassing of early limitations of externality and imperfect humaneness, the Bible records a widening range of moral obligation. This increasing universality in the ethics of the Old Testament was closely associated with the development of monotheism. A growing internationalism in Israel's life and thought furnished the necessary basis for a growing monotheism; tribal conditions had to be transcended before tribal gods could be eliminated; but when monotheism once secured a foothold, its ideal implications outran the actualities of the political situation. Faith in one God was in part the result of an increasingly cosmopolitan experience and, in part, the cause of a still more extensive vision of the range of moral duty. This interplay between developing international relationships and developing monotheism constitutes one of the most significant and fascinating aspects of the Old Testament.

As early as the eighth century B.C., Amos thought of Yahweh not only as the God of Israel but as the controlling deity of other nations, who punished the sins of Damascus,[1] Philistia,[2] Ammon,[3] and Moab,[4] and who was responsible for the migrations of the Ethiopians, Philistines, and Syrians, as he was for bringing Israel out of Egypt.[5] From such a theology ethical influences inevitably flowed, even amid the bitter hatreds of that early time. Amos vehemently attacked specific cases of international cruelty and chastened the pride of his people by asserting their equality with other races in the divine care—"Are ye not as the children of the Ethiopians unto me, O children of Israel? saith Yahweh."[6]

From this early beginning, monotheism and an international conscience grew together when they grew at all. Practical conditions, however, were hostile to both. In the eighth century Assyria utterly destroyed the Northern Kingdom and so attacked Judea that the Jews, invaded and ravaged, narrowly escaped a similar ruin. In the seventh century, Babylon destroyed Jerusalem and left the city and temple a "haunt of jackals."[7] The years from Amos' ministry through Jeremiah's were no congenial time for international goodwill, and the desire for vengeance rather than the celebration of human brotherhood represented the trend of the times. Even Jeremiah, while in contrast with his contemporaries he counseled submission to Babylon, could not draw the full inferences of universal moral obligation that were implicit in his idea of God; and his contemporary, Habakkuk, could get no further than the assurance that the terrible power of the conqueror was temporary and that his downfall would vindicate the moral order of Yahweh's world.

In view of the obsessing immediacy of national disaster, it is the more amazing that the high altitude of international vision and goodwill, surpassing all that had preceded it and standing solitary long afterwards, should have been reached in the desperate years of the Exile—"Yea, he saith, It is too light a thing that thou shouldest be my servant to raise up the tribes of Jacob, and to restore the preserved of Israel: I will also give thee for a light to the Gentiles, that thou mayest be my salvation unto the end of the earth."[8] For a long time, however, this comprehensive outlook on both God and man lacked widespread appreciation. The circum-

[1] Amos 1:3-5.
[2] Amos 1:6-8.
[3] Amos 1:13-15.
[4] Amos 2:1-3.
[5] Amos 9:7.
[6] Ibid.
[7] Jeremiah 10:22 (Moffatt translation).
[8] Isaiah 49:6; cf. Isaiah 42:1-4; 19:23-25.

stances of the returned exiles under Nehemiah and Ezra, struggling for existence against the penury of nature and the hostility of half-breed neighbors, made irresistibly for a policy of narrow exclusiveness. All mixed marriages with aliens were prohibited to Jews. Ezra even demanded that Jews put away non-Jewish wives and their children, dissolving families already established.[1] This attitude is of one piece with the story in the Book of Numbers according to which a plague slew twenty-four thousand of the people before its cause was located in an Israelite's marriage to a Midianite and was removed by the execution of the couple.[2]

Here was no fertile soil for ideas of inter-racial obligation. Upon the contrary, the desire for vengeance was commonly given free expression, as through Zechariah, who hoped for the Jews that "they shall devour all the peoples round about, on the right hand and on the left."[3] So, late passages, inserted in the Book of Isaiah, predicted the coming revenge of Israel—"That nation and kingdom that will not serve thee shall perish; yea, those nations shall be utterly wasted."[4] And so, in general, the imprecatory psalms heaped curses on the heads of all and sundry whom the psalmist regarded as enemies of his people—

> Pour out thine indignation upon them,
> And let the fierceness of thine anger overtake them.
> Let their habitation be desolate;
> Let none dwell in their tents.[5]

This attitude, however, did not go unrebuked, and two books in the late Old Testament specifically represent the larger view: the Book of Ruth, written to encourage a more generous inter-racial policy, and the Book of Jonah, written to enforce the world-wide mission of Israel.

The Book of Ruth was apparently directed against the policy of forbidding mixed marriages. It is an historic romance recounting the way in which its heroine, Ruth, a Moabitess, became the ancestress of David. To this end the fact that Ruth was a Moabitess is repeatedly stressed. She was "of the women of Moab," "the Moabitish damsel," "a foreigner," and five times, "Ruth the Moabitess."[6] Thus the story drives home the fact that she was an alien and, what is more, of a particularly hated race and

---

[1] Ezra 9:1—10:44.
[2] Numbers 25:6–18.
[3] Zechariah 12:6; cf. 9:1–8; 12:1–9.
[4] Isaiah 60:12; cf. 60:14–16; 61:5; 66:12.

[5] Psalm 69:24–25; cf. Psalm 59:13; 83:13–18; 109:8–15.
[6] Ruth 1:4; 2:6; 2:10; 1:22; 2:2; 2:21; 4:5; 4:10.

nation.[1] Yet, according to contemporary standards, she was an ideal woman, unforgetable in her fidelity, and, married to a Jew, she became, so the climax of the story runs, mother of a son who was "the father of Jesse, the father of David."[2] The book, that is, presents in story form an argument against the prohibition of mixed marriages between the Jews and neighboring peoples.

The Book of Jonah is a picturesque appeal for the universal mission of Israel, a plea in favor of international goodwill in place of vindictiveness and prejudice. It is thus one of the supremely important books, not only of the Old Testament but of all ancient literature, and its common caricature, as the narrative of a fish literally swallowing a man and disgorging him alive after three days, is one of the most regretable absurdities in the Western world's long mistreatment of the Bible. Conceivably the Book of Jonah may be an allegory. In that case, the prophet Jonah represents Israel, hating such alien peoples as Nineveh and reluctant to undertake the saving mission to the world at large which God intends. The flight of Jonah is Israel's refusal of her world-wide mission; the swallowing of Jonah is the Exile, and his disgorging, the return; the continued surliness of Jonah is Israel's post-Exilic blindness to her international obligations; the repentance of Nineveh is a prophecy of the world won to righteousness; and the sullen prophet at the allegory's end stands for the stubbornness with which Israel retains her nationalistic ill will. This allegorical interpretation, however, is not necessary to the understanding of the book and has been almost universally given up by scholars. The story may instead be understood as a vivid, dramatic parable intended to present a single lesson—the world-wide extension of God's care and the folly and wickedness of Israel's reluctance to share the divine spirit and purpose. As with the Book of Ruth so with the Book of Jonah, the lesson is made clear in the climax. The story ends with a vision of the all-merciful God, compassionate over Nineveh and calling his representative to a similar outreach of saving goodwill—"And Yahweh said, Thou hast had regard for the gourd, for which thou hast not labored, neither madest it grow; which came up in a night, and perished in a night: and should not I have regard for Nineveh, that great city, wherein are more than sixscore thousand persons that cannot discern between their right hand and their left hand; and also much cattle?" So the book ends—bootlessly if it is supposed to be literal history,

[1] Cf. Deuteronomy 23:3; Nehemiah   [2] Ruth 4:17.
13:1-2.

splendidly if it is seen to be an impassioned plea for Israel's world-wide responsibility as the missioner of the universal God.

Along with this extension of Israel's goodwill went a development of thought about war. At the beginning Yahweh himself was "a man of war"[1] and his prophets were leaders in battle. In the early days in Palestine, before outstanding individuals appeared in the prophetic succession, bands of prophets represented the most fanatic patriotism of the Hebrew tribes, and Saul's espousal of his people's cause against their enemies followed his falling under the spell of the prophets' frenzy.[2] Elisha was a prophet of war and a counsellor concerning strategy,[3] and both Elijah and Elisha were praised as being "the chariots of Israel and the horsemen thereof."[4] One has only to read the final address of the dying Elisha to his king to see how vehement an encourager of war the prophet was and how lusty a chaplain of the hosts of Yahweh.[5] In the latter part of the eighth century, however, another note was heard. In view of the unquestioned prevalence of war, the inveterate conditions producing it, and the apparent necessity of success in it to preserve national existence, this new note was and is one of the most astonishing elements in the Old Testament. That there was an irreconcilable conflict between the practises of war and the developing humaneness of the prophets and their ideas of God is clear in retrospect, but that it should have been clear in the eighth century and that even then the hope of a warless world should have been unequivocably stated, is amazing. There is nothing to compare with it in Egyptian or Babylonian literature, and in Greek literature, even a great anti-war drama, such as Euripides' "Trojan Women"—first performed in 415 B.C.—issues in no such positive demand for war's elimination as the Hebrews reached centuries before. The same prophet, Micah, who summed up the divine demand as doing justly, loving kindness, and walking humbly with God,[6] foresaw the consummation of such an ethic in a warless world—"They shall beat their swords into plowshares, and their spears into pruning-hooks; nation shall not lift up sword against nation, neither shall they learn war any more."[7] Difficult as the confident dating of specific passages may be, there is no mistaking the strength of this prophetic hope in Israel. Isaiah's notable passage announcing the coming of the "Prince of Peace" is pre-

[1] Exodus 15:3.
[2] I Samuel 10:9–11.
[3] II Kings 3:15 ff.
[4] II Kings 2:12; 13:14.
[5] II Kings 13:14–19.
[6] Micah 6:8.
[7] Micah 4:3; cf. Isaiah 2:4.

ceded by a picture of war's end—"All the armor of the armed man in the tumult, and the garments rolled in blood, shall be for burning, for fuel of fire"[1]—and the mission of Messianic Israel is portrayed as ushering in a new epoch in which "they shall not hurt nor destroy in all my holy mountain; for the earth shall be full of the knowledge of Yahweh, as the waters cover the sea."[2]

To be sure, this note was commonly drowned out in war's cacophony. The prophet Joel, probably writing during the miserable humiliations of the Persian period, left a book containing some of the most bloodthirsty passages in the Old Testament, calling for vengeance and inciting to battle. He even deliberately took the peaceful phrases of Micah and Isaiah and reversed them. "Beat your plowshares into swords," he cried, "and your pruning-hooks into spears."[3] Far from appreciating the pacifism of his predecessors and their dream of a fraternal world, his hope was in revenge—"Egypt shall be a desolation, and Edom shall be a desolate wilderness, for the violence done to the children of Judah."[4]

The Old Testament, then, ends with no unanimous consent to the great ideas of an all-merciful God, a world-wide moral obligation, and a brotherhood of man from which war has been banished. Such ideas, however, were there; the possibility of their fruition was rooted in the deep convictions of the prophets concerning them; to change the figure, though the slag of the Book was greater in the mass, diamonds of infinite value had been formed in it.

XII

On this important question of the range of moral obligation, the New Testament arrays itself on the side of the larger outlook and is unequivocal in its proclamation. "The field is the world"[5] has been the church's interpretation of Jesus' teaching from the beginning. Not only did his monotheism, taken morally in earnest, imply this, but his humane ethic likewise involved the overpassing of all national and racial restrictions. When, for example, in his dramatic portrayal of the last judgment, the nations of the world are gathered before the Messiah, the basis of estimate is a test which contains no special Judaistic adhesions but is simply humanitarian service to the needy—caring for the hungry and thirsty, for strangers, for the naked, sick, and imprisoned.[6] A Gentile, as readily as a Jew, might meet the test of so universal an ethic, and no question of race or nation is suggested by it.

[1] Isaiah 9:5–6.
[2] Isaiah 11:1–9.
[3] Joel 3:10.
[4] Joel 3:19; cf. 3:1–8.
[5] Matthew 13:38.
[6] Matthew 25:31–46.

Indeed, the parable of the Good Samaritan[1] was a deliberate attack on the limited range of moral responsibility popularly taught in Jesus' time. As Professor E. F. Scott says of the parable,

> It embodies Jesus' criticism of the common Jewish attitude in his day. It was assumed that humane obligations were strictly limited. A Jew owed no duty to a Gentile; a religious Jew must think of his own associates and not of strangers and outcasts. The Law, to be sure, enjoined love to one's neighbor,—but "who is my neighbor?" was a question warmly discussed in the Rabbinical schools, and it was answered, as time went on, in an ever narrower way. Jesus tells his parable in order to show that no restrictions can be drawn.[2]

Moreover, the reason why no restrictions can be drawn is plain: Jesus' ethical demands are so universally humane, evidenced in such service as the Good Samaritan rendered the needy man, that no race or nation can be picked out as singularly implied in them. Every man of every race is included in them by virtue of being human.

To be sure, the Christian scriptures retain unmistakable evidence of the struggle in which the early church was involved in thus breaking free from Jewish particularism and racialism. The Gospel of Matthew, for example, presents us with ambiguous testimony. On the one side, the Torah is declared permanently valid;[3] while its interpreters may not be worthy of imitation in their lives, they are to be obeyed in their teachings;[4] and Jesus' mission is limited to "the lost sheep of the house of Israel."[5] On the other side, the universalistic prophecy, "In his name shall the Gentiles hope," is applied to Jesus;[6] the parable of the husbandmen teaches the substitution of the Gentile church for rejected Israel;[7] love to all men is presented as true imitation of the Father;[8] terrific denunciation is visited on Jewish leaders[9] and cordial praise is bestowed on a Roman centurion;[10] Tyre, Sidon, and Sodom, pagan cities, are to be preferred in the judgment before Bethsaida, Chorazin, and Capernaum;[11] when the kingdom arrives, "many

[1] Luke 10:30–37.
[2] *The Ethical Teaching of Jesus*, pp. 84–85.
[3] Matthew 5:17–18.
[4] Matthew 23:2–3.
[5] Matthew 15:24.
[6] Matthew 12:15–21; cf. Isaiah 42:1 ff.
[7] Matthew 21:33–43.
[8] Matthew 5:43–48.
[9] Matthew 23:1 ff.
[10] Matthew 8:5–10.
[11] Matthew 11:21–24.

shall come from the east and the west, and shall sit down with Abraham, and Isaac, and Jacob," while "the sons of the kingdom shall be cast forth into the outer darkness";[1] at the judgment "shall be gathered all the nations";[2] and, in the meantime, the Christian mission is world-wide and inclusive—"Go ye therefore, and make disciples of all the nations."[3] This diversity of witness in the records is an evidence of their honest adherence to their sources. There was a bitter controversy over the universalizing of the Christian movement, but in the end the larger outlook was victorious.

An unlimited range of moral obligation was revealed in Jesus' teaching about the kingdom of God. This was his central message and in his thought of it there was, so far as the Gospels reveal, no nationalistic element. The coming sovereignty of God over all mankind was not hoped for by him as the victory of Israel over the world but as the arrival of a new era in which all men should live as sons of the one Father and brothers to one another; into this new kingdom men would come from east, west, north, and south, and sit down with Abraham, Isaac, and Jacob;[4] and the conditions of its enjoyment lay in a quality of character which had nothing to do with special race or nation—"Whosoever shall do the will of my Father who is in heaven, he is my brother, and sister, and mother."[5] Indeed, on this point, the comment of a Jewish scholar is relevant. Professor Klausner of the Hebrew University in Jerusalem, an ardent Zionist, criticizes Jesus for the very thing that elevates him in the estimate of his followers— the universality of his ethic:

> Judaism is a national life, a life which the national religion and human ethical principles (the ultimate object of every religion) embrace without engulfing. Jesus came and thrust aside all the requirements of the national life; it was not that he set them apart and relegated them to their separate sphere in the life of the nation: he ignored them completely; in their stead he set up nothing but an ethico-religious system bound up with his conception of the Godhead.
>
> In the self-same moment he both annulled *Judaism* as the *life-force* of the Jewish nation, and also the nation it-

---

[1] Matthew 8:11-12.   [4] Luke 13:28-29.
[2] Matthew 25:31 ff.   [5] Matthew 12:50.
[3] Matthew 28:19.

self as a nation. For a religion which possesses only a certain conception of God and a morality acceptable to *all* mankind, does not belong to any special nation, and, consciously or unconsciously, breaks down the barriers of nationality. This inevitably brought it to pass that his people, Israel, rejected him.[1]

The New Testament as a whole represents a movement which had broken away from its original moorings in Judaism and had taken to the open sea with no restrictions of race or nation. "God so loved the world"[2] was the essence of its gospel; "Whosoever believeth"[3] represented the inclusiveness of its fellowship; "There can be neither Jew nor Greek"[4] revealed its transcendence of racial lines; and its ultimate ideal was a kingdom of souls "of every tribe, and tongue, and people, and nation."[5] Such is the undisputed character of the New Testament. In its eyes God is one and mankind is one, and there are neither boundaries restricting moral obligation to a special sector of the field nor preferences of race and nation making duty to one relatively more important than to another. From the tribal ethic of the Bible's beginning to this world-wide gospel and this universal range of moral obligation, the Scriptures record one of the most momentous developments of thought and life in all history.

With regard to war, two factors prevented international conflict from being specifically dealt with in the New Testament as a pressing problem: the apocalyptic expectation of the world's immediate end, so that the gradual reform of social institutions was not in the picture, and the further fact that the first Christians had no responsibility for governmental policies or influence in determining them. Nevertheless, there is no mistaking the conscious conflict in the morals of the New Testament between the ethic of love on one side and bloody violence on the other. Jesus, in particular, faced a situation where this conflict was explicit. His contention with Pharisaic legalism is popularly understood, but his contention with the militant Zealots is not so clearly recognized. They were the flaming patriots of his day, proclaiming revolt against Rome, in the face of whose incitement to violence Jesus counseled non-resistance, love of enemies, prayer for persecutors—reliance, that is, on moral forces. He even went so far as to say

---

[1] Joseph Klausner: *Jesus of Nazareth*, translated by Herbert Danby, p. 390.
[2] John 3:16.
[3] *Ibid.*
[4] Galatians 3:28.
[5] Revelation 5:9.

that, when conscripted under the Roman law to go one mile in bearing a burden, a man should go two.[1] If it be said that, like Jeremiah's policy of submission to Babylon because revolt was useless, Jesus' counsel was partly prudent good sense under existent conditions, this may be granted. For the Jews to undertake bloody insurrection against Rome was folly, as the later event proved. But the ethic of Jesus, the very essence of his teaching and life, was far profounder than such a theory plumbs. It involved the idea that violence begets violence, ill will creates ill will, and that the only force adequate to stop the vicious circle is undiscourageable, sacrificial goodwill. In his eyes war meant an endless cycle of evil—"They that take the sword shall perish with the sword."[2]

In view of this total attitude of Jesus, it is an amazing piece of textual atomism to quote in support of war a sentence from one of his discourses—"Think not that I came to send peace on the earth: I came not to send peace, but a sword." The context is a flat denial of such an interpretation. "For," reads the following sentence, "I came to set a man at variance against his father, and the daughter against her mother, and the daughter in law against her mother in law: and a man's foes shall be they of his own household."[3] In other words, Jesus was speaking of the division in families that would be caused when some of the household became his disciples while the rest remained orthodox Jews, and, as the parallel passage in Luke makes evident,[4] 'sword' in this case was a symbol not of international bloodshed but of domestic strife. Indeed, the New Testament as a whole is so clearly committed to aversion against war that the thoroughgoing pacifism of the early church was in all probability a continuance of the common attitude of the first Christians.[5] It was only when Christians began to face public responsibilities, in the second and third centuries, that the long story of Christianity's compromise with the sword commenced. In the New Testament itself the universal fatherhood of God involves the universal brotherhood of man, and, so far as human agency is concerned, only moral forces are counted on to bring about the recognition of the one and the reformation of life to fit the other.

Inwardness, humaneness, and *universality* are thus the three

[1] Matthew 5:41.
[2] Matthew 26:52.
[3] Matthew 10:34-36.
[4] Luke 12:51-53.

[5] See Cecil John Cadoux: *The Early Church and the World,* chap. 6, "War," pp. 269-281; also *The Early Christian Attitude to War.*

major goals of ethical development in the thought of the Bible. At the start, external observance of tribal custom was sufficient; at the end, the good life involved being transformed by the renewing of one's mind. At first, outside one's social group ruthlessness was enjoined and within it justice was commonly denied; at the end, an ethic of love had been envisioned whose fulfilment is still the best hope of the world. At the beginning, no moral obligation extended beyond tribal boundaries; at the last, one mankind under one God claimed the sacrificial service of the good man without regard to race or nation.

Surely, all this has an important bearing on contemporary disparagement of the New Testament's ethic in general and Jesus' ethic in particular, based on the supposedly perverting effect of expecting an immediate end to the present age. Such an apocalyptic hope foreshortened the horizon and falsified the perspective, some say, so that only an impractical 'interim ethic' was left. Before one consents to such a judgment, opposing considerations should be given due weight. For one thing, in so far as the influence of apocalyptic hopes can be clearly discerned, they seem to have positively heightened and clarified moral ideas and ideals. They faced the early Christians with the absolute demands of God's realized sovereignty, confronted them with an imminent kingdom of perfect righteousness, and so called out not small prudential counsels for getting on in this world, but the highest, most unqualified insights as to eternal values. However inapplicable to immediate conditions in this present age some precepts in the New Testament may seem to be, the ethical ideals of the New Testament as a whole have gone ahead of the race like a pillar of fire by night and of cloud by day. They have been not so much proverbs of practical counsel as criteria by which all proverbs of practical counsel must ultimately be judged. In this result, apocalyptic hopes, with their challenge that Christians be prepared at once to face a kingdom of absolute righteousness, may well have played an important part.

For another thing, while apocalyptic forms of hope probably did exercise this influence, it is flying in the face of the evidence to explain the New Testament's ethic, as a whole, as dependent on and everywhere fashioned by apocalypticism. What have the parables of the Good Samaritan and the Prodigal Son, or the idea of love in the thirteenth chapter of First Corinthians to do with apocalypticism? Jesus' ethical teachings, so far as tradition was involved, were rooted in the prophecies and psalms of the Old

Testament, and their development can be traced directly back to these non-apocalyptic sources. Forgiveness of persecutors,[1] mercy toward sinners,[2] humaneness as true service to God,[3] the surrender of life's dearest loyalties when more imperative loyalties are at stake,[4] inwardness of spiritual quality as necessary to true goodness,[5] the finding of life by losing it in a high devotion,[6] the utter subjection of anxious care about transient things to care about abiding values[7]—such characteristic teachings of Jesus, even when their statement happens to be set in an eschatological framework, have another source than apocalypticism, and they are not so demonstrably fashioned by it that, without it, we can be sure they would have been very different. Indeed, if the urgent imminence of the kingdom were the real architect of the New Testament's ethic, how should one explain such similarity of ethic as exists between the Johannine writings and the rest of the Christian scriptures? For far from being Johannine, apocalypticism was fairly well read out of the record in the Fourth Gospel.[8] Yet many of the same emphases which are ascribed to apocalyptic influence are present in John, as well as in the Synoptics and Paul.

For another thing, the criterion by which ethical teaching is to be judged is never the mental category in which it happens to arise. Moral ideals were developing throughout the ancient world —in Egypt, Babylonia, Persia, Judea, Greece—and effective influences were flowing back and forth among them. The mental categories in which these developments of moral idea and ideal were taking place were various—sometimes apocalyptic, more often not—and in no case can one judge the value of the ethical insights that emerged by the mental patterns which happened to give them temporary housing. This certainly seems to be true in the New Testament, where both apocalyptic and non-apocalyptic categories exist and yet where the major ideas that rose in the non-apocalyptic Old Testament sustain their continuous development. If some one notes, as we have already noted, the influence of early Christian hopes of Christ's immediate return on the church's aloofness from remedial civic and social tasks and from

---

[1] Matthew 5:43-48.
[2] Luke 15:1 ff.
[3] Matthew 25:31 ff.
[4] Luke 14:26 (cf. Matthew 10:37). Far from being a disparagement of the family, this statement of utter devotion to God in terms of surrendering family ties, when that is called for, is evidence of Jesus' supreme estimate of the family, as the value most difficult for a man to give up.
[5] Matthew 5:27 ff.
[6] Matthew 10:39.
[7] Matthew 6:19 ff.
[8] This subject will be treated more fully in chap. VI, sec. XI, p. 286 ff.

all sense of responsibility for the improvement of social institutions, the answer seems plain. The barrier to early Christian participation in the tasks of civic and cultural life was not alone the apocalyptic idea but even more the prevailing practical circumstances of social and political life. It is to be remarked that when, at last, the way was open for Christians to become potently effective in the affairs of state and society, not all the apocalyptic ideas in their scriptures or in their current thinking prevented their acceptance of the responsibility.

Finally, the course of thought we have been tracing in this chapter is adverse to those who claim apocalypticism as the real creator of the New Testament's ethic. From the beginning of the Bible to the end runs the development of inwardness, humaneness, and universality as the major qualities of the good life. This development began long before apocalyptic hopes were dreamed of; it passed through days when they were a ruling category in Christian thinking to later days when in wide areas of the church the old Jewish forms of expectation were sublimated, spiritualized, and explained away. Neither in its sources, its main channel, nor its outcome was this stream of development so dependent on any special category as to give that category a just claim to have determined the stream's direction.

CHAPTER IV

THE IDEA OF SUFFERING

I

The development of a high concept of God in terms of complete power and complete goodness necessarily involved the Biblical writers in a correlative problem concerning the explanation of suffering. John Stuart Mill made the classic statement of the modern theist's difficulty when he called it "the impossible problem of reconciling infinite benevolence and justice with infinite power in the Creator of such a world as this."[1] So modern a phrasing of the matter, involving mature ethical monotheism, is far distant, both in mental category and in circumstantial setting, from the questions which the early Hebrews asked about trouble's meaning. Then, as now, such questions were pressing and acute; men faced, not only with emotional wretchedness but with mental bafflement, the apparently senseless incidence of misery upon mankind. At first, however, the Bible represents these questions as asked by men in whose world unity, sole sovereignty, and merciful character had not been dreamed of as attributes of God.

In general, the early Hebrews, like other primitive peoples, explained their happiness or misfortune as due to the favor or disfavor of the gods. Our modern, urban society, with its ubiquitous evidence of man's control over nature and his own fate, makes much less obvious than nomadic society did man's real dependence on extrahuman powers. Under primitive conditions man was so at the mercy of wind and storm, heat and cold, drought and rain, mysterious diseases and unpredictable disasters, that the first, natural explanation of his good or evil fortune was sought in the will of superhuman forces. In this sense primitive peoples were and are profoundly 'religious,' with a pervasive consciousness of constant and inescapable dependence on their divinities, quite unfamiliar to a modern city-dweller. Whatever good or evil fortune befell the individual or his social group seemed to the primitive mind a conscious expression of favor or disfavor on the part of

[1] *Essay on Theism* (1904), Part II, p. 80.

superhuman powers, and the first explanation of prosperity or calamity was that something must have been done which either pleased or displeased the gods.

Here, as elsewhere behind the Biblical record, is visible the ancient background of the animistic ages, whose haunting ways of thinking persisted long after their specific forms had gone. To the animist the extrahuman powers were unaccountably capricious and whimsical—uncertain wills, whose reasons for acting were commonly obscure if not inscrutable. The problem, therefore, was not to justify the gods ethically; they were not conceived in ethical terms so as to make that need apparent. The problem of evil, to the primitive mind, was more naïve—what could man do so to please the capricious divinities as to win superhuman favor and support and thus insure himself against calamity?

Mainly practical though this phrasing of the problem seems, it was associated with intellectual questioning and bewilderment. Out of the Semitic background from which the Hebrews came, a Babylonian psalm has been preserved, voicing the baffled endeavor of ancient minds to discover what kind of conduct met the whims of a god:

> What, however, seems good to one, to a god may be displeasing.
> What is spurned by oneself may find favour with a god.
> Who is there that can grasp the will of the gods in heaven?
> The plan of a god is full of mystery,—who can understand it?
> How can mortals learn the ways of a god?
> He who is still alive at evening is dead the next morning.
> In an instant he is cast into grief, of a sudden he is crushed.[1]

That the variations of human fortune were thus due to the caprice of deities and that in their favor and disfavor lay the origin of all man's happiness and misery, seemed self-evident. From this premise came the momentous corollary that if, for example, a family was fortunate, the gods were pleased with it, and if, instead, disaster befell a household, divine displeasure was the reason. This was the first simple formula in explanation of suffering, and the practical conclusion was that life's main business lay in so conducting affairs as to win the approbation and avoid the dislike of the superhuman powers.

The conduct of affairs proper to this end, however, was not at first merely or mainly moral. The exigent needs of the primitive

[1] A penitential psalm attributed to Tabi-utul-Enlil, King of Nippur, as quoted by Morris Jastrow, Jr.: *Aspects of Religious* *Belief and Practice in Babylonia and Assyria*, p. 333.

community—rain, fertility of soil and herd, victory in war—
were not obviously associated with ethical quality and behavior.
The satisfaction of such needs seemed to depend on the power of
those mysterious arbiters of destiny, the gods, whose reasons for
giving or withholding benefits were difficult to know. If rain was
wanted, therefore, not improved moral character in the people but
successful magical practise in the cult was first suggested. So the
Zulus in time of drought slew a "heaven bird" that the god, melt-
ing with grief, might weep and thus cause rain. Indeed, Christians
in Palermo once dumped an image of St. Joseph into a garden
that he might see how dry it was, and swore to leave him there in
the sun until it rained.[1] In whatever century such practises occur,
we are dealing with primitive religion, and in such practises primitive
religion is characteristically dealing with the problem of suffering.

While far advanced, even in its earliest documents, beyond the
purely animistic stage, the Old Testament often reflects this primitive endeavor to please Yahweh by non-ethical acts and so to
avoid the misery of his displeasure. Thus when Yahweh for no apparent reason sought to slay Moses at a wayside inn, the swift circumcision of Moses' son stayed the tragedy;[2] when Saul sought
God's guidance in a campaign against the Philistines by augury
and it was withheld from him, the reason turned out to be Jonathan's eating of a little honey in contravention of a taboo;[3] and
when Saul tried to injure David, David said to him, "If it be
Yahweh that hath stirred thee up against me, let him smell an
offering."[4] Indeed, the whole complex of taboo, custom, and rite,
revealed in the Old Testament, went back originally to this primitive desire to do something, however non-moral or bizarre, so to
Yahweh's taste that it would ward off the troubles that he held in
his control. However rationalized and sublimated they were in
later usage, circumcision, laws of clean and unclean foods, various
types of human and animal sacrifice, and all manner of prohibitory
taboos, had in their primitive background the belief that disaster
could be avoided only through Yahweh's favor, and that Yahweh's
favor depended on a multitude of actions which had no ethical
content whatever. Even so great a prophet as Ezekiel indiscriminately mingled moral and merely ritualistic acts as alike indispensable in the avoidance of Yahweh's wrath.[5]

[1] James George Frazer: *The Golden
Bough; A Study in Magic and Religion*
(abridged ed., 1935), p. 75.
[2] Exodus 4:24-26.
[3] I Samuel 14:24-30, 36-43.
[4] I Samuel 26:19 (marginal translation).
[5] Ezekiel 18:5-9; 44:9; 33:25-26.

The first phrasing of the problem of suffering in the Old Testament, therefore, might be put thus: men are afflicted because Yahweh is displeased; he is displeased because of something men have done or left undone; the only solution is to discover what has aroused Yahweh's dislike and to act accordingly.

II

The collapse of this original phrasing of the problem followed of necessity from the development of monotheism in Israel and especially from the ascription of high moral quality to God. The divine powers, in Hebrew thinking, ceased being many and became one, and, no longer a being of unaccountable caprice, the one God was seen as steady and dependable character—

> The Rock, his work is perfect;
> For all his ways are justice:
> A God of faithfulness and without iniquity,
> Just and right is he.[1]

This concept of God as "powerful Goodness," to use Benjamin Franklin's phrase, far from solving the problem of suffering, restated it in a much more difficult form than it had had in earlier days. Then the search for ways of acting that would please the gods had indeed been baffling, but now a moral puzzle was added to man's bewilderment. How could God's powerful goodness be reconciled with the cruel injustice of man's experience? Though the thinking of our animistic ancestors may seem to us naïve, it remains true that a multitude of whimsical gods, so constituted that they are likely to be pleased or displeased by almost anything, is not incongruous with the welter of man's joys and miseries, befalling him, at least when superficially observed, with irrational capriciousness. A rapacious man prospers, a generous man suffers tragedy; needed people die young, worthless scoundrels reach a ripe old age; some children are blessed from birth, others are cursed with idiocy or disease; of two families of like quality and conduct, one experiences habitual good fortune, the other continuous adversity. Such facts perplexed the primitive, as they perplex the modern, mind. Life, then as now, often seemed a helter-skelter affair of pleasure and wretchedness befalling men with no discernible relation to their moral quality. All this was not ill explained by primitive thought as due to hypersensitive, easily irritated gods, capricious in favor, the occasions of whose good

[1] Deuteronomy 32:4.

and ill will were only with difficulty known to man. When, however, this diversity of gods was gathered up into monotheism and, for the whimsical nature of the divine powers was substituted the ineffable goodness and justice of the one God, how then could the inequity and cruelty of man's experience be explained?

The more profoundly the Jews, therefore, believed in God as "powerful Goodness," the more baffling they found the mystery of trouble's incidence on man. In a new form the modern mind faces a similar situation, when it endeavors to hold a theistic, rather than a materialistic, philosophy. When thoroughgoing materialism is accepted—a merely physical cosmos, lacking spiritual origin, purpose, or destiny, with man and his esthetic and ethical values only a transient fortuity—there is no further mystery in suffering. Still difficult to endure, it is not at all difficult to explain. Rather, suffering is what we might expect in a world where all our conscious, and still more our spiritual, experiences are alien and accidental intruders. When, however, theism is accepted and the unity of the universe is conceived in terms not of physical cohesion only but of moral purpose also, then the appalling tragedies of man's personal and social life become not merely hardships difficult to bear but an intellectual problem difficult to solve. So, of old, as the Hebrews elevated their idea of the character and omnipotence of God, they found the apparent inequities of life not less but more bewildering.

The persistence with which, in religion as everywhere else, old formulas are stretched to cover new situations is interestingly exhibited in the Hebrew handling of this situation. The basic idea of the earlier formula—all good or ill fortune springs from the pleasure or displeasure of the gods—was retained but the terms were reinterpreted: the gods became God, and what pleased or displeased God was described in ever more emphatically ethical terms. The new formula, in consequence, was that man's happiness and misery come from God as the evidence of his favor or disfavor; that one thing supremely pleases God, moral goodness, and one thing supremely he hates, moral evil; that whenever men are fortunate they must have been virtuous and whenever they are wretched they must have transgressed; that all human suffering is thus punishment for sin—"Shall not the Judge of all the earth do right?"[1]

For centuries, insistence on this formula seemed to the Hebrews their only way of maintaining faith in God's integrity. Around the

[1] Genesis 18:25.

formula powerful influences gathered, the like of which, in every age and among all peoples, have constituted the strength of orthodoxy. The ideas on which the formula was based came out of ancient ancestral traditions; the logic of the doctrine was unassailable once the premises were granted; great prophets, such as Amos, Micah, and Jeremiah, held stoutly to it; and the formula was confirmed and solidified by the final rewriting of the Hebrew historical narratives to illustrate the thesis that every calamity in Israel's record had been a definite punishment for Israel's transgression. From such influences came an established doctrine, the orthodoxy of a large part of the Old Testament, that all human suffering presupposes corresponding sin. God is absolutely just; his rewards and punishments are here and now equitably apportioned; all prosperity is award for antecedent goodness; all disaster is penalty for antecedent sin—such was the Old Testament's long sustained theodicy.

The modern mind stands in amazement before this thesis, which for centuries seemed to the Jews entirely certain and which seems to us entirely incredible. The backdrop of legend, which in the ancient world made life's history on the earth seem a matter of centuries, has for us been lifted, revealing a vista of uncounted millenniums of organic life, suffering unfathomable agony long before man was here to sin at all. Moreover, far from judging the major sufferers to be the major sinners, the supreme heroes of the race are in our eyes its martyrs and sacrificial servants who have drunk the hemlock or borne the cross. So obvious, therefore, does it appear to us that suffering is woven into the very fabric of creation and that the mark of rank in nature is capacity for pain, that a difficult *tour de force* of historic imagination is demanded if we are to understand the Old Testament's point of view. It should in fairness be said, however, that the reason for this contrast does not lie in the superiority of the modern mind but rather in the long-accumulated presuppositions with which we start and the area of human relationships within which our ideas of justice move. We are concerned about justice to the individual, and that obviously is not done here and now in such fashion that from any person's good or evil fortune we can confidently argue back to his previous good or evil conduct. Socrates drinking the hemlock, Christ on his cross, Hugh Latimer burned at the stake, Lincoln martyred when he was profoundly needed—such events, to say nothing of commoner experience, make it impossible for us to say that all suffering is penalty for corresponding sin. In this, however, we are thinking of individual persons, each having status and rights of his own, while the early Hebrews were thinking of something else altogether.

The reason for the plausibility of the orthodox formula—all suffering is punishment for sin—was that, at the beginning of its use, the Hebrews were thinking of justice in relation to the social group rather than to the individual. Here, once more, we run upon that determinative matter without understanding which the Old Testament is everywhere obscure, the late and gradual emergence of individual personality out of corporate personality. "It seemed eminently natural, accordingly, to the ancient Hebrew," writes Professor Paton, "that Yahweh should deal with the group rather than the individual, and should bring the punishment of the sinner, or the reward of the righteous, upon his family, his clan, or his nation, rather than upon himself."[1] Thus, when Korah and his fellow conspirators rebelled against Moses, Yahweh's first intention was to destroy the entire people. Against this Moses protested, "Shall one man sin, and wilt thou be wroth with all the congregation?" and when the penalty did fall with fatal consequence both on the rebels themselves and on "their wives and their sons and their little ones" but the rest of the people were spared, far from seeming unjust, such limitation of punishment seemed to him merciful.[2] Similarly, when David had broken a primitive custom by taking a census of the people and a subsequent pestilence was interpreted, in accordance with the orthodox formula, as divine penalty, David prayed that the nation as a whole might be spared—"Lo, I have sinned, and I have done perversely; but these sheep, what have they done?"—but it did not occur to him that his clan could escape sharing his punishment, for he also said, "Let thy hand, I pray thee, be against me, and against my father's house."[3] So, when Pharaoh withstood Yahweh's will for Israel, all the first-born of Egypt, both of man and cattle, were slain as a penalty,[4] and "the iniquity of the fathers" was conceived as justly visited "upon the third and upon the fourth generation" of their offspring.[5] Reward and retribution, therefore, were to the early Hebrews not individual but social phenomena, and only upon this basis could the doctrine of happiness as always reward for virtue and trouble as always punishment for sin have rested so securely and so long.

[1] Lewis Bayles Paton: "The Hebrew Idea of the Future Life," in *The Biblical World*, "New Series," Vol. 35 (1910), p. 340.
[2] Numbers 16:20–35.
[3] II Samuel 24:17.
[4] Exodus 12:29.
[5] Exodus 20:5.

In any society taken as a whole, enough moral evil can be discovered to furnish plausible basis for interpreting the society's suffering as retribution. Granted the idea of social solidarity so complete that all members of a clan, tribe, or nation may justly be punished for what any member does, and one black sheep can furnish iniquity enough to satisfy the requirements of explanation when tragedy befalls the group.

A typical Hebrew prophet of the eighth century, for example, would have explained Belgium's disaster in 1914 as God's punishment for Belgium's sin. Only so, in his opinion, could the justice of God have been maintained, for how could a righteous deity permit a people so to suffer if they did not deserve it? To doubt the existence of sufficient sin in Belgium to justify her calamity would have seemed to a Hebrew prophet denial of God's righteousness. The prophet, therefore, would have discovered sin in Belgium, perhaps lighting on King Leopold's misgovernment of the Belgian Congo, and so would have justified God in visiting on the nation the consequence of such transgression. The Kaiser accordingly, while hated as the ravisher of the people, would have seemed to the prophet, as the Assyrian king seemed to Isaiah, the appointed minister of Yahweh's wrath—"Ho Assyrian, the rod of mine anger, the staff in whose hand is mine indignation!"[1] Thus having found in the nation iniquity enough to deserve the national disaster, the prophet would have felt that he had vindicated God's ways to man and had confirmed Yahweh's sole sovereignty by subsuming alike the suffering of the victim and the cruelty of the invader under the divine administration of justice.

In this fashion the established formula—all trouble is deserved punishment—was stretched to cover the entire history of Israel. Always it was possible to discover enough sin in the nation as a whole to justify the punishments of Yahweh on the nation as a whole. So ran the argument and appeal of Zephaniah when the Scythians came, of Joel when the locusts came, of Jeremiah when the Chaldeans came. So Isaiah, when Judah lay desolate, saw in the disaster not disaster only but penalty for social sin, because of which "the anger of Yahweh" was "kindled against his people."[2] Granting the premise in the prophets' thought, the logic of this thesis was unassailable. All suffering comes from God—"Shall evil befall a city, and Yahweh hath not done it?";[3] God is inflexibly just and, therefore, sends suffering only when it is de-

[1] Isaiah 10:5.   [3] Amos 3:6.
[2] Isaiah 5:25.

served; all suffering must, in consequence, be deserved punishment; and the sin punished is the disobedience of the nation or of individuals within it, which brings rightful penalty upon the whole people—such for centuries was the orthodox teaching of Hebrew religion.

III

This experiment in justifying God's ways with man was bound to break down when justice to the individual became a vital matter of concern. The suffering of Belgium, as a whole, may plausibly be interpreted as punishment for national sin, but when individual personality is singled out and the character and fortunes of Cardinal Mercier, let us say, are clearly visualized and deeply cared about, then the formula, 'all suffering is deserved punishment,' becomes precarious if not incredible. Certainly *his* suffering was not plainly due to *his* sin.

The development of Hebrew thought on this question, as on others, was thus profoundly affected by the emergence of individual personality out of the social mass, and this crucial phase of Hebrew thinking was associated with Jeremiah. To be sure, he found the public woes of Israel no mystery; the old formula adequately covered the case as he saw it. The national sins were so heinous and persistent that no collective retribution could be too severe to be deserved. Furthermore, Yahweh had been longsuffering and patient; more speedy and drastic punishment would have befallen Israel had not Yahweh in mercy repeatedly postponed his wrath until he was "weary with repenting."[1] In soundly orthodox fashion Jeremiah thus used the old doctrine to explain the woes of the nation. His individual woes, however, presented to him a mystery, which in turn emphasized the mystery of personal suffering all about him. Through the experience of his own isolated and afflicted life he looked at other personalities, singly seen and individually cared about, and was far too honest not to report what he saw—prosperous sinners escaping penalty and innocent sufferers enduring tragedy. Jeremiah, therefore, who exercised a potent influence on many developments in Hebrew thinking, was among the first, if not himself the very first, to raise the problem of suffering in its new form:

> Righteous art thou, O Yahweh, when I contend with
> thee; yet would I reason the cause with thee: wherefore

[1] Jeremiah 15:6.

doth the way of the wicked prosper? wherefore are all
they at ease that deal very treacherously? Thou hast
planted them, yea, they have taken root; they grow, yea,
they bring forth fruit: thou art near in their mouth, and
far from their heart. But thou, O Yahweh, knowest me;
thou seest me, and triest my heart toward thee . . . .[1] Why
is my pain perpetual, and my wound incurable, which re-
fuseth to be healed? wilt thou indeed be unto me as a deceitful brook, as waters that fail?[2]

Obviously a new factor had come upon the scene to shake confidence in the old formula. The separate individual to whom
personally, apart from all questions of collective reward and
retribution, justice was *due* but was not *done*, rose into Hebrew
thinking with disturbing effect. The dark riddle of innocent suffering here passed into its most baffling presentment, and the unanswered "why—?" which centuries afterward sounded from the
cross, was raised explicitly by Jeremiah.

The association of this emergent problem with the break-up
of the nation at the time of the Exile was further illustrated by
Jeremiah's contemporary, Habakkuk:

O Yahweh, how long shall I cry, and thou wilt not
hear? I cry out unto thee of violence, and thou wilt not
save. Why dost thou show me iniquity, and cause me to
look upon perverseness? for destruction and violence
are before me; and there is strife, and contention riseth
up. Therefore the law is slacked, and justice goeth forth
not unto victory; for the wicked doth compass about the
righteous; therefore justice goeth forth perverted.[3]

Art not thou from everlasting, O Yahweh my God,
my Holy One? we shall not die. O Yahweh, thou hast
ordained him [the Chaldean] for judgment; and thou,
O Rock, hast established him for correction. Thou that
art of purer eyes than to behold evil, and that canst not
look on perverseness, wherefore lookest thou upon them
that deal treacherously, and holdest thy peace when
the wicked swalloweth up the man that is more righteous
than he?[4]

[1] Jeremiah 12:1-3.
[2] Jeremiah 15:18.
[3] Habakkuk 1:2-4 (marginal translation).
[4] Habakkuk 1:12-13.

In such passages from Jeremiah and Habakkuk we face the perennial glory of the true prophets—their courage in acknowledging facts of experience that contradict accepted theories. Without blinking or evasion, these passages state the raw truths of experience which the current theology was inadequate to explain. Such perplexed why's and wherefore's as Habakkuk, for example, uttered concerning the problem of suffering are the more revealing because the prophet was loyally endeavoring to make the old orthodoxy work. He still could affirm that the Chaldean conqueror was acting under Yahweh's commission as the agent of divine retribution. While the old formula, however, was in his mind, the old confidence it had once inspired was not in his heart. The wide margin of mystery which it left unexplored and unexplained was to him painfully visible. In particular, he kept seeing the baffling personal injustice involved when "the wicked doth compass about the righteous," and, even when he thought of the nation's collective problem, his solution was not so much to blame present social tragedy on antecedent social sin as to believe that justice, now denied, would come in time— "Though it tarry, wait for it; because it will surely come, it will not delay."[1] Even when applied to the national problem, therefore, the old formula under the shock of Exilic disaster began to prove inadequate.

As the years passed, the problem of suffering thus moved into a new phase, dominated by two factors: a high, monotheistic doctrine of a just and merciful God and a growing care about the personal rights of individual people. These two factors, far from simplifying the problem, profoundly complicated it. Belief in many whimsical gods had left large leeway for capricious injustice, and collective retribution had made plausible the explanation of all suffering as punishment. When, however, the religious imagination began visualizing the divine-human relationship in terms of an all-powerful and benevolent God dealing with separate, individual lives, the problem of evil was brought to its climactic difficulty. Was God fairly administering justice to men, one by one? With that question the Old Testament was ever afterward vitally concerned. It has been said that the central problem of the religions of India is suffering, while the central problem of Hebrew religion is sin. Partially justified as such a distinction is, it can easily be exaggerated. Some of the most commanding ideas and most significant theological con-

[1] Habakkuk 2:3.

troversies in the Old Testament, from the days of the Exile on, were associated with the struggles of Judaism over this confusing and often agonizing problem of individual injustice in a world governed by "powerful Goodness."

IV

In this endeavor to reconcile the omnipotence of a good God with the facts of personal experience, four major lines of thought were followed out.

1. Suffering on the part of the individual was explained as deserved retribution for the individual's own sin. This extension of the old formula to cover the new case was to have been expected; in one realm or another every generation subsumes new facts under venerable theories rather than change the theories to conform with the facts. Such persistence of an ancient piece of mental furniture was seldom more stubbornly illustrated than by the long continuance in Judaism of the doctrine that, in the case of the individual as of the social group, all suffering is deserved punishment. Many faithful Jews, anxious to vindicate God's justice, saw no way of doing it if personal wretchedness were not exactly commensurate with preceding personal sin. Since Yahweh was flawlessly righteous and since—there being as yet no confident expectation of a future life—his justice had to be perfectly administered here and now, there seemed no solution unless all happy and prosperous people had been correspondingly good and all unhappy and afflicted people correspondingly wicked. Under duress of this theodicy, loyal Jews argued back from good fortune to good morals and from ill fortune to evil morals, and thereby found themselves at last in a position where theological theory and the facts of experience were in headlong collision.

This endeavor to make the old theory fit individual suffering, as it had seemed to fit social calamity, was stoutly prosecuted by Ezekiel. His older contemporary, Jeremiah, may first have set the theme which he elaborated; certainly this is true if two verses attributed to Jeremiah were really his—"In those days they shall say no more, The fathers have eaten sour grapes, and the children's teeth are set on edge. But every one shall die for his own iniquity: every man that eateth the sour grapes, his teeth shall be set on edge."[1] Ezekiel's argument was a painstaking explication of this doctrine.[2] Retribution is not transmissible;

[1] Jeremiah 31:29-30.   [2] See chap. II, pp. 67 ff.

fathers cannot hand on unexpiated penalty to their sons; even
within the family, every individual is so isolated from every
other that punishment is strictly apportioned to each member
according to his own sin—such was the new teaching of Ezekiel.
"The soul that sinneth, it shall die: the son shall not bear the
iniquity of the father, neither shall the father bear the iniquity
of the son; the righteousness of the righteous shall be upon him,
and the wickedness of the wicked shall be upon him."[1]

In this endeavor to explain all personal suffering as deserved
punishment, Ezekiel desired to vindicate Yahweh's justice. The
afflicted and resentful people in exile were tempted to blame
their calamitous estate on God's inequity. Centuries afterwards,
Jews still were rebelliously inquiring why God spares the wicked
and destroys his own people—"Are the deeds of Babylon better
than those of Sion?"[2] This reaction to national distress Ezekiel
faced in Babylon itself in the popular complaint that "the way
of the Lord is not equal."[3] The prophet, therefore, rose in defense
of divine fair play, and asserted that Yahweh's rewards and
retributions, in dealing not only with the nation but with individuals, were exactly just. So far did this Calvin of the Old
Testament carry his rigorous logic that he denied the possibility
of inheriting evil's consequence and asserted that absolute justice
is done to all individuals here and now in this present world.
He denied that righteous lives can exercise saving power—
"Though these three men, Noah, Daniel, and Job, were in it
[the land], they should deliver but their own souls by their
righteousness, saith the Lord Yahweh."[4] To be sure, Ezekiel's
ultimate purpose was merciful; he insisted thus on the individual's
control of his own destiny in order that he might open the door to
effective personal repentance and reformation.[5] Nevertheless, the
consequence of this extreme individualism was to make every
sufferer bear not only his suffering but in addition the odium of
having sinned enough to deserve it. "I will judge you, O house of
Israel, every one according to his ways, saith the Lord Yahweh."[6]

Thus the new way of thinking rose vehemently in revolt
against the old idea of collective punishment and collective reward as adequately explaining trouble. The individual had become a matter of concern too clamorous to be neglected, and the

[1] Ezekiel 18:20.
[2] II Esdras 3:31.
[3] Ezekiel 18:25–30; 33:17–20.
[4] Ezekiel 14:14. On pre-Exilic story of

Job, see *International Critical Com-
mentary* on *Job*, pp. xxv–xxvi.
[5] Ezekiel 18:27–28.
[6] Ezekiel 18:30; 33:20.

justice due him too important to be denied. The resultant doctrine
became post-Exilic orthodoxy in Judaism, and was with tireless
repetition presented from every angle by the friends of Job. At
first they tried to be comforting, interpreting Job's trouble as
disciplinary rather than punitive, but soon, with the hard rigor
of convinced logicians accepting an unquestioned premise, they
were arguing back from Job's misery to his antecedent and
corresponding sin. He must have sinned egregiously, they said,
to have deserved such tragedy, and, had he not deserved it,
God's justice could not have allowed it. These friends of Job
furnish one of the most illustrious examples in literature of utter
logic being utterly wrong.

> Remember, I pray thee, who ever perished, being innocent?
> Or where were the upright cut off?
> According as I have seen, they that plow iniquity,
> And sow trouble, reap the same.
> By the breath of God they perish,
> And by the blast of his anger are they consumed.
> .   .   .   .
> Shall mortal man be more just than God?
> Shall a man be more pure than his Maker?[1]

To such insistence on the complete justice of God to every individual Job's friends repeatedly returned. God, they argued, will
not "pervert justice";[2] he never will "cast away a perfect man,"
nor "uphold the evildoers";[3] the wicked man, therefore, "travaileth with pain all his days,"[4] terrors "chase him at his heels,"[5] and
any triumph he may have "is short";[6] the just God allows trouble
to fall exclusively on evil men, so that all trouble reveals the
precedent wickedness of the sufferer, and to an afflicted person like
Job the proper message is, "God exacteth of thee less than thine
iniquity deserveth."[7] Indeed, so logically indispensable to sound
faith seemed such confidence in God's perfect individual justice
that Job, who denied it, faced the charge, "Thou art destroying
religion."[8] Thus in the dramatic presentation of the Book of Job
the orthodox formula was argued and reiterated against an innocent sufferer.

Aside from its literary excellence, the glory of this ancient

---

[1] Job 4:7–9,17.
[2] Job 8:3.
[3] Job 8:20.
[4] Job 15:20.
[5] Job 18:11.

[6] Job 20:5.
[7] Job 11:6.
[8] Job 15:4 as translated by John Edgar
McFadyen: *The Problem of Pain; A Study
in the Book of Job*, p. 100.

drama lies in the intellectual honesty of Job, who, faced on one side with a venerable theory and on the other with plain facts of experience, insisted that the facts must have precedence. He punctured the complacent acceptance of the current orthodoxy with insistent questioning—"Why?" and "Wherefore?"[1] The traditional claim that God marks the wicked for condign retribution and the good for appropriate reward Job opposed with a statement of observed fact, "He destroys the blameless and the wicked."[2] His friends had, parrot-like, recited the familiar formula,

> Yea, the light of the wicked shall be put out,
> And the flame of his fire shall not shine,[3]

but Job impatiently thrust into the discussion a matter of fact,

> How oft is it that the lamp of the wicked is put out?
> That their calamity cometh upon them?[4]

Far from finding life's fortunes neatly apportioned according to moral character, Job had watched evil men "spared in the day of calamity,"[5] and the refusal of his friends to see that fact, because they insisted on looking through an opaque theory, roused his indignation to extreme overstatement—

> Why are wicked men suffered to live,
> To grow old and wax mighty in power?
> Their seed is established before them,
> And their offspring in sight of their eyes.
> Their homes are strangers to terror,
> No rod of God is on them.
> Their bull doth unfailingly gender,
> Their cow never loses her calf.
> Like a flock they send forth their young children;
> Their boys and their girls dance.
> They sing to the timbrel and lyre;
> At the sound of the pipe they make merry.
> They finish their days in prosperity,
> And go down to Sheol in peace—
> Though they said unto God, 'O leave us,
> We desire not to know Thy ways.

---

[1] Job 3:11–12,20; 7:20; 10:2; 13:24; 21:4,7; 24:1.
[2] Job 9:22 as translated by Julius A. Bewer: *The Literature of the Old Testament in its Historical Development*, p. 320.
[3] Job 18:5 (marginal translation).
[4] Job 21:17.
[5] Job 21:30 (marginal translation).

Why should we serve the Almighty?
And what is the good of prayer?'
See! their fortune is in their own hand:
Nought He cares for the schemes of the wicked.[1]

This heretical rebellion against a venerable orthodoxy marks Job as one of the great nonconformists of history. His spirit was, indeed, subdued to a humbler and better balanced mood before the drama closed, but his mind, to the end, refused subjection to an old explanation of suffering that did not explain, and in his refusal Yahweh at last confirmed him and confounded his friends.

In the outcome, therefore, the higher levels of the Old Testament rejected the formula that all personal suffering is personal punishment. That sin brings penalty in one form or another, that

... they that plow iniquity,
And sow mischief, reap the same,[2]

the sober thought of Old and New Testament alike accepted. But while the course of cause and consequence still ran from sin to suffering, it could no longer be confidently traced back from personal suffering to personal sin. All wickedness brought trouble, but not all trouble was penalty for wickedness; sinners in the end suffered, but all sufferers were not necessarily sinners—such came to be the insight of the later Judaism.

2. The persistence of the old formula, however, was revealed in a second endeavor to make sense of the relationship between wrongdoing and disaster. Before surrendering altogether the idea that one could argue not only from sin to suffering but from suffering back to sin, the device of postponed penalty was brought into play. Both with regard to individual and social experience, the old orthodoxy tried to save itself by appending to its statement of the case, "Wait and see." So Habakkuk, acknowledging the appalling injustice of the nation's miseries, appealed to the future for the triumph of the righteous and the overthrow of the wicked—"Though it tarry, wait for it; because it will surely come."[3] Thus the cracking formula was given a new lease of life.

The Psalms—whether national or springing, as even national psalms must, out of personal experience and conviction—voice repeatedly the assurance that God's indefectible justice in appor-

---

[1] Job 21:7-16 as translated by J. E. McFadyen: *op. cit.*, p. 147.   [2] Job 4:8 (marginal translation).   [3] Habakkuk 2:3.

tioning reward and retribution, while not now evident, will be revealed in time.

> When the wicked spring as the grass,
> And when all the workers of iniquity do flourish;
> It is that they shall be destroyed for ever.[1]

> Praise ye Yahweh.
> Blessed is the man that feareth Yahweh,
> That delighteth greatly in his commandments.
> His seed shall be mighty upon earth:
> The generation of the upright shall be blessed.
> Wealth and riches are in his house;
> And his righteousness endureth for ever.
>
> .   .   .   .
>
> The wicked shall see it, and be grieved;
> He shall gnash with his teeth, and melt away:
> The desire of the wicked shall perish.[2]

So deep-seated was the Jewish conviction that goodness and prosperity, badness and adversity, must always travel as twins, that even when the observed facts denied the doctrine, the evidence of the doctrine's truth was confidently postponed to the future.

The classic utterance of this attitude is the Thirty-seventh Psalm. The believer in God is there admonished not to fret himself over the good fortune of evil-doers,

> For they shall soon be cut down like the grass,
> And wither as the green herb.[3]

According to this psalmist, patient righteousness will always live to see itself vindicated by prosperous circumstance, while inevitable adversity awaits the sinner—

> For yet a little while, and the wicked shall not be:
> Yea, thou shalt diligently consider his place, and he shall not be.[4]

Indeed, the old formula, amended by the codicil of postponed award, reaches in this psalm its amazing climax,

> I have been young, and now am old;
> Yet have I not seen the righteous forsaken,
> Nor his seed begging bread.[5]

[1] Psalm 92:7.
[2] Psalm 112:1-3,10.
[3] Psalm 37:1-2.
[4] Psalm 37:10.
[5] Psalm 37:25.

Seldom has the truth been better exemplified that we see not only with our eyes but with our mental predispositions and prejudices. Obviously, then as now, the only way in which one could find virtue and prosperity, sin and adversity, so exactly conjoined would be by looking at the facts through the foregone conviction that the sufferer must have been evil and the successful man virtuous, no matter what appearances might indicate.

The inevitable nemesis of such rationalization was popular doubt of God's justice. The formula by which the divine righteousness was defended was irreconcilable with experience, and the explanation of trouble offered by Yahweh's apologists did not explain it. Here, as has so commonly happened, the plain man was closer to the facts of life than the theologian, and the more the latter insisted on his sacred formulas, the more the former felt the urgency of his contradictory experience. Malachi found the people of his day denying any fair correspondence between quality of character and happiness of circumstance and saying, "Every one that doeth evil is good in the sight of Yahweh, and he delighteth in them; or where is the God of justice?"[1] The only answer Malachi had to give was the old formula with 'wait and see' appended. The righteous, he said, are in God's "book of remembrance," and the day will surely come, when Yahweh "will spare them, as a man spareth his own son that serveth him." Then the allocation of prosperity and adversity will make it easy to "discern between the righteous and the wicked, between him that serveth God and him that serveth him not."[2]

Malachi's indefinite extension of time for the postponed awards of God could not satisfy those who saw no justice done in their lifetime. At last, therefore, the horizons of 'wait and see' were extended farther yet, into a life after death. One of the major reasons for the emergence of the hope of resurrection in the Old Testament was its necessity as a fulfilment to the course of thinking we have been tracing. Complete justice was not done within one's lifetime; generations passed and still justice was not done; but in God's world justice must ultimately be done; and justice, according to the inveterate formula, must mean the accurate conjoining of prosperity with goodness and adversity with badness—such was the situation in Jewish thinking out of which came the hope of a resurrected life.

Thus, Job, beating his mind against the mystery of his distress,

[1] Malachi 2:17.   [2] Malachi 3:14-18.

dared hope for a vindication after death, and Daniel, amid national disaster, with no assurance of universal resurrection, still believed that "many of them that sleep in the dust of the earth shall awake, some to everlasting life, and some to shame and everlasting contempt."[1] Faith in a future resurrection, therefore, was not among the Hebrews an abstract theory, but was forged in the furnace of affliction. It was an appeal from the injustices of time to the justice of eternity.

> Though the mills of God grind slowly, yet
> they grind exceeding small;
> Though with patience he stands waiting, with
> exactness grinds he all [2]—

that is excellent Old Testament doctrine, and such indefectible justice, resolutely believed in, was postponed beyond death when on this side of death it plainly was not exemplified.

As a result of this development, a large area of earthly suffering was withdrawn from the application of the old formula. As any one could see, some trouble, social and personal, was deserved punishment for sin. But what of the rest?

3. In dealing with this problem, the disciplinary effect of suffering was, for some, a welcome solution. Even the friends of Job, stout protagonists of the old orthodoxy though they turned out to be, had known Job's apparent integrity so well that at first they tried interpreting his disasters not as punitive but as educative—

> Behold, happy is the man whom God correcteth:
> Therefore, despise not thou the chastening of the Almighty.[3]

Two influences in Jewish thinking naturally converged to make this explanation of trouble acceptable. First, as the idea of God was heightened into nobler meanings, nothing for which he was responsible could be conceived as aimless and, therefore, the suffering which he brought on men and nations could readily be thought of, not as retribution merely, but as purposeful discipline and chastisement. Second, the experienced fact was, then as now, that suffering well handled adds new dimensions to character, that indeed, the noblest attributes of man are inconceivable in an untroubled life. As Henry Ward Beecher said, "Manhood is the most precious fruit of trouble."[4] This experience the Jews

---

[1] Daniel 12:2.
[2] F. von Logau: "Retribution," from the "Sinngedichte," as translated by Henry Wadsworth Longfellow.

[3] Job 5:17.
[4] Sermon, "Bearing but not Overborne," in The Original Plymouth Pulpit, Vol. III, p. 74.

also had, as witness the passage in the Testaments of the Twelve Patriarchs, celebrating the triumph of wisdom in the midst of adversity:

> Get wisdom in the fear of God with diligence;
> For though there be a leading into captivity,
> And cities and lands be destroyed,
> And gold and silver and every possession perish,
> The wisdom of the wise naught can take away,
> Save the blindness of ungodliness, and the callousness
>   (that comes) of sin.
> For if one keep oneself from these evil things,
> Then even among his enemies shall wisdom be a glory to him,
> And in a strange country a fatherland,
> And in the midst of foes shall prove a friend.[1]

Such a passage reveals profound strength of character, not only unconquered but positively strengthened by adversity.

To be sure, the explanation of trouble as punishment held the center of the field. From the story of the Garden of Eden, where such natural hardships as earning one's livelihood by the sweat of one's brow, contending with weeds, bearing children with travail, and even wearing clothes, are interpreted as definite penalties for the sin of Adam and Eve, the Old Testament is haunted by the idea that adversity is retributive. Nevertheless, too many major achievements had been won through disaster, and too many great characters had shone out like a Rembrandt portrait from a dark background, for the educative meanings of affliction to be missed entirely. "Suffering accepted and vanquished," said Cardinal Mercier, "will place you in a more advanced position in your career, will give you a serenity which may well prove the most exquisite fruit of your life."[2] Such an experience was by no means unknown in Judaism and the later Old Testament gives clear expression to it:

> My son, despise not the chastening of Yahweh;
> Neither be weary of his reproof:
> For whom Yahweh loveth he reproveth,
> Even as a father the son in whom he delighteth.[3]

> The sufferer He saveth through suffering;
>   Adversity opens his ear.[4]

[1] The Testament of Levi, 13:7-8.
[2] Quoted by John A. Gade: *The Life of Cardinal Mercier*, p. 5.
[3] Proverbs 3:11-12.
[4] Job 36:15 as translated by J. E. McFadyen: *The Problem of Pain; A Study in the Book of Job*, p. 265; cf. Ezekiel 22:18-22.

"And some of them that are wise shall fall, to refine them, and to purify, and to make them white, even to the time of the end."[1]

4. Neither the punitive nor the disciplinary idea of suffering, however, carries us to the highest altitudes of Old Testament thought. *Suffering can be redemptive*—through that insight the great Prophet of the Exile made his supreme contribution and started on its influential history an idea that has been rightly called "the noblest creation of Old Testament religion."[2]

To be sure, Isaiah of Babylon did not give up the conviction that Israel in her disasters had been punished for her sins. "Behold, for your iniquities were ye sold,"[3] he told the people, and even when he comforted them it was by no denial of punitive trouble but by its assertion—"Jerusalem . . . hath received of Yahweh's hand double for all her sins."[4] His distinctive contribution, however, lay in his change of emphasis in dealing with his people's suffering. Instead of looking back to past sins as its explanation, he looked forward to redemptive consequences as its purpose. Thus, while the national disasters were in a real sense punitive, and while, deeper yet, they were disciplinary—a long suffering God purifying his people in the fires of affliction[5]—the crowning fact about them was their vicariousness. Suffering endured for the sake of others God used in the redemption of the world—this profound truth the Great Isaiah saw clearly for the first time in our Jewish-Christian tradition and stated it in the inspired "poems of the Servant of Yahweh."[6]

Presupposed in these poems was a fully developed, ethically serious monotheism, which included all mankind in its scope and set the redemption of all mankind as its purpose—"Yea, he saith, It is too light a thing that thou shouldest be my servant to raise up the tribes of Jacob, and to restore the preserved of Israel: I will also give thee for a light to the Gentiles, that thou mayest be my salvation unto the end of the earth."[7] In this divine purpose to save mankind, the prophet saw the sufferings of Israel playing an essential part. To be sure, at the time the prophet wrote, the nations scorned Israel and the interpretation of national disaster as penalty added disgrace to the catastrophe. But, said the prophet, even the heathen will yet see in Israel's sufferings

---

[1] Daniel 11:35.
[2] H. Wheeler Robinson: *The Religious Ideas of the Old Testament*, p. 176.
[3] Isaiah 50:1.
[4] Isaiah 40:2; cf. Isaiah 42:24–25.
[5] Isaiah 48:10.
[6] Isaiah 42:1–4; 49:1–6; 50:4–9; 52: 13—53:12.
[7] Isaiah 49:6.

another meaning altogether and will say, "He was despised, and rejected of men; a man of sorrows, and acquainted with grief: and as one from whom men hide their face he was despised; and we esteemed him not. Surely he hath borne our griefs, and carried our sorrows; yet we did esteem him stricken, smitten of God, and afflicted. But he was wounded for our transgressions, he was bruised for our iniquities; the chastisement of our peace was upon him; and with his stripes we are healed. All we like sheep have gone astray; we have turned every one to his own way; and Yahweh hath laid on him the iniquity of us all."[1]

In making possible this interpretation of suffering as redemptive, one cannot be sure what factors, in the prophet's mind, made the largest contribution. The redemptive effect of substitutionary suffering was not new, as a fact, in Israel's history, although as an idea it had never before been clearly stated. Moses was represented as identifying himself sacrificially with his people's lot until he desired no good fortune of his own apart from theirs—"Yet now, if thou wilt forgive their sin—; and if not, blot me, I pray thee, out of thy book which thou hast written"[2]—and from such beginnings an illustrious record of vicarious suffering had brought the national history to Jeremiah, who, only a few years before Isaiah of Babylon wrote, had lived and died in voluntary self-giving for the salvation of his people. Indeed, he had consciously recognized his afflictions as serving a divine cause, so that he could say to God, "Know that for thy sake I have suffered reproach."[3] Moreover, the saving efficacy of good lives in a community had been an implicit corollary of the old sense of social solidarity, as is picturesquely evidenced in Yahweh's consent to Abraham's argument that if there were even ten good men in Sodom it should not be destroyed.[4] How much more saving would the lives of good men be when they suffered for others willingly and innocently! Still further, the persistent association of sin with commensurate adversity naturally suggested the idea that adversity itself was expiatory. In later Judaism it was plainly taught that suffering propitiates God, even more than burnt-offerings, since the latter are a man's property while the former are borne in his own person, and that "chastisements wipe out all a man's wickednesses."[5] If suffering

[1] Isaiah 53:3–6.
[2] Exodus 32:32.
[3] Jeremiah 15:15.
[4] Genesis 18:22–32.

[5] Berakot 5a as quoted by George Foot Moore: *Judaism in the First Centuries of the Christian Era*, Vol. I, p. 547.

is thus in itself expiatory for the individual, why may it not be
so for society, especially if it is voluntarily chosen or innocently
and patiently endured? Never before the Great Isaiah, however,
had these facts of experience and foregleams of idea fallen together and caught fire. In him they became flamingly explicit
in some of the most exultant passages in Scripture, where appalling disaster was transmuted into spiritual triumph because it
was seen as redemptive.

One motive in the prophet's mind is self-evident. The national
tragedy had been so dreadful and the interpretation of the
tragedy as deserved punishment had added to cruel suffering a
dishonor so intolerable, that the very bearing of the disaster
demanded a new interpretation that would substitute constructive purpose for dour penalty, exalted meaning for disgrace. So
the prophet glorified the sufferings of the true Israel; punitive
they were but, as well, a martyrdom whose saving effects would
redeem the world and exalt the very Israel once doomed by them.

> But it pleased Yahweh to crush him:
> if he would make his soul an offering for sin,
> He would see calamity for length of days,
> but the purpose of Yahweh would succeed through him.
> As a result of the travail of his soul he would see light
> and be satisfied with the knowledge of his vindication.[1]

What this reinterpretation of Israel's tragedy did for those who
understood and believed it is plain. Their minds had faced backward toward preceding sin as their disaster's cause. The Great
Isaiah turned their faces forward toward redemption as their
disaster's purpose. In their thought of their tragedy a primary
emphasis on future outcome and meaning was substituted for
the old, exclusive emphasis on past transgression. Hope instead
of hopeless self-recrimination was put into the center of the picture.

To be sure, the prophet did not do this lightly, speaking
smooth things to comfort his people. The Suffering Servant was
not the whole of Israel but the saving minority, the faithful
remnant whom opposition could not tame nor any bribe seduce,
who with patient, uncomplaining willingness had taken on themselves the punishments that should have fallen upon others.
The very presentation of the Suffering Servant, therefore,

[1] Isaiah 53: 0–11 as translated by Julius　*ment in its Historical Development,* p. 210.
A. Bewer: *The Literature of the Old Testa-*

charged the people with guilt and faced them with shame. Seeing how the true Israel had suffered in their stead for sins which they had committed, they were called to penitence and through penitence to pardon and healing. The "poems of the Servant of Yahweh," were first of all ethically challenging and demanding. But they were comforting as well. Their moral appeal rested not so much on God's penal justice as on his redemptive power exercised through the substitutionary sacrifice of his people; their distinctive interpretation of suffering was cast into terms not of retribution but of salvation.

To be sure, the prophet gave no explanation of such substitutionary sacrifice, offered no theory as to the way in which the sufferings of Yahweh's Servant operated to save the world. Of this, however, we may be sure: if we could have seen into his mind, we should have found there no such Western legal theories as have shaped and conditioned our more modern ideas of atonement, but rather should have found the persistent background of conceptions involved in social solidarity. Behind the fifty-third chapter of Isaiah, in which the true Israel is personified and the Suffering Servant's willing, uncomplaining assumption of punishment due to others is dramatically described and exalted, lies the ancient concept of corporate personality.[1] According to that, the sin of one could be the curse of all, and now the Great Isaiah announced that the sacrifice of one—the Suffering Servant—would be the redemption of all. Moreover, the Great Isaiah enlarged the corporate group to include all mankind, one inter-related human family within which the sufferings of the true Israel could be applied to the good of the whole race. The passages on the Servant of Yahweh, therefore, are poetry, expressing insight rather than formulated doctrine, but the insight has turned out to be one of the most consequential in history. *If suffering, sacrificially borne for others, is redemptive, then suffering itself is redeemed.* In the Old Testament pain and sorrow started as disgrace—all adversity was the dishonorable symptom of preceding sin; but now the Great Isaiah lifted suffering out of its ignominy. It could be redemptive. Like the trespass-offering upon the altar, it could be a holy and saving sacrament,[2] so that Israel's troubles needed no longer to be regarded merely as the evidence of God's punitive displeasure, but could be glorified as the agency of his saving grace toward all mankind.

The amazement which the prophet felt at his own daring insight

[1] Cf. chap. II, pp. 55 ff.　　　　[2] Isaiah 53:10.

still breathes in the written word. He saw that he had had revealed to him a complete reinterpretation of his people's sufferings, which exalted what once had been merely terrible and made spiritually hopeful what at first had seemed infamous. No wonder that he wrote in poetry! No wonder that he began his mission with the resounding words, "Comfort ye, comfort ye my people, saith your God"![1] No wonder that he foresaw the incredulity with which many would hear his message, and ascribed to the Eternal an idea which seemed so to outreach the mind of man— "For my thoughts are not your thoughts, neither are your ways my ways, saith Yahweh. For as the heavens are higher than the earth, so are my ways higher than your ways, and my thoughts than your thoughts!"[2]

v

Nevertheless, when the Old Testament had interpreted some suffering as punitive, some as disciplinary, and some as redemptive, the residue of mystery was still baffling. Why God, combining endless power with complete goodness, should have made a world in which disaster indiscriminately falls with tragic incidence on good and evil, remained in large measure an unanswered question.

In India, belief in reincarnation had already stepped into this breach. If all souls now on earth are reincarnated existences, the doctrine that personal suffering is always deserved punishment can be made to work. On the basis of transmigration, whatever befalls one here can be attributed to unknown sins committed in previous, unknown incarnations. Had Job's friends held this doctrine, their problem in explaining Job's disasters would have been simplified; they could have located the wrongdoing, for which he was being punished, in a previous existence, safely sheltered from his recollection and, therefore, from his denial. The Hebrew mind, however, was far too factual and realistic to try this easy retreat into the obscurities of preëxistence. True to their racial characteristics, they could find no satisfaction in a solution so theoretically metaphysical and so entirely beyond the testing of actual experience. Rather than explain the mystery of suffering by such a method, they left it a mystery.

Toward the close of the Exile and afterwards, Persian influence powerfully affected Israel, and a dominant feature of Persian religion was the explanation of human good and evil as the

[1] Isaiah 40:1. [2] Isaiah 55:8-9.

reflected consequence of a profound division in the superhuman world. There, so Zoroastrianism taught, a kingdom of light and a kingdom of darkness opposed each other; while Ahura Mazda exercised sole sovereignty as the one true God, he was withstood by Angra Mainyu, a power, like God himself, without beginning, the creator of all evil and the perpetual foe of God and of good men.[1] The problem of evil was thus carried back to a precedent, continuous conflict in the cosmos, with God and his attendant hosts of angels contending against the prince of darkness and his devils. Here was an explanation of evil ready at hand for the Jews to accept, and the wonder is that, within the confines of the Old Testament, its influence is so slight.

The Hebrews, like all early peoples, believed in angels and demons. To the primitive mind the world was populous with spiritual agents who gradually fell into two groups, one favorable, and the other unfavorable, to man, and these were later definitely classified as angels and devils. Before the molding influence of Persia affected Israel, however, Hebrew demonology and angelology had been inchoate and unorganized. It was only after Zoroastrianism had affected Jewish thought that angels appear, as in the Book of Daniel, in a hierarchy under ruling archangels, and demons possess in Satan a sovereign chieftain. While, however, Zoroastrian angelology and demonology thus influenced Jewish thought, so that one might almost call Satan a native of Persia naturalized in Judea, and while in later Judaism and in Christianity this influence had a florescent development, its effect within the Old Testament bulks small.

Indeed, so far as Zoroastrianism's main thesis was concerned, asserting a continuous conflict between two principles in the universe symbolized as light and darkness, we have in Isaiah of Babylon an explicit denial: "I form the light, and create darkness; I make peace, and create evil; I am Yahweh, that doeth all these things."[2] Nowhere was Jewish monotheism more uncompromising than here; it refused to explain life's moral and practical evil by limiting the sole sovereignty and responsibility of God. Whatever else might be the explanation of the mystery, it was not to be found in blaming a prince of darkness, a kind of second deity and god of evil, as though by thrusting back the problem to such a personage the problem itself could be even a little solved.

[1] See H. V. Williams Jackson: "Ahri- [2] Isaiah 45:7.
man" in *Encyclopædia of Religion and
Ethics*, edited by James Hastings.

Hard though it must have been to say it, the Great Isaiah, facing Zoroastrianism's division of power between Ahura Mazda and Angra Mainyu, insisted that the one God alone was the responsible creator of the world, with its light and its darkness, its good and its evil.

Accordingly, in none of the great passages where the Old Testament wrestles with the problem of suffering does demonology play a significant part. In only three connections is Satan even mentioned in the Old Testament—once as evilly disposed to Job but doing nothing without God's permission,[1] once as tempting David to take a census,[2] and once as the symbolic adversary of Israel[3]—and nowhere are the tragedies of individuals or of nations fathered on him as though by that device the ultimate responsibility of God could be mitigated in the least. In the Book of Job, for example, while Satan appears as one of the dramatis personae in the prologue, the entire argument proceeds without the slightest reference to him, and the ultimate responsibility for the cosmic problem is clearly placed on God—"If it be not he, who then is it?"[4] Here, once more, Jewish thought refused an easy escape and faced, in its full, unqualified difficulty, the mystery of evil in a world whose God is both omnipotent and good.

This unresolved residue of mystery is the ultimate problem of the Book of Job. The fact that some calamity is punitive, that some is disciplinary, and that some may be explained by a future vindication, is clearly recognized, as we have seen. That the Book of Job never speaks of suffering as possibly redemptive is typical of the neglect with which the Great Isaiah's insight was treated for centuries. Even had that insight been present in the writer's mind, however, Job still would have faced an unexplained remainder of mystery, and his virtue would still have been, not that he solved the problem but that so candidly he recognized its insolubility. Job successfully resisted the temptation to construct a complete theory of God's justice; he had the courage to stop where his evidence ended; no ingenius metaphysic, as in India, or mythology, as in Persia, beguiled his mind into a solution that solved nothing. This candid acknowledgment of insufficient light for the understanding of God's ways with man is a perpetual memorial to the intellectual honesty of the unknown writer of the ancient drama.

[1] Job 1:6–12; 2:1–7.
[2] I Chronicles 21:1.
[3] Zechariah 3:1–2.
[4] Job 9:24.

His way of dealing with the resultant situation was typically Jewish in its religiousness. He fell back on a profound, interior experience of God. Concerning the divine administration of affairs he felt endless perplexity but of God himself he felt sure— so sure that he could, as he said, "give free course to my complaint" and "speak in the bitterness of my soul,"[1] as only those can who are at home in prayer. The consequence was a profound conviction that, while he did not know all the explanation of suffering, there was an explanation, and that beyond the solutions he could see lay not chaos and aimlessness but order and purpose. In the drama this attitude is educed by a vision of the natural universe—immense, orderly, mysterious, magnificent—before which Job is humbled. In that experience he finds not an explanation of evil but an assurance that there *is* an explanation; he issues from it not with a solution of the mystery but with a confidence in God which lights him through the mystery. All this is typical of the Old Testament, and in this Job is the religious Jew par excellence, resolving his difficulties by religious experience, not philosophical theory. Not the explanation that is clear to him but the God who is real to him is his final resource—

> I had heard of thee by the hearing of the ear;
> But now mine eye seeth thee.[2]

Alongside the Book of Job stands the Seventy-third Psalm— both of them important as portrayals of personal difficulty in dealing with the problem of evil. The psalm is intimately autobiographical. In it are vividly pictured the fear and faith, the doubt and trust, the cynicism and buoyant hope, between which at least one Jewish mind was torn as it tried to believe in God's justice in an unjust world. The writer begins with the victorious confidence which in the end crowned his struggle—

> Surely God is good to the upright,
> to such as are pure in heart[3]—

but straightway to the psalmist's memory recurs the long and bitter conflict that preceded his spiritual triumph. His feet had almost gone out from under him, he says; envious resentment at the "prosperity of the wicked" had brought him to the rim of utter cynicism—

[1] Job 10:1.
[2] Job 42:5.
[3] Psalm 73:1 as translated by Julius A.

Bewer: *The Literature of the Old Testament in its Historical Development*, p. 388.

> They are not in trouble as other men;
> Neither are they plagued like other men.
> Therefore pride is as a chain about their neck;
> Violence covereth them as a garment.
> Their eyes stand out with fatness:
> They have more than heart could wish.
> They scoff, and in wickedness utter oppression:
> They speak loftily.[1]

In the face of such rank inequity, disillusionment possessed him and he cried,

> Surely in vain have I cleansed my heart,
> And washed my hands in innocency.[2]

Then he went into the sanctuary and found insight and illumination. His cynical doubt seemed to him stupid and brutish. His soul, which had been "in a ferment,"[3] achieved peace, stability, and hope. Part of his solution lay in the ultimate ruin of the wicked, whose prosperity he had envied and whose arrogance he had resented; when he considered their "latter end," he foresaw them falling on their "slippery places," cast down to destruction, and "become a desolation in a moment."[4] But deeper than this unsatisfactory solution, this mere postponement of justice to a later day, went the real answer to the psalmist's question. Unlike the wicked, he possessed the intimate and sustaining companionship of God. Why should he envy them? Their goods could not compare with his good. Even while their prosperity continues, he cries,

> Nevertheless I am continually with thee:
> Thou hast holden my right hand.
> Thou wilt guide me with thy counsel,
> And afterward receive me to glory.
> Whom have I in heaven but thee?
> And there is none upon earth that I desire besides thee.
> My flesh and my heart faileth;
> But God is the strength of my heart and my portion for ever.[5]

Here, as in the Book of Job, the problem of evil is left an intellectual mystery but with a triumphant soul transcending it and carrying off a victory in the face of it through the inward awareness of a divine fellowship and the experience of an unconquerable hope.

[1] Psalm 73:5–8.
[2] Psalm 73:13.
[3] Psalm 73:21 (marginal translation).
[4] Psalm 73:17–19.
[5] Psalm 73:23–26.

Such endeavors to interpret suffering as we have traced, however, no more met with unanimous acceptance then than they would now, and of this the Book of Ecclesiastes is the evidence. This vivid and daring essay is as much concerned with the problem of evil as is the drama of Job or the Seventy-third Psalm, but with an approach and an outcome altogether different. To every attempted explanation of suffering he had heard, this writer gave a skeptical reply. He tossed aside the formula that suffering is deserved penalty and asserted instead a senseless, indiscriminate inequity in life—"All things come alike to all: there is one event to the righteous and to the wicked; to the good and to the clean and to the unclean; to him that sacrificeth and to him that sacrificeth not; as is the good, so is the sinner; and he that sweareth, as he that feareth an oath. This is an evil in all that is done under the sun, that there is one event unto all.¹" He had only scorn for the hope that just awards, now denied, would be rendered in the future, whether before death or afterwards—"For that which befalleth the sons of men befalleth beasts; even one thing befalleth them: as the one dieth, so dieth the other; yea, they have all one breath; and man hath no preëminence above the beasts: for all is vanity. All go unto one place; all are of the dust, and all turn to dust again. Who knoweth the spirit of man, whether it goeth upward, and the spirit of the beast, whether it goeth downward to the earth?"² If ever he thought of using pain and sorrow for purposes of personal discipline or of redemptive service, cynicism smothered the idea and, instead, he "commended mirth, because a man hath no better thing under the sun, than to eat, and to drink, and to be joyful."³

Here within the canon of Jewish Scripture, as in the Rubáiyát of Omar Kháyyám, popular futilism and pessimism were given forceful and fearless utterance. Here the creed of those who cried, "Where is the God of justice?"⁴ found an eloquent voice, and the spiritual insights by which the seers of Israel had tried to illumine the age-long problem of evil faced derisive denial. The very search for a solution to life's problem was to the writer only "a striving after wind,"⁵ and in the end, seeing wickedness in the place of justice and evil men where the righteous should

¹ Ecclesiastes 9:2–3.
² Ecclesiastes 3:19–21.
³ Ecclesiastes 8:15.
⁴ Malachi 2:17.
⁵ Ecclesiastes 1:13–14.

have been,[1] he "hated life,"[2] denied all moral government in the world, and concluded that although a man, in the intensity of his search, "see no sleep with his eyes day or night," he will never understand what life is all about.[3]

Here, as elsewhere, the Old Testament defeats all endeavors to force upon it interior self-consistency and harmony, and in its inclusion of many points of view, even though at odds with one another, it remains true to life. In the Old Testament's treatment of the problem of suffering are some of the most notable expressions in literature of ethical insight into the meaning of retribution, profound faith in the ultimate justice of God, personal courage in accepting trouble as self-discipline, spiritual understanding of vicarious sacrifice, and religious experience of a trustworthy God; and, accompanying all these, the refrain of the disillusioned also, "Vanity of vanities, all is vanity."[4]

VI

No line of developing thought ever ran directly from the Old Testament into the New; always the inter-Testamental period had to be traversed; and, while original contributions were not often made there, an influential redistribution of emphasis commonly occurred. With regard to the idea of suffering, the most notable effect of the era between the Testaments sprang from its accentuation of the apocalyptic hope. So vivid and obsessing did the expectation of an imminent Messianic age become, and so did the imagination of judgment day with its awards fill the popular mind, that the solution of the problem of life's injustice was seen mainly through apocalyptic hopes. Of this emphasis the Book of Enoch was typical—

Fear ye not, ye souls of the righteous,
And be hopeful ye that have died in righteousness.
And grieve not if your soul into Sheol has descended in grief,
And that in your life your body fared not according to your goodness,
But wait for the day of the Judgement of sinners
And for the day of cursing and chastisement.[5]

In one form or another, every suggestion made in the Old Testament concerning the problem of suffering is to be found

---

[1] Ecclesiastes 3:16.
[2] Ecclesiastes 2:17.
[3] Ecclesiastes 8:14-17 (quoted phrase as translated by Julius A. Bewer: *The Literature of the Old Testament in its Historical Development*, p. 333). Later hands added to Ecclesiastes a few notes of positive faith.
[4] Ecclesiastes 1:2.
[5] The Book of Enoch 102:4-5.

somewhere in the inter-Testamental books. Thus the Psalms of Solomon taught that "the Lord is gracious unto such as patiently abide chastening";[1] Second Esdras labored over the unsearchableness of God's ways and the limitations of man's intelligence;[2] and Fourth Maccabees, exalting the sacrifice of those who became "as it were a ransom for the sin of the nation," said that "through the blood of those pious men, and their propitiatory death, Divine Providence saved Israel."[3] Dominant, however, over the rest, and orienting them in one constant direction, was the final arbitrament of judgment day and the expected vindication of God's justice in reward and retribution.

In the New Testament these ideas, which thus had run a varying course in Jewish thinking, continued still to be the reliance of those who pondered the problem of suffering. They were, however, reorganized in the New Testament, so that, for reasons not easy at first to be sure about, the total effect was distinctive and original. Ideas, like people, being more than mere individuals, must be seen socially grouped to be understood, and the principle of their grouping often brings out results not to have been predicted from the separate ideas themselves. No one in the Old Testament or in the inter-Testamental period could have guessed the consequence that would emerge when old and familiar ideas of suffering were associated with the cross.

1. That some human pain and torment are punitive the New Testament clearly saw. Long before either the idea of natural law or any word to express it was known to man, the reign of moral law, stated in terms of cause and consequence, of sowing and reaping, was plain to the insight of the Bible. There is an inevitable relationship between the beginning and the ending of any course of behavior; he who travels a road must face the outcome of it; he who picks up one end of a stick picks up the other; there is in this universe something which discovers and sits in judgment on our spiritual mistakes—this was the clear conviction of the New Testament. In the Christian scriptures, however, the battle won in the Book of Job against the assumption that this explanation is adequate to cover all suffering was taken for granted. While the New Testament constantly argues from sin to consequent trouble, it never argues from trouble back to preceding sin as a necessary formula of explanation.

[1] 10:1–4 as translated by II. E. Ryle and M. R. James: *Psalms of the Pharisees*, p. 99.
[2] II Esdras, 4:7–11; 13–25.
[3] IV Maccabees, 17:19–21 as translated by W. R. Churton: *The Uncanonical and Apocryphal Scriptures*, p. 595.

Indeed, Jesus earnestly denied that one can assume previous wrongdoing because of present calamity. When the tower of Siloam fell and killed eighteen persons, the still popular theodicy of early Hebraism marked them out as especially wicked, but Jesus protested: "Those eighteen, upon whom the tower in Siloam fell, and killed them, think ye that they were offenders above all the men that dwell in Jerusalem? I tell you, Nay."[1]

Far from expecting the nice adjustment of happiness to moral merit and of adversity to sin, which once had seemed the indispensable condition of faith in divine fair play, Jesus saw the vast impartiality of nature's processes—God "maketh his sun to rise on the evil and the good, and sendeth rain on the just and the unjust."[2] When in a parable he described two houses on which alike "the rain descended, and the floods came, and the winds blew,"[3] one denoted a wise, and the other a foolish, life but on both of them with equal incidence the storm beat. That men face trouble with different qualities of soul and come through it to different issues was manifest but, as Jesus saw life, some trouble falls on all without regard to moral character. This impartiality of disaster's incidence had been a stumblingblock to the writer of Ecclesiastes, and that "all things come alike to all"[4] had been the bone of his contention. Jesus, however, seeing the fact as clearly as the ancient writer saw it, welcomed the unbending administration of the universe. In this regard he seemed to feel, long before men knew it, the steady inflexibility of God's cosmic method, its austere disregard of ethical considerations, its vast background of procedure without thought of human merit or demerit—a dependable, impartial training-ground for souls.

In the Fourth Gospel, written in Hellenistic Ephesus, where reincarnation was a common idea, as everywhere among the Greeks, Jesus is represented facing the old question of suffering as penalty—"As he passed by, he saw a man blind from his birth. And his disciples asked him, saying, Rabbi, who sinned, this man, or his parents, that he should be born blind? Jesus answered, Neither did this man sin, nor his parents."[5] As the Master saw it, life's cosmic setting was utterly unlike the old theodicy's imagination of it. Rain and sunshine, storm and flood, falling towers and tragic personal afflictions, came with equal

[1] Luke 13:4-5.
[2] Matthew 5:45.
[3] Matthew 7:24-27.
[4] Ecclesiastes 9:2.
[5] John 9:1-3.

impact upon both good and evil men. Jesus did not naïvely expect God to pay fair wages on a Saturday.

In the New Testament, as a whole, the crucifixion made this attitude imperative. Three crosses were on Calvary. One bore a flagrant and blasphemous criminal, another a penitent thief, the third the Christ. Golgotha was a terrific exemplification of the pessimist's saying, "All things come alike to all." In the light of it, whatever remained of the old theodicy, which deemed all suffering just punishment for the sufferer's sin, was doomed. On the central cross a character, "holy, guileless, undefiled, separated from sinners,"[1] was crucified, and such suffering was obviously not retribution. While, therefore, punitive trouble was a terrific fact in early Christian thinking—"He that soweth unto his own flesh shall of the flesh reap corruption"[2]—it never was treated as an adequate statement of suffering's cause.

2. That some trouble is disciplinary was similarly taken for granted. Even Jesus, we are told, "learned obedience by the things which he suffered."[3] The roll call of faith's martyred heroes, in the Epistle to the Hebrews, ends in an exhortation to the contemporary church[4] to bear gladly its afflictions, not as punishment, but as chastening. Far from being an occasion of shame, in the writer's eyes, the church's sufferings were a cause of hope, since their explanation lay not behind in past sin but ahead in future good consequence—"All chastening seemeth for the present to be not joyous but grievous; yet afterward it yieldeth peaceable fruit unto them that have been exercised thereby, even the fruit of righteousness."[5] This conviction that an untroubled life is uneducated, that to deal with tragedy is to handle reality and to deal well with it a great gain, that no softly-cushioned life ever can be wise or strong or good, runs throughout the New Testament. Not sporadic and occasional, but constant and fundamental is this treatment of affliction as opportunity, not disgrace, an indispensable implement for building faith and character, rather than a means for their destruction.

Here lies one of the major reasons for the difference in mood and feeling between the Jewish and the Christian scriptures. The New Testament does not contain a single idea about suffering whose premonition, and in some cases whose classic exposition, is not to be found in the Old Testament. Taken as a whole,

---

[1] Hebrews 7:26.
[2] Galatians 6:8.
[3] Hebrews 5:8.

[4] Hebrews, chaps. 11–12.
[5] Hebrews 12:11.

however—the "poems of the Servant of Yahweh" excepted—the typical Jewish treatment of trouble looks backward to antecedent conduct as the explanation, while the New Testament habitually looks forward to the high spiritual uses of affliction. In this regard the cross had done its work. There the most infamous torment had turned out to be the most effective agent in serving God's purpose for the world. The early Christians, therefore, intuitively treated suffering not as ignominy to be endured, but as opportunity to be used, and their typical attitude was positive and triumphant, as when Paul said, "We know that to them that love God all things work together for good."[1]

However clearly, therefore, abstract ideas about suffering may be found paralleling each other in the two Testaments, the resultant seeming identity is misleading. There is throughout the Christian scriptures a positive enthusiasm in the midst of trouble—"I overflow with joy," Paul wrote, "in all our afflic- tion"[2]—which is distinctive. Not the negative endurance of trouble but its positive use, not its explanation in the past but its purpose in the future, occupies the center of attention. Trouble is something to be strongly seized upon, so that no matter what befalls a man—the love of God being in his heart—it will issue in his good, will discipline him, not destroy him, and will finally find him wielding as a shining sword the very weapon of affliction lifted against him.

Thus, when Paul found himself in prison, his mind turned not to queries concerning the justice of his being there, but to the uses to which his imprisonment could be positively put: "Now I would have you know, brethren, that the things which happened unto me have fallen out rather unto the progress of the gospel; so that my bonds became manifest in Christ throughout the whole prætorian guard, and to all the rest; and that most of the brethren in the Lord, being confident through my bonds, are more abundantly bold to speak the word of God without fear."[3] Especially characteristic of Paul though this attitude is, it is the common quality of the New Testament as a whole, from the time Jesus' beatitude rested on the persecuted and afflicted,[4] to the later days when Peter wrote, "Insomuch as ye are par- takers of Christ's sufferings, rejoice."[5]

3. The Old Testament's conviction that the ultimate issue of

[1] Romans 8:28.
[2] II Corinthians 7:4.
[3] Philippians 1:12–14.
[4] Matthew 5:10–12.
[5] I Peter 4:13.

the human drama would be ethically satisfactory was carried over into Christian thinking, and there gained new dimensions and horizons. The one unifying factor that put sense into the strange and varied developments of Jewish apocalypticism was the urgent demand of the Jewish conscience that, one way or another, the cosmic process should not in the end be ethically unsatisfactory. What kind of outcome would be ethically satisfying was not in detail agreed upon, and one picture of it after another cluttered the apocalyptic imagination between the Testaments. In general, however, the Jews, carrying over their traditional association of goodness with prosperity and of badness with adversity, regarded as inadequate any solution that did not finally apportion endless reward to the righteous and endless retribution to sinners.

That the hope of an ethically satisfying outcome to creation should reappear in the New Testament was inevitable. The early Christians did not suppose the cross, for example, to be the end of the matter. The conviction which the Great Isaiah held with reference to the suffering Servant of Yahweh, Christians held with reference to Christ—"He shall see of the travail of his soul, and shall be satisfied."[1] That is to say, ultimately the human drama would work itself out, under the guidance of God, to a denouement which would justify the cost of the process and satisfy the claims of equity. Moreover, this belief in an equitable outcome to man's tragic experience was naturally phrased in the New Testament, as in the Old, in terms of adversity for the wicked and prosperity for the righteous in the world to come. When, therefore, the ideas of suffering as present punishment or as possible discipline failed to cover the case, the ancient appeal to patience was still in reserve—the injustices of time would be righted in eternity, and the scales, here unbalanced, would there hang even.

In no regard is the attitude of certain passages in the New Testament more troublesome to modern minds than in this insistence that eternal bliss for the good and eternal torment for the bad would be an ethically satisfying finale for the universe. When Jesus represented Abraham in Paradise saying to Dives in torment, "Son, remember that thou in thy lifetime receivedst thy good things, and Lazarus in like manner evil things: but now here he is comforted, and thou art in anguish,"[2]—as though such reversal of circumstance, issuing in a permanently divided

[1] Isaiah 53:11.   [2] Luke 16:25.

188 A GUIDE TO UNDERSTANDING THE BIBLE

humanity, some in bliss and some in torture, would be an ethically adequate ending to the human story—he spoke in the
traditional manner of Judaism, but the modern conscience
remains unconvinced. Unless our best ethical ideas are false,
such a denouement would be appallingly unsatisfying and universal annihilation would be far better.

Two considerations, however, tend to illumine this matter.
First, in every creative thinker there are bound to be, of psychological necessity, not only his own original insights but, as
well, the traditional backgrounds of idea from which his insights
start their pioneering, and along with this latter element go the
familiar mental patterns and phraseologies of his day. Were it
not for this traditional factor in the creative thinker, he could
not speak to his own generation at all. When Jesus, therefore,
pictured the finale of the universe in terms of the contemporary
mythology, with fire, worms, wailing, and gnashing of teeth for
sinners, and bliss for the righteous, he was using an old form of
imagination. That he did uncritically use it the records plainly
indicate[1] but, in every case, he employed it only as a familiar
setting in which to frame an attack upon current ideas concerning
the kind of conduct that was pleasing or displeasing to God.[2]
Thus, in one of his most cogent pleas for humanitarian service
as the test of true religion and the crucial point on which God
judges man—"I was hungry, and ye gave me to eat; I was
thirsty, and ye gave me to drink; I was a stranger, and ye took
me in; naked, and ye clothed me; I was sick, and ye visited me;
I was in prison, and ye came unto me"[3]—the scenery of the
parable is the old-fashioned eschatology. How much of this was
merely *ad hominem* and how much represented Jesus' personal
conviction concerning human destiny it is difficult to be sure,
just as when Plato used demonology to serve his purpose it is
difficult to know how literally he took the mental pattern he
employed. That apocalyptic elements, in general, and pictures
of future punishment, in particular, were carried over from
current Judaism into Jesus' thinking and speaking seems obvious.

A second consideration is that the point at issue, in all such
uses of current categories, is the substantial matter being phrased
rather than the form of phrasing. What the Jews and early
Christians were concerned about in their theories of final things
was an ethically satisfying issue to human destiny, and the

[1] See chap. VI, pp. 282-283.   [2] Matthew 25:31-46.
[3] E.g., Luke 16:19-31.

formulations of that conviction changed radically from imaginations of a restored Davidic kingdom, in early Hebraism, to Paul's picture of a universal victory of God, in which, whether in heaven, on earth, or in Sheol, "every knee should bow," and God "be all and in all."[1] If we are unwilling to welcome great matters, even when they come to us in obsolete vehicles of thought, it is of no use to read any ancient literature whatsoever. The vital matter in the New Testament's appeal from the injustice of the present world to the justice of the final arbitrament lies not in any special formulation, whether it be that of Jesus or of Paul, but in the deep conviction that the "one far-off divine event" will be ethically adequate.

Nevertheless, the old phrasing of this ultimate vindication of righteousness is often terribly present in the New Testament. In many passages it is obvious that the idea of God inherent in Jesus' thought has not yet found its logical conclusion; that what Jesus himself, thinking in terms of some of his own parables and of his own life-principles, could not have considered ethically satisfying—endless, hopeless torture, without constructive moral purpose and therefore without moral meaning—God is accused of inflicting, as judge of the world and arbiter of destiny. At this point some of the worst crudities of apocalyptic Judaism passed over into New Testament passages, such as one finds in the Book of Revelation.

The distinctive element in the New Testament's future hope, as a resource in present trouble, does not, however, lie in such passages. They could all be eliminated and the afflicted soul's reliance on future vindication would still be unimpaired. Still there would remain the assurance of eternal life, beginning here in a quality of spirit worth permanent continuance and going on, through death, to its fulfilment. In the light of this present possession, involving endless hope, affliction was not so much endured as rejoiced in by the early Christians, and of this spiritual triumph Paul's words are representative: "Wherefore we faint not; but though our outward man is decaying, yet our inward man is renewed day by day. For our light affliction, which is for the moment, worketh for us more and more exceedingly an eternal weight of glory; while we look not at the things which are seen, but at the things which are not seen: for the things which are seen are temporal; but the things which are not seen

---

[1] Romans 14:11; I Corinthians 15:28. See chap. VI, pp. 297–298.

are eternal. For we know that if the earthly house of our tabernacle be dissolved, we have a building from God, a house not
made with hands, eternal, in the heavens."[1]

This inner victory of the eternal over the temporal, here and
now as well as hereafter, is the original and creative element in
the New Testament's use of future hope to comfort present
sorrow. In Jesus' own recorded words, this emphasis appears in
the spiritual nature and present accessibility of the kingdom of
God—an emphasis that, in view of the postponed hopes of
Jewish apocalypticism, is very significant. According to Jesus,
the kingdom, while future in its full consummation, is also
immediately here, its doors wide open now to men of the kingdom's quality, and, far from being merely a future expectation,
entrance into it is the crowning privilege of the present. Whatever
Jesus may have carried over from the apocalyptic traditions of
his people, he struck here a note characteristic of himself and
gave his disciples not so much a quotation as a fresh insight of
his own.

To be sure, some students of the New Testament have been
so completely commandeered by apocalypticism that they insist
on interpreting all references to the kingdom in terms of its
categories. The kingdom, they think, must always mean a future,
imminent, catastrophic event. But in the rabbinical teaching, to
become unquestioningly obedient to the Law means here and
now "to take upon oneself the Kingdom of heaven." Why, then,
should this same emphasis be thought strange in Jesus or its
importance in his thinking be doubted when so many passages
seem plainly to suggest it:

> Verily I say unto you, Whosoever shall not receive
> the kingdom of God as a little child, he shall in no wise
> enter therein.[2]

> But if I by the Spirit of God cast out demons, then is
> the kingdom of God come upon you.[3]

> But when Jesus saw it, he was moved with indigna-
> tion, and said unto them, Suffer the little children to
> come unto me; forbid them not: for to such belongeth
> the kingdom of God.[4]

> And when Jesus saw that he answered discreetly, he

---

[1] II Corinthians 4:16—5:1.   [3] Matthew 12:28; cf. Luke 11:20.
[2] Mark 10:15.   [4] Mark 10:14.

said unto him, Thou art not far from the kingdom of God.[1]

Blessed are the poor in spirit: for theirs is the kingdom of heaven.[2]

And being asked by the Pharisees, when the kingdom of God cometh, he answered them and said, The kingdom of God cometh not with observation: neither shall they say, Lo, here! or, There! for lo, the kingdom of God is within you.[3]

The present, therefore, in Jesus' thought, was not simply Satanic, as current teaching claimed; the kingdom of God was an immediate experience as well as a future expectation and those who were in the kingdom, possessing, as they did, a life with eternal issues inherent in it, could triumphantly surmount affliction.

Once more we run upon the characteristic mood of the New Testament in dealing with suffering. The future life was of immense importance to the early Christians in facing suffering, but it was no longer mainly an apologetic means of vindicating the justice of God through postponed rewards and retributions. It was a singing assurance of present victory in the spirit, with all future triumphs presaged in immediate experience, and the result was positive jubilance in the face of even extreme disaster. "For I am already being offered, and the time of my departure is come. I have fought the good fight, I have finished the course, I have kept the faith: henceforth there is laid up for me the crown of righteousness, which the Lord, the righteous judge, shall give to me at that day; and not to me only, but also to all them that have loved his appearing."[4]

An ethically satisfying outcome to the cosmic process remained, therefore, the confidence of New Testament Christianity, as it had been the confidence of Old Testament Judaism. It gained new dimensions, however. Within the Christian scriptures it has no uniform and unanimous phrasing. It even rises in the end into a hope of universal redemption, when God will "sum up all things in Christ."[5]

4. Such developments of experience and thought no more took the sting of inexplicable mystery out of suffering in the New

---

[1] Mark 12:34.
[2] Matthew 5:3.
[3] Luke 17:20–21.

[4] II Timothy 4:6–8.
[5] Ephesians 1:10.

Testament than they did in the Old. The cry of the psalmist was echoed on the cross—

> My God, my God, why hast thou forsaken me?
> Why art thou so far from helping me, and from the
>   words of my groaning?[1]

In the New Testament, therefore, as in the Book of Job, deeply religious spirits, often unable to explain the afflictions which God permitted, fell back nevertheless on God himself. To trust God when one can clearly understand his ways has always been but a slight indication of serious religion. A scientist steadily believes in the law-abiding nature of reality even when he is baffled in his endeavor to discern the laws; so the saints have understood God well enough to maintain faith in him even when they could not understand his plans and policies. The real triumphs of the spirit have been customarily won by those who trusted God when his ways were inexplicable. Indeed, the major function of religion, in the experience of its great exemplars, has been not so much the explanation of life, as life's conquest— the winning of spiritual triumph in the midst of mysterious adversity. Jesus is never represented as saying, "I have explained the world," but he is reported to have said, "I have overcome the world."[2] The bestowal of interior power thus to rise above trouble and carry off a victory in spite of it seemed to the early Christians a supremely vital function of religion, and this power they found through their faith in, and experience with, an availably present Spirit. Far from being driven away from God by unexplained suffering, therefore, they were driven to him. As Paul implies, trouble has a tendency to "separate us from the love of God"[3] but, in it, by God's grace we can be "more than conquerors,"[4] and early Christianity was all on the side of the latter possibility. In the New Testament, what began in the Book of Job was consummated—"Though he slay me, yet will I trust in him."[5]

In this is revealed one of the most important of all developments in the conception of religion's meaning. Primitive religion uses its gods for ulterior purposes, seeks to gain control over them and thus to win material favors from them. Mature religion rests in God himself as greater than any of his gifts. In primitive

[1] Psalm 22:1.
[2] John 16:33.
[3] Romans 8:35 (marginal translation).
[4] Romans 8:37.
[5] Job 13:15 (King James Version).

religion the gods are means to ends; in mature religion God is an end in himself. Such devotion to the eternal Goodness for his own sake, rather than for the sake of anything externally to be gotten from him, is therefore one of the clearest manifestations of serious faith, and in the Old Testament Habakkuk gave it typical expression:

> For though the fig-tree shall not flourish,
> Neither shall fruit be in the vines;
> The labor of the olive shall fail,
> And the fields shall yield no food;
> The flock shall be cut off from the fold,
> And there shall be no herd in the stalls:
> Yet I will rejoice in Yahweh,
> I will joy in the God of my salvation.[1]

Such an attitude was characteristic of New Testament Christians. They did not make fortunate circumstance a pre-condition of faith in God; they were not fair-weather saints, finding in adversity an occasion for disbelief or disillusion; they did not expect wholly to understand life but they did expect triumphantly to handle it, surmount its difficulties, and prove themselves spiritually superior to its hardships. The afflictions that their ideas of God did not enable them to explain, their inward experience of God enabled them to overcome.

The New Testament itself is full of trouble. It begins with a massacre of innocent children; it is centered in the crucifixion; it ends with a vision in which the souls of the martyred saints under the altar cry, "How long, O Master?"[2] The Book was written by men whose familiar experiences were excommunications, persecutions, and martyrdoms. Their faith was not like a candle flame, easily blown out by a high wind, but like a great fire fanned into a more powerful conflagration. In consequence, while the New Testament is supremely a book of hardship and tragedy, it is far and away the most exultant and jubilant book in the literature of religion.

5. The climactic element in the New Testament's contribution to the understanding of suffering is to be found in its treatment of vicarious self-sacrifice. The Great Isaiah, with his interpretation of Israel's tragedy as redemptive martyrdom, never had a thoroughly sympathetic and understanding successor until Jesus came. Indeed, the ideas with regard to the saving office of suf-

---

[1] Habakkuk 3:17–18.   [2] Revelation 6:10.

fering which the Great Isaiah had put into deathless song were
so little grasped that Professor J. M. Powis Smith can say:

> How unacceptable that message was to Deutero-
> Isaiah's times and how unintelligible it was is evidenced
> by the fact that, so far as we have any information,
> not a single follower of this interpretation was forth-
> coming among his prophetic contemporaries and suc-
> cessors, and no reference even is made to this substitu-
> tionary interpretation of suffering until IV Maccabees....[1]

In the endeavor to understand the sacrificial experience of Jesus,
however, the Great Isaiah received his long postponed coronation.

To explain the resemblance between the "poems of the Servant
of Yahweh" and Christ's ministry by supposing that the former
contains a clairvoyant prediction of the latter, is, of course, to
turn the relationship between the two upside down. What really
happened was that, after five centuries of neglect, the Isaian
passages on the Suffering Servant of the Lord were used by the
early Christians as a means of interpreting the necessity and the
significance of Christ's unmerited suffering. In the preaching of
the first disciples, as recorded in Acts and made clear in the
wording of the Revised Version, the title 'Servant' was applied
to Jesus in a way which inevitably suggests the Isaian source.[2]
When Philip presented the gospel to the Ethiopian eunuch, he
started with Isaiah's fifty-third chapter and "beginning from
this scripture, preached unto him Jesus."[3] In Peter's great
passage on Christian suffering, salient verses from the same
chapter are quoted,[4] and the Epistle to the Hebrews refers to
Christ's cross in terms of it.[5]

Some, indeed, are convinced that before the early church thus
began interpreting the sacrifice of Christ in Isaian terms, Jesus
himself, with his selective response to his religious heritage,
saw in the prophet's Suffering Servant the real meaning of
Messiahship and the directive principle of his own mission.
Certainly, according to the Gospels, Jesus had pondered the
writings of Isaiah. When he announced the purpose of his mission
in Nazareth's synagogue, he read from the prophet's sixty-first
chapter,[6] and when he answered the emissaries of John the

---

[1] *The Moral Life of the Hebrews*, p. 163.   [4] I Peter 2:22–25.
Cf. IV Maccabees 1:11; 9:29; 17:21–22.   [5] Hebrews 9:28.
[2] Acts 3:26; 4:27,30.   [6] Luke 4:16 ff.
[3] Acts 8:27–39.

Baptist he alluded to it.[1] The very word 'gospel'—good tidings—apparently came from the Great Isaiah.[2] Only one direct quotation from the fifty-third chapter is ascribed to Jesus—"I say unto you, that this which is written must be fulfilled in me, And he was reckoned with transgressors"[3]—but apparent intimations that Jesus had the Suffering Servant in the center of his thought are elsewhere discoverable. The ancient prophet had told his people that they should be "redeemed without money,"[4] that the "righteous servant" would "justify many" and that he "bare the sin of many";[5] Jesus said that he came "to give his life a ransom for many";[6] "The Son of man goeth," said Jesus at the Last Supper, "even as it is written of him."[7] Where else in the Old Testament, argue some, could he have found this conception of suffering saviorhood if not in the Great Isaiah? It may well be, therefore, that as Dr. James Moffatt puts it, "The suffering Servant conception was organic to the consciousness of Jesus, and that He often regarded His vocation in the light of this supremely suggestive prophecy."[8]

At any rate, a redemptive idea of suffering, which had begun as an individual intuition centuries before, became in the New Testament the organizing center of the gospel. Far from being simply punitive, educative, or inexplicably mysterious, suffering was understood in terms of saviorhood. So the Fourth Gospel reports Jesus as saying, "Except a grain of wheat fall into the earth and die, it abideth by itself alone; but if it die, it beareth much fruit."[9] Affliction, being thus redemptive, was in consequence itself redeemed; "Christ crucified," whom Paul rightly called a stumblingblock to Jews and foolishness to Gentiles, was proclaimed as the wisdom and power of God;[10] and, not stopping with any negative apologetic to explain the cross, the early Christians positively gloried in it[11] and made it their ambition to know "the fellowship of his sufferings."[12]

It would be difficult to exaggerate the difference in this regard between the Old and New Testaments, taken as wholes. The inveterate Jewish association of goodness with prosperity and of

---

[1] Matthew 11:2 ff.; cf. also Isaiah 35:5.
[2] Isaiah 40:9; 52:7.
[3] Luke 22:37; Isaiah 53:12.
[4] Isaiah 52:3.
[5] Isaiah 53:11,12.
[6] Mark 10:45.
[7] Mark 14:21.
[8] James Moffatt: *The Theology of the*

Gospels, p. 149. Cf. Ernest Findlay Scott: *The Kingdom and the Messiah*, chap. 8; Henry Wheeler Robinson: *The Cross of the Servant*, chap. 3.
[9] John 12:24.
[10] I Corinthians 1:23–24.
[11] Galatians 6:14.
[12] Philippians 3:10.

badness with adversity here broke down completely and the supreme sufferer became the highest revelation of God and the noblest ideal of man. No theory of the way in which vicarious sacrifice operates to redeem mankind was explicitly set forth; current forms of thought, such as those associated with animal sacrifices[1] or with inherited concepts of corporate personality,[2] were commonly in the Christian consciousness; but the power of self-sacrifice as an indispensable factor in saviorhood was none the less the orienting truth of early Christianity. The result was revolutionary. At the center of the first church's experience was a momentous tragedy—innocence outraged, wisdom overthrown by ignorance and bigotry, a supreme soul done to death by the hatred of little men and the ruthlessness of an inhuman government. Here were the factors which for ages had made men wish, as Job's wife advised, to curse God and die. Here was the kind of inequity that had made the Book of Ecclesiastes plausible and that seemed to justify the doubts of skeptics and the despair of pessimists. Instead, there issued from this tragedy a radiant and confident faith in God. Far from being cradled in fortunate circumstance, Christianity began in the kind of disastrous experience commonly supposed to make faith in God impossible—the worst triumphing over the best, the needed good dying young, goodwill ground under the heel of malevolence, and no equity anywhere—and, instead of faith meeting defeat, it achieved victory; the tragic cross proved to be so saving a force that it redeemed tragedy itself.

At the beginning of the Old Testament all suffering was regarded as punishment for previous sin, but in the New Testament we read, "What glory is it, if, when ye sin, and are buffeted for it, ye shall take it patiently? but if, when ye do well, and suffer for it, ye shall take it patiently, this is acceptable with God. For hereunto were ye called: because Christ also suffered for you, leaving you an example, that ye should follow his steps."[3]

Indeed, the possible uses of suffering were so far exalted and suffering itself was so clearly seen to be an integral part of the universe, not an alien intruder in it, that God himself was portrayed as the eternal Sufferer. Through the many differences that distinguish conflicting views of the divine nature in the Bible, one common strand of idea runs—God is in earnest, he cares, he is no metaphysical abstraction but a living being with

---

[1] E.g., Hebrews, chaps. 8–10.   [3] I Peter 2:20–21.
[2] E.g., "As in Adam all die," etc.

purposes, devotions, and affections. Hosea heard him say, "My heart is turned within me, my compassions are kindled together,"[1] and Isaiah says of him, "In all their affliction he was afflicted, and the angel of his presence saved them: in his love and in his pity he redeemed them; and he bare them, and carried them all the days of old."[2] In the New Testament this insight is fulfilled in a God "rich in mercy,"[3] who "so loved the world, that he gave his only begotten Son,"[4] and whose seeking, sacrificial compassion is incarnate in the suffering Christ. In this regard, thought had traveled a long way from the legend of the Garden of Eden, according to which trouble first entered the world as penalty. In the New Testament suffering is carried up into the heart of God himself; it is seen as no intruder in the universe, as though by some fortuity it had slipped in, or as an afterthought had been introduced as retribution. Suffering, sacrificially assumed for the sake of saving and serving others, has in the New Testament become an attribute of the divine nature itself. So ennobled, it is both a requisite and an evidence of the divine nature in man, no longer the mark of shame but the badge of honor. So Paul is proud to bear in his body "the marks of the Lord Jesus,"[5] and behind this personal glorying in self-sacrifice he has a cosmic outlook upon suffering as belonging to the very warp and woof of the universe—"The whole creation groaneth and travaileth in pain together until now."[6]

VII

Despite the importance of these five trends of New Testament thought with reference to suffering, it would be a mistake to regard them as covering the whole attitude of early Christians toward human affliction. Both Judaism and Christianity were, and if true to their heritage still are, aggressive faiths, not teaching resignation to life's evil but vigorous attack upon it. To picture the great Hebrew prophets as wrestling with the problem of evil as though it were mainly an affair of apologetics, demanding intellectual explanation, is to misrepresent the prophets altogether. Human affliction, especially the monstrous inhumanity of man to man, was to them a practical, rather than a theoretical, problem; it represented not only a conflict of ideas but a conflict of individual and class interests, a struggle for justice in personal

[1] Hosea 11:8.
[2] Isaiah 63:9.
[3] Ephesians 2:4.

[4] John 3:16.
[5] Galatians 6:17 (King James Version).
[6] Romans 8:22.

character or social organization against selfishness, ill will, and inequity. Ideas and tasks are always closely inter-related in any progressive development, but one may fairly say that the Hebrew prophets gave their conscious attention, not so much to the explication of the idea of suffering as to the task of eradicating the needless exhibitions of suffering caused by human cruelty. The problem of evil represented to them not merely something to be thought about but something to be done.

Of this prophetic tradition Jesus and his early disciples were the inheritors. They thought through one of the most radical revolutions in religious theory ever achieved in human history, but they never lost sight of the centrality of their task. They had come, as their enemies said, to turn "the world upside down,"[1] and they knew it. Their eyes were forward toward "a new heaven and a new earth."[2] While their minds worked upon the problem of suffering—exploring its retributive and disciplinary aspects, its saving power in the form of self-sacrifice, its future solutions in the eternal realm, and its inexplicable residue of mystery—their practical devotion was given to the kind of world where man's monstrous cruelty to man would end.

Where suffering is concerned, therefore, the New Testament is not only a thoughtful but a militant book. A great war is on, as the Christian scriptures see the case, between the hosts of good and evil. To be sure, the mythological paraphernalia of inter-Testamental Judaism, shaped probably by Zoroastrian influence, is often used in picturing this conflict. Satan and his devils are familiar personages in the New Testament and to their machinations is ascribed every manner of human affliction, great and small.[3] As in the Jewish Bible, however, they never are used as a means of solving the ultimate problem of evil in the cosmos; they remain an imaginative phrasing of the malevolent forces which convulse the world, and their existence is no more taken as an explanation of the problem's origin than is the existence of evil men. Whether in terms of demonic ill will or in less picturesque phrasings, evil in the New Testament is faced not mainly as a fact to be explained but as a force to be conquered. In this militant and aggressive task, early Christians conceived themselves as "God's fellow-workers,"[4] each striving to be "a good soldier of Christ Jesus."[5]

[1] Acts 17:6.
[2] Revelation 21:1.
[3] See the author's book, *The Modern Use of the Bible*, Lecture IV, sec. 3.

[4] I Corinthians 3:9.
[5] II Timothy 2:3.

Indeed, whereas at the Bible's beginning the practise of religion is in large measure a means of escaping trouble, at the Bible's end the practise of religion is a sure means of getting into trouble. The Master deliberately called his disciples to courses of action that involve suffering:

> Behold, I send you forth as sheep in the midst of wolves.[1]
>
> Blessed are ye when men shall reproach you, and persecute you, and say all manner of evil against you falsely, for my sake.[2]
>
> Then shall they deliver you up unto tribulation, and shall kill you: and ye shall be hated of all the nations for my name's sake.[3]
>
> They shall put you out of the synagogues: yea, the hour cometh, that whosoever killeth you shall think that he offereth service unto God.[4]
>
> If any man cometh unto me, and hateth not his own father, and mother, and wife, and children, and brethren, and sisters, yea, and his own life also, he cannot be my disciple.[5]
>
> Then said Jesus unto his disciples, If any man would come after me, let him deny himself, and take up his cross, and follow me.[6]

Discipleship to Jesus, therefore, while it saved men from lower orders of suffering, such as penalty for sin, called men to the higher order of self-sacrifice.

Modern knowledge has thrown special illumination on this area of thought. Suffering, far from being in itself a curse, is an essential, integral part of sentient living, the necessary concomitant of organic experience. As life evolved from mollusk toward man, each higher range involved increased capacity for pain. Always in the organic world it is the best who can suffer most, and man outranks the lower orders of existence, not simply in range of intelligence and creativity, but in depth, expanse, and poignancy of feeling and therefore of sensitivity. One major mark of rank in the organic world is the capacity to suffer.

Indeed, out of such sensitiveness has come man's greatness.

[1] Matthew 10:16.
[2] Matthew 5:11.
[3] Matthew 24:9.
[4] John 16:2.
[5] Luke 14:26.
[6] Matthew 16:24.

Much of man's thinking has been born out of his distress and bafflement in the presence of a painful problem. The aim of life, therefore, is not to abolish suffering, for that would be to abolish sensitivity, but to eliminate its cruel, barbarous, and useless forms, to elevate and sublimate its expressions and uses, to make it humane, stimulating, unselfish, and creative. Some suffering is needless, brutal, ruinous, but when Shelley speaks of

> a nerve o'er which do creep
> The else unfelt oppressions of this earth,[1]

he is recognizing the hall mark of creative character. So Jesus said, "Inasmuch as ye did it unto one of these my brethren, even these least, ye did it unto me."[2]

The New Testament, therefore, glories in an expansion of sensitiveness, in a keen and often suffering awareness of sins and brutalities which others take for granted, in a poignant sense of contrast between the actual and the possible, in a sacrificial assumption of vicarious toil and trouble. No story of the development of the idea of suffering in the Bible could rightly end except with this outlook on the regenerative task, both personal and social, in which all Biblical ideas culminate. The Jewish-Christian religion has always *involved* a philosophy but it has never *been* a philosophy. In its most essential nature and most continuous meaning, it was and is costly adventure for the kingdom of God.

---

[1] "Julian and Maddalo," lines 449–450.   [2] Matthew 25:40.

CHAPTER V

THE IDEA OF FELLOWSHIP WITH GOD

I

The meaning attributed to prayer is one of the most reliable tests of any religion, and developing quality in prayer is an inevitable accompaniment and indication of religious progress. Nowhere more clearly than in this realm do we find in the Bible the record of deepening spiritual life. Alike according to the New Testament and to the later Judaism, the individual soul had immediate access to God. Whether it was a psalmist praying on his bed at night[1] or Jesus going into his chamber and shutting the door,[2] communion with God was the privilege of sincerely seeking souls anywhere and at any time. Said an ancient rabbi: "It is as when a man utters his thought in the ear of his fellow, and he hears him. Can you have a God nearer than this who is as near to his creatures as mouth to ear?"[3]

For evident reasons, however, such praying was unthinkable in the early beginnings of Hebrew religion.

1. The primitive conceptions of Yahweh made him personally unapproachable. When first the tribes of Joseph met him at Sinai and he came down in "thunders and lightnings, and a thick cloud upon the mount," nothing remotely like the interior practise of the presence of God was suggested by the scene. Rather, "all the people that were in the camp trembled"[4] and, far from desiring intimate fellowship with their new deity, "they said unto Moses, Speak thou with us, and we will hear; but let not God speak with us, lest we die."[5] So long as such fearful awe was central in the people's attitude toward Yahweh, approach to him would be not direct but indirect; Moses and Aaron and their successors would address him on behalf of the tribe but, one by one, the

[1] Psalm 63:5-6.
[2] Cf. Matthew 6:6.
[3] As quoted by George Foot Moore: *Judaism in the First Centuries of the Christian Era*, Vol. I, p. 369.
[4] Exodus 19:16.
[5] Exodus 20:19.

tribesmen would have as little as possible to do with so dangerous a deity.

Moreover, quite apart from the fulminating fearfulness of Yahweh, as at first conceived, he was not, even in his most gracious aspects, so much the friend of individual souls as the leader and war lord of the tribal confederation. Dealing with him, therefore, was primarily a tribal matter. To be sure, individual needs were doubtless presented to any god the tribe believed in, but the characteristic approach to Yahweh on the part of the common people was at first public, and it could become private, involving so intimate a thing as inward communion, only when, long afterwards, the individual had escaped submergence in the social group and had become in his own right a recognized object of divine care. This idea, however, is only vaguely discernible before Jeremiah, and its effective popular influence on the meaning and practise of prayer was long postponed.

2. Another negative factor, making the later conceptions of prayer at first unthinkable, was the localization of Yahweh's worship. The animistic habit of ascribing to a god a local dwelling-place and of going to the sacred spot if one wished to deal with the god persisted in manifold forms long after animism itself had been left behind. The early strata of the Old Testament are full of intimations that, far from being spiritually available to the seeking soul at any place or time, Yahweh was to be sought only at his special shrines—"In every place where I cause my name to be remembered I will come unto thee."[1] The Old Testament as a whole represents an era from which the cruder practises of animism had been elided, but all the more impressive are the obvious remnants of the original primitivism, such as holy trees. It was under the sacred terebinth at Moreh[2] and at the terebinths of Mamre[3] that Yahweh appeared to Abraham. Gideon was called to his mission by an angel of Yahweh "under the terebinth which was in Ophrah,"[4] and at Shechem there was a sacred tree to which references are made from the legends of the patriarchs[5] to the story of Joshua's final charge to his people.[6] One who has seen, all the way from Korea to Arabia, the persistent continuance of such cult practises as these references indicate cannot mistake the meaning of the tamarisk of Beer-sheba,[7] the burning bush

---

[1] Exodus 20:24 (marginal translation).
[2] Genesis 12:6-7.
[3] Genesis 18:1 ff.
[4] Judges 6:11.

[5] Genesis 35:2-4.
[6] Joshua 24:25-29.
[7] Genesis 21:33.

of Sinai,[1] the palm-tree of Deborah,[2] or the tamarisk-tree in Jabesh.[3] Indeed, as late as the eighth century Hosea denounced the popular religion of his day for its worship "under oaks and poplars and terebinths."[4] Similarly there were sacred springs[5] and sacred caves,[6] and, in general, shrines so numerous that, when the prophetic demand for the centralization of worship in Jerusalem arose, Jeremiah described his people as playing the harlot "upon every high mountain and under every green tree."[7]

Such sacred places, taken over from the Canaanites, and transformed by a process of syncretism into shrines of Yahweh, were assumed without complaint in the earliest traditions of Israel. Stories grew up around the local holy places, as at Bethel, where a typical legend records the way in which the patriarch Jacob discovered Bethel to be the "house of God."[8] Even when the cruder forms of animism and fetishism had been outgrown, this persistent localization of Yahweh's available presence long continued, not altogether surrendering its hold on the worship and popular imagination of Judaism until after the destruction of the temple in 70 A.D. From Hannah offering mental prayer without audible words before the Ark of Yahweh in Shiloh[9] to Daniel in exile, praying thrice daily with his windows open toward Jerusalem,[10] many doubtless used the inherited idea of a local shrine as a trellis upon which grew a devout spiritual fellowship with God and a vivid sense of his reality. The Old Testament, however, as we shall see, clearly reveals the inner perplexity and the outward conflict involved as religious thought and practise moved from primitive shrines toward the idea of Jesus: "Neither in this mountain, nor in Jerusalem, shall ye worship the Father. . . . God is a Spirit."[11]

3. A further negative influence, inhibiting the approach to God in private prayer, sprang from the external nature of the methods traditionally used for securing superhuman guidance and support. In the primitive religion from which, as from a dim hinterland, the Hebrew faith emerged, approaching any god to learn his will and get his backing involved not so much the fulfilment of inward spiritual conditions as the successful working of a magical technique. According to repeated indications in the Old

---

[1] Exodus 3:2–5; Deuteronomy 33:16.
[2] Judges 4:5
[3] I Samuel 31:13.
[4] Hosea 4:13.
[5] E.g., Genesis 16:7.
[6] E.g., I Kings 19:9.

[7] Jeremiah 3:6; cf. Deuteronomy 12:2; Isaiah 57:5; I Kings 14:22–23.
[8] Genesis 28:10–22.
[9] I Samuel 1:9–13.
[10] Daniel 6:10.
[11] John 4:21,24.

Testament, for example, casting lots, Urim and Thummim, before a sacred image, the ephod, was a recognized method of securing Yahweh's judgment between two alternatives and so learning his will. David, we read, wishing divine guidance in his military strategy, "said to Abiathar the priest, . . . I pray thee, bring me hither the ephod. And Abiathar brought thither the ephod to David. And David inquired of Yahweh, saying, If I pursue after this troop, shall I overtake them? And he [Yahweh] answered him, Pursue."[1] It is clear here, as elsewhere, that the ephod was a piece of religious apparatus for ascertaining the divine will. That the ephod was a metal image which could be idolatrously used is evident from Gideon's manufacture of one out of the jewelry of the Ishmaelites, after which, said a later writer, "all Israel played the harlot."[2] Far from being reprehensible at first, however, an ephod was an indispensable instrument of a priest's technique, as when, for example, Abiathar "came down with an ephod in his hand,"[3] by which David "inquired of Yahweh."

Moreover, the method of such inquiry seems from the record clear. Casting lots was a familiar way of thrusting a decision back on God, as even the late Book of Proverbs shows—

> The lot is cast into the lap;
> But the whole disposing thereof is of Yahweh.[4]

When, for example, the taboo of total abstinence from food, which Saul had announced in the midst of the battle, had been broken and Yahweh had withdrawn his guidance, lots were cast to locate the guilt. "Then said he [Saul] unto all Israel, Be ye on one side, and I and Jonathan my son will be on the other side. And the people said unto Saul, Do what seemeth good unto thee. Therefore Saul said unto Yahweh, the God of Israel, Show the right. And Jonathan and Saul were taken by lot; but the people escaped. And Saul said, Cast lots between me and Jonathan my son. And Jonathan was taken."[5]

In this passage, as in others, the Greek Septuagint Translation of the Old Testament, begun in Alexandria around 285 B.C., apparently goes back to an earlier Hebrew manuscript than our English Versions represent. According to the Septuagint, Saul asked Yahweh to give Urim if he or Jonathan was guilty, and to give Thummim if the guilt lay with the people. That is, Urim

[1] I Samuel 30:7-8.
[2] Judges 8:24-27.
[3] I Samuel 23:6-12.
[4] Proverbs 16:33.
[5] I Samuel 14:38-42.

and Thummim were the holy lots or dice by casting which before a sacred ephod the will of Yahweh could be ascertained. So, when Saul had forfeited Yahweh's favor, "Yahweh answered him not, neither by dreams, nor by Urim, nor by prophets,"[1] and this method of learning Yahweh's will is reflected in Moses' command to inquire "by the judgment of the Urim before Yahweh."[2] When one endeavors, therefore, to reconstruct in imagination the religious life and practise of the early Hebrews, one must visualize them as presenting to their deity questions capable of a *yes* or *no* reply and then as casting lots with a cry like Saul's, "Show the right," and as accepting the arbitrament of the dice as the revealed will of the Lord.

Later the ephod, together with the Urim and Thummim, was sublimated and rationalized, becoming part of the priest's symbolical dress and no longer functioning as at first.[3] Even after the Exile, however, the ancient emblems possessed almost, if not quite, magical significance,[4] and the Hebrew word for the Law, the revealed will of God, *Torah*, very probably goes back to the Hebrew word for casting lots, *yarah*.[5]

Important as this primitive method of dealing with Yahweh was, it did not stand alone. Dreams, for example, were given a high place as media of divine revelation;[6] omens were trusted, such as the first word to be uttered at an expected meeting,[7] or a chance action regarded as a sign,[8] or wind in the mulberry-trees taken as Yahweh's command to join battle;[9] and, in general, dealing with the superhuman world suggested nothing so simple and spiritual as private communion in prayer, but rather a whole array of magical techniques and, from the modern point of view, incredible superstitions.

4. Interpenetrating the negative factors already mentioned was the practise of animal sacrifice as the characteristic way of approaching God. After the final destruction of the temple in Jerusalem, Jewish rabbis began teaching prayer as a substitute for the old offerings. So Rabbi Abahu said: "What shall replace the bullocks we formerly offered to Thee? 'Our lips,' in the prayer we pray to Thee. So long as the temple stood we used to

[1] I Samuel 28:6.
[2] Numbers 27:21.
[3] Exodus 28:6–35.
[4] Nehemiah 7:65; Ezra 2:63.
[5] Adolphe Lods: *Israel from its Beginnings to the Middle of the Eighth Century*, translated by S. H. Hooke, p. 297.

[6] Genesis 20:3; 26:24–25; 28:10–16; 31:24; 37:5; 41:1; 46:1–4; Judges 7:13–15; I Kings 3:5–15; etc.
[7] I Samuel 14:8–15.
[8] Genesis 24:12–14.
[9] II Samuel 5:22–24.

offer a sacrifice and thus atonement was made; but now we have nothing to bring but prayer."[1] Such a statement correctly represents two significant historical matters: first, personal prayer had been developing within the framework of the sacrificial system—

> Let my prayer be set forth as incense before thee;
> The lifting up of my hands as the evening sacrifice;[2]

and second, the approach to God by way of animal offerings had been so central in Judaism that, while the sacrifices were always accompanied by supplications, they had competed with personal prayer, had furnished for many people a public substitute for it, so that when the bloody altars were gone a devout rabbi could mingle his exaltation of private communion with the lament, "We have nothing to bring but prayer."

Animal sacrifice among the Hebrews was, of course, rooted far down in the primitive customs out of which their later faith emerged. The Old Testament contains clear evidence that in the earlier days not only animal but human sacrifice as well had been the common practise: "Yahweh spake unto Moses, saying, Sanctify unto me all the first-born, whatsoever openeth the womb among the children of Israel, both of man and of beast: it is mine."[3] That the actual slaying of first-born children was here intended is made evident in the fifteenth verse of the same chapter. There a special codicil is added, "but all the first-born of my sons I redeem," which doubtless represents one of the most important developments in ancient religion, the allowance of an animal substitute for a first-born human child. As though to leave no possibility of doubting the terrible meaning of this ancient law, it is reproduced in another passage—first, the original, absolute requirement, "All that openeth the womb is mine," and, appended, the merciful codicil, "All the first-born of thy sons thou shalt redeem."[4] In one place, however, the original demand for the sacrifice of first-born sons, as of first-born beasts, stands not only unmistakable in meaning but unrelieved by any exception: "The first-born of thy sons shalt thou give unto me. Likewise shalt thou do with thine oxen, and with thy sheep."[5]

---

[1] As quoted by George Foot Moore: *Judaism in the First Centuries of the Christian Era*, Vol. II, p. 218.
[2] Psalm 141:2.
[3] Exodus 13:1–2.
[4] Exodus 34:19,20; cf. Numbers 18:15.
[5] Exodus 22:29–30.

The archeological evidence in Palestine reveals with pitiful adequacy the common sacrifice of little children as offerings to the gods. That the worship of Yahweh was at times associated with this ancient abomination is clear from the indignant protests of the prophets. Not only are specific instances recorded—the children of Jephthah, Ahaz, and Manasseh,[1] for example—but as late as the eighth century the prophet Micah pictured a devotee appeasing Yahweh by offering up his son,[2] and in the seventh century Jeremiah vehemently denied that commands to slay the first-born had been given by Yahweh.[3] In the next generation Ezekiel tried another apologetic: granting both that the command to sacrifice children was in the Law, as it obviously was, and that Yahweh was responsible for its presence there, he asserted none the less that Yahweh had given "statutes that were not good, and ordinances wherein they should not live," for the ultimate purpose of punishing them with such desolation that they might recognize the divine hand in their tragedy.[4]

In the end, animal sacrifice was altogether substituted for human sacrifice, and this provision, represented as a merciful evidence of Yahweh's grace, was made picturesque in the legendary story of Abraham and Isaac.[5] "Take now thy son, thine only son, whom thou lovest, even Isaac, and get thee into the land of Moriah; and offer him there for a burnt-offering"— such is the command, representative of ages of primitive custom, which Yahweh lays on Abraham. A more moving portrayal of the meaning of child sacrifice to a good father could hardly have been written than this story furnishes; the profound loyalty involved in child sacrifice, holding nothing back that religious obligation might require, is recognized; and the story's obvious objective is reached when "Abraham lifted up his eyes, and looked, and, behold, behind him a ram caught in the thicket by his horns: and Abraham went and took the ram, and offered him up for a burnt-offering in the stead of his son."

Animal sacrifice, therefore, deeply rooted in traditional custom and congenial with contemporaneous Semitism, was the central act of Hebrew worship. No one idea of the meaning of such sacrifice can adequately cover the varied factors that entered into its significance. It was a gift to God, and the word commonly used to represent it, *minhah*, is used also of a present offered to

---

[1] Judges 11:30–39; II Kings 16:3; 21:6.
[2] Micah 6:1–8.
[3] Jeremiah 7:31; 19:5; 32:35.
[4] Ezekiel 20:23–26.
[5] Genesis 22:1–18.

a man or of tribute paid to a king. Such a gift might spring from varied motives—gratitude, homage, or the desire to curry favor—but obviously in the background of the practise of animal sacrifice was the idea that God liked this form of gift and profited by it. The fat and blood of the sacrifice were the "bread of God,"[1] and, however symbolical this idea became in later Judaism, its origin was as plainly literal as were identical ideas concerning pagan deities,

> Which did eat the fat of their sacrifices,
> And drank the wine of their drink-offering.[2]

Blended with such primitive conceptions was the idea of the sacred bond created between man and man and between man and deity, whether by sharing in a common feast or by having the blood of the sacrifice applied both to the sacred altar and to the persons of the devotees.[3] And always in the hinterland of animal sacrifice lurked age-old ideas of the magical potency of blood as a powerful agency of deliverance if rightly used[4] and a supernatural peril if wrongly handled.[5]

So long as animal sacrifice, interpreted in such terms, was the major method of approaching deity, it is clear that worshipers could not conceive an approach so simple and spiritual as solitary praying to the "Father who seeth in secret."

II

The fact that private prayer was not typical of the early life of Israel is disguised in the Hebrew stories of the patriarchs by their free and easy conversations with their god. Just as the Homeric heroes are on intimate speaking terms with the deities of Greece, so in the patriarchal narratives the ancient worthies of Israel dealt with Yahweh. Abraham, in particular, is represented as entertaining Yahweh at dinner and extensively conversing with him as a familiar friend.[6] That such stories represent the exceptional experience of the heroic figures only would be evident even if they were taken at their face value, whereas their actual worth lies in their revelation of later ideas and ideals, pre-Exilic to be sure, read back into early times.

The true state of the case is made plain when we trace the

[1] Leviticus 21:6,8,17,21; 22:25; Ezekiel 44:7; Numbers 28:2,24.
[2] Deuteronomy 32:38.
[3] Exodus 24:4-8.
[4] E.g., Exodus 12:12-13.
[5] E.g., I Samuel 14:32-35.
[6] Genesis, chap. 18; cf. 12:1 ff.; 13:14-18; 22:1 ff.

strange and fascinating change of meaning that took place in the word 'holy' as in successive ages it was applied to things divine. Beyond the power of anachronisms to conceal, this word moves through the Bible correctly representing in its altering significance the progress of the Hebrew-Christian idea of God and of the basic conditions of approaching him.

In its primitive meaning holiness was associated with the range of ideas and practises covered by our word 'taboo.' That is to say, anything holy was dangerous to meddle with, and, far from having ethical connotation, holiness meant unapproachableness. Repeatedly in the early records, for example, the adjective 'holy' is applied to the Ark, and the significance of the attribute was revealed when Uzzah, inadvertently touching the sacred fetish, fell dead in consequence,[1] or when the men of Beth-shemesh, looking into it, suffered such devastating penalty that they sent it from their borders, saying, "Who is able to stand before Yahweh, this holy God?"[2] Whatever was holy was thus full of a mysterious and perilous potency with which the prudent would have as little as possible to do.

The fact that Sinai was the "holy mountain" accounted for the elaborate precautions taken that the people should not touch it.[3] Repeatedly in the early laws the command to observe some negative taboo was reënforced by the penalties of violated holiness—"Ye shall be holy men unto me: therefore ye shall not eat any flesh that is torn of beasts in the field."[4] To say that the Sabbath is sacred is to say that it is inviolable—"Ye shall keep the sabbath therefore; for it is holy unto you: every one that profaneth it shall surely be put to death."[5] If bread is consecrated, it may be eaten only by the priests at the appointed time; otherwise "it shall not be eaten, because it is holy."[6] As H. Wheeler Robinson puts it, "Sacred objects can be touched only under the strictest precautions; they are as dangerous to the uninitiated as the switchboard of an electrical power-house might be to a child."[7]

Early stories such as the encounter with Yahweh at the burning bush, where Moses was warned to put off his shoes because the spot was "holy ground,"[8] reveal the way in which this dread of holy things and places and this need of insulations against their

---

[1] II Samuel 6:6-9.
[2] I Samuel 6:19-21.
[3] Exodus 19:12-14.
[4] Exodus 22:31.
[5] Exodus 31:14.

[6] Exodus 29:34.
[7] *The Religious Ideas of the Old Testament*, p. 131.
[8] Exodus 3:5; cf. Joshua 5:15.

dangerous potency issued in sacred rites and customs. Wherever the attribute of holiness was present, there some one or something was hedged about with sanctity, so that contact was dangerous unless meticulous care was taken to fulfil the prescribed conditions of approach. Out of this soil grew the luxuriant crop of ceremonial laws and customs which characterized the primitive religion of the Hebrews, as of all early peoples. Taboos on eating fat and blood,[1] rules concerning clean and unclean foods, detailed directions concerning the dress of the officiating priests, insistence on ceremonial exactness in sacrifice—these and similar legalisms have as part of their background and explanation the sense of sanctity and inviolability in things divine, demanding punctilious care to make human relationships with them safe and profitable. And because the priests were considered the expert initiates who alone knew the ways of the god and therefore monopolized fitness to approach him, their developing power among the Hebrews, as among all early peoples, became immense. Far from being synonymous with goodness or righteousness, therefore, 'holiness,' at the first, suggested the aloofness and inviolability of the god. Even when later connotations began to appear, the earlier ones persisted, as Joshua's words reveal: "Ye cannot serve Yahweh; for he is a holy God; he is a jealous God."[2] One does not go into one's room and shut the door to commune in secret with such a diety.

As the centuries passed, however, 'holiness' changed its meaning, and in the change can be seen the increasing possibility of private prayer. One of the ascending roads traveled by the idea carried it away from its old associations with perilous potencies in things divine into new associations with majesty, grandeur, and transcendence as attributes of God. Still the flavor of the ancient idea was recognizable when Isaiah saw the Most High seated on his throne, with the seraphim chanting above him, "Holy, holy, holy, is Yahweh of hosts."[3] Such a God was not lightly to be approached; an inviolability not to be profaned lay deep in Isaiah's thought of the Eternal; but reverence had taken the place of dread as the corollary of holiness, majesty had displaced the former dangerousness of the deity, and the response demanded from man by the holiness of the Most High had become thoroughly ethical.

Up this road Jewish thought traveled as monotheism became

[1] Leviticus 3:17.   [3] Isaiah 6:1–3.
[2] Joshua 24:19.

increasingly the faith of the people. Not unapproachableness in the old sense but greatness in power and righteousness in character came to be recognized as the qualities of God—

> Thy way, O God, is in holiness:
> Who is a great god like unto God?[1]

Of this changed meaning the "Holiness Code" in Leviticus[2] is representative. An Exilic codification of moral, ritual, and ecclesiastical usages for Jews in general and for the new temple at Jerusalem in particular, it labored with exacting care to secure ceremonial purity. There is no mistaking the flavor of the old word 'holy' in the writer's insistence on correctness of ritual in approaching Yahweh. The basis of all the rules and regulations is repeatedly stated: "I Yahweh your God am holy."[3] Along with moral commands against such evils as child sacrifice, adultery, and sexual perversion are detailed injunctions concerning ceremonial observances, reminiscent of the old taboos. But to the writer God is no longer an anthropomorphic deity in the old sense; he is the one God, omnipotent and altogether righteous, transcendent in majesty and in rightful claim on man's devotion; and his holiness is expressed in his exclusive right to Israel's worship and service.

Behind this "Holiness Code" one feels the conflict of the exiles in Babylon, refusing to surrender their religious peculiarities to a contaminating heathenism, and marking off with new sharpness the distinguishing features of their faith. There is for them only one God—he is holy, his land is holy, his nation is to be a holy people—and while the indiscriminate mixture of moral and ceremonial elements carries over old ideas even while it ventures into new ones, there is an evident elevation of the idea of holiness into terms of the divine majesty, and of the Most High's exclusive claim on man's devotion.

More important, however, for future religious development than this translation of holiness from primitive untouchableness into majestic greatness and exclusive sovereignty was the baptism of the idea into moral meanings. This was one of the major achievements of the prophets. They took a word, with its accompanying ideas, which at first had possessed no ethical significance at all, and they made it one of the great words in the moral vocabulary of the race. Isaiah of Jerusalem is notable for the way

---

[1] Psalm 77:13 (marginal translation).   [3] Leviticus 19:2; cf. 20:26; 21:8.
[2] Leviticus, chaps. 17–26.

in which, far ahead of his time, he translated the idea of holiness into ethical meanings. Again and again he returned to this matter as though deliberately trying to take a word whose cogency every one acknowledged and make it connote a range of meaning it had never suggested before. "Ah sinful nation," he cried, "a people laden with iniquity, a seed of evil-doers, children that deal corruptly! they have forsaken Yahweh, they have despised the Holy One of Israel,"[1] and then he uttered one of the most solemn and moving denunciations of moral wrong and one of the most momentous pleas for social justice in ancient literature. As though it were the nub of his message, he said, "Yahweh of hosts is exalted in justice, and God the Holy One is sanctified in righteousness."[2] Then, in contrast with this view, having described the loose and cynical ways in which popular thought referred to "the Holy One of Israel,"[3] he went on to announce with vehement earnestness the real meanings of holiness in terms of personal morals and social righteousness. Isaiah is thus one of the supreme examples in history of a religious teacher who, instead of discarding an ancient word, encrusted with inadequate and mistaken meanings, chose to reinterpret it. From the day when in the temple he saw the vision of the thrice-holy God and inwardly made the response of moral repentance and devotion, he saw holiness in terms of goodness.

What Isaiah of Jerusalem did so well, Isaiah of the Exile carried further—"For thus saith the high and lofty One that inhabiteth eternity, whose name is Holy: I dwell in the high and holy place, with him also that is of a contrite and humble spirit, to revive the spirit of the humble, and to revive the heart of the contrite."[4] Here we find both the exaltation of the meaning of holiness into terms of transcendent greatness and, as well, the deepening of its meaning into terms of goodness and mercy. Primitive ideas of dreadful unapproachableness in deity had been left behind; the concept of divine sanctity had been sublimated into terms of transcendent purity; and instead of 'holiness' meaning aloofness, it could itself characterize a humble and contrite heart. The changing meanings of holiness in the Bible are thus among the most indicative signs of progress, and obviously by the time the Isaiah of the Exile wrote, some men were praying in secret to the holy God.

So far as popular acceptance was concerned, however, this

[1] Isaiah 1:4.
[2] Isaiah 5:16.
[3] Isaiah 5:18-19.
[4] Isaiah 57:15.

reinterpretation of the idea of holiness was halting and unsure. Commonly the old connotations clung to the concept of the holy, whether in gross or attenuated forms. It outgrew the crude ideas of Yahweh's terribleness but it still retained the idea of his exclusiveness—a jealous god, with a special land and a chosen people. Holiness still meant separateness—sanctity in nation and in temple hedged about with ceremonial precautions. The old ideas of taboo were there, although sublimated and refined. "In general," says Dr. John Peters, "throughout the later literature the exclusive idea rather than the ethical idea is prominent."[1] Indeed, to the very last, the old associations of the word were retained in the architecture of the temple. There increasing holiness was denoted by increasing remoteness from the common man, until, farthest away of all, absolutely inviolable to the ordinary worshiper, the acme of sanctity and separateness, stood the Holy of Holies, into which even the high priest went only once a year.

All the more surprising, therefore, is the ultimate association of the word with the most intimate and inward experience known to the Bible—"the communion of the Holy Spirit."[2] No other word, used throughout the Book, so reversed in the end the most characteristic meanings with which it started as did the word 'holy.' At the beginning, Yahweh on Sinai protected his terrible sanctity from the approach of common men: "Yahweh said unto Moses, Go down, charge the people, lest they break through unto Yahweh to gaze, and many of them perish. And let the priests also, that come near to Yahweh, sanctify themselves, lest Yahweh break forth upon them."[3] In the end, God dwelt not on a smoking mountain nor in temples made with hands, but through his Spirit in the inner man, and this Spirit, his renewing and sustaining presence within the soul, was designated by the adjective 'holy,' which once had stood for aloofness and unapproachableness. This complete alteration of meaning in a word continuously employed throughout the Book is one of the most notable evidences of the development that the Book records.

In only two Old Testament passages does the phrase 'holy Spirit' occur: once, in a late psalm where a devout soul prays,

Cast me not away from thy presence;
And take not thy holy Spirit from me;[4]

[1] *The Religion of the Hebrews*, p. 304.   [3] Exodus 19:21–22.
[2] II Corinthians 13:14.   [4] Psalm 51:11.

and once in an Isaian confession of sin, where God is described
as "he that put his holy Spirit in the midst of them."[1] What thus
barely began in the Old Testament, however, became one of the
early church's most characteristic modes of thought and expression. In God, the Creator-Father, and in Christ, the revelation
of the divine character, the first Christians fervently believed,
but all this became inward and empowering only when the Spirit
entered and possessed them. According to the New Testament,
this experience of the indwelling presence of God is the essential
source of the Christian's power[2] and of his peace and joy;[3] it is
the best gift which the Father can bestow on his children;[4] it
is the secret alike of moral renewal[5] and of practical guidance;[6]
it furnishes the interior standards of motive and behavior which
must not be violated;[7] whatever else in Christian faith is valuable,
even though it be the love of God, becomes effective only when
this experience makes it inwardly real;[8] and the temple is easily
dispensable since to every Christian it can be said, "Know ye
not that your body is a temple of the Holy Spirit which is in
you?"[9] Moreover, in all these passages, as in many more, this
most inward dealing of God with man, this climax of divine-
human intimacy, is described as the work of "the *Holy* Spirit
which dwelleth in us."[10] How long a journey this use of the adjective reveals, since the tribesmen of Israel trembled before the
holy mount!

That the meaning of prayer must inevitably have changed in
the course of this development is obvious. At Sinai it meant the
approach to Yahweh of a single representative, who spoke for
all the people; in late Judaism and early Christianity it meant
the immediate access of soul to Oversoul, spiritually conditioned
and inwardly achieved, each man for himself "praying in the
Holy Spirit."[11] One does not mean by this that other elements of
the original tradition are not present in the New Testament's
thought of holiness. A certain awe is implied in the word's use,
a sense of inviolable sanctity,[12] but always the implications are
ethical. "Holiness and sincerity,"[13] "righteousness and holiness,"[14]
"holy and without blemish before him in love"[15]—such are the

[1] Isaiah 63:10–11.
[2] Acts 1:8.
[3] Romans 14:17.
[4] Luke 11:13; John 14:26.
[5] Titus 3:5.
[6] Acts 13:2.
[7] Ephesians 4:30.
[8] Romans 5:5.
[9] I Corinthians 6:19.
[10] II Timothy 1:14.
[11] Jude, vs. 20.
[12] E.g., Hebrews 8:2 (marginal translation); II Corinthians 7:1.
[13] II Corinthians 1:12.
[14] Ephesians 4:24.
[15] Ephesians 1:4.

associations of the word. To be holy means to have "a heart of compassion, kindness, lowliness, meekness, longsuffering; forbearing one another, and forgiving each other."[1] And when Peter, in his First Epistle, harked back to the old code in Leviticus, he lifted its meaning out of ceremonial exclusiveness into universal morality: "Like as he who called you is holy, be ye yourselves also holy in all manner of living; because it is written, Ye shall be holy; for I am holy."[2]

This development from the unapproachableness to the immediate accessibility of God, and from magical and ceremonial conditions of divine fellowship to the moral fitness of a sincere soul, represents one of the most permanently valuable contributions of Hebrew-Christian religion. The author of the Epistle to the Hebrews was historically correct when at this point he set the new dispensation in contrast with the old:

> For ye are not come unto a mount that might be touched, and that burned with fire, and unto blackness, and darkness, and tempest, and the sound of a trumpet, and the voice of words; which voice they that heard entreated that no word more should be spoken unto them; for they could not endure that which was enjoined, If even a beast touch the mountain, it shall be stoned; and so fearful was the appearance, that Moses said, I exceedingly fear and quake: but ye are come unto mount Zion, and unto the city of the living God.[3]

III

The Old Testament indicates two main highways up which the idea and the practise of fellowship with God moved into more spiritual meanings, and, strangely enough, one of them ran not around but through the vast sacrificial system with its bloody altars and ritual observances. Indeed, the modern mind misjudges the ancient situation when it centers attention on the prophets as the creators of the dominant attributes of Judaism. They were the most notable series of ethical teachers in the ancient world and the fountainhead of the noblest moral qualities in the Hebrew faith, but the great prophetic writers were comprehended within four centuries, and not only the legal but the sacrificial system preceded, underlay, and outlived them all. Had not the sacrificial

[1] Colossians 3:12–13.
[2] I Peter 1:15–16; cf. I Thessalonians 3:13; Hebrews 12:9–11; Romans 12:1; Ephesians 5:27; etc.
[3] Hebrews 12:18–22.

system itself, therefore, been adaptable to spiritual uses, so that devout souls could find in it ever deepening meanings, the religion of Israel would never have reached the heights that it attained. However one may prefer prophet to priest, two facts about priestly rites may not be forgotten if religious history is to be understood—first, forms of ritual stubbornly persist while the interpretations of them fluidly change; and second, so varied may these interpretations be that the most illiterate peasant and the most erudite philosopher can devoutly observe the same ceremonial, each seeing in it what each brings eyes to see. This is true in Christianity today and, even with regard to animal sacrifices, it was true in ancient Israel.

Originally, as in all nomadic societies, the priestly offices were functions of the tribal chief. The father of the family or the patriarch of the clan slew the animal and poured or rubbed its blood upon the sacred stone or altar as the portion of the god.[1] There was no order of hereditary priests, and the sacrifices, long after the settlement in Canaan, were apparently few in kind and simple in observance—principally the peace-offering, where the fat and blood were given to Yahweh and the people feasted on the flesh, and the burnt-offering, where the whole animal was burned upon the altar. With increasing complexity in Israel's social life, however, came corresponding developments in ritual and priesthood, especially after royal families began copying, in temple architecture, modes of worship, and priestly prerogatives, the models of Phœnicia. The priesthood became hereditary, a separate, professional class, and the sacrifices so increased in number and in the complexity of their attendant rites that one scholar points to the change as "perhaps the most striking and convincing proof of development the Old Testament affords."[2]

Two new kinds of sacrifice of major importance were added after the Exile—the trespass-offering, a sacrifice of restitution either for wrong done to man or as tribute due to Yahweh, and the sin-offering, an expiation for the unwitting guilt of the people. Together with the peace-offering and the burnt-offering, inherited from earlier times, these constituted the four main types of sacrifice in the second temple, and around them grew up a vast and complicated network of punctilious observance.[3] In these

[1] Cf. I Samuel 14:33-35.
[2] H. Wheeler Robinson: *The Religious Ideas of the Old Testament*, p. 144; cf. John Punnett Peters: *The Religion of the Hebrews*, chaps. 7-8.
[3] See George Foot Moore: "Sacrifice," in *Encyclopædia Biblica*, edited by T. K. Cheyne and J. Sutherland Black.

offerings of slain beasts, whatever form they took, the mysterious efficacy of the blood was assumed. The ancient taboo continued to the end—the blood must not be eaten.[1] Sometimes it was sprinkled on the altar;[2] sometimes it was poured out at the altar's foot;[3] in either case it was given to God, for whom the altar stood. With such primitive, animistic ideas the sacrificial system of Israel was thoroughly impregnated, so that, if one is to understand the problem of an intelligent and ethically-minded Jew in the post-Exilic era, one must imagine him, with animistic ideas no longer in his head, bound by the ties of inheritance, tradition, and sacred custom to the animistic practise of animal sacrifice. As always in similar situations, the first solution was not the abolition of the sacred custom but its reinterpretation.

In general, the method of this reinterpretation seems plain. The sacrifices stood in the Law as the command of Yahweh, ordained by his grace as a means of approach to his favor. The more definitely the written law became established as canonical and regarded as infallibly inspired, the more surely could the explanation of the sacrifices be transferred from the realm of animistic superstition, where they really started, to the realm of sacred observance ordained by God and for that reason faithfully to be maintained. They could be entered into, then, with no knowledge of or sympathy with the original ideas associated with them. They could be seen as God's provision for the confession and pardon of sins and the reëstablishment of personal and national relationships with the Most High. If to sophisticated thought the irrationality of bloody altars as a means of divine placation and fellowship became troublesome, the use of symbolism could come to the aid of the devout worshiper, as it has done in every other developing religion, Christianity not least of all. So meanings could be read into the sacrifices that were not seen there at first, and what the spiritual vision of the devotee saw to be true about God and man and duty he could find pictured in the liturgies of the temple.

Obviously, even animal sacrifice, shocking to modern sensibilities but universal in the ancient world, was susceptible of such symbolical interpretation. While some, therefore, among the great prophets turned away from it as too misleading to be useful, others, like Ezekiel, clung to it and, by giving it sublimated meanings, made it a servant of their spiritual lives. Circumcision

[1] Leviticus 7:27.
[2] Leviticus 1:5.
[3] Leviticus 4:7.

also originated in primitive, animistic ideas, but as early as the seventh century it was given an ethical significance: "Yahweh thy God will circumcise thy heart, and the heart of thy seed, to love Yahweh thy God with all thy heart, and with all thy soul."[1] Similarly, one of the most radiant of the psalms,[2] written *con amore* by a soul whose trust in God was intimate and sustaining, reveals a spiritual experience, which, far from being troubled by the temple and its smoking altars, found there delight and sustentation:

> One thing have I asked of Yahweh, that will I seek after:
> That I may dwell in the house of Yahweh all the days of my life,
> To behold the beauty of Yahweh,
> And to inquire in his temple.

In consequence, it is not alone to the prophetic tradition, with its distaste for priestcraft and animal offering, that we must look in the Old Testament to find personal prayer. Intimate, interior, spiritual communion with God flourished in association with the temple ritual; it found there encouragement and inspiration; it even used the sacrificial system as a trellis to grow upon. Today, though a Christian be as thoroughgoing as the Quakers in discarding ritual, he must none the less appreciate the often superior quality of inward spiritual life and outward social service on the part of those who in the sacrifice of the Mass see Christ verily present. So the true saints of Judaism were doubtless often to be found not with the prophets, who scorned the temple ceremonies, but with the devotees whose hearts were lifted up with the evening sacrifice.

The Books of Ezra and Nehemiah, for example, represent the passionate devotion of the post-Exilic community, rebuilding the holy city and temple and restoring the sacrifices. From the inception of the enterprise in the decree of Darius, "Concerning the house of God at Jerusalem, let the house be builded, the place where they offer sacrifices,"[3] to the festal celebration of ultimate success—"They offered great sacrifices that day, and rejoiced"[4]—the religious life of the restorers of Zion centered in the altar. Writes Professor George Foot Moore:

> There is no doubt that the Israelites in all ages firmly believed in the efficaciousness of sacrifice to preserve and restore the favour of Yahwè. In times of prosperity

---

[1] Deuteronomy 30:6; cf. 10:16.
[2] Psalm 27.
[3] Ezra 6:3.
[4] Nehemiah 12:43.

they acknowledged his goodness and besought its continuance by sacrifice; in times of distress they multiplied sacrifices to appease him and make him again propitious. The worship of God by sacrifice and offering was, indeed, the central thing in their religion, we might almost say *was* their religion.[1]

Certainly one could say this of Ezra and Nehemiah. Yet the latter especially was one of the most notable exemplars of personal prayer in the Old Testament. All his labors were "begun, continued, and ended" in prayer. His narrative is interlarded with swift, ejaculatory appeals to God,[2] sometimes ethically dubious as when he calls down divine wrath on his enemies, sometimes high-minded and devout, but always revealing an intimate sense of the spiritual presence and availability of the living God. When in the royal audience he prepared to make his plea for Jerusalem's rebuilding, he inwardly "prayed to the God of heaven";[3] when he and his fellows labored on Zion amid bitter enemies, he reports, "We made our prayer unto our God, and set a watch against them day and night";[4] and when he laid down his finished work, he exclaimed, "Remember me, O my God, for good."[5] Clearly, to men like this the sacrificial system was not a substitute for the interior practise of God's presence but rather the "outward and visible sign of an inward and spiritual grace."

Similarly the Book of Daniel, written in the second century B.C., represents a type of Judaism in which new apocalyptic hopes were blended with the old devotion to temple and sacrifice. According to the story, indeed, it was when the heathen king was sacrilegiously dishonoring the vessels "taken out of the temple which was in Jerusalem" that the king's fate was sealed and his doom announced.[6] Daniel, however, even though pictured in exile, far from the ruined site of Jerusalem and its desolated altars, was not far from his God. Personal prayer runs through the entire book, and thrice daily, with his windows open toward Jerusalem, Daniel communed with the God of Israel.[7]

It is in the Psalter, however, that the development of personal prayer within the sacrificial system is most convincingly made

[1] "Sacrifice," pars. 46–47 in *Encyclopædia Biblica*, edited by T. K. Cheyne and J. Sutherland Black.

[2] E.g., Nehemiah 4:4; 5:19; 6:9,14; 13:14, 22,29.

[3] Nehemiah 2:4

[4] Nehemiah 4:9.

[5] Nehemiah 13:31.

[6] Daniel, chap. 5.

[7] E.g., Daniel 6:10; 2:17–18, 20–23; 9:3–19.

evident. The Forty-second and Forty-third Psalms belong together—a moving song of inward spiritual struggle and triumph.
The experience revealed was intimately personal—

> My soul thirsteth for God, for the living God.

The ultimate hope of peace for the psalmist's troubled soul, however, led straight to the temple and its altar—

> Oh send out thy light and thy truth; let them lead me:
> Let them bring me unto thy holy hill,
> And to thy tabernacles.
> Then will I go unto the altar of God,
> Unto God my exceeding joy.

Nothing more inwardly personal is easily imaginable than the experience represented in the 116th Psalm. The entire hymn is
written on the theme of confidence in and gratitude for the
privilege of prayer—

> I love Yahweh, because he heareth
> My voice and my supplications.
> Because he hath inclined his ear unto me,
> Therefore will I call upon him as long as I live.

Yet, here also, the climax of the psalmist's experience was reached
in the "sacrifice of thanksgiving"—

> In the courts of Yahweh's house,
> In the midst of thee, O Jerusalem.
> Praise ye Yahweh.

While, as we shall see, not all the Psalter can be truly called the
hymn book of the second temple, wide areas of it are correctly
represented by that title.[1] Many of the psalms were sung by
temple choirs as an accompaniment to animal sacrifice, as one
post-Exilic description makes vivid and picturesque: "When the
burnt-offering began, the song of Yahweh began also, and the
trumpets, together with the instruments of David king of Israel.
And all the assembly worshipped, and the singers sang, and the
trumpeters sounded; all this continued until the burnt-offering
was finished."[2] Such was doubtless the usage of Psalm Sixty-six, a
hymn of gratitude, which, however public and national in its
deliberate significance, could have been written only by a devout

---

[1] See Julius A. Bewer: *The Literature of*
the Old Testament in its Historical Develop-
ment, pp. 347 ff.

[2] II Chronicles 29:27–28.

soul with a profound religious life. Here, as elsewhere, we find mingled together an inner experience of divine-human fellowship and a sacramental experience in the public sacrifice:

> I will come into thy house with burnt-offerings;
> I will pay thee my vows,
> Which my lips uttered,
> And my mouth spake, when I was in distress.
> I will offer unto thee burnt-offerings of fatlings,
> With the incense of rams;
> I will offer bullocks with goats.
>
> . . . . . .
>
> If I regard iniquity in my heart,
> The Lord will not hear:
> But verily God hath heard;
> He hath attended to the voice of my prayer.
> Blessed be God,
> Who hath not turned away my prayer,
> Nor his lovingkindness from me.[1]

Indeed, no such abbreviated statement as we here are making, with a few quotations from the Hebrew Psalms, can begin to do justice to the Psalter as a compendium of all the moods and attitudes, conflicts, desires, and aspirations of the human soul in its relationships with God. There are psalms of personal religion, craving inward fellowship with God or rejoicing in the experience of it, and there are patriotic psalms—pleas for national deliverance, praise for national success, songs of battle, and pæans of victory. There are private psalms, springing from the most intimate experiences of trust and fear, of joy and woe, and there are public psalms in which the great congregation expressed the common need, hope, gratitude, and praise of all. There are royal psalms voicing the festival spirit of celebration at the court, praying for help in the king's need and for blessing on the king's rule, and there are psalms in which the common man poured out his hope and trust in God amid the ordinary happiness, suffering, and drudgery of daily life. There are teaching psalms, not so much characterized by supplication as by affirmation, and there are psalms of desperate petition and intercession, welling up out of profound need. As for spiritual quality, the Psalms range from dire, vindictive pleas for vengeance to aspirations so high and timeless that no generation can outgrow them. The Psalter comprehends all kinds of prayer. Petition is there, penitence and con-

[1] Psalm 66:13-15, 18-20.

fession, thanksgiving and praise, the experience of trustful serenity, the affirmation of confident faith, the enjoyment of divine companionship, the inward conquest over temptation and trouble, the rededication of the life to God, the triumphant consciousness of released power.

When, therefore, the wide ranges of the Psalter associated with the services and sacrifices of the temple are taken into account, the progressive spiritualizing of the sacrificial ritual becomes evident. Even in the early days, Hannah, the mother of Samuel, came to the shrine of Yahweh to pray concerning a personal and family matter,[1] and in the second temple, as the Psalter reveals, the individual, as such, had part in the sacrifices, not simply as a member of the nation but in the light and right of his own private needs.[2]

> Come, and hear, all ye that fear God,
> And I will declare what he hath done for my soul[3]—

that is personal gratitude.

> Judge me, O Yahweh, for I have walked in mine integrity[4]—

that is a personal protestation of innocence.

> So will I compass thine altar, O Yahweh;
> That I may make the voice of thanksgiving to be heard[5]—

that is personal praise.

> . . . I will declare mine iniquity;
> I will be sorry for my sin[6]—

that is personal penitence.

> My God, my God, why hast thou forsaken me?
> Why art thou so far from helping me, and from the words
>   of my groaning?[7]—

that is personal despair. Granted that, as in modern hymnals, expressions of religious need and aspiration originally born out of individual experience were often used in public application and became the voice of the whole people, still the very poignancy that made them thus generally applicable came from the intensely intimate experience in which they started. And when one recalls

---

[1] I Samuel 1:9 ff.
[2] See Julius A. Bewer: *The Literature of the Old Testament in its Historical Development*, pp. 371 ff.
[3] Psalm 66:16.

[4] Psalm 26:1.
[5] Psalm 26:6–7.
[6] Psalm 38:18.
[7] Psalm 22:1.

that, as Professor Bewer puts it, "Alongside of the public worship for the whole community there were certain occasions for the individual worshipper when he poured forth his thanksgiving or his petition in the temple,"[1] it is evident that the old sacrifices had been progressively spiritualized into new meanings.

To multitudes the assurance of reëstablished fellowship between God and his children that the liturgies of the temple brought to the worshiper deepened the interior experience of personal communion. When, therefore, the sacrifices were finally abolished with the destruction of the second temple in 70 A.D., Judaism, like Christianity, was not without resource. What had been solidly built within the ritual scaffolding remained secure, and the rabbis taught the people that "just as the worship of the altar is called worship, so prayer is called worship."[2]

IV

Long before Roman armies demolished the temple on Zion, however, the sacrificial system had been attacked by the prophets as a peril to true religion. All sacramental systems lend themselves to two uses—they can be either supports to a genuinely spiritual faith or substitutes for moral character and conduct in seeking the divine favor. This ambiguous meaning of temple rites was obvious in Israel. The sacrifices were confided in by good men as the outward symbols of forgiven sin and reëstablished fellowship with God, but they were also confided in by evil men as an efficacious technique for placating God regardless of one's ethical life. This latter fact bulked so large in the thought of the greatest of the prophets that, even had they granted the best elements in the sacrificial system, they would still have felt that the perversion of the best was the worst.

Alongside the growth of personal prayer within the liturgical framework, therefore, went its development not only apart from the sacrifices but in opposition to them. From the standpoint of the prophetic conscience, the offering of animals as a placation of Yahweh and the punctilious rites associated with the temple's smoking and bloody altars, were either altogether an abominable superstition or else were a once meaningful tradition dangerously corrupted by misuse. The more the prophets interpreted God and his holiness in terms of goodness, the more exclusively did goodness constitute the sole path to the divine favor. And beyond

---

[1] *Op. cit.*, p. 371.
[2] As quoted by George Foot Moore: *Judaism in the First Centuries of the Christian Era*, Vol. II, p. 218.

moral indignation at liturgical substitutes for goodness, the scorn which some prophetic passages pour on animal sacrifices suggests intellectual contempt as well. That the holy God should have pre-arranged the punctilious offering of beasts as a technique by which his own feelings and attitudes were to be affected involved an imagination of God far too childishly anthropomorphic for the prophetic mind to credit or respect. Apart from the sacrificial system, therefore, and commonly in positive aversion to it, pro-phetic thinking blazed a new trail into the experience of prayer.

Before the Exile the written law was still plastic and uncanoni-cal, in the making rather than set and rigid. Amos, therefore, felt free to doubt even the existence of a sacrificial system during the idealized days of Israel's pristine loyalty to Yahweh—"Did ye bring unto me sacrifices and offerings in the wilderness forty years, O house of Israel?"[1] The negative answer expected to this ques-tion was made more explicit in the next century by Jeremiah's representation of Yahweh saying, "I spake not unto your fathers, nor commanded them in the day that I brought them out of the land of Egypt, concerning burnt-offerings or sacrifices."[2] Clearly, then, one prophetic doctrine taught that the entire system of animal offerings was a late accretion, beginning not with Yahweh's original law but in the degenerate influences of Canaanitish baals. Even when sacrifice was not so drastically eliminated from Israel's early tradition, the prophetic conscience denied all efficacy what-ever to animal offerings. They furnished no true way of approach-ing Yahweh, said Micah—"Wherewith shall I come before Yah-weh, and bow myself before the high God? shall I come before him with burnt-offerings, with calves a year old? will Yahweh be pleased with thousands of rams, or with ten thousands of rivers of oil?"[3] Such liturgies of blood and smoke, said Amos, were the objects not of divine acceptance but of divine contempt—

> I hate, I despise your feasts, and I will take no delight in your solemn assemblies. Yea, though ye offer me your burnt-offerings and meal-offerings, I will not accept them; neither will I regard the peace-offerings of your fat beasts. Take thou away from me the noise of thy songs; for I will not hear the melody of thy viols. But let justice roll down as waters, and righteousness as a mighty stream.[4]

[1] Amos 5:25.
[2] Jeremiah 7:22.
[3] Micah 6:6–7.
[4] Amos 5:21–24.

If Hosea puts milder words upon Yahweh's lips, the meaning is none the less clear—"I desire goodness, and not sacrifice; and the knowledge of God more than burnt-offerings."[1] As for Isaiah of Jerusalem, words can hardly carry a heavier weight of indignant aversion than the passage that begins—"What unto me is the multitude of your sacrifices? saith Yahweh: I have had enough of the burnt-offerings of rams, and the fat of fed beasts; and I delight not in the blood of bullocks, or of lambs, or of he-goats."[2]

The two perennial temperaments of religion—the ethical and the liturgical—thus had representatives in the development which the Old Testament records. Personal prayer emerged from both, but with a difference. The great prophets were inwardly laid hold on by a sense of divine compulsion. The "word of Yahweh" took possession of them with an oppressive and yet exhilarating mastery, in which a consciousness of first-hand dealing with the living God was inherent. "The Lord Yahweh hath spoken; who can but prophesy?"[3] said Amos. "Yahweh spake thus to me with a strong hand,"[4] cried Isaiah. In such experiences nothing external stood between the soul and God; the divine Spirit was an immediate, personal presence, awesome and masterful, directing thought and compelling action. To the prophet, therefore, prayer was no appendage to a sacrificial system and required no smoking altar for its support. Rather, prayer was the immediate response of man to God's approach, involving inward communion and ethical devotion, and was itself the fountainhead of whatever moral value any public ceremony might possess.

It is significant that with Elijah, first of the succession of outstanding prophets, is associated a story that ever since in the Hebrew-Christian heritage has represented this profoundly inward concept of prayer. At the sacred mountain, whither he had fled in desperate need of spiritual reinforcement, Elijah faced first a strong wind, then an earthquake, and then a fire, but in these outward shows of physical power God was not present. Then came "a still small voice. And it was so, when Elijah heard it, that he wrapped his face in his mantle, and went out, and stood in the entrance of the cave. And, behold, there came a voice unto him."[5] This ancient portrayal of a prophet's communion with his divinity—so impressive that even Mendelssohn's music can hardly heighten its meaning—represents truly the immediacy of access

---

[1] Hosea 6:6.
[2] Isaiah 1:11.
[3] Amos 3:8.

[4] Isaiah 8:11.
[5] I Kings 19:9-13.

to God that the prophets experienced and that later, both in Judaism and in Christianity, wielded a profound influence as the highest type of prayer.

In the Old Testament, Jeremiah is the chief expositor of this heritage. In his young manhood he supported the Josian reform by which local high places were abolished and sacrificial worship centered in Jerusalem. Whatever may have been his attitude at that time toward animal offerings on Zion, in the end he lost confidence in their value, discredited their origin, and denied Yahweh's pleasure in them—"Your burnt-offerings are not acceptable, nor your sacrifices pleasing unto me."[1] Even the temple itself, used as a pious substitute for social justice, he scathingly denounced, and threatened it with the same destruction that had fallen on Yahweh's former shrine at Shiloh.[2] In his own experience, prayer, associated with neither temple nor altar, was an intimate, familiar colloquy between his soul and God. To any one with stiff and formal attitudes in religion, Jeremiah's prayers are even today positively sacrilegious. He argued with God, questioning him— "Wherefore doth the way of the wicked prosper?"—and contending with him because all they are "at ease that deal very treacherously";[3] he accused God of acting as though he were a mere wayfarer in Israel's land instead of being one who deeply cared for it, and cried, "Why shouldest thou be as a man affrighted, as a mighty man that cannot save?";[4] he complained at God's seeming desertion, saying, "Wilt thou indeed be unto me as a deceitful brook, as waters that fail?";[5] and in his despair he pleaded with God in terms that knew no restraint—"Hast thou utterly rejected Judah? hath thy soul loathed Zion? why hast thou smitten us, and there is no healing for us? ... Do not abhor us, for thy name's sake; do not disgrace the throne of thy glory: remember, break not thy covenant with us."[6]

With only three characters in the Old Testament are prayers like this associated—Moses,[7] Job,[8] and Jeremiah—and in each case not doubt but assurance of God is in the background, and the very intimacy with which the soul bares its complaints and carries on its struggle in prayer is testimony to the utter genuineness of the experience. Only those who know God as Jeremiah did—"My strength, and my stronghold, and my refuge in the day of afflic-

---

[1] Jeremiah 6:20.
[2] Jeremiah 7:1–26.
[3] Jeremiah 12:1–2.
[4] Jeremiah 14:8–9.
[5] Jeremiah 15:18.
[6] Jeremiah 14:19, 21.
[7] Exodus 5:22–23; Numbers 11:11–15.
[8] Job 10:2–21; 13:24—14:6.

tion"[1]—can so make free with him. With entire unconstraint Jeremiah found thus in solitary prayer immediate entrance into the divine presence and, sensitive, poetic spirit though he was, lacerated by national calamity and individual rejection, he was accustomed to go out from this interior resource to face the world again, having heard Yahweh say to him, "I will make thee unto this people a fortified brazen wall . . . I am with thee."[2] It is not strange, therefore, that when temple and altar were destroyed by Nebuchadnezzar, and the exiles in Babylon, bereft of their sacrificial system, were in confusion, Jeremiah's faith was expressed in a message to them concerning personal prayer—anywhere, in any land, sacrifices or no sacrifices, the God of Israel was saying to his people, "Ye shall call upon me, and ye shall go and pray unto me, and I will hearken unto you. And ye shall seek me, and find me, when ye shall search for me with all your heart. And I will be found of you, saith Yahweh."[3]

In this approach to personal prayer the influence of the prophets was by no means confined to the prophets, and of this fact the Psalter gives abundant evidence. Hymn and prayer book of the second temple it may have been, but obviously some of the psalms could never have been sung in connection with the sacrifices, and may well be grouped, as Professor Julius Bewer suggests, under the caption, "Private Worship outside of the Temple."[4]

> For thou delightest not in sacrifice; else would I give it:
> Thou hast no pleasure in burnt-offering.
> The sacrifices of God are a broken spirit:
> A broken and a contrite heart, O God, thou wilt not despise[5]—

such a psalm is a direct reflection of the prophetic spirit, and must have been distinctly displeasing to the priests until some later hand added the incongruous anticlimax,

> Do good in thy good pleasure unto Zion:
> Build thou the walls of Jerusalem.
> Then wilt thou delight in the sacrifices of righteousness,
> In burnt-offering and whole burnt-offering:
> Then will they offer bullocks upon thine altar.[6]

In this typical contrast within the present Fifty-first Psalm, the recurrent conflict of prophet and priest in the Psalter is made

---

[1] Jeremiah 16:19.
[2] Jeremiah 15:20.
[3] Jeremiah 29:1–14.
[4] *The Literature of the Old Testament in its Historical Development*, pp. 377–394.
[5] Psalm 51:16–17.
[6] Psalm 51:18–19.

explicit. Devotees of the sacrificial system are well represented, as we have seen, but with catholic inclusiveness, like a true hymnal, the Psalter gives large place to the attitude of the prophets:

> Sacrifice and offering thou hast no delight in;
> Mine ears hast thou opened:
> Burnt-offering and sin-offering hast thou not required.[1]

> I will praise the name of God with a song,
> And will magnify him with thanksgiving.
> And it will please Yahweh better than an ox,
> Or a bullock that hath horns and hoofs.[2]

> I will take no bullock out of thy house,
> Nor he-goats out of thy folds.
> For every beast of the forest is mine,
> And the cattle upon a thousand hills.
> I know all the birds of the mountains;
> And the wild beasts of the field are mine.
> If I were hungry, I would not tell thee;
> For the world is mine, and the fulness thereof.
> Will I eat the flesh of bulls,
> Or drink the blood of goats?
> Offer unto God the sacrifice of thanksgiving;
> And pay thy vows unto the Most High;
> And call upon me in the day of trouble:
> I will deliver thee, and thou shalt glorify me.[3]

The prophetic influence, therefore, was effective far beyond the ambit of the prophets themselves and, as the Book of Proverbs shows, became part of the homely common sense of many of the people:

> To do righteousness and justice
> Is more acceptable to Yahweh than sacrifice.[4]

> The sacrifice of the wicked is an abomination to Yahweh;
> But the prayer of the upright is his delight.[5]

Thus, both within the sacrificial system and in antagonism to it, personal prayer developed as the characteristic approach to God, and the way was prepared for the typical attitudes and ideas of the New Testament.

[1] Psalm 40:6.
[2] Psalm 69:30-31.
[3] Psalm 50:9-15.
[4] Proverbs 21:3.
[5] Proverbs 15:8.

V

Indeed, both the priestly and the prophetic heritage entered into early Christianity. Jesus himself taught a faithful observance of the Law.[1] He was a lover of the temple[2] and a pilgrim to the sacrificial feasts,[3] and his first disciples, far from breaking with the ceremonial requirements, continued to be such thoroughgoing Jews that the ultimate surrender of circumcision and of kosher food nearly disrupted the church.[4] Even after the inhospitality of Judaism had outlawed the Christian movement from the sacrifices and the destruction of Jerusalem had finally ended them, the Old Testament was still the Christian Bible, and some disposal had to be made of its ceremonial codes. In Judaism this problem was solved, in part, by substituting the reading of the laws of sacrifice for their outward observance. God was represented by one of the ancient rabbis as saying, "When they read before me the laws about sacrifices, I will impute it to them as if they offered the sacrifices before me, and will have mercy upon them for all their misdeeds."[5] Christian ideas, however, soon moved too far away from either the practise or the perusal of sacrificial laws as a means of reconciliation with God for the early Christian to be content with such a solution.

A typically Christian way out is offered in the Epistle to the Hebrews. Here the ancient Jewish sacrificial system is represented as the temporary foreshadowing of an eternal truth. The temple in Jerusalem was "a sanctuary of this world,"[6] a mere preparatory symbol of "the true tabernacle"[7] in which God and the soul deal with each other in intimate spiritual fellowship. The offering of unwilling beasts was morally ineffective—"For it is impossible that the blood of bulls and goats should take away sins"[8]—and the only redemptive offering is voluntary self-sacrifice such as that of Christ who "offered up himself."[9] The Jewish priesthood was a temporary makeshift, bringing oblations which needed constantly to be repeated,[10] with no final efficacy in reconciling the soul and God, and so they were the dim foreshadowing of Christ's true priesthood, who has "entered in once for all into

[1] Matthew 5:18; Luke 16:17; Matthew 8:4; Luke 5:14; 17:14; Matthew 23:23.
[2] Mark 11:15-17; Matthew 26:55.
[3] Luke 2:41-42; Mark 14:1-2.
[4] E.g., Galatians, chap. 2.
[5] As quoted by George Foot Moore: *Judaism in the First Centuries of the Christian Era*, Vol. II, pp. 14-15.
[6] Hebrews 9:1-10.
[7] Hebrews 8:2; 9:11 ff.
[8] Hebrews 10:4.
[9] Hebrews 7:26-27; 9:14.
[10] Hebrews 10:3.

the holy place, having obtained eternal redemption."[1] Thus the writer moves from one element of the old system to another, interpreting each as a transient intimation of abiding spiritual experience. As a result, the literal and tangible sacrificial apparatus of the Jews became to the Christians symbolic of another kind of religious system altogether, whose temple is heavenly, not earthly, whose high priest once for all has entered the holy place of divine communion, where believing souls may follow him,[2] whose sacrifice is voluntary self-giving, and whose consequence is an open way for all to "draw nigh unto God."[3]

While, however, New Testament Christianity disposed of the ceremonial laws in the Old Testament so that the ancient rites were sublimated into Christian meanings, by that very process the ancient rites were given an extended influence. A large area of historic Christian theology would have been completely altered if ideas of atonement, especially as related to the blood of Christ, had not been carried over from primitive concepts associated with animal sacrifice.[4] Christianity left the rubric of bloody altars far behind, but mental patterns are too stubbornly persistent to be so easily cast off, and even yet semimagical ideas concerning the potency of blood, from the earliest documents of the Old Testament, are woven into some Christian hymns, sermons, and prayers. In this regard Judaism has escaped from its own cult of sacrifice more completely than has Christianity.

Influential as the old sacrificial system continued to be in Christian thinking, it was the prophetic tradition with reference to personal prayer that more powerfully affected the New Testament. Jesus may have reverenced the ceremonial heritage of his people, but he himself was in the true succession of the prophets, especially Hosea and Jeremiah. Reared in Galilee, his spiritual life had been nourished in the synagogue. "For the vast majority of Jews," writes Professor George Foot Moore, "not alone in the dispersion but in Palestine itself, the synagogue had become, long before the destruction of the temple, the real seat of religious worship, though so long as the temple stood they may not have used of it the word 'worship' historically appropriated to the sacrificial cultus."[5] In the synagogue, therefore, as well as in the temple, Jesus prayed, but neither temple nor synagogue sufficed for his fellowship with God. Twice he quoted Hosea, on the ceremonial

[1] Hebrews 9:12.
[2] Hebrews 10:19.
[3] Hebrews 7:19; 10:22.

[4] E.g., Hebrews 9:13–14.
[5] *Judaism in the First Centuries of the Christian Era*, Vol. II, p. 12.

law, "I desire mercy, and not sacrifice, "[1] and his indignant distaste for hypocrites who "love to stand and pray in the synagogues"[2] was openly expressed. Alone with the door shut, in desert places, or among the hills[3] Jesus was accustomed to pray; and even when in the Garden of Gethsemane his disciples were with him, we read, "He was parted from them about a stone's cast; and he kneeled down and prayed."[4]

It is this habit of private prayer that, rather than ceremonial worship, characterizes the New Testament. The disciples were devout Jews, trained not only in the ritual of their faith but in the more mystical fellowship that could say, "The nearness of God is my good, "[5] and

> He that dwelleth in the secret place of the Most High
> Shall abide under the shadow of the Almighty.[6]

Yet when they heard Jesus in his personal devotions, the experience seemed to them so fresh and new that they said, "Lord, teach us to pray."[7] From this beginning prayer moved out into the early church and so into the New Testament. With the ancient altars no longer standing, with the sacrificial cultus interpreted as a mere foreshadowing of the access to God that Christians spiritually enjoyed, with the growing rituals of the new churches still plastic and unformed, personal prayer became the typical method of divine fellowship. Men were to pray "without ceasing"[8] and "in every place."[9] Indeed, the New Testament lives and moves and has its being in the atmosphere of informal, unconventional, spontaneous, intimate prayer.

This involved the complete supersession of those limitations which at the beginning of Hebrew history had made such praying unthinkable. Far from being unapproachable, God's dwelling-place was within the spiritual life of his children. Whether this immediacy of God was described in Pauline terms as God's Spirit, carrying the divine presence and power into the Christian's inner life,[10] or in Johannine terms, as God himself dwelling in his people,[11] the accessibility of the divine grace and help was everywhere pro-

---

[1] Matthew 9:13; 12:7.
[2] Matthew 6:5.
[3] Matthew 6:6; Mark 1:35; Matthew 14:23.
[4] Luke 22:41.
[5] Psalm 73:28 as translated by J. M. Powis Smith in *The Religion of the Psalms*, p. 152.
[6] Psalm 91:1.
[7] Luke 11:1.
[8] I Thessalonians 5:17.
[9] I Timothy 2:8.
[10] I Corinthians 3:16.
[11] John 14:23; I John 4:12.

claimed. No longer interested merely in the destinies of corporate groups, God was conceived as caring for persons one by one, so that prayer was a transfiguring individual experience—"As he was praying, the fashion of his countenance was altered."[1] Instead of being localized in any shrine, the early church rejoiced in the liberation of the divine presence from all Gerizims and Jerusalems to the universality which the Fourth Gospel announces— "God is a Spirit: and they that worship him must worship in spirit and truth."[2] Instead of involving bizarre and ominous signs or magical apparatus, dealing with God was an affair of interior communion, and while a few stories still reflect belief in dreams[3] as a means of divine revelation, and once the casting of lots[4] is used to secure divine guidance, the characteristic and habitual practise of early Christians in approaching God was direct and simple prayer. Instead of allowing any unethical substitutes for spiritual fellowship with God, God was so conceived in terms of goodness that there could be no companionship with him without ethical likeness to him.[5] As for the sacrificial system, that had been displaced by a moral and universally applicable substitute—"Present your bodies a living sacrifice, holy, acceptable to God, which is your spiritual service."[6]

VI

This development of deepening meaning in fellowship with God was accompanied by significant changes in the idea of faith. Always the possibility of fellowship with God is dependent upon one's faith. As the Epistle to the Hebrews says, "He that cometh to God must believe that he is, and that he is a rewarder of them that seek after him."[7] In general the characteristic emphasis of the Old Testament is not upon belief but upon obedience, and the test of religious rightness is not one's faith but one's deeds. Indeed, in no particular is the distinction between the Testaments much more marked than in the slight stress on faith in the Old and the centrality of it in the New. Even in a familiar passage, where Habakkuk says, "The righteous shall live by his faith,"[8] the marginal rendering is doubtless correct, "in his faithfulness," and —as when Isaiah foresees "the righteous nation which keepeth

[1] Luke 9:29.
[2] John 4:20-24.
[3] Matthew 1:20; 2:12,13,19; 27:19.
[4] Acts 1:24-26.

[5] I John 4:7-8.
[6] Romans 12:1.
[7] Hebrews 11:6.
[8] Habakkuk 2:4.

faith"[1]—this ethical significance, akin to fidelity, is the familiar meaning of faith in the Old Testament.[2]

In the New Testament, however, faith, meaning something other than faithfulness, is central in the religious experience, and its various phrasings furnish a valuable clue to the dominant ideas of the writers.

1. In the Synoptic Gospels—Matthew, Mark, and Luke—faith is a humble, hearty confidence in God's power and goodness and a potent laying hold on his proffered help. In Jesus' first preaching it is associated with repentance—"Repent ye, and believe in the gospel"[3]—as though to turn from old sins were the negative, and to exercise a new faith were the positive, aspect of becoming his disciple. Everywhere in the Synoptics, faith is the precedent necessity if any mighty work is to be done or any divine help received,[4] and when real faith is present, even though it be "as a grain of mustard seed," it releases such power that it can move mountains.[5] "All things are possible," said Jesus, "to him that believeth."[6]

2. In Paul's writings this meaning of faith is casually present[7] but he goes much further. In the background of his experience and thought is a different set of ideas and problems from those familiar in the Synoptics. The Jewish legal system, now left behind, had once been the means by obedience to which he had sought 'justification'; now faith—the whole-hearted self-committal of a man to Jesus Christ by which the entire personality is transformed—is the sole ground of any one's acceptance with God.[8] The cross of Christ, "unto Jews a stumblingblock, and unto Gentiles foolishness,"[9] is to Paul the cardinal element in the divine self-revelation, and faith is the attitude toward Christ of acceptance, trust, appropriation, by which the salvation offered in the cross becomes effective in the believer.[10] Goodness had once been the work of a strenuous will endeavoring to obey God's law; now, to Paul, goodness is the overflow of an inner life which by faith has welcomed the indwelling Spirit.[11] Religious experience had been to Paul a difficult struggle; now by faith he is so joined with Christ that there is a mutual interpenetration of the divine and the human, so that "it is no longer I that live, but Christ liveth in

---

[1] Isaiah 26:2; cf. Hosea 4:2.
[2] See, however, Genesis 15:6.
[3] Mark 1:15.
[4] E.g., Mark 10:52; Matthew 9:22; 13:58; 15:28.
[5] Matthew 17:20.
[6] Mark 9:23.
[7] I Corinthians 13:2.
[8] Romans 3:21–22,26,28; 4:22–25; 5:1–2.
[9] I Corinthians 1:23.
[10] Romans 3:24–25.
[11] Galatians 5:4–6.

me."[1] At every point, therefore, faith means to Paul that vital self-committal to Christ which so opens the life to him and appropriates his spirit that by it men become sons of God.[2] Far from being primarily opinionative, faith is an act of the whole personality, so appropriating the divine that a good life inevitably ensues—"with the heart man believeth unto righteousness."[3]

3. In the Epistle to the Hebrews the reader moves into another set of ideas altogether. There, after the Neo-Platonic fashion, are two worlds—visible and invisible, temporal and eternal, earthly and heavenly, shadow and substance, foregleam and fulfilment. Such is the cosmic outlook that everywhere dominates the thought of the Epistle, and faith means the power by which we can live in both worlds, grasping the assurance of things hoped for ere the fulfilment has actually come, and holding a conviction of things not seen even while we are pressed upon by the visible.[4] This is the quality of all the heroes of faith in the eleventh chapter: in one world they live as though another world were real; on one level of being they grasp the surety of a higher level; amid the transient they are convinced of the permanent; and so they endure, "as seeing him who is invisible."[5]

4. In the Fourth Gospel we move into still another set of ideas which strongly affect the phrasing of faith. Throughout the Gospel, John is concerned with the persuasive presentation of the doctrine that Jesus is the Son of God, and his primary aim is to win men to believe in Christ as such.[6] This determines the principal significance of faith in the Fourth Gospel—it means both an intellectual conviction that Christ is the Son of God and a personal self-commitment to him because of that. The Gospel, that is, reflects the kind of experience doubtless familiar in a Hellenistic city such as Ephesus, as converts were won to Christianity. First, they were attracted to Christ; going deeper in acquaintance with his life and ministry, they found in him the satisfaction of their religious needs; through this experience they progressed in knowledge of him until at last they believed in him as the Son of God. That is to say, in John's Gospel faith is not so much the beginning as it is the end of the process of conversion.

In the Synoptics, for example, faith is the precedent condition of Jesus' miracles while in the Fourth Gospel faith is the consequence

[1] Galatians 2:20.
[2] Galatians 3:26.
[3] Romans 10:10.
[4] Hebrews 11:1.

[5] Hebrews 11:27.
[6] E.g., John 1:34,49; 3:18; 9:35-38; 10:35-36; 11:4,27; 20:30-31.

of Jesus' miracles—"Believe me for the very works' sake";[1] "Though ye believe not me, believe the works";[2] he "manifested his glory; and his disciples believed on him," after his first miracle;[3] and, when a nobleman's son was healed, he "himself believed, and his whole house."[4] To put the matter another way, in John's Gospel faith does not generally come before knowledge, but knowledge before faith. Men are drawn by the attraction of Christ, his works and his cross,[5] and, entering into a satisfying experience with him, come first to know him and then to believe on him as the Son of God. They "knew . . . and they believed"[6] is the distinctive Johannine order. Uniquely characteristic of John though this phrasing of faith is, at the heart of it is still the vital self-commitment of person to person—"Every one that beholdeth the Son, and believeth on him";[7] "He that believeth on me";[8] "Believe in God, believe also in me."[9] Such faith is not simply doctrine; it is an intellectual conviction born out of a profound, spiritual experience.

5. In some later writings of the New Testament, however, faith is primarily belief in dogma. This phrasing of faith, impossible in the first years of the Christian movement, emerged only when the convictions of the church were so well formulated that the acceptance of orthodox teaching could be a major criterion of Christian discipleship. So in the Epistle to Titus and in the Epistles to Timothy faith is primarily intellectual assent to the standard convictions of the church. The ideal is to hold "faith and a good conscience" against heretics,[10] to be true to the "faith of God's elect,"[11] not to "fall away from the faith"[12] but to withstand contrary opinions, "which some professing have erred concerning the faith."[13] This doctrinal conception James presents negatively, disparaging faith as compared with works, on the ground that, belief being a matter of opinion, "the demons also believe, and shudder";[14] and Jude presents it positively, exhorting his brethren "to contend earnestly for the faith which was once for all delivered unto the saints."[15]

So varied are the New Testament's conceptions of one of the

[1] John 14:11.
[2] John 10:38.
[3] John 2:11.
[4] John 4:53.
[5] John 12:32.
[6] John 17:8 (but see John 6:69).
[7] John 6:40.
[8] John 12:44; 14:12.
[9] John 14:1.
[10] I Timothy 1:18–20.
[11] Titus 1:1.
[12] I Timothy 4:1.
[13] I Timothy 6:20–21.
[14] James 2:19–20.
[15] Jude, vs. 3.

most central and influential ideas of early Christianity. Yet through all these diversities of phrasing—whether faith was thought of as a power-releasing confidence in God, or as self-commitment to Christ that brought the divine Spirit into indwelling control of one's life, or as the power by which we apprehend the eternal and invisible even while living in the world of sense, or as the climactic vision of Christ as the Son of God which crowns our surrender to his attractiveness, or as assured conviction concerning great truths that underlie and constitute the gospel—always the enlargement and enrichment of faith was opening new meanings in the experience of fellowship with God and was influencing deeply both the idea and the practise of prayer.

VII

Revelatory as are such changes in the concept of worship and of the faith that underlies it, it is the content of the prayers recorded in the Bible that most plainly reveals development in thought and life. In one characteristic realm after another, changing ideas of prayer were accompanied by changing substance in the prayers themselves.

1. There was, for example, an unmistakable growth in magnanimity. Many of the early petitions are demands on God for vengeance after the manner of Samson's dying cry, "O Lord Yahweh, remember me, I pray thee, and strengthen me, I pray thee, only this once, O God, that I may be at once avenged of the Philistines for my two eyes."[1] Between this petition and the prayer of the dying Stephen, the first Christian martyr, "Lord, lay not this sin to their charge,"[2] lies a long road of ethical ascent.

This road, obvious as it is in retrospect, was not easily visible in advance, and some of the greatest souls in the Old Testament were laggards in traveling it. Jeremiah, pouring out before God everything he felt, poured out his vindictiveness: "Bring upon them the day of evil, and destroy them with double destruction";[3] "Deliver up their children to the famine, and give them over to the power of the sword; and let their wives become childless, and widows; and let their men be slain of death, and their young men smitten of the sword in battle. . . . forgive not their iniquity, neither blot out their sin from thy sight; but let them be overthrown before thee; deal thou with them in the time of thine anger."[4] A notable amount of praying in the Old Testament is

---

[1] Judges 16:28.
[2] Acts 7:60.
[3] Jeremiah 17:18.
[4] Jeremiah 18:21,23.

thus cursing, and lest Christians should assume too much credit in this regard, a similar abuse of prayer, all the more inexcusable because sinning against light, stands in the New Testament—"How long, O Master, the holy and true, dost thou not judge and avenge our blood on them that dwell on the earth?"[1] The writer of Lamentations, bewailing the miserable estate of desolated Zion, cried, "Do unto them, as thou hast done unto me";[2] Nehemiah, rebuilding the walls of Jerusalem, besought Yahweh against his foes, "Cover not their iniquity, and let not their sin be blotted out from before thee";[3] and in the Psalter are outbursts of vindictiveness the singing of which in the second temple seems scarcely credible:

> Let their table before them become a snare;
> And when they are in peace, let it become a trap.
> Let their eyes be darkened, so that they cannot see;
> And make their loins continually to shake.
> Pour out thine indignation upon them,
> And let the fierceness of thine anger overtake them.[4]
>
> Let his children be fatherless,
> And his wife a widow.
> Let his children be vagabonds, and beg;
> And let them seek their bread out of their desolate places.
> Let the extortioner catch all that he hath;
> And let strangers make spoil of his labor.
> Let there be none to extend kindness unto him;
> Neither let there be any to have pity on his fatherless children.[5]

Sincere praying is always a revelation of character, and generosity in prayer waited of necessity for magnanimity in spirit. When Jeremiah bade the exiles in the city of Babylon "pray unto Yahweh for it; for in the peace thereof shall ye have peace,"[6] we see the dawning of a better day, whose full light, however, did not come before Christ—"Love your enemies, do good to them that hate you, bless them that curse you, pray for them that despitefully use you";[7] "Father, forgive them; for they know not what they do."[8]

2. The recorded prayers of the Bible disclose also a growing universality of interest and care. The tribal and national limitations

[1] Revelation 6:10.
[2] Lamentations 1:22.
[3] Nehemiah 4:5.
[4] Psalm 69:22–24.
[5] Psalm 109:9–12.
[6] Jeremiah 29:7.
[7] Luke 6:27–28.
[8] Luke 23:34.

of early Hebrew thought and life were necessarily reflected in Hebrew praying. Even when the petitions of the Old Testament concerning public matters are not vindictive, they are commonly nationalistic, as, for example, the Isaian plea for divine interposition in Israel's desperate need,[1] or Daniel's great prayer for his people,[2] or the ejaculatory supplications of Ezekiel,[3] or the elaborate petitions in the Books of Ezra and Nehemiah.[4] Only occasionally does mankind as a whole appear as the object of intercession.

In the Psalter, however, the wider outlook finds expression:

> God be merciful unto us, and bless us,
> And cause his face to shine upon us;
> That thy way may be known upon earth,
> Thy salvation among all nations.
> Let the peoples praise thee, O God;
> Let all the peoples praise thee.
> Oh let the nations be glad and sing for joy;
> For thou wilt judge the peoples with equity,
> And govern the nations upon earth.
> Let the peoples praise thee, O God;
> Let all the peoples praise thee.[5]

In this regard, Jewish prayer ranged over a wider ambit than Jewish law. To the very end the Law was particularistic—its duties intended for Jews only, its rights fully accorded neither to foreigners outside the Jewish community nor to casual sojourners and slaves within it. The same limitation in the scope of law existed in Athens, where, in order to avail himself of legal rights, a sojourner had to secure a citizen as patron, where slaves were, generally speaking, outside the privilege of the laws altogether, and where the 'barbarians' beyond the borders were not within the legal purview.[6] It was the glory of Roman jurists in the early centuries A.D. that they first conceived the *jus gentium*, the natural law of all peoples, as incorporating the duties and rights which belonged to human beings everywhere. In Judaism, however, prayer outran law, aspiration surpassed enactment, and the universal God was approached in intercession as

> . . . the confidence of all the ends of the earth,
> And of them that are afar off upon the sea.[7]

[1] Isaiah 63:15—64:12.
[2] Daniel 9:4–19.
[3] Ezekiel 9:8; 11:13.
[4] Ezra 9:6–15; Nehemiah 9:6–37.
[5] Psalm 67:1–5.

[6] R. M. MacIver: *The Modern State*, pp. 103–104.
[7] Psalm 65:5 (To be sure, this may refer only to the Jews of the Dispersion).

Not only Christianity but the later Judaism was the enriched inheritor of this growing universality of interest and care. So a Jewish teacher of the fourth century A.D., Rabbi Joshua, said: "Hast thou ever seen the rain fall on the field of X who is righteous, and not on the field of Y who is wicked, or the sun shine upon Israel who are righteous, and not upon the nations who are wicked? God makes the sun shine both upon Israel and the nations, for He is good to all."[1] Whether this passage is a reflection of Jesus' words[2] or Jesus' words a reflection of similar teachings in the Judaism of his day, it is a true intimation of the growing universality of the better sort of Jewish teaching, and especially in praying the outreach of intercession to all humanity was perceived by some as the corollary of monotheism—

> O thou that hearest prayer,
> Unto thee shall all flesh come.[3]

In the New Testament the world as the subject of redemption is continually present either in the foreground or in the background of the recorded prayers. Paul's description of God as the "Father, from whom every family in heaven and on earth is named"[4] is typical. Even in the intercessory prayer of Jesus for his disciples at the Last Supper, where he is represented as saying, "I pray not for the world," the world still remains the ultimate object of his care: "As thou didst send me into the world, even so sent I them into the world . . . . that the world may believe that thou didst send me."[5] From the beginning of the gospel, when Jesus taught his disciples to pray, "Thy kingdom come,"[6] to the end of the New Testament with its dream of worshiping hosts, crying, "The kingdom of the world is become the kingdom of our Lord,"[7] the range of Christian intercession keeps the whole earth in view.

3. The prayers of the Bible plainly indicate a deepening sense of sin. In the early days of Israel with their morality of outward custom, when wickedness was the violation of tribal taboos, penalty a tribal misfortune in consequence, and the cure public reform and obedience, the prayers of confession were congruous with such ideas. It is typical of Israel's early repentances that only when the people were "sore distressed" by national defeat did

[1] As quoted by C. G. Montefiore in *The Beginnings of Christianity*, edited by F. J. Foakes Jackson and Kirsopp Lake, Part I, Vol. I, p. 40.
[2] Matthew 5:45.
[3] Psalm 65:2.
[4] Ephesians 3:15.
[5] John 17:18,21.
[6] Matthew 6:10.
[7] Revelation 11:15.

they recognize that they had wickedly disobeyed Yahweh, and so cried unto him, "We have sinned against thee."[1] At the first, therefore, penitence was a public rather than a private matter, and the sense of sin concerned the violated customs of the social group rather than the inner quality of the individual. Far down in Israel's history such ideas, associated with corporate personality, deeply affected the praying of the people. The sin confessed was not so much personal unworthiness as national misdeeds, and the misdeeds were not alone the evil work of the living but of the ancestral generations whose iniquities were still involving their offspring in penalty. Out of this range of thought came the re-iterated confessions of sin for both contemporaneous and historic national sin: "We acknowledge, O Yahweh, our wickedness, and the iniquity of our fathers";[2] "We have sinned against Yahweh our God, we and our fathers";[3] they "stood and confessed their sins, and the iniquities of their fathers";[4] "For our sins, and for the iniquities of our fathers, Jerusalem and thy people are become a reproach to all that are round about us."[5]

This sense of corporate disobedience involving both present and past generations became more acute as national calamities increased. The Jews faced a difficult and momentous dilemma: either the accumulated miseries of Israel were due to Yahweh's failure as a powerful god, or else he was the one true God who, with righteous judgment, had decreed their national distress as punishment. Many a nation, facing a similar dilemma, had chosen the former and easier alternative; it was Israel's distinction that she chose the latter. In the face of abysmal wretchedness she asserted the sole sovereignty and the unfailing justice of her God, and interpreted her calamities as his appointment in punishment for her sins.

In Exilic and post-Exilic times, in consequence, the sense of guilt deepened in Judaism and the prayers of confession and peni-tence became poignant and, at times, almost abject. When Ezra cries, "Thou our God hast punished us less than our iniquities deserve,"[6] or a prayer in the Book of Nehemiah says, "Thou art just in all that is come upon us; for thou hast dealt truly, but we have done wickedly,"[7] or Daniel exhausts tautology in confessing, "We have sinned, and have dealt perversely, and have done

---

[1] Judges 10:9–10.
[2] Jeremiah 14:20.
[3] Jeremiah 3:25.
[4] Nehemiah 9:2.
[5] Daniel 9:16.
[6] Ezra 9:13.
[7] Nehemiah 9:33.

wickedly, and have rebelled,"[1] we see the self-accusation which resulted from the acceptance of national misfortune not as an evidence of Yahweh's weakness in protecting his people but as proof of his inflexible righteousness. It is characteristic of the worship of the post-Exilic temple, therefore, that the two forms of sacrifice added to the rubric were the trespass- and the guilt-offerings, both expiations of sin, and that, in general, the sense of public guilt in the later Old Testament is poignant and profound.

Indeed, so extreme is it that at times it seems to modern minds morbid, but this judgment is qualified when one recalls the historic setting. National self-accusation was the price paid by the Jews for two of their most valuable possessions—their *monotheism*, for only by interpreting their public misery as the just penalty for their own sins could they assert Yahweh's omnipotence and righteousness; and their *social conscience*, for only by thinking of Israel as a continuous community, irrefragably bound together across the generations by the eternal laws of moral cause and consequence, could they explain their fate. Those moderns who too superficially account for religion by Freudian formulas and, in particular, conceive it habitually as a mere mechanism of escape from disliked realities, should take the measure of this area of Judaism. The Jews, who might have blamed their calamities on Yahweh's failure as a god and so might have evaded a crushing sense of their own guilt, chose not this easier path but one of the most difficult ever traveled by the mind of man. They accused themselves of sin so heinous as to deserve their suffering and at their best exhibited a spirit of contrition and humility which has entered into the abiding spiritual heritage of the race.

With the individual's emergence from his primitive estate as a mere item in the social whole, prayers of confession gained a new dimension—acknowledgment of personal unworthiness was added to national penitence. Moreover, the poignancy of the sense of public guilt was reflected in private self-accusation, and the issue is seen in such prayers as the psalmist's confession of deep-seated sinfulness,

> Behold, I was brought forth in iniquity;
> And in sin did my mother conceive me,[2]

and in such cries as Job's,

---

[1] Daniel 9:5.   [2] Psalm 51:5.

> Wherefore I abhor myself,
> And repent in dust and ashes.[1]

Here appears one of the major paradoxes of the spiritual life, of which the Bible gives vivid illustration—the more self-respect men achieve, the more they are plunged into self-depreciation. Only when personality has emerged from the social mass into a high status of its own, as possessing spiritual value and possibility, can the sense of failure, in falling short of personality's promise, become acute. The more elevated the standards, the more inevitable humility becomes; only when men think highly of themselves do they begin to think humbly of themselves, so that self-respect and self-depreciation, instead of being antithetical, are two sides of the same experience.

Of this paradox the later Old Testament and all the New Testament are illustrations. Instead of being a passing phase of the social group, individual, personal life was progressively gaining a distinct and profound value of its own, and the higher personality thus rose in ideal, the farther it could fall by comparison. So the Book of Job, whose hero gives a consummate portrayal of a good man's life,[2] makes its hero say also, "Behold, I am of small account;"[3] and the Fifty-first Psalm, whose writer sees that God desires "truth in the inward parts," is correspondingly penitent—

> Wash me thoroughly from mine iniquity,
> And cleanse me from my sin.
> For I know my transgressions;
> And my sin is ever before me.[4]

This juncture of high personal self-estimate and profound personal humility is a main attribute of the New Testament's thought. When Jesus set in contrast a self-righteous Pharisee, saying to God, "I thank thee, that I am not as the rest of men," and a contrite publican, praying, "God, be thou merciful to me a sinner,"[5] he was both summing up the best of his race's teaching on the true spirit of confessional prayer and indicating to his disciples the self-depreciation which must follow any such estimate of personal worth and possibility as he himself believed in. Not many prayers are preserved for us in the New Testament, but one cannot read the Pauline and Johannine letters without feeling that the obverse side of such an ideal as Christ had brought was a pro-

---

[1] Job 42:6.
[2] Job, chap. 31.
[3] Job 40:4.

[4] Psalm 51:2–3.
[5] Luke 18:9–14.

found humility about man's moral estate. The Prodigal's contrition—"Father, I have sinned against heaven, and in thy sight: I am no more worthy to be called thy son"[1]—is implied in many a New Testament passage.

In this realm of confessional prayer, however, the New Testament still needs the supplementation of the Old. Social penitence did not rise naturally from the individualistic conditions that faced early Christianity. The great prayers of the Bible concerning national failure and social sin are still the gift of the Old Testament.

4. With these progressive tendencies toward increased magnanimity, inclusiveness, and humility in prayer went a deepening spirituality in the content of the petitions. In the early stages of Biblical history men regarded the major good of existence as physical—ample creature comforts, a long life, a large family, and victory in war—and for these benefits the Hebrews besought Yahweh. The Deuteronomic ideal of a people blessed of God was summed up in such details as a multiplying population, ample harvests, plenty of wine and oil, fruitful flocks, freedom from disease, and ability to "consume all the peoples" that were hostile.[2] With these for the main objects of petition, prayer was naturally evoked by their lack, and it was typical of early Hebrew as of all immature praying that the negative rather than the positive purpose of prayer was prominent. Like the sailors in the 107th Psalm who, "at their wits' end" in a storm, "cry unto Yahweh in their trouble," or like the mariners with Jonah who, amid the "mighty tempest," "cried every man unto his god,"[3] men were driven to prayer by physical peril. So Jeremiah condemned his people for habitual neglect of Yahweh, to whom, however, "in the time of their trouble they will say, Arise, and save us."[4]

In Old Testament times the problem of subsistence was frequently so difficult and national calamities fell with such repeated dreadfulness that much of the supplication recorded was motived by crisis and was aimed at material recovery. If the New Testament contains less of such petition than the Old, an important part of the explanation lies in the difference of circumstance. When in the Book of Lamentations we read of mothers under stress of famine eating their own children,[5] of women ravished, princes

---

[1] Luke 15:18–19.
[2] Deuteronomy 7:12–16.
[3] Jonah 1:4–5.

[4] Jeremiah 2:27.
[5] Lamentations 2:20.

"hanged up by their hand," little children stumbling under their burdens, and the mountain of Zion become a haunt of foxes,[1] we cannot wonder that the people poured out their hearts "like water before the face of the Lord."[2] Quality in prayer depends not alone on spiritual insight but on social circumstance. So long as wars are fought, prayers to the god of battle will be offered as they were in ancient Israel,[3] and, so long as economic destitution remains, men who despite it believe in God will offer materialistic prayers. That men should pray for the reform of the social order is generally recognized, but it is less commonly recognized that on the reform of the social order depends in considerable measure the spiritualizing of prayer.

To the credit of the later Judaism, therefore, stands the deepening spiritual quality of its petitions despite the material evils afflicting the people. The Book of Deuteronomy, which in many passages gives color to Lord Bacon's saying that "prosperity is the blessing of the Old Testament,"[4] says also that "man doth not live by bread only."[5] The recognition of this fact is the glory of Israel's praying at its best:

> Give thy servant therefore an understanding
> heart to judge thy people, that I may
> discern between good and evil.[6]

> Search me, O God, and know my heart:
> Try me, and know my thoughts;
> And see if there be any wicked way in me,
> And lead me in the way everlasting.[7]

> As the hart panteth after the water brooks,
> So panteth my soul after thee, O God.
> My soul thirsteth for God, for the living God.[8]

> Whom have I in heaven but Thee?
> and having Thee there is naught on earth that I desire.[9]

> Create in me a clean heart, O God;
> And renew a right spirit within me.

[1] Lamentations 5:8-18.
[2] Lamentations 2:19.
[3] E.g., Numbers 10:35; I Samuel 7:8; II Chronicles 14:11; II Chronicles, chap. 20.
[4] "On Adversity," No. V of *Essays or Counsels Civil and Moral*.
[5] Deuteronomy 8:3.

[6] I Kings 3:9.
[7] Psalm 139:23.
[8] Psalm 42:1-2.
[9] Psalm 73:25 as translated by Julius A. Bewer in *The Literature of the Old Testament in its Historical Development*, p. 390.

> Cast me not away from thy presence;
> And take not thy holy Spirit from me.[1]

This deepening spiritual quality in prayer is shown in the thanksgivings with which the Scripture abounds. When men receive what they have petitioned God for with an urgent sense of need, they are grateful. Typical thanksgivings in the earlier period were associated, therefore, with victory in war,[2] or with the fertility of the land, "flowing with milk and honey."[3] The Hebrew mind was too realistic ever to outgrow the grateful sense of solid value in material blessings, and in this refusal of an ascetic spirituality showed its health. In the great psalms of thanksgiving —the 103d, for example—the physical basis of life was not forgotten as a cause of gratitude, but thankfulness ranged up into other areas also, such as forgiven sin, the visible execution of divine justice, and the saving experience of divine mercy. At their best the Psalms overpassed the gifts of God in gratitude for God himself—

> Enter into his gates with thanksgiving,
> And into his courts with praise:
> Give thanks unto him, and bless his name.
> For Yahweh is good; his lovingkindness endureth for ever,
> And his faithfulness unto all generations.[4]

In the New Testament the chief office of prayer, whether in petition or thanksgiving, is concerned with spiritual welfare. Bread is not forgotten and, as the symbol of life's physical basis, is made an object of request in the Lord's Prayer. But the predominant and almost exclusive concern of early Christian praying with moral and spiritual quality is unmistakable. That the disciples may "stand perfect and fully assured in all the will of God";[5] that they may be "perfect in every good thing to do his will";[6] that in the face of persecution they may speak their message "with all boldness";[7] that they "may be filled with the knowledge of his will in all spiritual wisdom and understanding, to walk worthily of the Lord unto all pleasing, bearing fruit in every good work, and increasing in the knowledge of God"[8]—such are the characteristic petitions of the New Testament. Those who make the effect of prayer on material conditions the test of its efficacy have little rootage for their ideas in New Testament soil.

[1] Psalm 51:10-11.
[2] Genesis 14:19-20.
[3] Deuteronomy 26:5-10.
[4] Psalm 100:4-5.
[5] Colossians 4:12.
[6] Hebrews 13:21.
[7] Acts 4:29.
[8] Colossians 1:9-10.

This is evident alike in early Christian thanksgiving and inter-cession. Paul thanked God for personal victory over sin,[1] for the church's victory in the proclamation of its faith "throughout the whole world,"[2] for the lives of faithful Christians,[3] and for de-liverance "out of the power of darkness" into "the kingdom of the Son of his love."[4] When he interceded for his friends he de-sired for them abounding love, increasing knowledge, the fruits of righteousness, and discernment to perceive and approve moral ex-cellence, so that they might be "sincere and void of offence."[5] The great tradition of intercession, with which in the Hebrew writings the names of Moses, Samuel, and Jeremiah were chiefly associated,[6] was fulfilled in the New Testament where prayer for one another was continually urged and exemplified.[7] Such inter-cession, however, uniformly concerned the spiritual estate of the church and its members, as in Paul's petition for his Ephesian friends:

> For this cause I bow my knees unto the Father, from whom every family in heaven and on earth is named, that he would grant you, according to the riches of his glory, that ye may be strengthened with power through his Spirit in the inward man; that Christ may dwell in your hearts through faith; to the end that ye, being rooted and grounded in love, may be strong to apprehend with all the saints what is the breadth and length and height and depth, and to know the love of Christ which passeth knowledge, that ye may be filled unto all the fulness of God.[8]

Before the quality and range of such petition much of the his-toric and contemporaneous practise and theory of prayer in the church should stand ashamed. Supplication for material benefits was the primitive beginning of prayer, and the development of Biblical thought in this regard is measured by the distance be-tween two typical intercessions:

> God give thee of the dew of heaven,
> And of the fatness of the earth,

---

[1] Romans 7:25.
[2] Romans 1:8.
[3] Philippians 1:3; I Thessalonians 1:2–8.
[4] Colossians 1:12–13.
[5] Philippians 1:9–11.

[6] Jeremiah 15:1; cf. II Maccabees 15:14; The Assumption of Moses 12:2,6.
[7] E.g., I Thessalonians 5:25; Hebrews 13:18.
[8] Ephesians 3:14–19.

> And plenty of grain and new wine:
> Let peoples serve thee,
> And nations bow down to thee:
> Be lord over thy brethren,
> And let thy mother's sons bow down to thee:
> Cursed be every one that curseth thee,
> And blessed be every one that blesseth thee.[1]

They are not of the world, even as I am not of the world. Sanctify them in the truth: thy word is truth. . . . Neither for these only do I pray, but for them also that believe on me through their word; that they may all be one; even as thou, Father, art in me, and I in thee, that they also may be in us: that the world may believe that thou didst send me.[2]

5. Accompanying such developments as we have noted in the substance of Biblical prayers, an even more profound change was in process: praying, employed at first as a means of persuading a god to do man's will, grew to be used as a means of releasing through man whatever was God's will. Primitive religion everywhere involves the endeavor, whether by sacrificial gifts or magical methods, to gain influence with superhuman powers so as to command their services. "O my Lord," said an Arab on a robber-raid, "I say unto Thee, except Thou give me a camel to-day with a water-skin, I would as it were beat Thee with this camel stick!" When, at evening, the raiders returned successful, the Arab said, "Now ye may know, fellows, ye who blamed me when I prayed at dawn, how my Lord was adread of me to-day!"[3] At the stage of development represented by such an attitude, the value of religion was measured by the control given the devotee over superhuman powers and, so far as prayer was used, its object was to persuade a god to do the bidding of a man.

In early nomadic and agricultural society, for example, when the weather was the determiner of destiny for herds and crops, religion was utilized as a means of bringing rain. Prayers for rain, as well as imitative magic to produce it, were and are a commonplace in primitive faiths. In ancient Athens the people prayed, "Rain, rain, O dear Zeus, on the cornland of the Athenians and on the plains"; in Rome one writer set the old piety of folk who prayed to Jupiter for showers, and went home from the temple

---

[1] Genesis 27:28–29.
[2] John 17:16–17, 20–21.
[3] See Charles M. Doughty: *Travels in* *Arabia Deserta* (3d ed., 1925), Vol. II, p. 241.

streaming wet themselves with the ready answer, in contrast with the then impiety, when, as he said, "we are no longer religious, so the fields lie baking"; in Upper Burma in recent times the people prayed to their tree-spirit, "O Lord, have pity on us poor mortals, and stay not the rain"; and wherever primitive religion is found today it includes means, magical or otherwise, of so gaining influence over superhuman powers as to control wind and rain, and even the sun and moon.[1]

This idea of prayer was obviously prevalent in early Biblical thought. In compliance with Joshua's demand,

> . . . the sun stood still, and the moon stayed,
> Until the nation had avenged themselves of their enemies,[2]

and while this story at first was poetry it was later taken as prosaic fact. As for rain, a man of prayer, like Samuel, powerful in his influence with Yahweh, was supposed to be able to dictate its coming—"I will call unto Yahweh, that he may send thunder and rain; and ye shall know and see that your wickedness is great, which ye have done in the sight of Yahweh, in asking you a king. So Samuel called unto Yahweh; and Yahweh sent thunder and rain that day: and all the people greatly feared Yahweh and Samuel."[3] In the traditional stories of Elijah, his control over rain was represented as one of the major factors in his public power, for so had the disposal of the weather been put in his hands that he could say: "As Yahweh, the God of Israel, liveth, before whom I stand, there shall not be dew nor rain these years, but according to my word."[4] Indeed, in the dramatic narrative of the contest on Mount Carmel between Elijah and the priests of Baal, Yahweh's swift answer to the prophet's prayer for lightning decided the issue.[5] Primitive ideas of prayer were thus thoroughly impregnated with the hope of gaining control over superhuman powers.

A less obtrusive but no less revealing evidence of this is the reluctance of any superhuman spirit to let his name be known. Possession of the name of either man or god conferred on the possessor control over him—such was and still is the well-nigh universal belief of primitive religion. "Hence," says J. G. Frazer, "just as the furtive savage conceals his real name because he fears that sorcerers might make an evil use of it, so he fancies that his gods

---

[1] See James George Frazer: *The Golden Bough; A Study in Magic and Religion* (abridged ed., 1925), pp. 159, 160, 118, 78–80.

[2] Joshua 10:12–13.
[3] I Samuel 12:17–18.
[4] I Kings 17:1.
[5] I Kings 18:37–40.

must likewise keep their true names secret, lest other gods or even men should learn the mystic sounds and thus be able to conjure with them."[1] In the Old Testament, accordingly, when Jacob asked the superhuman wrestler his name, he was rebuffed;[2] when Manoah asked "the angel of Yahweh" for his name, the answer was, "Wherefore askest thou after my name, seeing it is secret";[3] and when Moses sought to learn Yahweh's name, he received no clearer reply than "I AM THAT I AM."[4] In consonance with this traditional attitude, the Jews, from reverential motives, substituted *adonai*, meaning 'lord,' for the sacred name in their reading of the Scriptures; as a consequence, in the thirteenth century Christian Hebraists mistakenly used the consonants of the name *jhwh* with the Hebrew vowels of *adonai*, thus getting *Jehovah*; but behind this later mystification lay in primitive times the recognized unwillingness of any god to surrender possession of his secret name, lest the possessor thereby gain control over him. As the centuries passed, such magical connotations of the holy name fell away; the 'name of God' became synonymous with his personality, his dignity, character, and purpose; prayer in his name, which at first implied the supplicant's desire to control the divine will, came at last to mean the supplicant's submission to the divine will; and the remote and sublimated leftovers of this ancient idea still remain in prayers offered in the name of Christ.

The earliest Hebrew petition, however, with its rootage deep in primitive religion, sought with unabashed desire the means of persuading or coercing God to do the bidding of a man. With this for their philosophy, men bargained with their gods as Jacob did,[5] or argued with them, as the Hebrews from Joshua[6] to Joel[7] argued with Yahweh that if he did not save them his reputation would suffer loss. No development in Biblical praying is more important, therefore, than its gradual reorientation until God's will, not man's, became central and controlling. This change was bound to occur as the idea of God was elevated, until in him was seen to dwell not only power but wisdom and goodness. So Jeremiah's companions in disaster asked him to pray that "God may show us the way wherein we should walk, and the thing that we should do."[8] With God conceived as infinitely wise and good, reasonable

---

[1] See J. G. Frazer: *op. cit.*, pp. 260–262.
[2] Genesis 32:29.
[3] Judges 13:17–18 (marginal reading).
[4] Exodus 3:13–14.
[5] Genesis 28:20–22.
[6] Joshua 7:9.
[7] Joel 2:17; cf. II Kings 19:16–19; Daniel 9:19.
[8] Jeremiah 42:3.

prayer must be conceived not as a means of forcing on God the bidding of man, but as a means of releasing through man the purpose of God. So the greater praying of the Old Testament rose, as in the Fortieth Psalm, to say, "I delight to do thy will, O my God."[1]

In the New Testament this radical reorientation of prayer became controlling. Still the older usages persisted. James even illustrated the efficacy of petition by Elijah's power to prevent and produce rain,[2] but the characteristic and original quality of New Testament prayer is of another stuff altogether. "If we ask anything according to his will, he heareth us"[3]—that is the organizing idea of typical Christian praying. God's will came first, infinitely wise and good, and prayer was intended not to change but to release it, not to gain power over it but to open the door for its complete expression. The pith of the Lord's Prayer, therefore, is "Thy will be done."[4] As New Testament Christians *thought* that they might understand the divine will, and as they *labored* to give it effective application, so they *prayed* that nothing within themselves might impede or balk it. Prayer was a means of alignment and coöperation with God, and its effect was not the substitution of something else for the divine will but the divine will's powerful and transforming release into the world. With good reason, therefore, the essence of characteristic Christian praying has been found in the Garden of Gethsemane. There the clinging residue of primitive magic was entirely laid aside. The crude superstition of man's prayer as a means of instructing God or altering his intention was overpassed and praying became both congruous with the Christian idea of God and effectively powerful in spiritual result— "Abba, Father, all things are possible unto thee; remove this cup from me: howbeit not what I will, but what thou wilt."[5]

From vindictiveness to magnanimity; from tribalism to universality; from the regret of penalized men over broken taboos to the penitence of humble men over personal guilt; from supplications for physical benefits to prayer as the fulfilling of interior conditions of spiritual growth; from the desire to impose man's will on a god to the desire that God's will should be done through man—such are the developments revealed in the recorded prayers of the Bible.

[1] Psalm 40:8.
[2] James 5:17-18.
[3] I John 5:14.

[4] Matthew 6:10.
[5] Mark 14:36.

VIII

Such developments, however, while they immeasurably deepened and expanded the meaning of personal prayer, did not solve the problem of public worship, which the early Christians only temporarily escaped when they left the temple and the synagogue. Jesus himself was reported to have said that "where two or three are gathered together in my name, there am I in the midst of them,"[1] and very early in the New Testament's narrative we are made aware of a strong, corporate solidarity in the nascent churches. The new disciples, whether with Jewish or Gentile backgrounds, found in the Christian community not only a transforming experience of divine grace but a sustaining experience of human fellowship, and, in whatever other ways this fellowship functioned, it was bound to express itself in corporate worship. Many a problem of inherited ritual the first Christians sloughed off in leaving the temple and synagogue, but many new ones faced them as soon as they inaugurated what the Epistle to the Hebrews called, "our own assembling together."[2] Indeed, so central were these problems to certain of the early Christians that Professor E. F. Scott can say of religion: "For some it is an inward fellowship with God, for some an inspiration to right living, for some the highest exercise of reason. There are others, and the author of Hebrews was one of them, for whom religion consists above all in *worship*."[3]

The fact that the Old Testament continued to be the Christian Bible made the earliest worship of the new assemblies by no means an innovation. At the beginning, their "psalms and hymns and spiritual songs"[4] were probably taken over and adapted from the older heritage, and while the evidence on this matter is scant, the devotional services of the early churches doubtless leaned heavily on the Old Testament, especially the Psalter, and even on the customs of the synagogue. Such data as we have suggests informality and spontaneity as characteristic of the first Christian worship, held in private houses[5] and unequipped with symbolic pomp and circumstance. Indeed, in Corinth the worship was accompanied by emotional ecstasies, plunging the devotees into mysterious trances and finding utterance in enthusiastic, although unintelligible, eloquence. On this disorderly emotionalism Paul

[1] Matthew 18:20.
[2] Hebrews 10:25.
[3] *The Literature of the New Testament*, p. 201.
[4] Colossians 3:16; Ephesians 5:19.
[5] Colossians 4:15; Romans 16:5.

put the stamp of his disapproval,[1] but it indicates in how informal, spontaneous, and non-liturgical an atmosphere some, at least, of of the first churches worshiped.

Such simplicity, however, was transient. The liturgical heritage of Judaism, the psychological and practical needs of the worshiping group, and the inexorable pressure of ideas and customs in the Mediterranean world, especially in the mystery religions, presaged the development in Christianity, as in other faiths, of ritual and sacrament. How specifically influential the mystery religions were in the formulation of the consequence is a moot matter. Certainly they were the most vital and popularly important religious movements in the social matrix where Christian worship took shape. At many points they were sufficiently akin to Christianity so that their prevalence furnished a favorable preparation for the gospel. They had inculcated a deep sense of sin and a conscious need of personal salvation; they had overpassed national and racial lines and had made religious faith a matter of individual conviction; they had emphasized faith in immortality and the need of assurance concerning it; they had bound their devotees together in mystical societies of brethren fired with propagandist zeal; and they had accentuated the interior nature of religious experience in terms of an indwelling Presence, through whom human life could be 'deicized.' When, therefore, we find them also possessing sacraments, fairly magical in their efficacy—especially baptisms, whether of water or of blood, and sacred meals that conferred union with the deity—the query inevitably rises in how far in these regards they influenced Christianity.[2]

Whatever may be the solution of this difficult and perhaps insoluble problem, the evidence of the New Testament is clear that an organized cultus, with accompanying ideas of sacramental efficacy, was already in process of formation before the canon closed. Baptism was the normal, if not the indispensable, condition of membership in the church,[3] and so magical an efficacy did some ascribe to it that, at least in Corinth, there were baptisms on behalf of the dead.[4] The profoundest experiences of Christian conversion—especially remission of sins,[5] the death of the old life and the resurrection of the new,[6] and incorporation into the body of

[1] I Corinthians, chaps. 12–14.
[2] See Samuel Angus: *The Mystery-Religions and Christianity*, for discussion and bibliography.

[3] I Corinthians 12:13; Galatians 3:27; Acts 2:37–38; etc.
[4] I Corinthians 15:29.
[5] Acts 2:38; I Peter 3:21.
[6] Romans 6:2–4; Colossians 2:12.

Christ[1]—were associated with baptism. At first the ritual was doubtless figurative, a ceremonial cleansing in water, which was regarded as symbolizing, rather than effecting, the purification of the inner life, and the origin of which lay in the baptism of John and kindred customs rather than in the sacraments of the mystery religions. Paul even thanked God that he himself had baptized none of the Corinthians save two, together with the household of Stephanas, saying, "Christ sent me not to baptize, but to preach";[2] in the Fourth Gospel John's baptism in water is explicitly subordinated to Christ's baptism in the Holy Spirit;[3] and in the Epistle to the Hebrews "the teaching of baptisms" is put among the rudimentary principles, to be accepted, indeed, but beyond which those need to go who are pressing on "unto perfection."[4] This, however, is not the whole story. The Fourth Gospel attributes to Jesus the words, "Verily, verily, I say unto thee, Except one be born of water and the Spirit, he cannot enter into the kingdom of God";[5] the Epistle to Titus says the same thing in other language—"He saved us, through the washing of regeneration and renewing of the Holy Spirit";[6] and in the Shepherd of Hermas, which in some of the earliest canons was included in the New Testament, the baptismal water is called "the seal of the Son of God" into which they descend "dead," and out of which they come "alive."[7] Whether or not the sacramental ideas of the mystery religions directly affected Christianity, the New Testament indicates a budding sacramentalism whose rootage one would less expect to find in Judaism than in the Hellenistic cults.

As for the Lord's Supper, it began so simply that at first every meal where disciples ate together was a sacred communion, and their ordinary bread and wine were memorials of their Lord's sacrifice. This led to such disorders, however, at least in the Corinthian church, where, as Paul said, "one is hungry, and another is drunken,"[8] that the Eucharist was separated from common occasions and became a definite, symbolic act. As to this act's precise meaning in the first churches, evidence is scarce and decision difficult. The original associations of the Supper were with the Jewish Passover,[9] a corporate communion of God's people protected by the saving blood of the paschal lamb. That

---

[1] I Corinthians 12:13,27; Ephesians 4: 4-5.
[2] I Corinthians 1:13-17.
[3] John 1:33.
[4] Hebrews 6:1-2.
[5] John 3:5.

[6] Titus 3:5.
[7] The Shepherd of Hermas, translated by Charles H. Hoole, "The Ninth Similitude," xvi, p. 146.
[8] I Corinthians 11:20-22.
[9] I Corinthians 5:7.

the Eucharist was, therefore, a commemoration[1] followed naturally from its origin. This, however, does not exhaust the meaning
of the rite in the New Testament. Alike in the sacred meals of
Judaism and of paganism, another idea had from primitive times
been dominant—by eating the sacrificed and dedicated food,
union was consummated between the worshiper and his deity.
Was this idea in Paul's mind when he implied that eating of the
heathen feasts was a real "communion with demons," and that
in the same mystical sense the "cup of the Lord" and the "table
of the Lord" conferred on Christians union with Christ?[2] Was
this the meaning of the Fourth Gospel also when it put on the
lips of Jesus words of high sacramental import—"Verily, verily,
I say unto you, Except ye eat the flesh of the Son of man and
drink his blood, ye have not life in yourselves. He that eateth
my flesh and drinketh my blood hath eternal life; and I will
raise him up at the last day. For my flesh is meat indeed, and
my blood is drink indeed. He that eateth my flesh and drinketh
my blood abideth in me, and I in him"?[3] At any rate, even
within the New Testament the Eucharist, along with baptism,
was exalted as an essential element in the new Christian cult
and so mystical were some of its suggested interpretations that
Principal J. G. Simpson writes, "it must be frankly admitted
that . . . none of the explanations which have divided Christendom
since the 16th cent., not even the theory of transubstantiation
when precisely defined, can be regarded as wholly inconsistent
with the language of Scripture."[4]

While the New Testament, therefore, records the development
of personal prayer as the habitual maintenance of an interior
spiritual communion with the Unseen Friend, it also records the
beginning of a new cultus. In place of the synagogue came the
church; in place of circumcision came baptism; in place of the
temple altars came the acceptance of Christ's sacrifice in the
Lord's Supper; and while only the first suggestions of the early
Catholic rubric are within the canon, these suggestions are there,
presaging, as they are seen in retrospect, the repetition of all
the good and evil fortunes that in every age and faith have
attended sacramentalism. The subsequent centuries have wit-
nessed endless conflict over the Christian cultus, but one element
in the long development of Biblical experience and thought

---

[1] I Corinthians 11:24.
[2] I Corinthians 10:16–21.
[3] John 6:53–56.

[4] Closing paragraph of "Eucharist," in
Hastings' *Dictionary of the Bible*, One Vol.
Edition, p. 246.

concerning fellowship with God has remained as the common and unifying gain of all—"Thou, when thou prayest, enter into thine inner chamber, and having shut thy door, pray to thy Father who is in secret."[1]

No such statement as we have made can adequately portray the experiential meaning of such prayer to New Testament Christians. When, centuries later, Brother Lawrence described prayer as establishing oneself "in a sense of God's presence by continually conversing with Him,"[2] he was true to the best tradition of the Gospels and Epistles. This interior divine fellowship, when a man fulfilled its conditions, became "in him a well of water springing up unto eternal life."[3] Prayer was not instructing God concerning human wants, for "your Father knoweth what things ye have need of, before ye ask him."[4] Prayer was not begging a reluctant deity for his best gifts, as though he were an unjust judge or a surly neighbor in bed with his children unwilling to arise and answer a call for help—although if patience in prayer could accomplish its end even in such cases, how much more with the righteous and merciful God![5] Prayer was first of all the maintenance of an habitual spiritual companionship— "I am not alone, because the Father is with me."[6]

From this central fountainhead new meanings streamed into practises that had long been traditional with praying people. Prayer in the New Testament church was, in part, a form of spiritual self-discipline, associated at times with ascetic usages such as fasting.[7] Prayer was a process of purification from which forgiven souls emerged cleansed from old stains of unpardoned guilt.[8] Prayer was an appeal to the divine arbitrament against the condemnation and derision of the world, a protestation of innocence against the false judgment of men, an appeal to the future against the mistaken present.[9] Prayer was thanksgiving and praise, the joyful overflow of gratitude and hope, even amid difficult or desperate circumstance.[10] Prayer was a means of securing divine guidance, so that a man, not only in general but in particular surrendering himself to superhuman direction, could know God's will and do it.[11] Prayer was the

[1] Matthew 6:6.
[2] *The Practice of the Presence of God the Best Rule of a Holy Life*, "First Conversation."
[3] John 4:14.
[4] Matthew 6:8.
[5] See Luke 11:5-13; 18:1-8.
[6] John 16:32.
[7] Acts 14:23; I Corinthians 7:5.
[8] I John 1:9; 5:16.
[9] Acts 4:24-31; II Thessalonians 3:1-2.
[10] Acts 16:25; Philemon, vss. 4-5; Colossians 1:12; I Thessalonians 5:18.
[11] Acts 1:24-26; I Timothy 5:5.

affirmation of confident trust, the centering of attention on faith, not fear, on assets rather than liabilities, on the help of God rather than the troubles of life.[1] Prayer was a potent force which released divine power not only for spiritual peace but for bodily health, and which at times wrought miracles of healing.[2] Prayer was the overflow of an unselfish love seeking the welfare of one's friends.[3]

All such traditional usages of prayer, however, are in the New Testament illumined by a central sun. The believer lives in God and God in him; the soul has immediate access into the divine presence and is, indeed, the very temple in which God's Spirit dwells; so that, whatever else may be granted or withheld in prayer, the sustaining companionship of the Unseen Friend is constant and assured. In this regard St. Augustine truly reflected the early Christian faith at its best—"Give me Thine own self, without which, though Thou shouldst give me all that ever Thou hast made, yet could not my desires be satisfied."[4]

[1] Cf. Ephesians 1:3–15; Hebrews 13:6.
[2] James 5:14–15. See Alexis Carrel: *Man the Unknown*, pp. 147–150, for a modern scientific confirmation.
[3] Colossians 4:12; James 5:16.
[4] As quoted by Mary Wilder Tileston: *Prayers Ancient and Modern* (new and revised ed.), p. 275.

CHAPTER VI

THE IDEA OF IMMORTALITY

I

A modern behaviorist, holding that a human being is simply a physical organism with its various functions, draws the inevitable inference that no continued life after death is possible. The early Hebrews, starting with a similar idea, came to no such conclusion. While they believed that man was a body with breath for his soul, blood for his life, and organs whose functions were both physical and psychical, the earliest Hebrews of whom we have record were convinced that dead men were not altogether dead. What remained existent after death was not soul conceived as an immaterial reality, for no such idea dawned on the Hebrews until ages later, when Greek influence was felt in Judaism. Human beings after death were, to the early Hebrews, still bodies, attenuated leftovers and shadowy replicas of the flesh, and these existences beyond the grave the Old Testament called *rephaim*—that is, shadows or ghosts.

That the dead were thus not sufficiently dead to cease being matters of concern to the living is made clear both by direct statement and indirect intimation in the Old Testament.

1. As among all early peoples, necromancy, dealing with the dead, was an active superstition among the Hebrews. In the background of such wizardry were doubtless the same influences, especially dreams, that have commonly persuaded primitive peoples of the continued existence and influence of the dead. Man's mind at first did not value waking experience above sleeping as a clue to truth, and far down in history, dreams, instead of being discredited as unreliable witnesses to fact, were given supernormal importance as revelations. When, therefore, a living man dreamed, let us say, of his dead father, and in his dream conversed with his sire and saw him act, the door was opened to the conviction that the dead were not dead, and to the still further belief that the dead, being mysterious and possibly dangerous presences, needed to be rightly dealt with.

Such ideas always have given rise to a special class of people, witches and wizards, who practise necromancy, and in the Old Testament they are repeatedly mentioned in terms of denunciation. The Deuteronomic law commanded the extirpation of any one who could be called "an enchanter, or a sorcerer, or a charmer, or a consulter with a familiar spirit, or a wizard, or a necromancer."[1] Isaiah poured scorn on "them that have familiar spirits" and on "the wizards, that chirp and that mutter,"[2] and the later law of Leviticus twice returned to the same attack.[3]

The most picturesque passage in the Old Testament in illustration of such prevalent beliefs concerns the Witch of Endor, whom Saul consulted in order to seek counsel from the dead Samuel. One notes the weird night scene, the underground setting, the fact that only the witch is reported to have seen Samuel, the complete credulity of Saul, Samuel's rising out of Sheol in bodily form, clothed in a robe and physically recognizable, and, implied in the whole story, the popular prevalence of such necromancy in making use of the still-existent dead.[4]

2. By all analogy we should expect to find ancestor worship associated with this range of ideas about the afterworld. In the Old Testament, however, the actual practise of worshiping ancestors had been so far overpassed that while one first-rate scholar says, "There is a growing consensus of opinion that the Hebrews, like all other peoples at a certain stage of thought, worshipped these spirits,"[5] another first-rate scholar says, "The alleged indications of Ancestor Worship are all exposed to more or less serious objections."[6]

What we do have in the Old Testament is a mass of evidence that the dead were of profound importance to the living, that elaborate ceremonies and popular customs were involved in dealing with them, and that such observances were concerned both with the veneration due from the living to the departed and with the possible good or evil that might come from the departed to the living. Many mortuary customs which persist today—putting food on graves, as in China, for example, or flowers, as with us—are traceable to primitive endeavors to please and placate the spirits of the deceased, and similar offerings

[1] Deuteronomy 18:10–11; cf. Exodus 22:18.
[2] Isaiah 8:19–20.
[3] Leviticus 19:31; 20:6.
[4] I Samuel 28:3–25.

[5] Henry Preserved Smith: *The Religion of Israel*, p. 25.
[6] E. Kautzsch: "Religion of Israel," in Hastings' *Dictionary of the Bible*, Extra Vol., p. 614.

to the dead in Old Testament times should be so understood.[1] General analogies with Egyptian and Babylonian folk-ways confirm this, and in detail the kinship of Hebrew and Semitic mortuary customs is clear in such observances as offering one's cut hair to the dead or making incisions in the flesh to establish blood-covenant with the dead.[2] The persistence of such rites among the Hebrews is indicated by their condemnation in both early and late codes of law. So Deuteronomy said, "Ye shall not cut yourselves, nor make any baldness between your eyes for the dead,"[3] and Leviticus still found it necessary to insist, "Ye shall not make any cuttings in your flesh for the dead."[4]

Indeed, it has been supposed by some that the teraphim, household gods,[5] were originally images of ancestors; that they were honored as such and were part of the apparatus of popular religion;[6] that mortuary customs which the prophetic school later condemned grew up around them;[7] that the right of performing the necessary ceremonies for one's ancestors devolved upon a son and that this fact underlay both the sense of tragedy in being sonless and the practises of levirate marriage and of adoption to avoid such disaster;[8] and that this set of ideas and customs was an integral part of the whole clan organization of early Israel. "From such a mass of evidence," says Lods, "it would seem that we are warranted in the conclusion that before their entry into Canaan the Hebrew tribes must have possessed a fully organized cultus of the ancestors of families and clans."[9] At any rate, there can be no doubt, in view of the evidence presented by mortuary customs, that early Hebrews felt a deep concern for dealing effectively with the influence of the still-existent dead.

II

As for the dwelling-place of the *rephaim*, the Old Testament leaves us in no uncertainty. The Hebrew cosmos was three-storied: the sky, or heaven, above; the flat earth beneath; and, under that, Sheol, the abode of the departed. In this regard, primitive

[1] E.g., II Chronicles 16:14.
[2] Isaiah 22:12; Jeremiah 7:29; Amos 8:10; Micah 1:16; Ezekiel 7:18; 27:31. See W. Robertson Smith: *Lectures on the Religion of the Semites*, pp. 323-326.
[3] Deuteronomy 14:1; cf. 26:14.
[4] Leviticus 19:28.
[5] Genesis 35:4; 31:19, 30-35; I Samuel 15:23; 19:13,16; II Kings 23:24.

[6] Hosea 3:4.
[7] Cf. Deuteronomy 26:13-14.
[8] Cf. Genesis 15:2-3; 30:3-8; Deuteronomy 25:5-10.
[9] Adolphe Lods: *Israel from its Beginnings to the Middle of the Eighth Century*, translated by S. H. Hooke, p. 229; cf. R. H. Charles: *Eschatology; Hebrew, Jewish and Christian*, pp. 21-33.

Greek and Hebrew conceptions were practically unanimous, and Sheol in the Old Testament was of one piece with Hades in Homer's poems. The dead in Hades, as the Iliad and Odyssey pictured them, were not souls, in the later Platonic sense, but vaporous bodies. Just as Samuel came up from Sheol in visible presence, clothed as he was on earth, so the shade of Patroklos is described in the Iliad as "in all things like his living self, in stature, and fair eyes, and voice, and the raiment of his body was the same." Yet, despite this earthly verisimilitude, the difference made by death was profound, for when Achilles "reached forth with his hands" he "clasped him not; for like a vapour the spirit was gone beneath the earth with a faint shriek."[1] So Odysseus found the shade of his mother wholly insubstantial,[2] and even valiant heroes were reduced in Hades to ghosts so feeble that a draught of the fresh blood of sacrificial victims was necessary to rouse them to action.[3]

In general conception and in many particular details the similarity between Hades and Sheol is plain. In the Hebrew underworld, the prophet still wore his ghostly mantle and kings sat on shadowy thrones.[4] The dreariest words in the vocabulary were used about the dwelling of the dead and its inhabitants. It was the land of the "dark" and of "forgetfulness,"[5] of "silence"[6] and of "destruction."[7] Far from being consulted as "the knowing ones," its inhabitants were conceived by those who had renounced necromancy as neither knowing nor caring about anything on earth:

> His sons come to honor, and he knoweth it not;
> And they are brought low, but he perceiveth it not of them.
> Only for himself his flesh hath pain, and for himself
> his soul mourneth.[8]

As though to leave us in no doubt about this shadowy half reality of Sheol, Isaiah drew a picture of it with even its royal tenants rising to greet newcomers and saying, "Art thou also become weak as we?"[9]

[1] *The Iliad of Homer Done Into English Verse:* by Andrew Lang, Walter Leaf, and Ernest Myers, Bk. xxiii, pp. 452, 453.

[2] *Homer; The Odyssey, With an English Translation,* by A. T. Murray, Vol. I, Bk. xi, pp. 401–403.

[3] *Ibid.,* Bk. xi, pp. 393, 397.

[4] I Samuel 28:14; Isaiah 14:9.

[5] Psalm 88:12.

[6] Psalm 94:17.

[7] Job 26:6 (marginal translation).

[8] Job 14:21–22 (marginal translation).

[9] Isaiah 14:9–10.

Clearly, therefore, no hope was associated with Sheol. It was the sad, inevitable end of man, "the house appointed for all living."[1] To go there was to lose real existence and the pious sick could pray,

> Oh spare me, that I may recover strength,
> Before I go hence, and be no more.[2]

The best to be said for Sheol was that life on earth might become so wretched that Sheol's very negativeness would be a relief. Job, finding his existence intolerable, craved the unreality of the underworld, too empty of positive content to involve the sufferings of earth:

> There the wicked cease from troubling;
> And there the weary are at rest.
> There the prisoners are at ease together;
> They hear not the voice of the taskmaster.
> The small and the great are there:
> And the servant is free from his master.[3]

While the early Hebrews, therefore, believed in existence after death, it was so pallid and unreal, in an underworld so undesirable, that no hopes were associated with it. Until far down in their history, all the vivid and enheartening hopes of the Hebrews were concerned with the future of their nation on earth—

> . . . thy seed shall be great,
> And thine offspring as the grass of the earth.[4]

As for those who went "down into the pit," they were

> . . . as a man that hath no help,
> Cast off among the dead.[5]

In suggesting the literal location of Sheol—an underworld beneath the surface of the ground and as geographically real as any place on earth—the Old Testament is clear and explicit. When, for example, Moses executed Yahweh's wrath against the rebellious sons of Korah, they were dropped alive into Sheol through the yawning ground—"The ground clave asunder that was under them; and the earth opened its mouth, and swallowed them up, and their households, and all the men that appertained unto Korah, and all their goods. So they, and all that apper-

---

[1] Job 30:23.
[2] Psalm 39:13.
[3] Job 3:17–19.

[4] Job 5:25.
[5] Psalm 88:3–5.

tained to them, went down alive into Sheol: and the earth closed upon them."[1]

Such was the beginning of the Bible's conception of the afterworld, and the development of thought from this crude primitiveness of Sheol to the New Testament's doctrine of eternal life constitutes one of the most significant contributions of the Scriptures to religious history.

III

Among the factors that played a part in this development, the enlarging idea of God was prominent. Sheol was an inheritance in Hebrew belief from a past long antedating the introduction of the people to Yahweh. At first, therefore, Yahweh as the storm god of Sinai, or as the war god of the migrant tribes, or even as the agricultural god of Canaan, had nothing to do with Sheol; the underworld of the dead was outside his realm.

Commonly in ancient mythologies, the gods of the nether world were not the gods of the earth's surface. So it was in Greece, where Hades had its own deity; and so it was in Babylonia. The Babylonian Sheol, called Aralû, was a great cavern in the bowels of a mountain under the earth;[2] it was without light, covered with dust and filth, its inhabitants eating dust save as offerings of food were received from the sacrifices of the living; and the shades who dwelt there were no longer under the domain of the gods of earth but had deities of their own, supremely Nergal. To be sure, in the Old Testament no gods of Sheol are specifically named, but Dr. Paton is probably correct in thinking that we have the faded reminiscence of them in such personifications as "Death shall be their shepherd"[3] or "He shall be brought to the king of terrors."[4] Moreover, it is not unlikely that the death angels of later Judaism were the old gods of the underworld, reduced, according to the habit of early religions, to the subordinate position of spirits.[5]

In any case, the Old Testament repeatedly reveals that, at first, Yahweh had no control over Sheol; he was god of the earth, then god of the sky, but at the gates of the underworld relation-

---

[1] Numbers 16:31–33; cf. Psalm 63:9; 86:13; Ezekiel 26:20; 31:14; 32:18,24.
[2] Cf. Jonah 2:6.
[3] Psalm 49:14.
[4] Job 18:14.
[5] See Lewis Bayles Paton: "The Hebrew Idea of the Future Life," in *The Biblical World*, "New Series," Vol. 35 (1910), pp. 159–171, for influence of Babylonian thought on Hebrew thought of life after death.

ships with him ceased. The Eighty-eighth Psalm is explicit on this point:

> . . . My life draweth nigh unto Sheol.
> I am reckoned with them that go down into the pit;
>
> .   .   .   .   .
>
> Like the slain that lie in the grave,
> Whom thou rememberest no more,
> And they are cut off from thy hand.[1]

Similarly, the sick Hezekiah shrinks from death believing that it separates from Yahweh:

> For Sheol cannot praise thee, death cannot celebrate thee:
> They that go down into the pit cannot hope for thy truth.[2]

Whether within the Old Testament, where the psalmist is convinced that

> The dead praise not Yahweh,
> Neither any that go down into silence,[3]

or in Jewish literature outside, as in Ecclesiasticus—"Who shall give praise to the Most High in the grave?"[4]—or in the Book of Baruch—"The dead that are in the grave, whose breath is taken from their bodies, will give unto the Lord neither glory nor righteousness"[5]— we have the persistent tradition that death breaks off all relationships between man and Yahweh.

One of the major factors, therefore, both in redeeming Sheol itself from its original negativeness and in arousing hope of resurrection from it to full life again, was the extension of Yahweh's sovereignty to the nether world. As Yahweh overpassed early limitations in the thinking of his people until he was recognized as God of heaven and earth, the question of his power over the realm below the earth was inevitably raised, and the forces which had expanded his sway elsewhere tended to include also under his domain the abode of the *rephaim*. The Old Testament still retains the early evidences of this new theology, explicitly contradicting the older restriction on Yahweh's power.

The first motive, of which we have expression, for thus extending Yahweh's rule to Sheol, was the desire that unpunished men might not escape justice there. So Amos represented Yahweh as

---

[1] Psalm 88:3–5; see also vs. 11.
[2] Isaiah 38:18.
[3] Psalm 115:17; cf. 6:5; 30:9; 118:17.
[4] Ecclesiasticus 17:27.
[5] Baruch 2:17.

saying, "Though they dig into Sheol, thence shall my hand take them,"[1] and Deuteronomy pictured him in a threatening mood:

> For a fire is kindled in mine anger,
> And burneth unto the lowest Sheol.[2]

In a word, the nether world, at first for the sake of justice, was gradually taken possession of by Yahweh's expanding power, until Isaiah could challenge Ahaz to ask a sign of God "either in the depth, or in the height above"[3]—that is, in Sheol or in heaven.

Without understanding this gradual expansion of the divine sovereignty until, at least in the imagination of a few, the entire Hebrew cosmos with its three levels—sky, earth, and underworld —were under Yahweh's sway, we cannot feel the full force of one of the supreme passages in the Old Testament. It was new theology when it was written, an immortal expression of man's faith in the universal presence and availability of God, and it was phrased in terms of the threefold Hebrew cosmos with the triumphant conviction that Yahweh was inescapably present throughout the whole of it:

> Whither shall I go from thy Spirit?
> Or whither shall I flee from thy presence?
> If I ascend up into heaven, thou art there:
> If I make my bed in Sheol, behold, thou art there.
> If I take the wings of the morning,
> And dwell in the uttermost parts of the sea;
> Even there shall thy hand lead me,
> And thy right hand shall hold me.[4]

Along this line of development hope traveled that Sheol might not be the last word in the story of man. "God," cried the psalmist, "will redeem my soul from the power of Sheol."[5] Moreover, with the divine sovereignty thus extended to the dead, and with the divine character conceived increasingly in terms of righteousness, Sheol itself was bound to be transformed. It gradually ceased being inane and meaningless, a non-moral land of darkness and forgetfulness. It became ethically significant, with rewards and punishments administered to its inhabitants. And, at last, along with the transformation of Sheol itself into

---

[1] Amos 9:2.
[2] Deuteronomy 32:22.
[3] Isaiah 7:11.

[4] Psalm 139:7–10.
[5] Psalm 49:15.

a morally meaningful place, came the hope of restoration from it to full life again.

IV

In achieving this result, the developing idea of man was also influential. So long as man was more or less completely submerged in the social mass, his personal fortunes beyond death would be imagined and cared for dimly, if at all. The continuing social group was the reality on which attention was centered and in which all hope inhered. This is the meaning of Hezekiah's words:

> They that go down into the pit cannot hope for thy truth.
> The living, the living, he shall praise thee, as I do this day:
> The father to the children shall make known thy truth.[1]

When, however, the individual as a personality with rights of his own began to stand free from social submergence, the question of his fate after death was inevitably raised.

Apparently it was the demand of the individual for justice that pushed this issue to the fore. At first, justice had especially concerned the social group as a whole and Yahweh was held to be inflexibly fair in dealing with the clan or nation, thought of *en masse*. With the increasing discrimination of the individual, however, as a center of keen interest, it became clear that the problem of life's justice to him is a much more complicated and difficult affair. So the Book of Job wrestled with the apparently insoluble dilemma—Yahweh just, and yet not always just to persons one by one, within their lifetime on the earth.

It is in the Book of Job, therefore, that we find what has been called "the first tentative demand for a life beyond death."[2] That this demand sprang from considerations of equity to the individual is made clear in the drama. Job, a virtuous man, suffering incredible afflictions and so facing in acute form the problem of life's injustice, blazed tentative trails toward a solution. One of these was the hope of at least a temporary restoration from Sheol and a vindication of his character at the judgment seat of God. Sheol itself was to Job what it was to his contemporaries, "the land of darkness and of the shadow of death"[3] but, all the more because of that, his demand for individual justice led him to hope that the inanity of Sheol was not God's last word to a mistreated man. Out of this situation rose

---

[1] Isaiah 38:18-19.   [3] Job 10:21.
[2] H. Wheeler Robinson: *The Religious Ideas of the Old Testament*, p. 94.

Job's conviction that, in a special case like his, Sheol might turn out to be only an intermediate state with a final vindication of righteousness afterwards. At times he denied such expectation and was hopeless:

> As the cloud is consumed and vanisheth away,
> So he that goeth down to Sheol shall come up no more.[1]

But even in those dark hours hope rose:

> Would'st thou but hide me in the nether world,
>   concealing me until thy wrath is over,
>   and then remember me when it is time!
> If only man might die and live again,
>   I could endure my weary post until relief arrived;
> thou would'st call, and I would come,
>   when thou didst yearn for life that thou hadst made.[2]

And in one passage Job's conviction was expressed with notable strength:

> Still, I know One to champion me at last,
>   to stand up for me upon earth.
> This body may break up, but even then
>   my life shall have a sight of God;
> my heart is pining as I yearn
>   to see him on my side.[3]

Taken in connection with the rest of the drama, this passage indicates no generally accepted doctrine of resurrection from Sheol and no widespread application of hope, but it does show that the idea of resurrection was in the air. Indeed, the Greek Septuagint Translation of the book climaxes Job's restoration to prosperity with this significant addition not in the Hebrew: "And it is written that Job will rise again with those whom the Lord doth raise."[4] In his realistic facing of life's frequent injustice to individuals and in his hope, however tentative and limited, that restoration from the underworld might bring vindication, Job blazed a trail which afterward became a heavily traveled road. The more the values and rights of personality were recognized and the more the concept of divine justice was applied to individuals, the more Job's clue was followed. Even Tenny-

---

[1] Job 7:9; cf. 14:7–12.
[2] Job 14:13–15 (Moffatt translation).
[3] Job 19:25–27 (Moffatt translation).

[4] See John Edgar McFadyen: *The Problem of Pain; A Study in the Book of Job*, pp. 248–249.

son's "In Memoriam" is to be found in the tradition which
Job inaugurated:

> Thou wilt not leave us in the dust:
> Thou madest man, he knows not why,
> He thinks he was not made to die;
> And thou hast made him: thou art just.

v

Even more influential in its permanent effect on the Biblical
hope of real life after death was the growing experience of personal religion as an inward, intimate relationship between the
soul and God. At first Hebrew religion, being altogether tribal,
involved no such interior meaning for individuals. In any powerful
spiritual movement, however, such as Israel's faith involved,
mysticism is bound to emerge despite all obstacles; special personalities, at first few in number but increasing by contagion,
find their religious experience becoming within themselves a
profound resource, a "fountain of living waters," an intimate,
sustaining fellowship with God. Whenever, in any religion, this
development takes place, the sense of essential timelessness in
the experience is not far off and the hope is sure to rise that such
a fellowship contains the prophecy of its own continuance.

When, for example, Jeremiah, thrown back on God amid the
social disintegration of his time, entered into a trustful reliance
on Yahweh—"my strength, and my stronghold, and my refuge
in the day of affliction"[1]—he was unwittingly blazing a trail
toward faith in immortality. He never himself followed it to
its conclusion; in his long and self-revealing book there is no
indication that he thought much about Sheol or thought of it
differently from his contemporaries, or had the slightest hope
of resurrection out of it. Despite that, however, he made an incalculable contribution to the inwardness of the soul's relationship
with God, and from that experience, at last, came the assurance
that what is in quality so timeless will not come to a futile
finale in the nether world.

When a late Isaiah represents God as saying, "I dwell . . . with
him also that is of a contrite and humble spirit, to revive the
spirit of the humble, and to revive the heart of the contrite,"[2]
the question rises in the mind of one who understands from
within what the implied experience means: If God so cares for
persons one by one and so dwells in them with creative power,

[1] Jeremiah 16:19.   [2] Isaiah 57:15.

is it not impossible that the relationship will be summarily terminated at death? However many individuals in Israel may have failed to raise this question or, raising it, may have left it shrouded in doubt or negatively answered, the question was bound to be raised by some and answered affirmatively.

As a whole, the Old Testament gives no clear reply to this question. The intimations of faith in the resurrection of the dead are few in number and late in date. Two of the Psalms, however, move up from a description of inward communion with God toward an expectation of release from Sheol:

> Nevertheless I am continually with thee:
> Thou hast holden my right hand.
> Thou wilt guide me with thy counsel,
> And afterward receive me to glory.
> Whom have I in heaven but thee?
> And there is none upon earth that I desire besides thee.
> My flesh and my heart faileth;
> But God is the strength of my heart and my portion for ever.[1]

> I have set Yahweh always before me:
> Because he is at my right hand, I shall not be moved.
> Therefore my heart is glad, and my glory rejoiceth:
> My flesh also shall dwell in safety.
> For thou wilt not leave my soul to Sheol;
> Neither wilt thou suffer thy holy one to see corruption.
> Thou wilt show me the path of life:
> In thy presence is fulness of joy;
> In thy right hand there are pleasures for evermore.[2]

Along this road from inward, personal religion to the assurance that God's care for the soul is too eternal in quality to be stopped by death, Hebrew-Christian thought traveled to its most distinctive idea of eternal life.

VI

Another influence which raised the question of restoration from Sheol was the Hebrew expectation of a coming Messianic age, "the most striking and characteristic feature of the religion of Israel." To be sure, this expectation was social; it concerned the nation as a whole; but by indirection it brought the Jews face to face at last with the inescapable problem of individual destiny after death. The Messianic hope in a rudimentary form

[1] Psalm 73:23–26.   [2] Psalm 16:8–11.

began with the sudden glory of David's kingdom. From a whipped and humiliated people, burdened by the Amorites among them and the victorious Philistines over them, the Hebrews under David's leadership sprang through swift conquest into an unexpected domain reaching from the borders of Egypt to the gates of Damascus. The glory of this kingdom caught the national imagination and established the first pattern of Messianic hope. David's domain was soon lost and the memory of its splendor was metamorphosed into hope of its restoration. At first this expectation was doubtless emotional in its appeal, as Mussolini stirs Italians now by pictures of a new Roman Empire, but as the centuries passed and the powerful theological conviction that Israel was a chosen people in special covenant relationship with Yahweh blended with the national dream, the coming Messianic age became increasingly a fixed idea and a cherished dogma. That the "day of Yahweh" would come, and Israel be triumphant over her enemies, thus vindicating Yahweh's choice of her and proving him to be God of gods, became a settled conviction of the nation even before the Exile.

During and after the Exile this Messianic expectation became for obvious reasons even more emphatic and assured. It furnished to a distressed nation, suffering intolerable trouble, a psychological compensation. From the humiliation and disillusionment of the present a Jew could retreat into the vivid hope of a Messianic future, when David's glory would be restored, with much more besides, and Israel would be triumphant over the world. This doctrine, which before the Exile had become orthodoxy, became during and after the Exile a psychological necessity, and its practical effect in holding together a distracted people and sustaining them through one disaster after another was incalculable.

The form taken by this Messianic hope varied from age to age. Even in the eighth century B.C., while the "day of Yahweh" meant to popular expectation a nationalistic victory, to Amos it meant a day of judgment on Israel's sins.[1] By the time Greek domination was in full swing, however, the outlines of typical Jewish Messianism were established, as the Book of Daniel makes evident. The power of heathenism, as the writer saw it, had been incarnate in one world empire after another, each of them in turn afflicting Israel, the people of God. Four imperial representatives of heathenism, in particular, he visualized—the Babylonian, Median, Persian, and Greek—all of them pictured

[1] Amos 5:18-20.

270 A GUIDE TO UNDERSTANDING THE BIBLE

as beasts which rise to power and then disappear. Israel, however, was not beast but "son of man," the people of the one true God; Israel alone had incarnated Yahweh's purpose and at a definite, date in the future would sweep into world power over the ruins of the fallen heathen realms. This kingdom of God, inaugurated by Israel's victory, would be eternal, the final consummation of Yahweh's will for man.[1]

The Book of Daniel was thus the first of a long series of Jewish apocalypses which present, amid many differences, certain common characteristics. They all spring out of a background of national distress; they all are utterly pessimistic about the present, which is ruled by heathenism; they all are absorbed in expectations of a future that stands in vivid and glorious contrast with the present; they all see the possibility of this future's achievement only through the supernatural and miraculous act of God; and they all are so eager for escape from unbearable oppression that they set the time for this divine invasion of the world immediately ahead. Within this general framework the apocalyptic expectations are variously phrased. In particular, the personalization of the Messiah as an existent supernal being, waiting the set hour to leave the sky and lead his hosts to victory, appears in some apocalypses but not in others. The general framework, however, outlined in the Book of Daniel remains characteristic of them all.

Obviously this Messianic hope was social rather than individual, but because it was the typical and controlling Jewish way of visualizing a worth-while future it was bound to become entangled, one way or another, with the idea of Sheol and what might come after it. The more the glorious reign of God on earth was believed in and the more vividly its splendors were imagined, the more surely the question of individual destiny was pushed to the fore: Should the beneficiaries of this divine consummation be only the fortunate persons who happened to be alive on the surface of the earth when the great day arrived? It was not they who had borne the burden of patient endurance and sacrifice, walking, as it were, in a "burning fiery furnace." The faithful servants of Yahweh, who amid untold distresses had been true to their trust and held Israel together as Yahweh's witness in the world, were in Sheol. How could the social hope of a Messianic reign on earth be ethically complete, if those who had sacrificed little or nothing enjoyed it and those who had given

[1] Daniel 7:1–27.

all for it remained unblessed in the nether world? Moreover, should not its ethical completeness be emphasized by the resurrection also, to proper punishment, of those whose cruelties had desolated the saints?

A new road was opened, therefore, through the Messianic expectation into a hope that at least some of the *rephaim* in Sheol would be restored to life. So in the Book of Daniel we find this conviction stated: "Many of them that sleep in the dust of the earth shall awake, some to everlasting life, and some to shame and everlasting contempt,"[1] and in two late Isaian passages a similar expectation is expressed: "He hath swallowed up death for ever; and the Lord Yahweh will wipe away tears from off all faces; and the reproach of his people will he take away from off all the earth: for Yahweh hath spoken it";[2] "Thy dead shall live; my dead bodies shall arise. Awake and sing, ye that dwell in the dust; for thy dew is as the dew of herbs, and the earth shall cast forth the dead."[3]

It is to be noted that in these passages the hope of resurrection is not universal. In Daniel many, but not all, shall rise, and in the Isaian hope the restoration which is joyfully proclaimed is explicitly limited to Israelites. Of heathen oppressors it is said, "They are dead, they shall not live; they are deceased, they shall not rise."[4] Thus even in the latest documents of the Old Testament the expectation of any resurrection out of Sheol is restricted and partial and is so infrequently expressed that, beyond the few passages which we have quoted in this chapter, no others intimate belief in a future life. It is not strange that, when Jesus came upon the scene, the Sadducees, the ultra-conservatives of their day, who accepted only the earlier books of the Old Testament and refused credence to the new ideas of the later literature, held "that there is no resurrection."[5]

VII

Indeed, the factors that made headway toward Hebrew faith in immortality difficult were very powerful.

1. The prophetic movement, in its endeavor to purge Israel's religion of its worst primitivism, waged a stout contest against the cult of the dead. As we have seen, consultation with the dead, placation of the dead, and accompanying practises of

---

[1] Daniel 12:2.
[2] Isaiah 25:8.
[3] Isaiah 26:19.

[4] Isaiah 26:14.
[5] Acts 23:8.

necromancy and necrolatry were firmly intrenched in the early traditions of the Hebrews. Indeed, since the Old Testament represents mainly a purified Judaism, such ideas and practises probably exercised, at the beginning, a much more predominant influence than the documents now indicate. Against this entire cult of the dead the prophetic movement waged a tireless battle.

The early prophets, however, and, for the most part, the later prophets too, provided no alternative ideas to take the place of those they were destroying. They did not believe in any resurrection from Sheol; they simply attacked, as dangerous to Yahweh's sole claim on worship and service, the tangled mass of wizardry and demonolatry associated with the dead. In a word, their message in this regard was negative, and its first effect was to take from the dead in Sheol and from Sheol itself even such significance as they had hitherto possessed. In the primitive religion that lay behind Yahweh's introduction to Israel, the dead had been at least "knowing ones" to be consulted, vivid significance existed in the popular picture of Sheol and its inhabitants, and active commerce was carried on between the dead and the living. All this the prophets undertook to wipe out. In so far as they succeeded, they reduced the dead to even more utter deadness than primitive paganism had attributed to them. The prophetic hostility against mortuary superstition, therefore, had its first result in demolishing the only way of thinking vividly concerning the dead that the Hebrews had possessed.

The consequence of this is evident in the passages where Sheol is pictured as utterly negative and the dead as utterly inactive and inane. Once the *rephaim* had been worth consulting; now they had been stripped of one attribute after another until they were powerless. "Thus," as Dr. Paton puts it, "the victory over necrolatry was won, but at the cost of the extinction of even a rudimentary belief in immortality."[1]

2. By this process of negation, emptying Sheol of such positive meaning as it had possessed, the Hebrew mind was driven, even more certainly than it might otherwise have been, to picture hope in terms of physical resurrection out of Sheol. The more the nether world was denied vivid reality, the more hope, when it rose at all, was coerced into one pattern of imagination—reëmbodiment and restoration to the surface of the earth. In Hebrew

[1] Lewis Bayles Paton: "The Hebrew Idea of the Future Life," in *The Biblical World*, "New Series," Vol. 35 (1910), p. 258.

thinking, so far as any worth-while future life was concerned, it was that or nothing.

So persistent has been the influence of this idea of bodily resurrection, belief in which is still affirmed by millions of Christians in their recitation of the creeds, that its origins are worth special consideration. All the major elements in Hebrew thought about the dead conspired to make bodily resuscitation the only way of picturing hope.

Belief in the geographical reality of Sheol, as a definite place in the underground portions of the earth, worked to this end. Those who died did not, in Hebrew imagination, vaguely disappear. They went "down into the pit";[1] they dwelt in "the nether parts of the earth."[2] Sheol was as definitely a place beneath as the sky was a place above,[3] and a synonym for dying was to say, "The earth swallowed them."[4] Therefore, the dead, who were so realistically pictured as going, one might say, from one floor of the cosmos down to another, could be as realistically pictured as coming back again. This, indeed, was the characteristic Hebrew way of visualizing hope for the dead.

Moreover, the fact that in Hebrew thought the body was regarded as the essential constituent of the man worked to the same end. By Plato's time Greek philosophy had conceived the soul as immaterial, but such metaphysical generalization was alien from the realistic, dramatic, picturesque methods of the Hebrew mind. Since, therefore, man was unimaginable to the Hebrews without a body, life after death was naturally pictured as the resuscitation of the embodied life and its restoration to the land of the living. Always Hebrew hope of immortality, when it existed at all, concerned the whole man and not a disembodied wraith. When Enoch was translated or Elijah, escaping death, was raised to the sky, the whole man went. This way of thinking held firm from the beginning to the end of the Old Testament and long afterward. When, either in the Persian or the Hellenistic period, a writer said, "Thy dead shall live," he used as a parallelism, "My dead bodies shall arise,"[5] and one of the familiar prayers of subsequent Judaism ends with the words, "Blessed art Thou, O Lord, who dost return souls to dead bodies."[6]

[1] Psalm 28:1; Isaiah 38:18.
[2] Ezekiel 26:20; 31:14.
[3] Job 11:8; Isaiah 29:4.
[4] Exodus 15:12.

[5] Isaiah 26:19.
[6] As translated by George Foot Moore: *Judaism in the First Centuries of the Christian Era*, Vol. II, p. 215, q.v.

With regard to this identification of life with body, one naturally thinks of the influence of Egypt, where a unique climate made possible the mummifying of bodies as the seat of continued life. At any rate, the Hebrew mind habitually dramatized its immortal hopes in terms of physical resurrection.

Another factor which emphasized this pattern of thought was the desire of the individual Israelite, if he was to have any immortality, to have it as a member of the Messianic kingdom on earth. Greek thought of eternal life, at its higher levels, early became individualistic; it concerned the escape of the soul to the pure world of spirit, immaterial and invisible. Hebrew thought, however, while it developed a strong tradition of personal value and possibility, did it within the framework of a predominant social expectation. Always the ultimate goal and consummation of God's purpose was the divine sovereignty made manifest in the Messianic age. When, therefore, the individual hope of future life began to arise, it was phrased, as in Daniel, in terms of a commonwealth on earth, to have part in which was the highest conceivable desire of man. But if one is to join in the victorious Messianic age on earth, he must be fully restored to life, reëmbodied, and made a real man again.

Whether one thinks of Sheol as a literal "pit" beneath the ground, or of man as basically a body, or of the enjoyment of future life as sharing in the Messianic age on earth, bodily resuscitation is demanded, and since all three of these ideas were operative in the Hebrew mind, there was no escaping their coercion. Future hope and physical resurrection were done up in one bundle of thought. In view of the body's visible decomposition, however, such a way of picturing hope was not easy to believe, so that one reason for the long sustained negativeness of the Old Testament on the subject of life after death may well have lain in the difficulty of imagining resurrection.

3. A further difficulty lay in the fact that the early traditions of the Semitic race were negative about return from Sheol. To be sure, there were ghosts which, in Hamlet's phrase, revisited the glimpses of the moon,[1] but even in English speech 'ghost' and 'gust' come from the same stem and represent something atmospheric and insubstantial. Genuine resurrection to real life does not appear in the Babylonian legends. There Aralû is often "the land of no return,"[2] and Gilgamesh, speaking of Eabani,

[1] Act I, Sc. IV.

[2] As translated by Stephen Herbert Langdon: *Semitic Mythology*, p. 161.

says, "My friend whom I loved has become like clay. . . . Shall I not also like him lay me down to rest, and not arise for ever-more?"[1] This was precisely the note of David's lament for his child, "I shall go to him, but he will not return to me."[2] When to such influences from ancient racial tradition and from the controlling patterns of contemporary thought was added the fact that prophetic orthodoxy in Israel had held out no hope of a future life for the individual, it is not strange that even in the Old Testament's later writings we have explicit and con-vinced denials of such hope.

The Eighty-eighth Psalm, for example, was written by an out-spoken skeptic on this subject[3] and the Book of Ecclesiastes was scornful in its denials:

> For that which befalleth the sons of men befalleth beasts; even one thing befalleth them: as the one dieth, so dieth the other; yea, they have all one breath; and man hath no preëminence above the beasts: for all is vanity. All go unto one place; all are of the dust, and all turn to dust again.[4]
>
> For to him that is joined with all the living there is hope; for a living dog is better than a dead lion. For the living know that they shall die: but the dead know not anything, neither have they any more a reward; for the memory of them is forgotten.[5]

Nevertheless, the very scorn of such denials reveals the reality and prevalence of the ideas they disdain. The hope of future life for individuals expanded and grew strong. Between the Testaments the affirmations of it became convinced and unequivocal: "Sheol also shall give back that which it has received";[6] "The earth shall restore those that are asleep in her, and so shall the dust those that dwell therein in silence."[7]

VIII

That the influence of Persian religion, which affected Hebrew thinking from the late Exile on, encouraged the developing hope of life after death and helped to shape its form, seems probable.

---

[1] Gilgamesh Epic, VIII, v, 36 f. as trans-lated by Lewis Bayles Paton: "The Hebrew Idea of the Future Life," in *The Biblical World*, "New Series," Vol. 35 (1910), p. 161.

[2] II Samuel 12:23.

[3] E.g., Psalm 88:3–12.

[4] Ecclesiastes 3:19–20.

[5] Ecclesiastes 9:4–5.

[6] The Book of Enoch 51:1.

[7] II Esdras 7:32.

276 A GUIDE TO UNDERSTANDING THE BIBLE

Indeed, in four major apocalyptic matters a close affinity exists between Zoroastrianism and the later Judaism: the separation of the righteous from the wicked at death; their distinct estates, the one blessed and the other miserable, between death and the resurrection; the general raising of all the dead at once; and the last judgment with its eternal consequences. Such affinities between two religions, however, may not hastily be interpreted as the mere unilateral influence of one upon the other. Some scholars even think that the Zoroastrians borrowed apocalyptic ideas from the Jews, and, while this is improbable, it is also improbable that the Jews came by their ideas merely by grace of Zoroastrian influence. Such conceptions were rather common property, developing by an inner logic out of the primitive background, and if the Jews borrowed largely from the Zoroastrians, as they probably did, it was because they found in Zoroastrianism a kindred set of mental categories.

Whatever may be true about the effect of Persian ideas on Judaism's thought of the future life, it is clear that between the Testaments there was a powerful swing of faith toward convinced hope. To the Judaism of that period, Sheol still remained the abode of the dead; bodily resurrection from it was the characteristic way of picturing hope; and this resurrection, associated with the coming of the Messianic kingdom, was staged, in the dramatic imagination of the people, as a general judgment day. The more orthodox party in Israel, represented later by the Sadducees, denied all this and held to the negative attitude of the Torah and the prophets. The liberal party, represented later by the Pharisees, accepted the new teaching and won to its credence and support the more religious Jews. Thus the future hope, all the more welcome because it furnished compensation for a humiliating present, became a dominant factor in Judaism.

To the advancing thought involved in this process the moral meaninglessness of the primitive Sheol became intolerable, and between the Testaments we find a change taking place in the descriptions of the underworld itself. The demand for diverse fates in Sheol, corresponding with diverse character, had already been voiced by Isaiah[1] and Ezekiel,[2] and this demand became ever more imperative. In the Book of Enoch, written in the first two centuries B.C., Sheol is divided into four parts, two each for the wicked and the righteous. One contains the wicked

[1] Isaiah 14:18-20.　　　　　　　[2] Ezekiel 32:18-32.

who in torment await the resurrection day, when final penalties will be adjudged; another contains the wicked who already have been punished and for whom there is to be no resurrection; another contains the moderately good who await their reward at the judgment; another contains the faithful saints who enjoy Paradise until their rising at the last day to eternal blessedness.[1]

In this transformation of Sheol, as in other regards, a florescent development of Jewish thought took place between the Testaments. The details of the various books are confused and contradictory. Always in the background is the persistent idea of Sheol, but as in the Greek Orphic cults Hades became an intermediate state where souls were punished and purged until, fully cleansed, they could ascend to the blessed life with God, so Sheol among the Jews became intermediate and preparatory, leading up to the judgment day and its eternal awards. As such, the idea is still immensely influential under the guise of the Roman Catholic purgatory, for purgatory is simply Sheol developed and sublimated.

Within this general framework, however, the details of the inter-Testamental books are too varied to be reduced to harmony. Sometimes there is one resurrection, accompanied by the final judgment, sometimes two resurrections, the first partial, the second for all the dead, with a millennial reign between; sometimes only the righteous are to be raised, sometimes both righteous and wicked; in some writings the dead come back to live on earth under familiar, material conditions; in others the transcendental and supernatural quality of the resurrected life is emphasized. Throughout this confused and difficult struggle of Hebrew imagination with its intractable heritage of primitive idea, only one thing is entirely clear: a deepening certainty that death is not the end, that moral destinies include a future life, that it requires the eternal to complete the temporal.

At one point there appeared an emergent idea so radical in its nature as to constitute a departure from traditional Judaism. About 100 B.C. the Messianic kingdom on earth became to some of the Jews an inadequate picture of the final consummation of God's purpose for man. The earth was seen to be no proper theater for an eternal staging of divine redemption. To give up the hope of the Messianic reign on earth would have been an impossible break with a cherished pattern of faith. The Jews, therefore, did not elide from their thinking the earthly reign of the Messiah,

[1] The Book of Enoch, chap. 22.

but limited it in time. It was to last a thousand years—that is to say, a long time but not endlessly. So began the idea of a millennium, which even yet in Biblical fundamentalism exercises a potent sway over the imagination of many Christians, and upon which the curiosity of the credulous has worked for centuries in an endeavor to predict "times and seasons." The millennium came into Hebrew thought as a means of putting a time limit to the hitherto endless extension of the Messianic age on earth. It sprang from a desire not to emphasize the Messianic realm but to circumscribe it; it originated in a more spiritual conception of the world's finale than could be satisfied by a nationalistic victory or by any kind of social order imaginable on earth. This limitation of the Messianic age opened the door to a notable expansion and heightening of hope. Man's destiny lay beyond Sheol, beyond bodily resurrection and judgment day, even beyond the Messianic age. All these became inherited scenery, retained, but no longer regarded as the ultimate goal. The consummation of the will of God for the righteous lay in heaven, after this earth had been utterly destroyed.

This development of thought and imagination tended to escape from old nationalistic and materialistic conceptions of the Messianic reign. Its pictured rewards became heavenly rather than earthly. It lent itself to an increasing emphasis on the fate of the individual soul apart from the nation. It rose above the old geographical realism into sublimated interpretations of the future. However limited the effect of such ideas on the apocalyptic writings, their importance was very great. The New Testament stemmed out from this branch of Jewish eschatology.

Indeed, one area of Jewish thought, centering in Alexandria, was so deeply influenced by Hellenistic ideas that its Hebrew distinctiveness was well-nigh lost. The Wisdom of Solomon, in the Apocrypha, represents this submergence of Jewish apocalyptic in Greek philosophy. The writer of this book returns repeatedly to the subject of the future life, but for him Sheol has vanished, bodily resurrection has become both incredible and undesirable, and the Messianic age has so lost its dramatic staging and its vivid importance that the most explicit reference to the idea simply says that the righteous

> . . . shall judge nations, and have dominion over peoples;
> And the Lord shall reign over them for evermore.[1]

[1] The Wisdom of Solomon 3:8.

The characteristic ideas of Hellenism, however, are present in this book in full force. The soul is immaterial and preëxistent, and each soul, when born into the world, receives a body appropriate to its quality;[1] the body is a clog on the soul, a prison in which spirit is immured while here on earth;[2] the death of the body is a blessed release from imprisonment, and at death the righteous pass to an immediate reward.[3] Here we find, growing in Judaism under Greek influence, a specific idea of the immortality of the soul as distinct from the resurrection of the body, and this doctrine rises into notable expression:

> . . . The souls of the righteous are in the hand of God,
> And no torment shall touch them.
> In the eyes of the foolish they seemed to have died;
> And their departure was accounted to be their hurt,
> And their journeying away from us to be their ruin:
> But they are in peace.[4]

IX

In passing from pre-Christian Judaism into the New Testament, we cross a boundary line into no strange country; the same ways of thinking used by Palestinian Jews to express their future hopes were used also by the first Christians. In the teaching attributed to Jesus in the Synoptic Gospels are the five major elements characterizing the picture of life after death to which in his youth he was accustomed.

1. Sheol—called Hades in the New Testament—was still the place to which the soul went at death. It involved, however, no longer a listless and negative existence. It was under the sovereignty of God, and rewards and penalties were there administered. It was, in a word, recognizably the same Sheol that had developed in the imagination of later Judaism, an intermediate state between death and resurrection. When Jesus said to the thief upon the cross, "To-day shalt thou be with me in Paradise,"[5] 'Paradise,' as usage then current shows, meant not eternal heaven but the portion of Sheol where the righteous were rewarded even before the resurrection. So too in Jesus' parable, the poor man, dying, went to "Abraham's bosom," while the rich man "in Hades" was in torment, and between the two a

---

[1] *Ibid.*, 8:20.
[2] *Ibid.*, 9:15.
[3] *Ibid.*, 4:7-15.
[4] *Ibid.*, 3:1-4. Cf. Josephus: *Antiquities*,

Bk. xviii, chap. 1, par. 5, and *The Wars of the Jews*, Bk. ii, chap. 8, par. 11, for similar ideas among the Essenes.
[5] Luke 23:43.

great gulf was fixed.[1] The very words in which this scene is depicted were taken from the literature of the time[2] and refer not to final destinies in an eternal heaven and hell, but to the intermediate fate of the dead in the time between decease and resurrection. It should be noted, however, that Jesus is reported to have used the word Hades only three times,[3] twice with an obviously figurative significance—Capernaum brought "down unto Hades"[4] and "the gates of Hades shall not prevail against" the church[5]—and only once, in the parable just quoted, in any such way as to throw light on his opinions. From this one use of the word we may infer that Sheol was an inherited factor in Jesus' thinking, with which he dealt little, if at all, so that his characteristic and original contribution to immortal hope was not phrased in terms of it.

2. The supernatural advent of the Messiah is prominent in the reported words of Jesus. Indeed, this inherited phrasing of hope is so clearly set forth that it seems impossible to read it away, to ascribe it altogether to the disciples' misunderstanding, to poetize it or otherwise dispose of it except by taking it as a familiar, contemporary way of thinking used by Jesus when he imagined the end of the present evil age and the inauguration of the kingdom of God. Even the accent of immediacy is in Jesus' words about the coming Messiah,[6] and alike in direct statement and in parable his reported teaching shows the influence of the prevalent Jewish apocalypticism.[7]

3. The resurrection of the body stands clear in Jesus' reported teaching. He used the word and the idea behind it, in common with his contemporaries, as a natural vehicle for expressing hope of victory over death. Continued life after Sheol meant to him not the escape of an individual soul to the realm of 'pure being' or reabsorption into the eternal Spirit, but the shared life of a divine kingdom. To be readily imagined, this had to be in some sense an embodied life, however sublimated body might become. At any rate, unless the records utterly misrepresent him or his disciples completely misunderstood him, Jesus shared with his race expectation of a bodily resurrection from Sheol.

[1] Luke 16:19-31.
[2] E.g., II Baruch 51:11; IV Maccabees 13:15,17. See William Adams Brown: The Christian Hope, p. 84.
[3] Matthew 11:23; 16:18; Luke 16:23.
[4] Matthew 11:23.
[5] Matthew 16:18.
[6] Matthew 16:27-28.
[7] E.g., Mark 13:35-37; Matthew 25: 1-13; 24:37-44. For contemporary reaction against overstressing the effect of apocalyptic ideas on Jesus' teaching, see Charles Harold Dodd: The Parables of the Kingdom.

In the Fourth Gospel he is explicitly quoted on this matter[1] but, even if this saying be read out of the record, evidence remains, especially the narrative of his conversation with the Sadducees about the nature of the resurrected body.[2] Jesus joined issue with his opponents, not on the doctrine of the Messianic age and a resurrection preceding it, but on their too gross conceptions concerning it. "They that are accounted worthy to attain to that age," he said, "and the resurrection from the dead, neither marry, nor are given in marriage: for neither can they die any more: for they are equal unto the angels; and are sons of God, being sons of the resurrection."[3] Indeed, quite apart from special quotations, a reëmbodied life, however rarefied and sublimated, was involved of necessity in the whole dramatic picture of the future which Jesus shared with his race and time.

4. The final judgment is present as a dominant factor in this picture. As Jesus is reported to have spoken, there are to be not two resurrections with an earthly kingdom between, but one resurrection, after which comes a general assize, inaugurating the Messianic age. This kingdom, far from being earthly, is itself to be heavenly and eternal. Jesus' picture of the consummation of mankind's life is thus freed from popular trappings of materialism and nationalism, and the Messianic age itself becomes so spiritual that those who attain to it are conceived "as angels in heaven."[4] In this regard Jesus was at one with the best tradition of his people. Both the Book of Enoch[5] and the Apocalypse of Baruch[6] use the same comparison with angels in giving an ethical and spiritual interpretation to Israel's hope. It is impossible, therefore, clearly to distinguish, in Jesus' thought, the kingdom on earth from the eternal destiny of the righteous in heaven, for the former idea has been so elevated and sublimated that it blends with the latter. Thus to "inherit eternal life"[7] and to "enter into life"[8] mean the same thing as to "inherit the kingdom"[9] and to "enter into the kingdom."[10] In a word, the idea of the kingdom of God was interpreted by Jesus in terms of spiritual quality, so that in a real sense men enter the kingdom now and find in the future age the flowering out and full release of the life with God and with one another that begins here. While, however, the Messianic age was thus deprived by Jesus of its

[1] John 5:28–29.
[2] Luke 20:27–40.
[3] Luke 20:35–36 (marginal translation).
[4] Matthew 22:30.
[5] The Book of Enoch 104: 4,6; 51:4.
[6] II Baruch 51:10.
[7] Mark 10:17; cf. Mark 10:30.
[8] Matthew 18:8; 19:17.
[9] Matthew 25:34.
[10] Mark 9:47; Luke 18:24.

early, crude characteristics, the picturesque inauguration of it by a last judgment was still retained, and repeatedly appears in his teaching.[1]

5. Hell, as the ultimate destination of the wicked, was another inherited factor in the thinking of Jesus. His word for it, *Gehenna*, "the Valley of Hinnom," is familiar in the writings of the later Judaism. The Valley of Hinnom[2] was a gorge outside the gates of Jerusalem where in earlier days idolaters had sacrificed their children to Molech. After Josiah's reforms and his pollution of the accursed spot, it became an object of horror to the Jews and was used for the incineration of refuse and of the bodies of animals and criminals, and in general for the disposal of anything noisome and unclean. The origin of the historic Hebrew picture of hell, therefore, may with some accuracy be located: "He defiled Topheth, which is in the valley of the children of Hinnom, that no man might make his son or his daughter to pass through the fire to Molech."[3]

Later, the Talmudic theology represented the mouth of hell as being in this valley, and drew the picture with vivid detail: "There are two palm-trees in the valley of Hinnom, between which a smoke arises. . . . And this is the door of Gehenna."[4] Hell itself, according to the teaching of the apocalyptic writings, was a great abyss full of fire,[5] in the midst of the earth, and so vividly were its tortures imagined and the satisfaction of the righteous in the contemplation of them conceived that, according to Charles' understanding of the text, a notorious element in the later Christian doctrine of hell appears in a Jewish book, probably written during Jesus' lifetime:

> . . . Thou wilt look from on high and wilt see thy
>   enemies in Ge(henna),
> And thou wilt recognise them and rejoice,
> And thou wilt give thanks and confess thy Creator.[6]

In the first three Gospels, the word *Gehenna* is often used in the original Greek,[7] and there is nothing in its usage to distinguish its meaning from its Judaistic heritage. The "whole body" is likely to be "cast into hell";[8] there "both soul and body" may

---

[1] E.g., Matthew 16:27; 25:31–33.
[2] Cf. Nehemiah 11:30; Joshua 15:8; 18:16; II Chronicles 28:3.
[3] II Kings 23:10.
[4] As quoted by J. T. Barclay: *City of the Great King*, p. 90.

[5] The Book of Enoch 18:11–16.
[6] The Assumption of Moses 10:10.
[7] E.g., Matthew 5:22,29,30; 10:28; 18:9; Mark 9:45–47.
[8] Matthew 5:29.

be destroyed;[1] there is "eternal fire,"[2] "the furnace of fire";[3] there is "weeping and the gnashing of teeth"[4] and "their worm dieth not."[5] In all this Jesus was a pensioner on contemporary Judaism even for the special phrases that he used.[6] As for the permanence of this torture chamber, while the Greek word, αἰώνιος may mean age-long, and the corresponding Hebrew word means the same, there is no clear reason for supposing that Jesus entertained any mitigating thought about what he called "eternal punishment,"[7] or saw any end to its quenchless fire. To be sure, in one passage the penalties of God are said to be graded to the degree of guilt;[8] from another passage one may infer that after the "last farthing" of penalty is paid the sinner may hope for escape;[9] from another passage one may argue that since only one sin can never be forgiven, "neither in this world, nor in that which is to come,"[10] there is the possibility of pardon for all other sins. Only by such dubious, and, in the last case, almost certainly mistaken inferences, however, can one introduce hope into Jesus' picture of Gehenna. The general statement still holds good that he took over the contemporary pattern of thought about hell, and, neither denying it nor seeming interested primarily in teaching it, he rather used it as a basis for redefining the qualities of character that are eternally disapproved by God.[11]

These five familiar elements in the Jewish thinking of Jesus' day—Sheol, the Messiah's coming, the resurrection, judgment day, and eternal punishment—are present in Jesus' reported teaching. In view of this fact it is the more astonishing that his advent did, in the end, make so epochal a difference in man's outlook on immortality.

X

This difference must be clear to the reader of the Scriptures as soon as he steps from the Old into the New Testament. In the Old Testament even the references to life after death are few; in the New Testament from the beginning the reader is in an atmosphere of radiant hope concerning life eternal. Moreover, when one adds to the Old Testament the later Jewish writings and moves from them into the Christian scriptures, a contrast

---

[1] Matthew 10:28.
[2] Matthew 25:41.
[3] Matthew 13:42.
[4] Matthew 8:12; 13:42,50; 22:13; 24:51; 25:30; Luke 13:28.
[5] Mark 9:48.

[6] E.g., Judith 16:17.
[7] Matthew 25:46.
[8] Luke 12:47-48.
[9] Matthew 5:25-26.
[10] Matthew 12:32.
[11] Matthew 25:41-46.

still is evident. "When we pass from Jewish literature to that of the New Testament," one scholar says concerning future life, "we find ourselves in an absolutely new atmosphere."[1]

This impression should not blind us to the continuance in the Christian scriptures of the patterns of thought and imagination which we have been describing. Indeed, the vividness with which the first Jewish Christians continued to use their inherited categories is obvious in the way they thought of Jesus' death, his intermediate stay in Sheol, and his bodily resurrection. Still in the Apostles' Creed millions of Christians confess their faith that Jesus, when he died, "descended into hell," that is, into Hades or Sheol, but the average person, making this confession, does not clearly visualize the literal, geographical significance that this idea had at the first in the New Testament. So realistically was the visit of Jesus to the nether world conceived that early Christian tradition pictured him as preaching the gospel to the *rephaim* there, thus giving them an opportunity for repentance and salvation. During the intermediate state between his cross and resurrection, when Jesus was in "Paradise"—that is, the fortunate area of the nether world—we read that "he went and preached unto the spirits in prison, that aforetime were disobedient[2]. . . . For unto this end was the gospel preached even to the dead, that they might be judged indeed according to men in the flesh, but live according to God in the spirit."[3]

Moreover, after this realistic and active stay in the nether world, Jesus' return to life on earth and, by ascension, to life in heaven, was presented in bodily terms and was picturesquely set in the framework of the three-storied Jewish cosmos. His resurrected body, as described in the assembled narratives of the New Testament, represents alike the original, primitive belief in a resuscitation of the flesh with all its earthly functions still intact and, as well, the later tendency to rarefy and spiritualize the idea of 'body' in the risen life. On one side, Jesus' body is real "flesh and bones";[4] it is the body that was laid in the tomb revivified so that the tomb is empty; it can be seen and handled; it bears still the wounds of the crucifixion; it can even eat food, and Jesus partakes of "a piece of a broiled fish" to prove it.[5] On the other side, his flesh functions in utterly unfleshly ways, appearing and disappearing, passing through closed doors, and at last ascending visibly by

[1] R. H. Charles: *Eschatology; Hebrew, Jewish and Christian*, p. 306.
[2] I Peter 3:19-20.
[3] I Peter 4:6.
[4] Luke 24:39.
[5] Luke 24:36-43; John 20:20-27.

levitation through the clouds into the sky.[1] However one may explain the rise of these stories, with their obvious conflict in the involved ideas of 'body,' their import is plain. In the New Testament, in so far as its sources were Jewish, the old dramatic picture of the future world still held sway, including Sheol and a physical resurrection to restored vitality on earth. Without such bodily restoration, so the narrative in Luke makes clear, only a ghost might return from Sheol—"They were terrified and affrighted, and supposed that they beheld a spirit"[2]—and the one satisfactory proof that the apparition was not a ghost but a resurrected man lay in the evidence of "flesh and bones."

This convinced belief in a resurrected body—howbeit full of confusion as to what 'body' meant—was the Jewish-Christian way of phrasing life after death. The history of this idea explains the wrestling of Paul over the problem of the Christian's resurrection. To him it was not a physical affair in any fleshly sense —"Flesh and blood cannot inherit the kingdom of God"[3]—but it was a bodily affair. Throughout the fifteenth chapter of First Corinthians the reader can feel Paul struggling to express his profound faith that the incorruptible part of man eternally survives his corruptible flesh. But always his Jewish heritage and training prevented his acceptance of the Greek idea of soul as immaterial, although he must have been acquainted with it. In the story of Paul's address to the Athenians, it is at this point that conflict becomes acute between his faith and theirs: "When they heard of the resurrection of the dead, some mocked."[4] Paul, however, was adamant upon this point. He wished not to be "unclothed" of his body in the future world, but "clothed upon" with a new body,[5] a fit spiritual organ and vehicle of his risen life. It seems clear, therefore, that Paul would be on the side of the more idealized and sublimated ideas of Christ's rising from the dead, and quite out of tune with stories about "flesh and bones" and meals of fish. In Paul's eyes the new organism given to the Christian, of whose resurrection Christ's was the prototype,[6] would be utterly different from this present flesh. The body, he wrote, "is sown in corruption; it is raised in incorruption: it is sown in dishonor; it is raised in glory: it is sown in weakness; it is raised in power: it is sown a natural body; it is raised a spiritual body."[7]

[1] John 20:26; Luke 24:31,51; Acts 1:9.
[2] Luke 24:37.
[3] I Corinthians 15:50.
[4] Acts 17:32.
[5] II Corinthians 5:4.
[6] I Thessalonians 4:14; I Corinthians 15:12 ff.
[7] I Corinthians 15:35 ff.

Furthermore, in the New Testament generally, this Jewish insistence on keeping the body, however rarefied and spiritualized, as part of the future hope, was associated with the Jewish apocalyptic drama—the sudden arrival of the Messiah on the clouds of heaven and the resurrection to eternal destinies.[1] Some of the conflicts already noted in the confused apocalyptic writings of the Jews reappear in the New Testament. The Book of Revelation, for example, is at odds with the Synoptic Gospels in having not one resurrection, but two, with a millennial reign of the Messiah on earth between them.[2] Only in this passage does the millennium appear in the New Testament. Starting some two centuries before, as a way of stating the long but limited extent of the Messiah's earthly reign, the millennium had been formalized and made literal in Jewish thought. So an Egyptian Jew, writing probably during the half century preceding the advent of Jesus, figured that since the world was created in six days, and each day is with the Lord as a thousand years, the world would last six thousand years, and that, since after the six days came a day of rest, the world would have a millennial 'Sabbath' when its history was over.[3] Thus from clever juggling with figures and texts came the literal significance of the famous Jewish-Christian millennium, which the Book of Revelation includes in its drama of the future.

If inherited categories and patterns of thought from the Jewish heritage thus persist into the New Testament, whence came the "absolutely new atmosphere" with regard to the hope of life eternal? The profound difference between typical passages in the New Testament, such as the fifteenth chapter of First Corinthians, and even the most confident passages in the Old Testament is striking. Yet the contrast is not explicable, so far as the New Testament as a whole is concerned, by basic change in the formal patterns of thought.

XI

There is, however, one New Testament book, the Fourth Gospel, where the inherited Jewish categories can be seen in process of reinterpretation. The reason for this rethinking of hope lies in the same factor—the influence of Hellenistic thought—that had caused in certain Jewish writings such as the Apocryphal book, The Wisdom of Solomon, the submergence of apocalyptic

[1] E.g., I Thessalonians 4:14–17.
[2] Revelation, chap. 20.
[3] The Book of the Secrets of Enoch

(Slavonic Enoch). See R. H. Charles: *Eschatology; Hebrew, Jewish and Christian*, p. 261.

drama. That the Fourth Gospel shows Hellenistic influence is clear. To be sure, this need not mean conscious dependence on special sources, such as Philo of Alexandria, as has been commonly thought, nor need it reveal any thoroughgoing knowledge of Neo-Platonic philosophy. The ideas of Hellenism were in the air, and in a city such as Ephesus, where the Fourth Gospel probably originated, they would impregnate the thinking and speaking of intelligent people as familiarly as general ideas of evolution and of a law-abiding cosmos do among us today. The Fourth Gospel, therefore, represents early Christianity as it moved out from its first Palestinian setting into the Hellenistic world. The book is not primarily or formally philosophy; it is preaching—the earnest endeavor to present Christ, and the "eternal life" he came to bestow, to the mind and conscience of a world thinking in Hellenistic terms. The opening verses, based on the idea of the Logos, would be understandable by all Ephesians who knew current thought, even though their special affiliations were as far apart as Stoicism, Neo-Platonism, Alexandrian Judaism, and Persian Zoroastrianism. All such schools of thought contained the idea of the Logos.

So far as future life was concerned, the Hellenistic hope, represented of old in the Orphic cults and moving through Platonic teaching into the characteristic thinking of cultured Hellenists, was phrased in terms of an immaterial soul escaping imprisonment in a material body. It was, therefore, critically at odds with the Hebrew phrasing. The Greeks taught the immortality of the soul; the Jews taught the resurrection of the body, an idea alien to the Greek mind at its best. Moreover, along with distaste for and disbelief in the idea of physical resurrection, the Greek mind could not be at peace with the apocalyptic drama in general, so that, from the beginning, Hellenistic Christianity questioned the inherited framework we have been describing. The Book of Revelation, for example, which is probably a Jewish apocalypse rewritten in Christian terms, was utterly uncongenial to Hellenists; it was, in consequence, opposed by the Eastern church when its admission to the sacred canon was pressed; and, in the end, it was accepted only after the use of allegory had substituted spiritual meanings for its literal intention.

The Fourth Gospel represents this Hellenistic attitude at work within the New Testament. As the Book of Revelation is early Christianity cast in the mold of Jewish apocalyptic, so the Fourth Gospel is early Christianity trying to commend itself to the Hellenistic mind and, in order to do this, setting itself to supersede the literal dramatics of the Jewish hope.

For example, judgment day, according to the Fourth Gospel, is not so much external and future as internal and present. It is removed from the outer world of picturable events into the inner world of spiritual experience. Repeatedly the Christ of the Fourth Gospel denies that his function is to sit in judgment on men, although in Jewish Christianity that aspect of his commission was magnified: "I came not to judge the world, but to save the world";[1] "Think not that I will accuse you to the Father";[2] "God sent not the Son into the world to judge the world."[3] In so far as divine judgment takes place, it is operative here and now, an inherent testing of life by its responses to opportunity, a constant interior arbitrament by which light shows up darkness—"He that believeth on him is not judged: he that believeth not hath been judged already.... And this is the judgment, that the light is come into the world, and men loved the darkness rather than the light."[4] In this view of divine judgment, which dominates the Fourth Gospel, Jewish dramatics have disappeared and only a spiritual residuum remains. Christ has so revealed light that God need not judge any man, because that light, by being what it is, reveals the status of men's souls: "For neither doth the Father judge any man, but he hath given all judgment unto the Son."[5]

Similarly, the triumphant arrival of the Messiah, in the Fourth Gospel, loses its theatricality and becomes a present, spiritual experience. The second coming of Christ is not so much a postponed, external event—if, indeed, any passage in the Gospel can be certainly interpreted to mean that at all—as it is an inward coming of Christ into the heart of the believer. The fourteenth chapter contains a deliberate discussion of this new view of Christ's coming, put upon the lips of Jesus as though he were presenting in advance a Hellenistic reinterpretation of the Jewish hope as it would appear in Ephesus at the end of the first century. He will not leave his disciples comfortless and desolate, he says, but will come to them and will manifest himself unto them; this coming is of such a kind, however, that it means his being in them and making his abode with them; far from being a visible, external manifestation, the world cannot see him, and only those who love him and are loved by him will inwardly know this divine parou-

[1] John 12:47.
[2] John 5:45.
[3] John 3:17.

[4] John 3:18,19.
[5] John 5:22; cf. John 8:15-16.

sia.[1] So radical a change was involved in this Hellenized version of the Messiah's coming that the Jewish objection to it is put upon the lips of "Judas (not Iscariot)" who marveled, we are told, at a second coming so inward and spiritual that it would not be dramatically obvious to the whole world.[2] This sublimated and spiritual understanding of Christ's coming dominates the Fourth Gospel.

Out of the same manner of thinking comes the Johannine idea of eternal life. The hope which the Synoptic Gospels had phrased in terms of the kingdom of God on earth is reinterpreted in terms of life eternal. Only three times in the Fourth Gospel is the kingdom even mentioned,[3] and in all three its spiritual, unworldly nature is emphasized. The great hope of this Gospel is not any kind of reign on earth but "eternal life," and even this, far from being a post-mortem goal, is a present, interior possession of the soul. "He that believeth hath eternal life";[4] "He that heareth my word, and believeth him that sent me, hath eternal life, and cometh not into judgment, but hath passed out of death into life";[5] "This is life eternal, that they should know thee the only true God, and him whom thou didst send, even Jesus Christ"[6]—this conception of immortal life as a present gift, inhering in the quality of spirit that Christ bestows, is characteristic of the Fourth Gospel. The writer even reveals his conscious awareness of the old view—physical resurrection to an earthly kingdom—and deliberately changes its meaning: "Verily, verily, I say unto you, The hour cometh, and now is, when the dead shall hear the voice of the Son of God; and they that hear shall live."[7] Note the "now is"! The dramatic scene of the general resurrection is spiritualized and made a present event in the souls of men. It is within the human spirit that the voice of Christ sounds and the dead rise to a new life which is eternal; there, in quality of living, men pass "out of death into life"; there, as the first Johannine Epistle puts it, "He that hath the Son hath the life; he that hath not the Son of God hath not the life."[8]

In consequence, for those who have received Christ, the entire issue involved in the future hope is already settled. They have been raised from the dead; they have passed through the judgment; they have been born again and entered the kingdom; they

[1] John 14:16-24.
[2] John 14:22.
[3] John 3:3; 3:5; 18:36.
[4] John 6:47.
[5] John 5:24.
[6] John 17:3.
[7] John 5:25.
[8] I John 5:12.

already possess eternal life. Physical death, therefore, is only an incident, so lacking in determinative power that, in a deep sense, it is no longer real: "Verily, verily, I say unto you, If a man keep my word, he shall never see death."[1] Only in the light of this range of thought can Jesus' reported words to Martha be understood: "Jesus saith unto her, Thy brother shall rise again. Martha saith unto him, I know that he shall rise again in the resurrection at the last day. Jesus said unto her, I am the resurrection, and the life: he that believeth on me, though he die, yet shall he live; and whosoever liveth and believeth on me shall never die. Believest thou this?"[2] Martha represents the Jewish belief in an external, postponed, physical resurrection; the Johannine Jesus represents the Hellenistic belief that both death and resurrection are spiritual states within the man.[3]

Far from being a matter of merely historic interest, this contrast in the New Testament between Jewish and Hellenistic ways of thinking about the future life has remained ever since an unresolved dilemma in Christianity. In general, the best thinking of the church has followed the Fourth Gospel, but always the old picturesque apocalyptic drama, with its intermediate state, bodily resurrection, theatrical parousia, and millennial reign, has lured the imagination of multitudes. Even within the Fourth Gospel occasional phrases suggest the older pattern of thought, such as, for example, Jesus' promise, "If I go and prepare a place for you, I come again, and will receive you unto myself; that where I am, there ye may be also,"[4] and his word to Peter, "If I will that he tarry till I come, what is that to thee?"[5] Moreover, in the Johannine thought of the future there doubtless is a consummation in time by which the quality of spirit constituting life eternal will be crowned. In this sense there is a "day of judgment,"[6] an ultimate denouement in which "the world passeth away, and the lust thereof,"[7] and an eternal fulfilment of the life in Christ that begins here. The wonder is not that such sublimated reminiscences of apocalypticism should be present, but that the Johannine writer should have commended so boldly to the early church so radical a rethinking of its hope.

One reason, therefore, for the "absolutely new atmosphere"

[1] John 8:51.
[2] John 11:23–26.
[3] On Johannine conception of eternal life, see E. F. Scott: *The Fourth Gospel; Its Purpose and Theology*, chap. 8.
[4] John 14:3.
[5] John 21:22. On John 5:28,29, see R. H. Charles: *Eschatology; Hebrew, Jewish and Christian*, pp. 370–372.
[6] I John 4:17.
[7] I John 2:17.

in the New Testament is to be found in this vivid apprehension of eternal life as a present possession, so real that he who has it has already received Christ's second coming, passed through the judgment, and been raised from the dead.

XII

The distinctive quality of the New Testament in this regard is not, however, to be explained merely by a shift of mental categories. Like everything else characteristic of the Book at its best, this also goes back to the influence of Jesus' personality. The profoundest note struck in the Old Testament in the development of a future hope came, as we have seen, from the experience of communion with God. Let the interior fellowship of a soul with God be once conceived in terms of mutual care, so that as the soul adores and trusts the Most High, the Most High values and supports the soul, and the corollary is bound to be drawn that such a relationship predicts its own continuance. Such divine friendship is, to use Johannine language, 'eternal life,' and unless the world is so topsy-turvy that its material structure abides and its spiritual meaning perishes, what is thus excellent is, as Emerson said, permanent. This has always been the implicit logic of faith in immortality when it has been most powerful and morally significant.

The deepest convictions of men in favor of future hope, therefore, have come not so much from those who have framed arguments for it as from those who have heightened life's spiritual value, given it new meaning, made it wealthy with fresh significance and purpose until it has seemed as though it ought to go on. The influence of Jesus in this realm cannot be understood without the apprehension of this major fact. He never argued for immortality. He did, however, introduce his disciples into a quality of life that incalculably elevated for them the significance of living. In particular, he made filial relationship with God a vital experience, and in so doing caused a fresh, original upthrust of confidence that death is an open door through which the soul's life with God moves on.

Indeed, the most characteristic thing Jesus is reported to have said about life after death makes this explicit. No one was surprised when, in speaking of the moral tests of future judgment, he took for granted the familiar thought patterns of his race and time. Once, however, he spoke about immortality not so much out of inherited frameworks of thought as out of his own vivid experience, and "when the multitudes heard it, they were astonished at his teaching."[1] What he said, in effect, was that when God enters into friendship with any personality, saying, "I am the God of Abraham, and the God of Isaac, and the God of Jacob," there is henceforth no doubt of the continued life of such friends of the Most High, for "God is not the God of the dead but of the living." That is, after he becomes the God of any soul he will never throw that soul away; the souls for whom God cares are always living, and not dead. The major influence of Jesus himself, therefore, in the matter of endless hope, sprang from the kind of life with God into which he introduced his followers. He moved them up into a quality of experience and a faith concerning it that made expectation of an endless future persuasively real.

How persuasively real he made it is clear not alone from their hopes for themselves but from their convictions concerning his own resurrection. The central factor in creating the difference between the Testaments with reference to life after death is the disciples' confidence that Jesus himself had been raised from the dead. Whatever opinion the modern mind may arrive at with regard to the origin and validity of the stories associated with Jesus' resurrection, the historic fact is clear that the first Christianity was essentially associated with a triumphant faith, not alone that death would be overcome but that it had been overcome. In this regard Paul was typical in insisting that if Christ had not been raised, his preaching was vain.[2]

The development of ideas and stories related with Jesus' resurrection presents one of the most tangled, if not altogether insoluble, problems faced by New Testament scholarship. The assembled documents, as they now stand, suggest that the empty tomb and the sight and handling of the risen body were the origin of confidence in the resurrection, and that the experience of the early Christians afterward went on to further visions of him, more spiritually conceived, as, for example, Paul's on the Damascus road. Careful study of the New Testament, however, throws doubt on this and suggests the possibility that the line of development may have been in precisely the opposite direction.

The New Testament plainly indicates two kinds of experience as bases of faith in Jesus' continued life—one, the empty tomb and its associated events; the other, appearances of the heavenly Christ to various people, especially to Paul at his conversion. Chronologically, the written records of these spiritual visions of the heavenly Christ are the earlier. The Epistles of Paul antedate

---

[1] Matthew 22:31–33.   [2] I Corinthians 15:14.

the Gospels, so that the first written testimony we possess to the resurrection of Jesus is I Corinthians 15:3–8, where Paul lists his own transforming sight of Christ as on a par with, and of the same sort as, all the other appearances of the risen Lord. The question inevitably rises: What if faith in Jesus' continued life originated in such spiritual experiences and was translated afterward into stories of physical resuscitation by the inveterate Jewish-Christian idea that without such revivification no life after death was conceivable?

Certainly it must be said that such experiences as Paul had on the Damascus road are intelligible and have often been reproduced in Christian history, but that as soon as we pass to the later writings, where the empty tomb and its related events are involved, we find ourselves amid dubious evidence and irreconcilable confusion. The earliest Gospel, Mark, has lost its original ending, as the Revised Version states, so that after verse eight of the final chapter we are dealing with a late addition not present in our oldest Greek manuscripts. As the main body of the Gospel is left, the story of the resurrection is reduced to terms so simple that only the finding of an empty tomb and the word of a young man that Jesus was not there remain; Jesus himself is not seen and the three women who found the tomb empty are too terrified to tell any one.

When we turn from this to the late addition to Mark's Gospel and to the narratives of the later Gospels, Matthew, Luke, and John, we find a florescent growth of story, full of irreconcilable details. In Mark one young man announces to the surprised visitors at the tomb that Jesus is risen; in Luke, two men; in Matthew, one angel; in John, two angels. In Mark, the women, coming from the tomb, say "nothing to any one"; in Luke they tell "all these things to the eleven, and to all the rest"; in Matthew, they depart quickly and run to bring the disciples word. Whereas in Mark three women visit the tomb, and in Matthew two women, and in Luke three women plus a larger group, in John only Mary Magdalene is thus early at the sepulcher and she tells the first news, not to the eleven, but only to Peter and "the other disciple whom Jesus loved." In Matthew Jesus himself meets the women as they run from the tomb to tell the disciples; in Luke he does not meet them; in John he meets only Mary Magdalene, not as she goes to tell the disciples about the empty sepulcher but after two disciples themselves have visited it. Neither in Matthew nor in Mark, even with the late addition, is there any account that the disciples themselves saw the empty tomb; in Luke Peter ran and looked into it; in John Peter and the "other disciple" both entered the sepulcher. As for specialties in the individual narratives, Matthew alone records the sealing and guarding of the tomb and he alone introduces an earthquake; Luke expands the story of the revelation on the road to Emmaus, which Mark's addition suggests, and introduces the meal of broiled fish partaken of by Jesus to prove the reality of his resuscitation; John alone, at the end of the century, narrates at length the conversation between Jesus and Mary Magdalene and records the scene between Jesus and Thomas and the appearance by the Sea of Galilee.[1]

No straightforward dealing with these and other similar facts can resolve their incompatibility into even the semblance of consistent narrative. Moreover, underlying such disharmonies is the still more substantial conflict, which we earlier noted, between two ideas of Jesus' resurrected body, one altogether fleshly, the other so spiritualized as to escape the trammels of a material organism.

It is not clear, therefore, whether within the New Testament itself the idea of Jesus' resurrection started with an empty tomb and moved on to such spiritual 'appearances' as Paul experienced, or, on the other hand, started with 'appearances,' such as Paul lists along with his own vision of the heavenly Christ, and moved on to stories of a physical disentombment, which, in Jewish-Christian thought, would be the necessary phrasing of a resurrected life. Certainly, if the idea of Jesus' risen life started with any factual element associated with an empty tomb, that element was never clearly visualized, even in the imagination of the first disciples, and is now confused for us in narratives that contradict each other on every important detail.

Moreover, when one takes the full measure of Paul's experience on the Damascus road and of his subsequent thinking about the risen life, both of the Lord and of his followers, there is a profound disparity between his spiritual conceptions and the stories of a revivified body with its physical functions intact. Paul did not believe in the resurrection of the flesh; he specifically denied that "flesh and blood" continued after death;[2] and the spiritual 'body' with which he wished to be clothed moved in new dimensions altogether, quite different from the Jews' resuscitated "flesh and bones." So, too, the heavenly Christ was to Paul a spiritual pres-

---

[1] Cf. Mark 16:1–20; Matthew 27:62–   [2] I Corinthians 15:50.
28:15; Luke 24:1–43; John 20:1—21:23.

ence. Being "the first fruits of them that are asleep,"[1] he had gone ahead into that new world where flesh was left behind, and the "spiritual body" was not similar to but utterly unlike the "natural body."[2] In the New Testament, therefore, our earliest written testimony to the resurrection of Jesus comes from one who devoutly believed that Christ was "raised on the third day"[3] but who could not, consistently with his other thinking, have conceived it as the revivification of a physical body. It is, therefore, entirely possible that the New Testament's radiant confidence in Jesus' continued life had more profoundly spiritual origins than an empty tomb. It may have begun in the ardent conviction of the disciples that they were still in communion with their Master, that death could not control him,[4] that he had appeared to them in self-revelations, whether outwardly visible, as psychic investigators like Dr. Frederic Myers would say,[5] or inwardly spiritual as the result of their own kindled faith. This type of experience, suggested not only in Paul but in some of the Gospel narratives,[6] may have been the beginning of the conviction that Jesus was not dead but alive, and the more physical representations of the disentombment may have been an aftermath, caused by the insistent belief of the Jewish-Christian mind that resurrection was of necessity involved in life after death.

The acceptance of such an hypothesis, however, leaves still unanswered a host of questions. No one who knows the full extent and complexity of the problem will be dogmatic about it. The tracing of the development of faith in Christ's risen life is still and probably always will be an unfinished task. Only one thing is certain—the towering faith of the New Testament that Jesus is alive. By whatever route the first Christians arrived at that faith, their arrival itself is clear. Their confidence in his continued life turned their dismay at Calvary into triumph, and without it some of the most characteristic elements in the New Testament— the radiant hope and joy of the whole Book, the Christ-mysticism of Paul, the shining reality of the eternal world in the Epistle to the Hebrews, and the enthusiastic acceptance of sacrificial hardship exhibited by the early church—are inexplicable. Fortunately, the sharing of this faith that Jesus is not dead, but alive, does not depend on any hypothesis as to its origin in the New Testament.

[1] I Corinthians 15:20.
[2] I Corinthians 15:35–44.
[3] I Corinthians 15:4.
[4] Romans 6:9.

[5] See Frederic W. H. Myers: *Human Personality and its Survival of Bodily Death.*
[6] E.g., Matthew 28:16–17; Mark 16:9–12.

XIII

Along with the Johannine interpretation of future hope in terms of eternal life and the victorious faith of the first Christians in their Lord's conquest of death, other elements, sometimes not easily blended into a consistent whole, contributed to the New Testament's distinctive faith in life after death. While Paul, for example, always expected the speedy advent of Christ, the old apocalyptic scheme with its dramatic details was in his thinking increasingly sublimated. The spiritualizing of the eschatological hope had its Pauline as well as its Johannine form. Already Christ dwelt in the Christian's heart by faith;[1] already the faithful enjoyed "every spiritual blessing in the heavenly places in Christ."[2] While, therefore, Paul longed for the great consummation, when at Christ's coming "the body of our humiliation" would be fashioned anew and "conformed to the body of his glory,"[3] this climactic experience became less an external and imposed event and more the fulfilment of the Christian's present blessedness. Apparently this emphasis affected Paul's imagination of the future, although how much it is difficult to say. The individual's immediate passage through death into eternal glory is even suggested, and Paul, facing life and death, was "in a strait betwixt the two, having the desire to depart and be with Christ; for it is very far better."[4] In his thinking, apparently, to be "absent from the body" was "to be at home with the Lord,"[5] and in the contemplation of this the external dramatics of the traditional apocalyptic tended to grow dim. Some have even thought that according to one passage Christ's second coming in glory will disclose the saints not in Sheol waiting to be raised, but in heaven with him waiting to join his triumph.[6] Whether Paul ever harmonized these various elements in his thinking and, if so, how he did it, we cannot know. One thing, however, is certain: with Paul as with the Fourth Gospel, the richness of present spiritual life in Christ was such that the central meanings of the apocalyptic drama tended to be conceived as already in spirit consummated for faithful believers. They had already been raised with Christ;[7] they were already "alive from the dead";[8] they already sat "in the heavenly places."[9] Death,

[1] Ephesians 3:17.
[2] Ephesians 1:3.
[3] Philippians 3:21.
[4] Philippians 1:23.
[5] II Corinthians 5:8.

[6] Colossians 3:4.
[7] Colossians 2:12; 3:1.
[8] Romans 6:13.
[9] Ephesians 2:6.

therefore, was to them an incident, a transition from this fleshly body to being "with the Lord."

A further problem of great interest concerns Paul's attitude toward the final estate of the wicked. If one accepts the account of the Apostle's preaching in Acts, he carried over into his Christian faith the Jewish doctrine "that there shall be a resurrection both of the just and unjust."[1] In Paul's Epistles, however, no such clear declaration is either made or implied. When Christ comes, Paul says in Second Thessalonians, the disobedient will "suffer punishment, even eternal destruction from the face of the Lord,"[2] but whether this involves a prior resurrection, on the one hand, or annihilation or endless torment, on the other hand, is not evident. Indeed, almost complete reticence characterizes Paul's Epistles with reference to the final estate of the wicked. It is worth noting, however, that in one passage the privilege of being made alive again is apparently confined to those "that are Christ's";[3] that, in another, attaining "unto the resurrection from the dead" is represented as the prize of high endeavor rather than as a universal fact;[4] that, in a third, an essential relationship is announced between the indwelling "Spirit of him that raised up Jesus" and the possibility of resurrection.[5] Logically, therefore, Paul could not have believed in the resurrection of the wicked; certainly they are not clearly placed in his picture of the ultimate outcome of the cosmos; whether they pass out of existence or remain in Sheol separated from Christ and his kingdom, it is difficult to say.

Paul's positive pictures of the ultimate triumph of God over all opposing forces at times suggest universalism—"all things" subjected to Christ and he in turn subjected to God, "that God may be all in all."[6] Whether this involved the annihilation of all opposing forces, demonic and human, or their redemption, or their reduction to utter impotence in Sheol is not made clear. In some passages the old idea of two realms, one of eternal blessedness and the other an alien one of rebellious souls in misery, seems to have been overpassed. As Christ is the Being in whom all things cohere and have their meaning, so it is God's purpose "through him to reconcile all things unto himself."[7] At his name "every knee" shall bow, and this will be true, says Paul, in all three levels of the

[1] Acts 24:15.
[2] II Thessalonians 1:7-9.
[3] I Corinthians 15:22-23.
[4] Philippians 3:10-11.
[5] Romans 8:10-11.
[6] I Corinthians 15:28.
[7] Colossians 1:19-20.

cosmos, "of things in heaven and things on earth and things under the earth."[1] All antagonistic "rule and all authority and power" shall in the end be "abolished,"[2] and God will "sum up all things in Christ."[3]

The New Testament, therefore, so far as faith in immortality is concerned, does possess an "absolutely new atmosphere." This newness, however, is strangely blended with old ways of thinking and nowhere is consistency to be found, either in the imaginative pictures or the intellectual categories used. That is to say, the New Testament is a living Book, representing new thoughts emerging out of old settings, and full of contrasts as individual minds and racial traditions contribute their distinctive qualities. Nevertheless, in this diversity there is unity—the "promise of the life which now is, and of that which is to come."[4]

Considered as a whole, the development of ideas in the Bible concerning the future life represents one of the most notable and influential unfoldings of thought in history. At the beginning, Yahweh is pictured, not only as indignant at man's eating of the "tree of the knowledge of good and evil"[5] and so becoming conscious of sin, but as being anxious lest man should "take also of the tree of life, and eat, and live for ever," and, in order to guard against this event, man is driven from Eden and its gates are guarded by "the flame of a sword which turned every way, to keep the way of the tree of life."[6] Thus, in the early Old Testament, Yahweh cherishes immortality as a divine prerogative which he will not share with man. As with social regimentation and behavioristic concepts of human nature, so too with the denial of immortality, what seems to many people a modern conclusion was, in fact, the primitive beginning. From that beginning the Bible records a long development of experience and thought consummated at last in Christ, "who abolished death, and brought life and immortality to light through the gospel."[7]

---

[1] Philippians 2:9–11.
[2] I Corinthians 15:24.
[3] Ephesians 1:10.
[4] I Timothy 4:8.

[5] Genesis 2:9.
[6] Genesis 3:22–24.
[7] II Timothy 1:10.

APPENDICES

APPROXIMATE CHRONOLOGY OF THE OLD
TESTAMENT WRITINGS

1. Before the time of David, 1000 B.C.
   Songs and lyrics, such as the song of Deborah (Judges, chap. 5);
   the song of the well (Numbers 21:17–18); the song of Lamech
   (Genesis 4:23–24); the taunt against the Amorites (Numbers
   21:27–30); etc.
   Oracles, such as Balaam's (Numbers, chaps. 23–24); the curse of
   Canaan (Genesis 9:25–27); the blessing of Jacob (Genesis
   49:1–27); etc.
   Sayings, such as Samson's riddle (Judges 14:14); Jotham's fable
   (Judges 9:7–15); etc.
   Possibly records of ancestral traditions, of the Exodus and the
   conquest, and quite probably notations of legal custom, afterwards incorporated in the early books of the Bible.
2. Between 1000 B.C. and 700 B.C.
   History, such as the achievements of Saul, David, and Solomon
   (parts of First and Second Samuel and of First Kings); beginnings of the royal annals and of the temple records; the rise and
   fall of Omri's dynasty (I Kings, chaps. 20–22; II Kings, chap.
   3; 6:24—7:20; 8:7–15; chaps. 9–10); etc.
   Songs and parables, such as praise of David's victories (1 Samuel
   18:7); Nathan's parable (II Samuel 12:1–4); David's lamentation
   over Saul and Jonathan (II Samuel 1:19 ff.); etc.
   Laws, especially the Book of the Covenant (Exodus 20:23—23:19)
   and the Decalogue of Exodus 34.
   Narratives, such as some stories of Elijah (I Kings 17:1—19:21);
   of Elisha (II Kings, chaps. 2–8 in part; 13:14–21); the Judean
   Document of early narratives (Yahwist) about 850 B.C.; the
   Ephraimitic Document (Elohist) about 750 B.C.
   The writings of prophets—Amos, about 750 B.C.; Hosea, beginning
   about 745 B.C.; Isaiah of Jerusalem, beginning about 738 B.C.;
   Micah, beginning about 725 B.C.
3. From 700 B.C. to the fall of Jerusalem, 597 B.C.
   Editorial combinations and completions—the combination of the
   Judean and Ephraimitic narratives; the first edition of the
   Books of Kings.
   Laws—the publishing of Deuteronomy, 621 B.C.
   The writings of prophets—Zephaniah about 627 B.C.; Jeremiah,
   beginning 626 B.C.; Nahum, about 610 B.C.; Habakkuk, beginning
   about 600 B.C.

4. From 597 B.C. to the rebuilding of the walls of Jerusalem, 444 B.C.
   Editorial work, such as the combination of the Judean and
   Ephraimitic Documents with Deuteronomy in the first six
   books of the Bible; the second edition of the Books of Kings;
   the edition of the stories of Joshua, Judges, and Samuel in the
   Deuteronomic tradition.
   Laws, especially the "Holiness Code" (Leviticus, chaps. 17–26)
   and the Priestly Code.
   The writings of prophets—Jeremiah, extending till after 585 B.C.;
   Ezekiel, 593–571 B.C.; Isaiah of Babylon (Isaiah, chaps. 40–55),
   between 546 and 539 B.C.; Haggai, 520 B.C.; Zechariah, chaps.
   1–8, beginning 520 B.C.; Malachi, about 460 B.C.; Obadiah, date
   uncertain; and various additions to the prophetic books, such
   as Amos 9:8–15; Isaiah, chaps. 56–66; chaps. 34–35; 11:10–16; etc.
   Poetry—The Lamentations, about 586–550 B.C.
5. From 444 B.C. to 100 B.C.
   History—the memoirs of Nehemiah, shortly after 432 B.C., and
   Ezra, shortly after 444 B.C.; the Books of the Chronicles,
   300–250 B.C.
   Poetry and general literature—the Books of Ruth, Proverbs, Job,
   Esther, Song of Solomon, Jonah, Ecclesiastes, and the completed
   Book of the Psalms.
   The writings of prophets—Joel, about 400 B.C.; Zechariah, chaps.
   9–11; additions to the prophetic books, such as Isaiah 19:1–25;
   23:1–14; chap. 33; etc.
   Apocalypses—Isaiah, chaps. 24–27; Daniel, 165 B.C.; Zechariah,
   chaps. 12–14.

APPROXIMATE CHRONOLOGY OF THE NEW
TESTAMENT WRITINGS

Early collections of the sayings of Jesus and notes on his life, written
   shortly after his death, possibly in Aramaic, and afterwards used in
   the compilation of the Gospels.
First and Second Epistles of Paul to the Thessalonians, 50–51 A.D.
The Epistle of Paul to the Galatians, 52–58 A.D., date contested.
The Corinthian correspondence, probably four letters now combined in
   First and Second Corinthians, 54–55 A.D.
The Epistle of Paul to the Romans, 56–57 A.D.
The Epistles of Paul to the Colossians, to Philemon, to the Ephesians,
   and to the Philippians, 59–61 A.D.
The Gospel according to Mark, about 70 A.D.
The Epistle to the Hebrews, 80–90 A.D.
The Gospel according to Matthew, 90–95 A.D.
The Gospel according to Luke, and The Acts, about 90 A.D.
The Book of Revelation, about 95 A.D.

The First Epistle of Peter, about 96 A.D.
The Epistle of James, about 100 A.D.
The Gospel according to John, and the three Epistles of John, about 100 A.D.
The Epistle to Titus and the two Epistles to Timothy, about 100 A.D., with earlier genuine portions from Paul probably included.
The Epistle of Jude, uncertain.
The Second Epistle of Peter, about 150 A.D.

SELECTED BIBLIOGRAPHY

GENERAL INTRODUCTION

Bewer, Julius August: *The Literature of the Old Testament in Its Historical Development*. Columbia University Press. Revised Edition, 1933.
Creelman, Harlan: *An Introduction to the Old Testament Chronologically Arranged*. The Macmillan Company, 1917.
Moore, George Foot: *The Literature of the Old Testament*. Henry Holt and Company, 1913.
Scott, Ernest Findlay: *The Literature of the New Testament*. Columbia University Press, 1932.
Lake, Kirsopp and Silva: *An Introduction to the New Testament*. Harper & Brothers, 1937.
Bacon, Benjamin Wisner: *The Making of the New Testament*. Henry Holt and Company, 1912.
Moffatt, James: *An Introduction to the Literature of the New Testament*. Charles Scribner's Sons, 1918.
Peake, Arthur Samuel: *A Critical Introduction to the New Testament*. Charles Scribner's Sons, 1910.

THE GENERAL DEVELOPMENT OF BIBLICAL IDEAS

Lods, Adolphe: *Israel from Its Beginnings to the Middle of the Eighth Century*, translated by S. H. Hooke. Alfred A. Knopf, 1932.
Lods, Adolphe: *The Prophets and the Rise of Judaism*, translated by S. H. Hooke. E. P. Dutton & Co., 1937.
Kautzsch, E.: "Religion of Israel," in *A Dictionary of the Bible*, edited by James Hastings and John A. Selbie, Extra Vol. Charles Scribner's Sons, 1905.
Peters, John Punnett: *The Religion of the Hebrews*. Ginn and Company, 1914.
Smith, Henry Preserved: *The Religion of Israel; An Historical Study*. Charles Scribner's Sons, 1914.
Leslie, Elmer A.: *Old Testament Religion in the Light of Its Canaanite Background*. The Abingdon Press, 1936.
Paton, Lewis Bayles: *The Early Religion of Israel*. Houghton Mifflin Company, 1910.

Meek, Theophile James: *Hebrew Origins.* Harper & Brothers, 1936.
Budde, Karl: *Religion of Israel to the Exile.* G. P. Putnam's Sons, 1899.
Cheyne, Thomas Kelly: *Jewish Religious Life After the Exile.* G. P. Putnam's Sons, 1915.
Robinson, Henry Wheeler: *The Religious Ideas of the Old Testament.* Charles Scribner's Sons, 1913.

Fairweather, William: "Development of Doctrine in the Apocryphal Period," in *A Dictionary of the Bible,* edited by James Hastings and John A. Selbie, Extra Vol. Charles Scribner's Sons, 1905.
Porter, Frank C.: *The Messages of the Apocalyptic Writers.* Charles Scribner's Sons, 1911.
Charles, Robert Henry, editor: *The Apocrypha and Pseudepigrapha of the Old Testament in English.* Oxford University Press, 1913.
Charles, Robert Henry: *The Religious Development Between the Old and New Testaments.* Henry Holt and Company, 1914.
Fairweather, William: *The Background of the Gospels; or Judaism in the Period Between the Old and New Testaments.* Charles Scribner's Sons, 1908.

Gilbert, George Holley: *Jesus.* The Macmillan Company, 1912.
Bousset, Wilhelm; *Jesus.* G. P. Putnam's Sons, 1906.
Headlam, Arthur Cayley: *The Life and Teaching of Jesus the Christ.* Oxford University Press, 1923.
Klausner, Joseph: *Jesus of Nazareth; His Life, Times, and Teaching,* translated from the original Hebrew by Herbert Danby. The Macmillan Company, 1929.
Mackinnon, James: *The Historic Jesus.* Longmans, Green, & Co., 1931.
Guignebert, Charles: *Jesus,* translated from the French by S. H. Hooke. Alfred A. Knopf, 1935.
Scott, Ernest Findlay: *The Validity of the Gospel Record.* Charles Scribner's Sons, 1938.

Dodd, Charles Harold: *The Apostolic Preaching and Its Developments.* Willett, Clark & Company, 1937.
Bacon, Benjamin Wisner: *Jesus and Paul.* The Macmillan Company, 1921.
Porter, Frank C.: *The Mind of Christ in Paul.* Charles Scribner's Sons, 1930.
Lake, Kirsopp: *Paul, His Heritage and Legacy.* Oxford University Press, 1934.
Scott, Ernest Findlay: *The Gospel and Its Tributaries.* Charles Scribner's Sons, 1928.
Sheldon, Henry C.: *New Testament Theology.* The Macmillan Company, 1911.

Morgan, William: *The Religion and Theology of Paul*. Charles Scribner's Sons, 1917.
McGiffert, Arthur Cushman: *A History of Christianity in the Apostolic Age*. Charles Scribner's Sons. Revised Edition, 1903.
Lake, Kirsopp: *Landmarks of Early Christianity*. Macmillan and Co., 1920.
Ropes, James Hardy: *The Apostolic Age in the Light of Modern Criticism*. Charles Scribner's Sons, 1906.
Carpenter, Joseph Estlin: *Phases of Early Christianity*. G. P. Putnam's Sons, 1916.
Scott, Ernest Findlay: *The Fourth Gospel; Its Purpose and Theology*. Charles Scribner's Sons, 1926.
Scott, Ernest Findlay: *The Epistle to the Hebrews; Its Doctrine and Significance*. Charles Scribner's Sons, 1922.

THE HISTORICAL AND RELIGIOUS BACKGROUND

Barton, George Aaron: *A Sketch of Semitic Origins Social and Religious*. The Macmillan Company, 1902.
Smith, William Robertson: *Lectures on the Religion of the Semites*. Third Edition, with Introduction and Additional Notes by Stanley A. Cook. The Macmillan Company, 1927.
Jastrow, Morris: *Hebrew and Babylonian Traditions*. Charles Scribner's Sons, 1914.
Gordon, Alexander Reid: *The Early Traditions of Genesis*. T. & T. Clark, 1907.
Wallis, Louis: *Sociological Study of the Bible*. The University of Chicago Press, 1912.
Wallis, Louis: *God and the Social Process*. The University of Chicago Press, 1935.
Rogers, Robert William: *Cuneiform Parallels to the Old Testament*. The Abingdon Press. Second Edition, 1926.
Caiger, Stephen L.: *Bible and Spade; An Introduction to Biblical Archaeology*. Oxford University Press, 1936.
Barton, George Aaron: *Archæology and the Bible*. American Sunday-School Union. Sixth Edition, Revised, 1933.
Breasted, James Henry: *The Dawn of Conscience*. Charles Scribner's Sons, 1934.
Moulton, James Hope: *Early Zoroastrianism*. Constable & Co., 1926.

Angus, Samuel: *The Environment of Early Christianity*. Charles Scribner's Sons, 1915.
Cadoux, Cecil John: *The Early Church and the World*. T. & T. Clark, 1925.
Jackson, F. J. Foakes, and Lake, Kirsopp: *The Beginnings of Christianity*, Part I, "The Acts of the Apostles," Vol. I. Macmillan and Co., 1920.

Deissmann, Gustav Adolf: *Light from the Ancient East*, translated by R. M. Strachan. Harper & Brothers. New and Completely Revised Edition, 1927.

Mathews, Shailer: *New Testament Times in Palestine 175 B.C.–135 A.D.* The Macmillan Company. New and Revised Edition, 1934.

Branscomb, Bennett Harvie: *Jesus and the Law of Moses.* R. R. Smith, 1930.

Case, Shirley Jackson: *The Evolution of Early Christianity; A Genetic Study of First-Century Christianity in Relation to Its Religious Environment.* The University of Chicago Press, 1914.

Angus, Samuel: *The Mystery-Religions and Christianity; A Study in the Religious Background of Early Christianity.* Charles Scribner's Sons, 1928.

Colwell, Ernest Cadman: *John Defends the Gospel.* Willett, Clark & Company, 1936.

Gilbert, George Holley: *Greek Thought in the New Testament.* The Macmillan Company, 1928.

Bacon, Benjamin Wisner: *The Gospel of the Hellenists*, edited by Carl H. Kraeling. Henry Holt and Company, 1933.

Bevan, Edwyn Robert: *Stoics and Sceptics.* Oxford University Press, 1913.

Cumont, Franz V. M.: *The Oriental Religions in Roman Paganism.* The Open Court Publishing Company, 1911.

Glover, Terrot Reaveley: *The Conflict of Religions in the Early Roman Empire.* Methuen & Co. Twelfth Edition, 1932.

Willoughby, Harold Rideout: *Pagan Regeneration.* The University of Chicago Press, 1929.

Jackson, Frederick John Foakes: *Josephus and the Jews; The Religion and History of the Jews as Explained by Flavius Josephus.* Harper & Brothers, 1931.

Bevan, Edwyn R., and Singer, Charles, Editors: *The Legacy of Israel.* Oxford University Press, 1927.

Schürer, Emil: *A History of the Jewish People in the Time of Jesus Christ; Being a Second and Revised Edition of "A Manual of the History of New Testament Times,"* translated by Sophia Taylor and Peter Christie (in five vols.). Charles Scribner's Sons.

Herford, Robert Travers: *Pharisaism; Its Aim and Its Method.* G. P. Putnam's Sons, 1912.

Moore, George Foot: *Judaism in the First Centuries of the Christian Era; The Age of the Tannaim.* Harvard University Press, 1927–1930.

Harnack, Adolf von: *The Expansion of Christianity in the First Three Centuries*, translated and edited by James Moffatt. G. P. Putnam's Sons, 1904.

Special Subjects

Pace, Edward: *Ideas of God in Israel; Their Content and Development.* The Macmillan Company, 1924.

Aytoun, Robert Alexander: *God in the Old Testament; Studies in Gradual Perception.* George H. Doran Co., 1923.

Smith, John Merlin Powis: *The Origin and History of Hebrew Law.* The University of Chicago Press, 1931.

Mitchell, Hinckley G.: *The Ethics of the Old Testament.* The University of Chicago Press, 1912.

Smith, John Merlin Powis: *The Moral Life of the Hebrews.* The University of Chicago Press, 1923.

Gray, George Buchanan: *Sacrifice in the Old Testament; Its Theory and Practice.* Oxford University Press, 1925.

Moore, George Foot: "Sacrifice," in *Encyclopædia Biblica,* edited by T. K. Cheyne and J. Sutherland Black. The Macmillan Company, 1903.

McFadyen, John Edgar: *The Problem of Pain; A Study in the Book of Job.* James Clarke and Company.

Peake, Arthur Samuel: *The Problem of Suffering in the Old Testament.* London, Robert Bryant, Charles H. Kelly, 1904.

Robinson, Henry Wheeler: *The Cross of Job.* Student Christian Movement Press, 1917.

Robinson, Henry Wheeler: *The Cross of Jeremiah.* Student Christian Movement Press, 1925.

Robinson, Henry Wheeler: *The Cross of the Servant; A Study in Deutero-Isaiah.* Student Christian Movement Press, 1926.

Smith, John Merlin Powis: *The Religion of the Psalms.* The University of Chicago Press, 1922.

McFadyen, John Edgar: *The Prayers of the Bible.* Hodder and Stoughton, 1906.

Hughes, Henry Maldwyn: *Ethics of Jewish Apocalyptic Literature.* London, Charles H. Kelly, 1909.

Scott, Ernest Findlay: *The Ethical Teaching of Jesus.* The Macmillan Company, 1934.

Smyth, Newman: *Christian Ethics.* Charles Scribner's Sons, 1908.

Robinson, Henry Wheeler: *The Christian Doctrine of Man.* Charles Scribner's Sons, 1911.

Leckie, Joseph H.: *The World to Come and Final Destiny.* T. & T. Clark, 1918.

Charles, Robert Henry: *Eschatology; Hebrew, Jewish, and Christian. A Critical History of the Doctrine of a Future Life in Israel, in Judaism and in Christianity; or Hebrew, Jewish, and Christian Eschatology from Pre-prophetic Times till the Close of the New Testament Canon.* The Macmillan Company, 1913.

Brown, William Adams: *The Christian Hope; A Study in the Doctrine of Immortality.* Charles Scribner's Sons, 1912.

INDEX OF SUBJECTS AND NAMES

Doughty, Charles M., 247 n., quoted on justice of Arabs, 20, 98
Dreams, 205, 232, 257
Dress of priests, 210
Drink in connection with temple sacrifices, 63

Eabani, 274
Earle, Alice Morse, 109 n.
Earth, hopes of undying nation on, 74; new heaven and, 198; no theater for staging divine redemption, 277; restoration of dead to surface of, 272; Sheol under, 259; Yahweh sovereign over, 26, 262 f. See Resurrection; World
Eastern church, 287
Ecclesia, Isaiah formed first, 63
Ecclesiastes, Book of, denial of divine justice to individuals, 69; denial of future life, 275; impartiality of disaster stumblingblock to, 184; plausible, 196; skeptical reply to problem of evil, 181
Ecclesiasticus, Book of, fatherly love indicated in, 37; Jesus may have read, 134
Economic, break-up into unequal classes, 61; class struggle translated into religious conflict, 20; conditions influenced monogamy, 126; destitution and materialistic prayers, 244; factor in Elijah's sponsorship of Naboth, 21; freedom of womanhood, 129 f.; inequities, Yahweh not identified with, 24; institution producing slaves not attacked by Jesus, 132; status not recognized in New Testament, 138; system, New Testament writers not responsible for public measures to improve, 80. See Civilization, Commercial
Eden, Garden of, 1, 8, 105, 128, 171, 197, 298
Edom, 101, 144
Egypt, David's domain extended to, 269; deliverance from, 50, 140; Joel's hope for revenge on, 144; moral ideals developing in, 150; influence from scattering of Jews to, 65; theological thinking of Hebrews affected by, 30; to be blessing in earth, 34; Yahweh exhibited power in, 18, 50
Egyptian, climate of, made possible mummifying of bodies, 274; contest with Babylonian army, 130; hope of physical resurrection, 85; idea of humaneness antedated Hebrews, 135; influence on Old Testament difficult to estimate, 135; Jew quoted on millennial Sabbath, 286; literature, no warless world in, 143, see also Ameni, Coffin Texts, Memphis, Pyramid Texts, Wisdom of Amenemope;

monotheism antedated Hebrews', 30; mortuary customs of, 259, 274; of third generation permitted to enter Jewish assembly, 101; tomb-chapel, idea of good man on, 135
Egypto-Babylonian culture, 135
El Shaddai, 1
Eliezer of Damascus, 109
Elijah, at mount of God, 2, 225; conservative, 21, 99; contest with the baals, 5, 20 f., 62; control of over rain, 248, 250; in despair of at overthrow of local altars, 27; influence on idea of Yahweh's supremacy, 22; praised as "chariots of Israel," 143; raised son of widow of Zarephath, 82; raised to sky, 273; represented monolatry in theology, 22; social justice of, 21
Elisha, 12; 143
Elkanah, 106
Elohim, 17 f.
Emerson, 291
Emmaus, revelation on road to, 294
End of world, 79. See Apocalyptic; Apocalypticism
Endor, witch of, 258
Enemies, Book of Esther enjoys pogrom of alien, 117; hatred of, enjoined, 6 ff., 115; in distress, 115 f.; Jesus counseled forgiveness of and love for, 137, 147; living and laboring among, 13, 219; retaliation on, celebrated in Psalms, 114, 141; to Hindu-Buddhism hunger and thirst man's worst, 96; vindication of Yahweh, triumph over, 269; Yahweh's punishments on children of his, 59. See Foreigners
English Versions (of the Bible), Elohim variously translated in, 18; euphemisms for slaves in, 107; misleading translations of *nephesh* in, 82; Septuagint used earlier mss. than represented by, 204; 'utterly destroy' given in margin as 'devote,' in, 7
Enoch, translated, 273
Enoch, Book of, describes Sheol, 276; solution of injustice in, 182
Environment, ability to resist, 72
Ephesus, 39, 184, 234, 287
Ephod, 204 f.
Ephraim, alliances after kingdom established in, 18 f.; Israelites in hill country of, 13, 16, 19; Micah of, 10
Ephraimite Document, 2
Epistles, of Paul antedate Gospels, 292 f.; presentation of God's crucial deed in, 49; rejoice in "adoption as sons," 51. See under separate titles

compensation for present, 190, 276; future, as physical resurrection, see Future Life; Resurrection; future, settled for Christians, 289; limitations of Messianic age expanded, 278; not associated with Sheol, 261; of future, undying nation, 74; of life eternal in New Testament, 283 ff., 292, 296, see Eternal Life, Idea of Immortality; sufferings, cause of, 185 f.

Horeb, 2

Hosea, all lands but Canaan unclean to, 22; denounced popular religion, 203; emphasis on individual by, 62, 66; evil traced to thoughts, by, 66; idea of God, of, 2, 22, 24 ff., 133 f., 197, 225; in succession of prophets, 40, 80, 230; opposed graven images, 10; opposition to baals, 14; quoted by Jesus, 230 f.; subject of slavery in abstract not raised by, 131

Human sacrifice, common, 206; deity rejoicing in, 7; of Agag, king of Amalek, 7, 100; of conquered enemies, 7; of crown prince of Moab, 12; of children, 60, 206 f., 211, 282; substitution of animal sacrifice for, 207

Humaneness, apocalypticism not source for, 150; commanded toward foes in misfortune, 115 f.; competes with ritual, 113; demand for, 131 ff.; development of, 133 ff.; Egyptians antedated Hebrews in, 135; goal of ethical development, 148 f.; grounded in estimate of personality, 136; hope of, for warless world, 143; of Jesus' monotheism, 144; overpassed national and racial restrictions, 144; quality of good life, 151; test of true religion, 188; to foreigners feared, 101 f.; within tribal group but not without, 100

Hymns, ideas of blood in, 230; in early Christian church, 251; of post-Exilic temple, 66, 220, 227

Hypocrites, Jesus' distaste for, 231

Idea of Fellowship with God, connection with emergence of individual, 65; in Isaiah, 267; in Job, 192; kinship between Testaments in, 89; chap. V, 201–256: early influences inhibiting approach to God in private prayer, 201 ff.; development of idea of holiness, 208 ff.; sacrificial system one highway toward spiritual fellowship with God, 215 ff.; the prophetic experience, another highway toward spiritual fellowship with God, 223 ff.; priestly and prophetic heritage in early Christianity, 229 ff.; changes in idea of faith, 232 ff.;

development revealed in changing substance of prayers in Bible, 236 ff.; public worship, 251 ff. See God, presence of

Idea of God, common strand through Bible, 196 f.; development of, through practical situations, 86; in New Testament, stems out from deed, 250; in terms of Jesus, 47 f.; in thought of Jesus, 72 f., 189; summary of Biblical, 53 f.; tribal, 65 f.; chap. I, 1–54: Yahweh becomes god of Israelites, 1 ff.; characteristics of Yahweh as mountain god, 4–10; storm god, 4 f.; god of war, 5 f.; tribal god, 6 ff.; anthropomorphic, 8 ff.; becomes territorial deity of Canaan, 10–17; geographical limitation of Yahweh, 11 ff.; becomes agricultural deity, 13 ff.; enlargement of idea of God, 17 ff.; god of sky, 17 f.; power outside own land, 18; inter-territorial worship, 18 f.; enlargement result of social conflict, 19 ff.; monolatry becomes theoretical monotheism, 22 ff.; struggle before ethical monotheism became common property, 26–31; centralization of worship, 27; spiritualized idea of God result of destruction of temple and Exile, 27 ff.; uniqueness of Old Testament monotheism, 29 ff.; monotheism involving an international outlook, 31 ff.; comparison between Testaments in idea of God, 35 ff.; influence of separation of church and synagogue, 37 ff.; influence of Jesus on Idea of God, 40 ff.; newness of Christian idea of God associated with Jesus, 42 ff.; effect of deifying Jesus on Christian thought, 46 ff.; God's saving deed center of New Testament interest, 49 ff.; origin of trinitarianism, 52 f.

Idea of Immortality, chap. VI, 257–298: idea of the dead in early Old Testament, 257 ff.; nature of Sheol, 259 ff.; enlarging idea of God factor in developing idea of afterworld, 262 ff.; emergence of individual from group influential in hope of restoration to full life, 265 ff.; personal religion as intimate relationship of soul and God influential on hope of real life after death, 267 f.; expectation of Messianic age influential on hope of restoration from Sheol, 268 ff.; factors making Hebrew faith in immortality difficult, 271 ff.; influence of Persian religion on hope of life after death, 275 ff.; familiar Jewish expressions of future hope attributed to Jesus in Synoptic Gospels, 279 ff.; New Testament's radiant hope concerning life

126; moral obligation universalized by, 144 ff.; name of, 44 f., 249; never broke away from Judaism, 71; nourished in synagogue, 230; parables of, see Parables; prayer of, 42, 121, 239, 247; personality in teaching of, 72 ff., 136; regarded evil as requiring action, 198; resurrection of, 284 f., 292 ff.; return of (second coming), 50 ff., 150 f., 288 ff., 296; Son of God, 50, 77, 234; soul and body not speculated on by, 88; suffering, Jesus' attitude toward, 184, 186, 199; suffering Servant of Yahweh, relationship to, 187, 193 ff.; sufferings of, Christians to partake in, 186; union of, with Christian, 252 ff., 296; universalism of, 239; used old ideas, 40; war, attitude toward, 148;

Jethro, 3

Jew. See Hebrew

Jezebel, 20 f., 58

Job, a great nonconformist, 167; argumentative in prayers, 226; Ezekiel refers to, 164; fell back on God in afflictions, 192

Job, Book of, ideal man pictured in, 132, 134 f., 242; importance as portrayal of problem of evil, 179 f., 266; intimation in, of hope of resurrection, 266; orthodox theory of suffering in, 165 ff.; Satan in prologue but not in argument, 178

Joel, argues with Yahweh, 249; bloodthirsty, 144; taught all trouble, deserved punishment, 159

Johannine writings, apocalyptic influences in, 150; eternal life in, 289, 296; ethic of, similar to rest of Christian scriptures, 150; flesh and spirit in, 122; immediacy of God described in, 231; need of interior deliverance in, 122 f.; presentation of Christ in, 43, 288; salvation in, 123; spiritualizing eschatological hope in, 296

John, Epistles of, humility about man in, 242 f.; love of brethren test of faith in First Epistle, 78, 139

John, Gospel of. See Fourth Gospel

John the Baptist, 194 f., 253

Jonah, Book of, appeal against racial prejudice, 33 f.; out-reach of divine mercy represented in, 117; pictures Jonah fleeing to another country to escape Yahweh, 12; pictures mariners crying to gods in storm, 243; possible allegory of, explained, 142 f.; written to enforce worldwide mission of Israel, 141 ff.

Jonathan, 204

Jordan, 21

Joseph, forgives brethren, 117; tribes of, 201

Josephus, 279 n.

Joshua, 5, 13, 202, 210, 248 f.

Joshua, Rabbi, quoted, 239

Josiah's reform, 27, 64; Deuteronomy, summary of ideals leading to, 101; Jeremiah's disillusionment over, 119; Jeremiah's early support of, 65, 226; pollution of Valley of Hinnom in, 282

Joy, 'heart' used to express, 83; in afflictions, 186; causes of Christians', 191, 214; New Testament most jubilant book, 193

Jubilee, year of, 132

Judah, Isaiah's argument at desolation of, 159; Isaiah from ruling class in, 63; Jehovah, not Babylonians, triumphed over, 31; kingship in, affecting ideas of sovereignty of God, 18; Solomon practised inter-territorial worship in, 18 f.

Judaism, a national life, 70, 146 f.; abolition of idolatry by, 10; Alexandrian, 39, 85, 287; ceremonial behavior in orthodox, 113; escaped from cult of blood, 230; Jesus never broke with, 71; legalism of, boast and disgrace, 112; liturgical heritage of, 252; prayer in late, 214, 238, 244; taught attack on evil, 197; Zoroastrian influence in, 176 f., 276. See Hebrew; Israel

Judas (not Iscariot), 289

Jude, 235

Judea, 150

Judean Document, 3

Judge, Christ denied function of, 288; 'Elohim' translated as 'judges,' 18; head of early Israel household, the, 57; widow mistreated by unjust, 76; Yahweh preached as, 24 f., 156

Judgment day, basis of estimate at, 144; dominant in inter-Testamental thought, 182 f.; in Enoch some await reward at, 276 f.; inauguration of Messianic age by, 281 f.; internal and present, 288; pagan cities preferred before Jewish at, 145; personal readiness to meet, 79; staged as general resurrection, 276; those who have received Christ, already passed through, 289; ultimate denouement, 290

Judith, 103

Jupiter, 247

Jus gentium, 238

Justice, affected by social solidarity, 58 ff., 67, 158; central ethical concept of Hebrews, 98; Egyptians' high standards of social, 135; Ezekiel's assertion of present justice, 163 f.; fair play within tribal group, 100; Isaiah of Jerusalem's plea for

268 f.; limited in time, 277 f.; no marriage
in, 281; resurrection associated with,
268 ff., 276, 281; social nature of, 144,
270; without dramatic staging in Wisdom
of Solomon, 278. See Kingdom of God
Metaphysics, Jews not interested in, 86, 88,
93, 176, 178
Micah (the Ephraimite), 10
Micah (the prophet), attacked animal offerings, 224; believed suffering punishment
for sin, 157; demanded decision of individuals, 62; foresaw warless world, 143;
quoted on Yahweh's requirements, 114;
slavery not discussed as institution by,
131
Midianite, 3, 141
Mill, John Stuart, quoted, 152
Millennial Sabbath, 286
Millennium, apocalyptic drama of, 290; be-
ginning of idea, 277 f.; in inter-Testamen-
tal books, 277; in only one New Testa-
ment passage, 286; in Revelation, 286.
See Messianic age
Mind, in Paul's usage, 90 f.
Miracles, 235, 256, 270
Miriam, 103
Mishpat, 98
Mission, of Christianity, 146; of Israel, 35,
114, 141 ff.; of Jesus in Matthew, 145 f.
Mixed marriages. See Marriage
Moab, 18 f.; 140
Moabites, enemies, lived among for genera-
tions, 13; forbidden to enter Hebrew
congregation, 101; Ruth a Moabitess,
141 f.; sacrifice crown prince, 12
Moffatt, James, quoted, 195
Molech, 18, 282
Mollusk, 199
Monogamy, 125 f., 130. See Marriage
Monolatry, 19, 22
Monotheism, attracted other races to syna-
gogue, 70 f.; common property of people
after struggle, 26 ff., 210 f.; contrast between Jewish and Christian, 52; cosmopolitan experience led to belief in, 139;
Egyptians antedated Hebrews in asserting, 30; Exile produced flower of, 28, 211;
freed from Old Testament particularisms,
38; in New Testament, 147; in relationship to problem of evil and suffering, 152,
155 f., 162, 177, 240, 265; Isaiah held, 29;
Jeremiah achieved ethical, 26; Jesus'
ethical, 40 ff., 144; Jewish, had character
of its own, 30; monolatry, monotheism
in bud, 22; moral ideas developed with,
23; moral meaning of, 41; not necessarily

grasped by practiser of monolatry, 19;
one of Jews' most valuable possessions,
241; outcome of belief in Yahweh's justice, 21; in poems of the Servant of
Yahweh, 31 f., 172; primitive Semitic,
suspected by some, 17 f.; supernational-
ism a corollary of, 139 f., 144, 239;
terminology of, inadequate to express
Christian thought, 52 f.; universality in
ethics associated with, 139, 144; writing
prophets move toward, 23
Montefiore, C. G., quoted, 37
Moore, George Foot, quoted, on belief of
Israelites in sacrifice, 218 f.; on Jehovah's
punishing religious treason, 31; on personal responsibility, 70; on synagogue as
seat of worship, 230
Moral. See Ethical
Moral obligation, Bible records widening
range of, 139; incompleteness in New
Testament's statement of, 80; limitation
of, in early Old Testament, 99–113, 144;
universalized in New Testament, 144–151
Moreh, 202
Mores, 110
Mosaic Law, 10, 15
Moses, argumentative in prayers, 226; God
discusses his name with, 1, 249; at burning bush, 209; beginning of Yahweh's
worship in time of, 2; command against
images pushed back to law of, 10; converts fellow tribesmen, 3; creative influence of, 4; executes Yahweh's wrath
on Korah, 158, 261; given physical vision
of Yahweh, 9; marriage of, 3; Platonic
ideas found in books of, 39; prophetic
figure, 21; sacrificially identified with his
people, 173; saved by circumcision of
son, 24, 154; with Yahweh at Mount
Sinai, 2, 14, 60, 201 f.
Most High, 5, 47 f., 210
Mother, 73, 125, 243
Mount Carmel, 5, 21, 248
Mount of Olives, 18 f.
Mountain, of God, 2 ff., 60, (215); Yahweh
a mountain god, 2, 4 ff., 17. See Sinai
Murder, 72, 112
Myers, Frederic W., 295
Mystery, in suffering, 156, 162, 176 ff.,
191 f.; in the Eternal, 53; problem of evil
a, 178, 180
Mystery religions, 80, 252 f.
Mythology, 188, 198, 262

Naaman, 12
Nabal, 109

107 f., 130 ff.; preferring bondage to freedom, 108

Smell, sacrifice accepted through sense of, 8 f., 154

Smith, George Adam, quoted, on monotheism of Great Isaiah, 29; on necessity of temple's destruction, 32

Smith, Henry Preserved, quoted, 258

Smith, J. M. Powis, 102 n., quoted, on absence of chivalry, 104; on Great Isaiah's ideas, 194; on rights of foreigners, 100

Smith, W. Robertson, quoted, on gods of heathenism, 60; on purpose of religion, 110

Social solidarity. See Corporate personality

Society, focus in Christianity's ellipse, 81; prerequisite of fortunate, 119; preserving institutions of, 79 f.; religion existed to preserve, 110

Socrates, 42, 157

Sodom, 103, 145, 173

Sodomy, 16

Sojourners in Israel, 131, 238

Solomon, 18 f., 105 f., 131; temple of, see Temple

Son, Abraham's plea for, 109; ceremonies for ancestors devolved on, 259; sacrifice of first-born, 206

Son of God, baptismal water, seal of, 253; Biblical quotations on, 50 f., 197, 289; John's teaching of, 234; kingdom of, see Kingdom of God; Paul's waiting for, 79; soul died for by, 77. See Jesus

Son of man, Israel, 270

Song of Songs, romance gaining recognition in, 124

Songs, accompaniment of sacrifice, 220, 224; in wine houses, 125 n.

Sonship to God, 51, 73, 122, 233 f., 291

Soul, "and God stand sure," 77; as breath, 82 f., 257; as function of material organism, 85; Christianity no circle with soul for center, 81; dead in Hades not, 260; fellowship for redemption of, 81; God's care for, 268, 291; God's relationship with, 75, 267, 291, see Fellowship with God, Idea of Fellowship with God; Greek teaching on, 79 f., 85, 88, 274, 279, 287; immaterial and preëxistent, 279; immortality of, 279, see Eternal life, Idea of Immortality; Jews never generalized about metaphysical, 86; Johannine idea of, 289; modern thought of, 93; not characteristic element of Hebrew personality, 84; Paul's thought of, 93, 285; temple where God dwells, 256; tran-

scends evil, 180; trouble faced with different qualities of, 184; value of, 77, 79 f.; word used for *psyche*, 89. See Idea of Man

Soule, George Henry, quoted, 20

Sowing and reaping, 183, 185

Spirit (God), God, a, 32, 35; Holy, see Holy Spirit; indwelling source of power, 52, 88, 192, 214, 225 f., 233; one, 52; *ruach* changed to mean, 87 f. See God

Spirit (man), body identified with, 83 ff.; Christ, life-giving, 92; contrast between flesh and, see Flesh; contrite, 267; Ezekiel appealed for new, 120; immured on earth, 279; man's distinguishing characteristic, 88; of man and beast in Ecclesiastes, 181; pure world of, 85, 274; quality of, 110, 118, 189; *ruach*, 87, see Ruach. See Man

Spirits, 18, 262

Springs, 203

Stade, D. Bernhard, quoted, 105

Stephanas, 253

Stephen, 236

Stoicism, 91, 287

Stones, 16, 74, 216

Suffering, as discipline, 170 ff.; as displeasure of Yahweh, 153, 155; as postponed penalty, 167 ff.; as punishment for national sin, 157, 239 ff.; as redemptive, 172 ff., 193 ff.; as retribution for individual sin, 163 ff.; as vicarious self-sacrifice, 173 f., 193 ff., see Servant of Yahweh; at heart of New Testament experience, 185, 193, 196; attribute of God, 196 f.; brief summary of Old Testament ideas of, 182; Cardinal Mercier quoted on advantages of, 171; central problem of India, 162; Christ's, 186, 194, 197; cross redeemed tragedy, 196; disciples called to, 199; early Hebrew phrasing of, 152 ff.; Ecclesiastes skeptical about, 181; future hope to comfort present, 190; in inter-Testamental books, 182 f.; inexplicable mystery in, 191 ff.; integral part of living, 185, 196, 199; interpretations not unanimous, 181; no mystery for materialists, 156; of church cause of hope, 185; problem of innocent, 160 f.; Satan not held responsible for, 178; Servant, 194 f., see Servant of Yahweh. See Idea of Suffering

Sun god, 30

Sun hymn, 30

Swords, 143 f.

Symbolism, 217, 229 f.

altar, prayer, 223; union of worshiper and deity in sacred meals, 8, 254
Worship of Yahweh, associated with child sacrifice, 207, see Child sacrifice; at high places of Canaan, 14 ff., 21 f., 26 f.; centralized, 27, 119; centrality of sacrifice in, 218 f.; delayed till Exodus, 1; effects of localization of, 202 f.; in post-Exilic temple, 241; inter-territorial, 18 f.; prostitution and sodomy crept into, 16; royal families copying Phœnician forms of, 216; synagogue seat of, 230; under likeness of bulls, 16

Xenophon, 42

Ya in cuneiform documents, 3 f.
Yahweh, a Kenite god, 3; and his angel, shading vague between, 11; anthropomorphism of, see Anthropomorphism; appeased by sacrifice, 113, 207, see Sacrifice, Animal sacrifice, Human sacrifice; as an agricultural god, 13 ff.; as baal, 14 ff.; as god of Sheol, 262 f.; as guide, 154, 204; as jealous god, 7, 17, 59, 210, 213, 298; as law-giver, 34; as lover of his people, 35; as mountain god, 2, 4 ff., 17; as personal god, 66; as sky god, 17 ff., 262; as storm god, 4 ff., 13; as supernationalistic, 18 f., 25; as territorial god of Canaan, 10 ff.; as tribal god, 6 ff., 20, 60, 64, 118, 158, 202 f., 269; as war god, 5 ff., 14 ff., 143, 202 f., 205; becomes god of Hebrews, 1 ff.; commands cruelty against Israel's rivals, 100; conversation of, with patriarchs, 8, 173, 208; day of,

269, 290; displeasure of, as cause of suffering, 155, fearfulness of, 60 f., 202; holiness of, 209, see Holiness; immortality of, 298; insistence of, on circumcision, 110, see Circumcision; justice of, 16, 21, 164, 265, see Justice; mercy of, 117, 133; moral character of, at lowest point, 24; name of, 249, see Elohim, El Shaddai, Lord; nature of, at beginning, 10, 298; omnipotence of, 241, see Omnipotence; poems of the Servant of, 172, see Servant of Yahweh; reputation of, involved if Hebrews not saved, 249; requirements of, 114; righteousness of, 241, see Righteousness; seen by Moses, 9; sovereignty of, 29; tradition in Israel's popular religion, 16; unapproachableness of, 201 f., 211; word, became 'Lord,' 45; worship of, see Worship of Yahweh. See God; Idea of God; Jehovah
Yarah, 205
Year of jubilee, 132

Zacchæus, 76
Zarephath, 82
Zealots, 147
Zechariah, 34, 141
Zedekiah, 131
Zephaniah, 159
Zeus, 2, 247
Zion, 28, 33, 67, 218 f., 223, 244
Zipporah, 24
Zophar, 53
Zoroastrian, 177, 276, 287
Zulus, 154

INDEX OF SCRIPTURAL REFERENCES

OLD TESTAMENT

337

Luke

John (The Fourth Gospel)